CW01217482

THE IRISH CORONER

The Irish Coroner

*Death, Murder and Politics in
Co. Monaghan, 1846–78*

MICHELLE McGOFF-McCANN

FOUR COURTS PRESS

Set in 10.5 pt on 12.5 pt Ehrhardt MT for
FOUR COURTS PRESS LTD
7 Malpas Street, Dublin 8, Ireland
www.fourcourtspress.ie
and in North America for
FOUR COURTS PRESS
c/o IPG, 814 N. Franklin St, Chicago, IL 60610

© Michelle McGoff-McCann and Four Courts Press 2023

A catalogue record for this title is available
from the British Library.

ISBN 978-1-80151-063-9

All rights reserved. No part of this publication may be reproduced, stored in or introduced into a retrieval system, or transmitted, in any form or by any means (electronic, mechanical, photocopying, recording, or otherwise), without the prior written permission of both the copyright owner and publisher of this book.

The author and publisher would like to gratefully acknowledge the financial support received from Monaghan County Council.

Printed in England by
CPI Antony Rowe, Chippenham, Wilts.

Contents

ILLUSTRATIONS	6
ABBREVIATIONS	7
ACKNOWLEDGMENTS	9
Introduction	11

Part I. Before the Famine

1	The reputation and authority of the coroners in nineteenth-century Ireland	21
2	William Charles Waddell	47

Part II. During the Famine

3	The Famine and moral ambiguity	69
4	Managing and investigating pauper death	102

Part III. After the Famine

5	Public welfare and justice	145
6	The value of a life: the emergence of the modern Irish coroner	174

Conclusion	203
Appendix 1: The coroners of Ireland (1871)	213
Appendix 2: Inquests and inquiries in William Charles Waddell's casebooks	216
BIBLIOGRAPHY	223
INDEX	240

Illustrations

FIGURES

1	Daguerreotype of William Charles Waddell, *c*.1875	65
2	Inquest page from William Charles Waddell's casebook	73
3	Inquests taken May 1846 to Dec. 1852	105
4	Panopticon architecture of Victorian gaols (1843)	108
5	George Wilkinson's workhouse plans (1839)	120

MAPS

1	County Monaghan (1890)	15
2	The townland of Lisnaveane, Co. Monaghan (1836)	49
3	Monaghan town and Monaghan gaol (1836)	110
4	Monaghan town, Monaghan workhouse and hospital (1908)	121

TABLES

1	Some of the offices held by Catholics in 1823	33
2	Schedule of payments coroners were authorized to make (1846)	44
3	Inquests taken from May 1846 to July 1847	72
4	Grain prices in Co. Monaghan in Oct. 1845 and Oct. 1846	80
5	Grain prices in Co. Monaghan in Oct. and Dec. 1846	82
6	Grain prices in Co. Monaghan in Dec. 1846 and Feb. 1847	84
7	Inmate population, available accommodation at Monaghan gaol in Dec. 1847	114
8	Deaths reported at Ulster gaols, 1845–52	115
9	Inquests at the workhouses supporting Co. Monaghan, 1848–50	119
10	Populations of workhouses supporting Co. Monaghan, Dec. 1846–Dec. 1849	135
11	Populations of workhouses supporting Co. Monaghan, 1853–5	155
12	Population of inmates, Co. Monaghan gaol, 1849–55	155
13	Supposed causes of 'mental disease' (1872)	191

Abbreviations

BMN	*Belfast Morning News*
BN	*Belfast Newsletter*
CB1	Casebook of William Charles Waddell (1846–55)
CB2	Casebook of William Charles Waddell (1856–76)
CB3	Casebook of William Charles Waddell (1876–7)
CSORP	(also CSO/RP) Chief Secretary's Office Registered papers
DD	*Dundalk Democrat*
DEM	*Dublin Evening Mail*
DIB	*Dictionary of Irish biography*
DUB	*Dictionary of Ulster biography*
FJ	*Freeman's Journal*
FRC	Famine Relief Commission papers
HC	House of Commons
LS	*Londonderry Standard*
MP	member of Parliament
NAI	National Archives of Ireland
NS	*Northern Standard*
NSW	New South Wales
ODNB	*Oxford dictionary of national biography*
OS	Ordnance Survey
POI	Prisons of Ireland
PRONI	Public Record Office of Northern Ireland
QC	queen's counsel
RM	resident magistrate
ROD	Registry of Deeds (Dublin)

Acknowledgments

This book became possible when I discovered that the missing Famine casebook of Co. Monaghan coroner William Charles Waddell had surfaced again, as its location was unknown for over 20 years. I am grateful to Catriona Lennon at Clones Library, who indulged my request to create a digital copy of the casebook so that I could begin my research remotely. Once I began reading the inquests, I could soon see that the material offered an incredible opportunity. Combining Waddell's first casebook (1846–55) with his second (1856–76) and third (1876–7) would provide a solid foundation to examine the role of the coroner and its social and political importance in nineteenth-century Ireland.

I also set out to write a history book on Co. Monaghan, tying it into national politics to demonstrate its significance and importance within the wider context of Irish historiography. I've had the privilege of being guided by experts who have welcomed me with a spirit of belonging and inclusion, as well as pride for our connection to the subject matter, which continues to inspire me. This study would not have taken shape if it weren't for the insight, encouragement and direction of Peter Gray, Queen's University Belfast. Peter helped me develop my knowledge and understanding of nineteenth-century Irish history, and supported my vision to write a detailed work. For this, I am truly grateful. The guidance I received from Olwen Purdue was equally invaluable. Olwen's timeliness in lending solid advice with meaningful, experienced focus helped me sharpen my skills and keep my head on straight. Big thanks also to Chris McGimpsey for responding so quickly to my request to identify Monaghan Orange Order documentation to support my thesis. Other academic supporters whose input I have valued include Lance Petit, Birkbeck University; Marie Coleman, Elaine Farrell, James Davis, Andrew Holmes and Fergal McGarry, Queen's University Belfast; Terence Dooley, Maynooth University; and my Irish Studies lecturers from St Mary's University, Twickenham, Ivan Gibbons, Michelle Paull, Anne Goudsmit, Keith Hopper and Richard Mills, whose expertise helped me gather my confidence when I needed it most.

Descendants of Waddell and family connections in Ireland and further afield supported me with documentation and 'positivity' in creating this book. I'm indebted to Hope Blundell (neé Waddell), great-granddaughter of William Charles Waddell, for flying to Belfast to meet with me, offering a variety of surprises related to my research, and for visiting with me every year to discuss updates on the progress of this project. Her friendship has been a special gift. Rory Hope, another Waddell (Hopes) descendant, provided me the opportunity to read and transcribe letters written to Waddell by his wife, Maria. This helped develop insight into their relationship and Waddell's family relationships. My deep gratitude also goes to Alistair and Angela McCrory, who allowed me to use the inquests from Waddell's second casebook, which they privately own. I give special thanks to the Irish Manuscripts Commission, who saw the value in my digital transcription of Waddell's inquests over the thirty-one years of his career and have agreed to work with me to see them published as well.

My very warm regards to Four Courts Press for their interest and understanding of what this book set out to achieve.

Across different countries and social circles, both physical and virtual, friends, family and colleagues supported me with encouragement along this journey. Monaghan is a special place, and so are the many who call it their home. Grace Maloney, Clogher Historical Society, and Alice O'Neill, SOLAS, are two women with whom, no matter how many years pass, we always pick up just where we left off. I greatly value their support and encouragement. I also want to thank Liam Bradley, County Monaghan Museum, and Deborah Flack, Clogher Historical Society, who have always offered opportunities to get my research in the public domain. Special thanks to Councillor Seán Conlon and Heritage Officer Shirley Clerkin for their interest in this project and for immediately understanding the value it brings to the history of Co. Monaghan.

Henry Skeath has been a supporter of mine for over two decades. He won't like the attention of being acknowledged, but I'm doing it anyway. Thank you, Henry, for all the research and debates.

I was fortunate enough to travel to public and private libraries and archives to conduct my research, meeting supportive staff, always willing to go the extra mile to provide me with records and additional information where they could. This includes the Public Record Office of Northern Ireland, Belfast; the British Library, London; Schomberg House, Belfast; the State Library of New South Wales, Australia; and Longleat House, Warminster, UK (Emma Challinor). I want to give special thanks to archivist Gregory O'Connor, National Archives, Dublin, who has since passed, who also had a passion for the history of the coroner in Ireland. Gregory always took the time to ensure I had what I needed and to fill me in on any overlooked sources in this area of Irish history.

Lastly, I thank my parents and all my McCann and McGoff family for their support, and especially my nieces and nephews, Sam, Connor, Cooper, Lorcan and Astrid, who I hope will take some inspiration from this work to challenge themselves with similar goals. You can do anything you put your mind to. Special heartfelt thanks to my sounding board, Jacqui McCann, for listening to a daily progress report on *The Irish coroner* over the past many years. And most of all, to my husband, Ryan McCann, for his patience and encouragement each step of the way.

Introduction

On Wednesday, 11 March 1847, Jane Forsythe opened the door of her mud walled cabin to Cecelia McPhillips who arrived with her four children all crying from hunger.[1] Jane lit a fire and placed the pot over the hearth so Cecelia could make dinner, which consisted of the meal she had gathered by begging throughout the Monaghan countryside. The children were fed and soon fell asleep on the hard dirt floor. Early the next morning, while the meal for breakfast was being prepared, Cecelia's young son, Pat, was sitting by the fire warming himself when suddenly his head fell to one side. The women feared he was dying. A bed of straw was made for the unresponsive boy and his mother placed him in it. Pat lay there quietly for about an hour until he stopped breathing and died.

At eight o'clock the next morning, among headstones in the grass at St Coleman's Church of Ireland graveyard, a woman was spotted with a spade, trying to bury a child. Benjamin Beatty, the schoolmaster of Clontibret parish, asked her why she would bury her child without a coffin. Cecelia replied that she could not secure one. Beatty told her he would not allow her to continue until he consulted with the archdeacon, Fr Russell, who was 'pain struck' when he heard the details of the situation. The priest gave Beatty money to buy the grieving mother some breakfast and to procure a coffin for the child. Russell then sent word to the police to investigate the circumstances around the child's death.

The archdeacon's communication prompted a request for an inquest to be conducted by William Charles Waddell esq. (1798–1878), who served as coroner in north Co. Monaghan over three decades from 1846 to 1878. On 15 March 1847, the details of the circumstances surrounding the sad story were captured, while the need for physical evidence required the examination of the body by Dr James Stanley Christian. He confirmed that the body of the little boy had no marks of external violence. On one foot was an ulcerated sore, the result of walking great distances with his mother in search of food. Pat's body was weak and greatly emaciated. Dr Christian considered that Pat McPhillips died as a result of exposure to cold and want of proper and nourishing food.[2] A review of Waddell's expenses revealed itemized fees paid for his travel, the housing of the body for two nights, a coffin and the interment of the body.

Coroners' inquests, like that of Pat McPhillips, captured thousands of deaths throughout the nineteenth century. While inquests from newspapers and official documents have been used to bolster other academic works, this book uses original

1 CB1, no. 23.42, Pat McPhillips, 15 Mar. 1847.   2 Ibid.

inquest reports written in a coroner's casebook as its key source material. These official investigations into the circumstances of those who died from starvation, disease, political and domestic murder, suicide, infanticide, misadventure and natural causes provide valuable insight into Irish society. They also represent the humanitarian aspect of the coroner's work and reveal the societal benefit of investigating sudden or suspicious deaths, particularly inquests held on the vulnerable, poor, sick or mentally ill.

I discovered Waddell's original handwritten casebooks by a combination of determination and serendipity. The books emerged at different times and not in succession. In 2001, I was first introduced to the second casebook (1856–76) when it was in possession of Alistair McCrory. I transcribed all the cases in order to transfer them into the public domain, and used them as source material for my book *Melancholy madness: a coroner's casebook*.[3]

It wasn't until twelve years later that I discovered Waddell's Famine casebook (1846–55) had been tucked away in the safe, uncatalogued, at the Clones Library. For years, it had been considered missing. This was the catalyst for initiating this study. The Famine casebook had been used many years earlier as supporting material for two local-history essays.[4] While those articles offer a glimpse at the tragic details of the suffering of the people and contribute to an understanding of social history in Co. Monaghan during the Famine, they also exposed a gap in the history of the county at that time. After the last article was written in 1995–6, it was believed by local historians that the book had vanished. Like the second casebook, I have now transcribed the Famine casebook as well, and it is a primary source for this study.

The Famine casebook (CB1) begins 7 May 1846 and ends 29 December 1855. Its survival opens up opportunities to approach the Famine through a new source. It provides insights into the work of the coroner and the official investigation of death during this critical time in Ireland's history. The casebook identified deaths as they occurred; trends and changes in behaviour over time are exposed, such as the impacts of legislative changes, inadequate local management of the crisis, the pressure on institutions, poor decision making by local relief officers, as well as social behaviour and changes in attitudes towards the poor.

The inquests align with other primary source materials, covering social and political events, to provide a more accurate and substantial view as to how and why such deaths occurred. The resulting work also questions the purpose of the coroner as a figure of authority in nineteenth-century Irish history. Examining the officialdom surrounding the investigation of death during the crisis supports

3 Michelle McGoff-McCann, *Melancholy madness: a coroner's casebook* (Cork, 2003). 4 Brian Ó Mórdha, 'The Great Famine in Monaghan: a coroner's account', *Clogher Record*, 4:1/2 (1961), pp 29–41; idem, 'The Great Famine in Monaghan (continued)', *Clogher Record*, 4:3 (1962), pp 175–86; Pilip Ó Mórdha, 'Summary of inquests held on Currin, Co. Monaghan victims 1846–1855', *Clogher Record*, 15:2 (1995), pp 90–100; idem, 'Addenda to the Summary of inquests held on Currin, Co. Monaghan victims 1846–1855', *Clogher Record*, 15:3 (1996), pp 158–9.

inquiry into the legal liability and evidence of (or lack of) for criminal charges or convictions in the period of the Famine and its aftermath.

Relying on Waddell's Famine casebook, this book offers, for the first time, a social history of Co. Monaghan during the Great Famine (1846–52) that examines the alignment of legislation, local mismanagement of the crisis and Waddell's inquests to reveal all factors that contributed towards the deaths. Famine historians have long sought to find evidence concerning those who emigrated and died. The most readily available documentation supporting Famine studies includes folklore accounts, newspaper coverage, government statistics and official papers. These primary sources reveal regional variations that help define the effects of the Famine and provide the opportunity to create an historical account of the conditions that impacted those persons that vanished, whether through emigration or death. Unlike any Famine history, Waddell's inquests offer the first-hand experience of a county coroner who worked at the coalface during the humanitarian crisis.

Over the course of developing my PhD thesis, in 2016, Waddell's third casebook (1876–7), which records the last 56 inquests and 64 inquiries that he conducted in his 31-year career, was discovered. It was bound and mislabelled at Clones Library, entitled *Inquisitions by Coroner Hugh Swanzy, 1876–1877, County Monaghan*. Now before me, I had every documented inquest and inquiry investigated by Waddell from the start of his journey as coroner, up to the last inquest he captured before his death.[5] CB2, covering the period from 7 January 1856 to 18 February 1876, combined with CB3, from 22 February 1876 to 21 September 1877, highlight post-Famine abuses of authority and power, familial and sectarian murders, inquests on beggars and mendicant strangers capturing evidence of the agricultural famine of 1877, and local management of the mentally ill and the poor. After poring over the entire collection of Waddell's work, I realized just how rare these records were and their value to Irish history.

There is no evidence that any other similar coroner's casebooks have survived from the nineteenth century. The current pool of literature on nineteenth-century Irish history indicates that Waddell's set of casebooks is one of a kind, so there are no others like it to draw comparisons. The Offaly Historical Society holds three casebooks from coroner James Dillon (1836–59), which give the name of the deceased, the date and location of the inquest, the names of witnesses and jurors, and the verdict of death.[6] These books do not contain the same valuable testimony of witnesses and doctors that exist in Waddell's casebooks. Only random inquests published in newspapers of the time include some, but still not all, of the original testimony and evidence provided at inquests. As this study will show, inquests published in newspapers should be examined with some scepticism, as facts and

5 The casebooks contain three different handwriting styles, one of which is Waddell's. This indicates that Waddell had some assistance or an assitant to rewrite his notes or transcribe onsite at the inquests. This study did not find any records of such persons. 6 James Dillon (1788–1859), King's Co. coroner of the Tullamore district, was responsible for the northern half of the county. Three casebooks were kept: casebook one (1836–40); casebook two (1846–54); and casebook three (1854–9).

commentary often do not always reflect important details that are captured in Waddell's casebook. Newspaper research, while often supportive and valuable in the absence of other primary sources, does not explicitly provide insight into the social and political conditions under which so many perished.

Very little has been published about the backgrounds of the men who served as coroners, and this book aims to address the absence of the coroner in Irish historiography using Waddell's work in Co. Monaghan during the period from 1846 to 1878 as a case study. It also places Waddell within the fabric of local government and society in Monaghan. How and why was he able to secure the role of coroner? How did he function and operate? Sources such as personal letters, wills, land records, deeds and official public papers, as well as his religious orientation, genealogy and membership to local groups and associations, help provide a comprehensive view of one coroner in Irish society. These documents help to establish his reputation and the impact this may have had on his work. Newspapers, both local and national, liberal and conservative, reported on inquests, but there also existed political stratagems behind publishing (or not) the work of the coroner. Questioning Waddell's personal politics and his duties as a coroner within the politically polarised environment of Co. Monaghan reveals the potential impact this had on the outcome of inquests and the course of justice. The patterns that emerge emphasize a modernisation of society within Co. Monaghan, representative of the country at large.

Since studies on the men who conducted inquests and served as coroners in local government are generally absent from administrative history, there are no other such studies with which comparisons can be drawn. However, by examining Waddell's inquests chronologically over thirty-one years, patterns of behaviour and ideologies are revealed that provide a clearer picture of the broader landscape of the coroner and his function within local government and nineteenth-century Irish society. Attitudes and behaviours of the elite in the management of local government in Co. Monaghan and the role of the coroner within it are also exposed. The function and potentially contentious political role of the coroner within local government and amongst the elite is examined and a new template for future studies for other sets of coroners' records for the nineteenth century emerges.

The purpose of the office and the inquest was to determine a cause of death and liability in cases of murder. Considering the coroner functioned within a colonial context, and in a politically polarized society, political and social complexities often shadowed the authority of the office. Property qualifications and social status were requirements to gain entry to the office, which reflected a bias towards the wealthy and social elite securing the role. Did scepticism around their investigations of death impact the confidence of their constituency? As Ireland began to modernize, the role of the coroner evolved from one held by men with inherited status into one that required candidates for the office who had 'merit' within professional society.[7]

---

7 Harold Perkin, *The rise of professional society: England since 1880* (London, 1989), p.380.

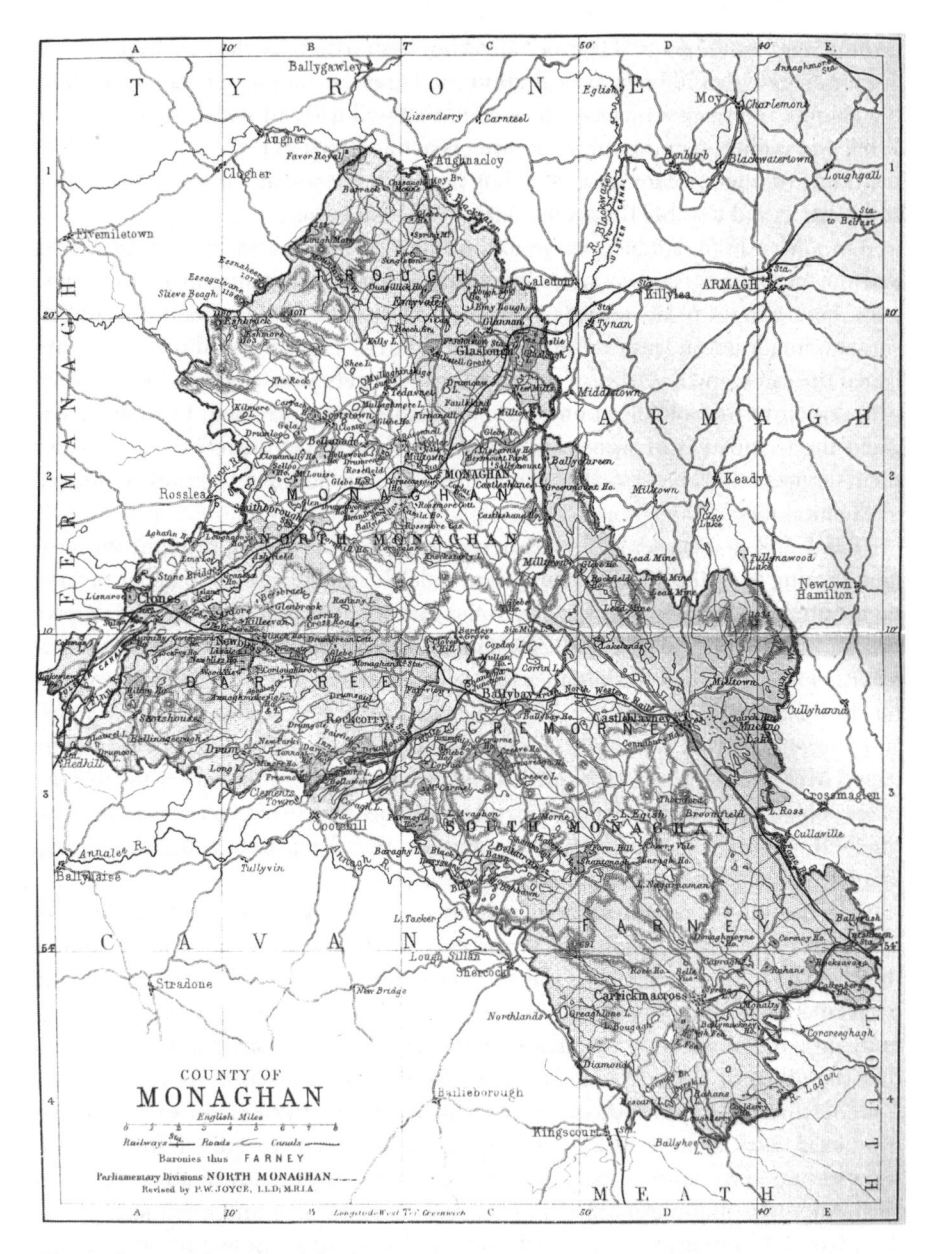

Map 1 County Monaghan (1890).

The transition of the position of the coroner relates to themes of popular politics, the development of democracy, the growth of the state and the rise of the professional society. Joseph Lee defines modernization as an improvement in the quality of opportunity where merit supersedes birthright in the distribution of income, status and power.[8] His work identifies Irish society as one held back by slow economic growth and sectarianism up to the 1840s, becoming one transformed by the Famine and the post-Famine process of vast political and social modernization. While the evolution of the role of coroner is not included in Lee's work, it provides the frame of reference for understanding how it developed as a political institution and contributed towards the modernization of Irish society.

On 1 May 1856, Waddell wrote to the editor of the *Londonderry Standard*, 'As a senior coroner of this county, I have had to resist many attempts to interfere with the discharge of my duties ...'[9] Waddell's letter reveals that there was conflict surrounding inquests, public inquiries into sudden or suspicious death that established the cause and a verdict of death. His experiences were shared widely by men who served in the role of coroner in nineteenth-century Ireland. Coroners navigated the trepidation of witnesses, grand juries' proclivity to refuse payment for their services and threats to abolish their role by MPs and grand juries comprised of the local elite.

The Chief Secretary's Office received complaints pertaining to and from coroners ranging from the interference of local officials and the peasantry in performing their duties, and abuses of authority, to the fear of violence to their person. 'I have conducted several murder inquests, examining evidence and interviewing witnesses, but this has put me in danger for my life,' stated William Mullock, coroner for the district of Banagher in King's Co.[10] Such experiences, like those of Waddell and Mullock, reflect the challenges of leading Ireland's only independent public court. Moreover, verdicts that revealed institutional corruption, government mismanagement, and neglect of marginalized groups put the coroner at odds with the local elite, of which Waddell was a member. W.E. Vaughan noted, 'An officious coroner was regarded as a constitutional nuisance'.[11]

A collection of various sources including the legislation, writings of coroners in official papers, and national newspapers reveal the challenges to the survival of the coroners' office. Critics of local government in Ireland highlighted that it was open to corruption, jobbery and inefficiency and the central government became more involved in the supervision of coroners and their function.[12] A trend emerges that the office of coroner was supported by the administration through legislation, but was often under threat of being abolished by grand juries and MPs who were local elites. On the surface, it appeared to be a financial burden they did not want to bear. This study considers how the role of coroner posed a real threat to local elites. An inquest could impose justice in cases of murder, without prejudice, based on forensic and medical evidence, along with witness testimony. The survival of the office can be attributed to its evolution from one where the holder

---

8 Joseph Lee, *The modernisation of Irish society, 1848–1918* (Dublin, 1989), p. ii.   9 *LS*, 1 May 1856.   10 Letter to Smith-Stanley from coroner, William Mullock, 29 Sept. 1832 (NAI, CSO/RP/1832/6202).   11 W.E. Vaughan, *Murder trials in Ireland, 1836–1914* (Dublin, 2009), p. 49.   12 Jobbery is the awarding of public contracts based on nepotism and patronage.

required patronage and property ownership to one where education, experience and professionalization became the essential requisites. As a result, the religions and education of the men serving in those roles began to change, and representation became fairer.

Political events and local tensions that contributed to sectarian murders investigated by Waddell require examination. Identifying the changing political landscape in the politically polarized society of Co. Monaghan offers the context of the tensions at the time of the murder. Crucially relevant to such murder investigations were the changing political parties in office, and the impact of legislation that contributed to rural violence and upset, which sometimes resulted in death. The link between the national political landscape and the changes in the history of the coroners' office is revealed.

This book is divided into three sections, each consisting of two chapters, arranged in chronological order: pre-Famine, Famine and post-Famine. Chapter one provides a history of the office of coroner, from the Act of Union until 1846, an area that is under-researched, and highlights the purpose of the role, the public opinion of the men who served as coroner and how it served as a contested form of authority nationally and locally. While from this public court emerge the moral and social values of the community, without significant numbers of named murderers in homicides or a higher rate of convictions at criminal trial, the coroner's role in government becomes tenuous. New legislation in 1846 helped encourage more autonomy for coroners, but under the careful management of central government. Chapter two introduces Waddell, his genealogy, biographical information from his personal life and an examination of his political and social position as an Ulster Presbyterian in the Monaghan landscape. It also examines his own participation as a juror in nineteenth-century Ireland, to frame his personal politics.

In section two, chapter three focuses on Waddell's work in his first fifteen months as coroner in Monaghan during the Famine. It examines the political and moral barometers of the community through the inquest evidence and verdicts. This chapter considers the authority of the coroner as well as instances where that authority was undermined. Chapter four examines the work of the coroner in identifying causes of death at workhouses and gaols, as they reflect the impact of legislation and local management of the poor, referred to in nineteenth-century Ireland as paupers. It reveals the coroner's legal obligation to investigate death within such institutions. The chapter also uses Waddell and his inquests as a case study to reveal moral ambiguity around priorities and fiscal decisions made by conservative local gentry that played a role in the death of local paupers.

In section three, chapter five uses Waddell's post-Famine inquests as a case study to review abuses of authority and power while he attempted to impose justice. Inquest findings often conflicted with the political and social values of the local elite, putting the coroner at odds with them. The chapter focuses on cases where a crime had been committed, particularly sectarian killings, testing whether the role of coroner was a contributing factor in convicting those accused of murder. Chapter six examines the national political landscape and its impact locally on Monaghan through the inquests captured by Waddell. It examines murders, accidental deaths and institutional death in a politically changing environment. It considers the moral compass of the verdicts in Waddell's casebooks as it reflects on the politics of Co. Monaghan and the signs of potential changes to come.

PART I

Before the Famine

I

The reputation and authority of the coroners in nineteenth-century Ireland

'[The] disgrace of the present system of coroners' inquests [is] a gross burlesque on jurisprudence.'[1]
—Sir Dominic John Corrigan, physician, 9 Sept. 1840

'Sire ... the fact is: Coroners in Ireland are (generally speaking) the lowest and most contemptible characters.'[2]
—Revd Peter Browne, dean of Ferns to Prince Frederick, duke of York and Albany, 7 June 1819

On 1 June 1819, William Gregory, the lord lieutenant's secretary, received a letter. It was sent by Reverend Peter Browne, dean of Ferns, who was outraged by the behaviour of a local coroner who was using British army soldiers to arrest a farmer for a debt, which provoked a mob of hundreds to appear and soldiers to open fire on the crowd.

> Glebe House, Ahascragh, Galway, 1 June 1819
> Sir, I deem it my duty as a magistrate to communicate to you the information of government a circumstance which took place here yesterday. A coroner came to this neighbourhood to arrest an individual for <u>Debt</u> – he had constables and a party of military though I cannot hear of any previous reason to allow such a man Troops.
> I have since been informed that these coroners constantly take soldiers and often commit violences for which there is no remedy as they (generally speaking) cannot pay damages.
> In the case alluded to, they made good their arrest, about five in the morning. At eight or nine, they reached this village (two miles) where a mob collected, but by the earnest entreaties of the prisoner, they used no violence – the mob followed at a great distance as some say (while others say closely)

---

1 *Dublin Evening Post*, 10 Sept. 1840.   2 Letter to Prince Frederick from Peter Browne, 7 June 1819 (NAI, CSO/RP/SC/1821/138).

and the soldiers commenced a firing and retreat till their ammunition was exhausted. The mob then followed and rescued the prisoner.

In this bloodless battle, I cannot hear of one on either side hurt. My reason for writing is merely a Doubt pertaining as to the precedence of making soldiers bailiffs in cases of Debts: for it (as in the case it did) might identify the desires and the wishes of the soldiers with the mobs and make them inefficient when really wanted.

Indeed it is improbable to conceive it accident, that a party should expend all their ammunition in an open road mostly on a mob of supposedly onwards of nine hundred (I heard of more but do not credit it) without hurting one and I think it equally improbable to believe a mob would entirely spare the soldiers without a previous understanding, for mobs are ferocious in success and hate soldiers intuitively.

I beseech you to consider the consequence of making soldiers trifling to mobs by employing them on services where they would rather assist than disperse rioters. Neither did I think it (when I played soldiers as a yeoman in 1798 and 1799) a matter of course that a soldier with a musket and bayonet was disarmed and in the power of a mob with sticks though his cartouche box was empty. Think not I am an advocate for Bloodshed, on the contrary: I know this business will cause it and I am assured every party near this will be attacked in consequence. Till something serious takes place, previous to it, I could send a prisoner to Biloe [sic] with a single Constable[3] – it would now require a Corporal and with the probability of Bloodshed. I beg you will excuse my presentation in communicating to you a circumstance which appears to me (perhaps erroneously) connected with the peace of this county and honour of the army.

Peter Browne
Dean of Ferns[4]

Browne's fury didn't stop there. He wrote several more letters, including one addressed to Prince Frederick, duke of York and Albany, who was the commander-in-chief of the British army. It stated,

Sire ... the fact is: Coroners in Ireland are (generally speaking) the lowest and most contemptible characters: the one alluded to in the enclosed keeps a low whiskey house in his own or his brother's name. Such a fellow is authorised to command the king's soldiers and officers and violate the peace under pretence of preserving it.[5]

---

3 Biloela gaol, Cockatoo Island, Sydney, Australia. 4 Letter to William Gregory from Peter Browne, 1 June 1819 (NAI, CSO/RP/SC/1821/138/C). 5 Letter to Prince Frederick from Peter Browne, 7 June 1819 (NAI, CSO/RP/SC/1821/138).

Evidence suggests that conscience got the better of Browne, as a second letter to the duke of York just a week later requested that the prince 'not misconstrue the complaint of the individual coroner, but of the general custom [of collecting debts]' as the coroner had contracted a fever in consequence of either the incident or 'excess' (implying alcohol) and was 'therefore not likely to err again'.[6] These letters are representative of others that were delivered to the highest-ranking government officials from local figures of authority complaining about the behaviour of coroners. Such reports raise questions as to the role and purpose of the coroner in Irish society.

A SHORT HISTORY OF THE CORONER AND THE INQUEST

The office of coroner first appeared in the twelfth century. It was believed to have been brought over from England and Wales as a result of the implementation of the Articles of Eyre in 1194. Richard I needed to raise funds for his expensive wars and introduced coroners to support his endeavours.[7] The coroner's initial purpose was to investigate unlawful deaths of Normans, and find deodands (funds, property or possessions) from those considered to have caused the deaths that could be claimed to help fund the state.[8] Throughout the Middle Ages in Ireland, some lives were given a monetary value, while others were not. If a 'king's Irishman', an Irish man working for the crown, was found murdered, a penalty/payment called an éraic was due.[9] For those deaths with value, the coroner would carry out an inquest by organizing a jury, examining the body, looking for wounds as a cause of death and documenting the proceedings. If a guilty party was not found for a 'murdrum' (murder), the local community could be fined. The men suitable for the role of coroner were expected to 'be persons honest, lawful and wise ... the most wise and discreet knights'.[10] The coroner shared some of the same responsibilities as the sheriff and both answered to the crown (hence the name 'crowner', which then became 'coroner').

On 1 January 1801, the United Kingdom of Great Britain and Ireland became a sovereign state established by the Act of Union.[11] Over the following century, some government departments were abolished and implementation of new legislation around public health, Poor Law and economic development gave way to new roles for civil servants and changes to local government. The police service was disassembled, reconstructed and re-established. Corruption, partisan politics and incompetence in the judicial system was seen as an embarrassment to the administration and, as a result, many legacy judicial positions were eliminated.[12] The office

---

6 Letter to Prince Frederick from Peter Brown, 14 June 1819 (NAI, CSO/RP/SC/1821/139).   7 R.F. Hunnisett, *The medieval coroner* (Cambridge, 1961), p. 2.   8 Ibid.   9 G.J. Hand, *English law in Ireland, 1290–1324* (London, 1967), p. 202.   10 3 Edw. I, c. 10 (25 Apr. 1275), Coroners Act.   11 40 Geo. III, c. 38 (1 Aug. 1800), Act of Union (Ireland).   12 Galen Broeker, *Rural disorder and police reform in Ireland, 1812–36* (London, 1970), p. 40.

of coroner sat within the magistracy, the responsibilities of the role being essentially a local independent judge. Irish coroners were compared to their English peers, who were considered 'magistrates of the people', and it became clear that, in Ireland, it was often a role that was viewed with disdain and disrespect in a highly politicized society.

The primary duties of the coroner were to investigate the causes and authorship of sudden, violent or otherwise unnatural deaths in the community and to collect debts or monies owed should a responsible person be found guilty of homicide by trial. The investigation of death and the inquest were intended to establish if a crime had been committed.[13] Inquests were initiated once the coroner was informed of a death by a local official or the constabulary and was then required by law to attend. The coroner's first duty was to have summonses sent to persons also required to attend including medical men, witnesses, and jurors. Inquests were open to the public and often held in the home where the body was laid, a local public house or, sometimes, the local courthouse. Witness testimony and medical evaluation of the corpse was assessed by the jury in order to reach a decision on the cause of death. The coroner's office was subject to more legislative transformation than others in the nineteenth century, owing to its connection to the investigation of murder.[14]

Pre-Famine Ireland is considered by many historians to have been a society in which recreational violence and assaults were common, and where inter-familial and sectarian homicide were endemic in many communities.[15] While the inquest was a public court intended to offer transparency into the circumstances that led to the taking of a life, and while it represented the authority of government and the need for social order and justice, it also exposed a society that was deeply politically divided.[16] The predominant belief was that those in Irish local government abused the system to support their own politics and interests, and many citizens were disturbed over how revenues were spent and misappropriated.[17] Legislative change in pre-Famine Ireland was also implemented to attempt to find men of wealth and respectable social status to serve in the role of coroner in order to prevent mismanagement and misappropriation of fees.

---

13 Sarah Tarlow, *Ritual, belief and the dead in early modern Britain and Ireland* (Cambridge, 2013), p. 84. 14 Vaughan, *Murder trials in Ireland, 1836–1914*, pp 41–2; Brian Farrell, *Coroners: practice and procedure* (Dublin, 2000), p. 21. 15 Scholars who have written on violence in Ireland including Broeker, *Rural disorder and police reform in Ireland, 1812–36*; Neal Garnham, *Courts, crime and the criminal law in Ireland, 1692–1760* (Dublin, 1996); Richard McMahon, *Homicide in pre-Famine and Famine Ireland* (Liverpool, 2013); Cormac Ó Gráda, *Ireland: a new economic history, 1780–1939* (Oxford, 1995); Stanley H. Palmer, *Police and protest in England and Ireland, 1780–1850* (Cambridge, 1988). 16 Michael Brown and Seán Patrick Donlan, 'The laws in Ireland, 1689–1850: a brief introduction' in Michael L. Brown and Seán Patrick Donlan (eds), *The laws and other legalities of Ireland, 1689–1850* (Farnham, 2011), p. 8. 17 Virginia Crossman, 'Peculation and partiality: local government in nineteenth-century rural Ireland' in Roger Swift and Christine Kinealy (eds), *Politics and power in Victorian Ireland* (Dublin, 2006), p. 133; Palmer, *Police and protest in England and Ireland, 1780–1850*, p. 127.

LOCAL GOVERNMENT: GENTRY, GENTLEMEN AND THE EDUCATED PROFESSIONAL

County government was led by the high sheriff, a man selected from the local Protestant elite, and nominated annually by the lord lieutenant. His primary role was to preserve the peace and the authority of the law. He then hand-selected a grand jury comprised of men of the county gentry, who would decide on county finances, particularly the maintenance and construction of roads, and determine if there was satisfactory evidence for criminal prosecutions to be carried out. Grand juries had a reputation for corruption and keeping their own best interests in mind.[18] Magistrates were also appointed based on wealth and social standing, although the Irish administration considered many to be unsuitable, sectarian, disreputable or simply unable or unwilling to attend to their duties.[19] Commissions were often handed to men as a result of patronage rather than qualifications, and in these jobs, they profited both financially and politically.[20] The landed elite were responsible for the administration of justice in local affairs, and if they could not participate, they supported men who in return protected their interests.[21]

The chief concern of the administration in the investigation of a sudden or suspicious death was to ensure it was managed by locally responsible men with experience in managing local affairs. They needed to have some background in fiscal management and responsibility, and the ability to exact justice in cases of murder. Similar to magistrates, coroners were expected to be men of good social standing. It was a public role that was secured by election; as such, it was an attractive position to men who wanted to improve their social status. Winning power and status was more difficult for some than others.[22] Entry into county society generally required wealth, property or a peerage, but professional standing could provide additional credibility.[23]

Gentlemen of the law, a growing middle class comprised of both Protestants and Catholics, were desirous of extending their connections. Members of the bar were more respected than solicitors and attorneys.[24] The social standing of a country lawyer occupied the same position in polite society as the country doctor and upper servants in the manor house.[25] Doctors also aspired to attain gentlemen status. Medicine in pre-Famine Ireland was considered a gentleman's career and offered those who could attain the education the opportunity to gain access to the social elite.[26] Professionally trained men who entered public office might

---

18 Virginia Crossman, *Local government in nineteenth-century Ireland* (Belfast, 1994), p. 29. 19 S.J. Connolly, 'Union government, 1812–23' in Vaughan (ed.), *A new history of Ireland*, vi: *Ireland under the Union, 1801–70, II* (Oxford, 1989), p. 69. 20 Broeker, *Rural disorder and police reform in Ireland, 1812–36*, pp 40–1. 21 Olwen Purdue, *The MacGeough Bonds of the Argory* (Dublin, 2005), p. 22. 22 Harold Perkin, *The rise of professional society: England since 1880* (London, 1989), p. 4. 23 Joanne McEntee, '"Gentlemen practisers": solicitors as elites in mid-nineteenth-century Irish landed society' in Ciaran O'Neill (ed.), *Irish elites in the nineteenth century* (Dublin, 2013), p. 99. 24 Ibid., p. 102. 25 Ibid., p. 100. 26 Laurence M. Geary, *Medicine and charity in Ireland 1718–1851* (Dublin, 2004), p. 151.

acquire the desired standing. A coroner operated his own legal court, which was the only independent public court in Ireland. He could also execute writs to have a man arrested and held, and secure property to be sold, with the revenue generated distributed to the plaintiff and the coroner. With this autonomy, the position of coroner could prove a powerful opportunity for someone who wanted to raise their rank in society.

REPUTATION OF CORONERS: CORRUPTION, INJUSTICE AND DRUNKENNESS

In order to gain a better understanding of the attitudes and opinions of the coroner in nineteenth-century Ireland, we can examine newspapers and literary fiction that offer portrayals of coroners that contemporary readers would have easily recognized and understood. Early nineteenth-century newspapers published a handful of stories on a few drunk or disorderly coroners and reports of poor behaviour appeared in parliamentary debates. One such incident was captured on 22 February 1837, when Co. Leitrim MP Lord Clements (1768–1854) stated that he was approached by one of his revenue officers to discuss the circumstances under which he needed a coroner, 'but the coroner, was as usual in Ireland, in gaol'.[27] Reference was made to the Co. Galway coroner Andrew Hosty, who was jailed by the head magistrate for contempt of court. Another incident appeared on 7 May 1842, when the *Manchester Courier* reported that a Dublin county coroner was brought to the head office in Dublin and charged with being drunk and disorderly. However, it is the portrayal of the coroner in the imaginative literature of Carleton, Boucicault, Griffin and Somerville and Ross that lends insight into the public view of the inquest. Their works reflect beliefs and a socio-historical context of the politics surrounding the coroner in his death investigations. The stage of the inquest is used in Carleton's fiction as a metaphor for suppression of political and economic crime. He also contributes to the stereotype of corrupt or incompetent figures of local government. The story 'The resurrections of Barney Bradley' (1841) features a farcical inquest in the countryside held by county coroner Casey, 'a vulgar man who loved his glass', who drinks whiskey throughout the proceedings.[28] He declares himself and the jury to be politically neutral as he begins the proceedings of the inquest,

> Gintlemen ... We want to identify ourselves with no party whatsoever ... I'm partly a government officer, and obedience is my cue; but as the county is divided into two parties, I feel it be my duty to hould myself neuther upon the one side. Hamim an diouol! Whisht wid yz, gintlemen, no cheerin![29]

[27] *Hansard 3*, xxxvi, 22 Feb. 1837, cc 863–958. [28] William Carleton, 'The resurrections of Barney Bradley' in *The fawn of Spring Vale, The clarionet, and other tales* (Dublin, 1841), iii, pp 261–328 at p. 289. [29] Ibid., p. 305.

Carleton puts dialect into the mouth of the coroner, and in doing so, he makes it clear that Casey is no gentleman. The story reveals that the 'corpse', Barney Bradley, is in fact alive, but the coroner must prove him dead. After several naggins of whiskey ordered and drunk by the coroner and the jury, a fight broke out among all participants including the audience at the inquest. Casey then toasted the crowd,

> Gintlemen ... I now propose the health of ould Ireland – a country, gintlemen, in which I am proud to say the law of inquest, gintlemen – the law of inquest – is better understood than in any other country under the sun. Gintlemen, 'Ould Ireland, the land of Inquests'.[30]

The story ends by describing how the coroner receives a 'flaybottomry and sound drubbing' and does not receive the fee for his services for the inquest. Casey is pained for being 'defrauded out of his money ... and [the fees for] two medical gintlemen to prove that he was dead'.[31] Overall, the story identifies several salient features of the political nature of the inquest: the disparity between the political parties, corruption and the indifference of local government towards uncovering the 'truth'.

A general mistrust of the investigation of death by the coroner is prevalent in other nineteenth-century literary texts. While Carleton's 'Barney Bradley' positioned the coroners' inquest as a topsy-turvy justice for a living corpse, 'The black prophet' (1847) depicts the coroner as unreliable and the inquest as a precarious miscarriage of justice. A man is found dead and the coroner is unable to conduct an inquest as he is purported to be gravely ill with typhus. Later it is revealed that he had simply experienced 'a severe wetting', had a cold and was recovered. The inquest finds Cornelius Dalton, a man wronged by his landlord, guilty of wilful murder, highlighting the contradictory nature of Irish justice.[32] Similarly, suspicion and greed surround an untimely death in Dion Boucicault's play 'Used up' (1844), where as a result of the coroner's inquest and writ of execution, the heirs and executors, i.e. debt collectors, would come to take possession of the estate.[33]

Several texts portray the coroner and inquest under the theme of Britishness and British justice in Ireland. An innocent man finds himself as a murder suspect and subject to a coroner's inquest in Gerald Griffin's 'Card drawing' (1827). The story depicts an inquest where a verdict of wilful murder is reached against an innocent Duke Dorgan, an Irish sailor serving in the British navy.[34] The tale highlights the injustices of the Irish courts of justice and frames the coroner and jury as representatives of administrative and judicial unfairness. The story represents different types of death, specifically death during war, while serving king and country

---

30 Ibid., p. 326. 31 Ibid., p. 305. 32 William Carleton, *The black prophet* (New York, 1881), p. 340. 33 Dion Boucicault, *Used up: a petite comedy, in two acts* (London, 1844). 34 Gerald Griffin, *Card drawing, The half sir, and Suil Dhuv the coiner* (Dublin, 1891), p. 67.

in military service, and death due to unjust British justice, or judicial murder.[35] A different dynamic is illustrated later in the century in Somerville and Ross' 'Some experiences of an Irish R.M.' (1899), in which a coroner's jury took a cautious view and reached a verdict of death by misadventure in a suspected murder case. However, the conservative resident magistrate (RM) feels it is his duty to 'call a magisterial inquiry to further investigate the matter', demonstrating that without a suspect named in the inquest verdict, the investigation needed closer examination.[36] The late nineteenth-century resident magistrate is a professional and an outsider attempting to impose order on Irish social chaos. This aspect of the text illustrates the modernization of the role as neither fees for profit nor a politicized subtext are imposed in executing the duties of coroner.

ISSUES WITH PAYMENT: DEBT COLLECTION AS COMPENSATION

Coroners were paid a fee per inquest plus a rate of mileage for travel expenses. Grand juries often refused to pay coroners' fees for various reasons, ranging from an inquest resulting in a verdict of death from non-violent causes to the grand jury simply wanting to keep costs down. Evidence suggests that inquests held on the poorest members in society – cottiers, beggars and other marginal groups – were considered a waste of public money by many Irish elites. The law could be used or ignored in any individual local court and issues regarding a lack of support and payment became abundant. In 1821, the four coroners covering Co. Cork, which is 120 miles in length and in some areas 54 in breadth, reported travelling up to 60 miles from home, often being detained for several days at considerable expense. Their petition highlighted,

> the arduous journey of the horses ... the great difficulties often arising in ascertaining the immediate cause of death ... inquests held in open fields ... the absence of surgeons or properly qualified medical persons ... and grand juries refuse to present any remuneration for those who have attended, and the friends of the deceased are frequently so poor as to be unable to bear the expense ...[37]

Co. Tipperary, infamous for outrages and high levels of death resulting from violence, was supported by seven coroners as well as the mayors of Clonmel and Cashel.[38] In 1819, the Tipperary coroners signed a letter addressed to Chief Secretary Charles Grant, stating that the grand jury was refusing to pay them more than the amount mandated by law and requesting that they be 'compensated for

---

35 Claire Connolly, 'The national tale' in Peter Garside and Karen O'Brien (eds), *The Oxford history of the novel in English*, ii: *English and British fiction 1750–1820* (Oxford, 2015), p. 229. 36 E.Œ. Somerville and Martin Ross, *Some experiences of an Irish R.M. with illustrations by Edith Somerville* (London, 1899), p. 61. 37 The coroners of Cork to Charles Grant, chief secretary of Ireland, 14 Apr. 1821 (NAI, CSORP/RP/1821/72). 38 Based on the group filing a petition it implies that the mayors were also magistrates. Two magistrates could hold an inquest when a coroner was not available.

their expenses or that they may not be liable to attend at inquests'.[39] Coroners and other officials from counties Down, Dublin, Limerick and Louth communicated similar grievances.[40] Across Ireland, a common trend emerged that coroners were not consistently compensated for their work, and, as a result, they often threatened not to perform their duties.

One advantage to the role of coroner in the first half of the nineteenth century was the power of debt collection. With the ability to execute writs, coroners could collect deodands as another means of compensation for themselves. This practice dated back to the Middle Ages and was no longer a part of the privileges of a coroner in England, but it was still practised in Ireland.[41] A deodand was a thing forfeited or given to the king, specifically, in law, an object or instrument that becomes forfeit because it has caused a person's death. The coroners were entitled to a fee for every inquest taken, as well as 13*s*. 4*d*. of the goods and chattels of a convicted murderer.[42] They were also allowed to inventory the goods of felons and fugitives and could exercise writs of execution with the same power as the sheriff.[43] Prison registers reveal that coroners' exchequers and writs were executed on felon inmates, with large sums confiscated from those incarcerated.[44] Sheriffs' sales and coroners' sales appeared in early nineteenth-century newspapers, showing they were still in practice. A coroner's sale published the name of the plaintiff and defendant, the auctioneer and when and where the goods named were being sold.[45]

However, as highlighted earlier by Peter Browne, dean of Ferns, some coroners were abusing their power by using public resources to collect debts as a result of matters other than death investigation. Although this behaviour was considered to be the 'general custom', it worked directly against the purpose of the office and its responsibility to the community. On 6 November 1821, in Co. Kildare, the chief magistrate of police, James Landy, wrote to Undersecretary William Gregory that two coroners, who were also sessions attorneys in the county, were executing writs on prisoners and laymen in the pursuit of matters other than the investigation of death.

---

39 The coroners of Tipperary to Charles Grant, 1 Sept. 1819 (NAI, CSO/RP/1822/1139). 40 Charles Clarke Hughes, MD, member of the Royal College of Surgeons, Dublin, and Drury Jones, alderman, one of the coroners for County and City Dublin, to Charles Grant, 21 Mar. 1820 (NAI, CSO/RP/1820/659); James McCarthy, coroner for Co. Dublin to. Charles Grant, 13 Dec. 1821 (NAI, CSO/RP/1821/220); Paul Parks, one of the coroners of Co. Louth, Dundalk to William Gregory, the lord lieutenant's secretary, 22 May 1821 (NAI, CSO/RP/1821/424); William McCune, church warden, Downpatrick, to Henry Grattan, MP, 16 Oct. 1822 (NAI, CSO/RP/1822/1936). 41 3 Hen. VII, c. 1 (1487), Recognizances Act. 42 14 Edw. III, St 1, c. 8 (1340), Escheators and Coroners Act; Matt Dutton, *The office and authority of sheriffs, under-sheriffs, deputies, county-clerks and coroners in Ireland* (Dublin, 1721), p. 444. 43 Dutton, *The office and authority of sheriffs*, p. 444. 44 Denise M. Dowdall, *Irish nineteenth-century prison records: survey and evaluation* (Dublin, 2013), p. 42; NAI, Prison registers 1790–1924, 29 June 1846, book no. 1/10/7, 622; ibid., 21 May 1832, book no. 1/10/2, 236; ibid., 28 May 1846, book no. 1/10/7, 507. 45 *FJ*, 16 Mar. 1815, 22 Sept. 1815; *Saunders's News-Letter*, 6 Feb. 1827; *Sligo Journal*, 16 Mar. 1832; *Kerry Evening Post*, 26 Oct. 1836; *Dublin Morning Register*, 5 Mar. 1840; *Clare Journal and Ennis Advertiser*, 1 Jan. 1844.

Annfield, Kilcullen, Co. Kildare, 6 November 1821
Dear Sir,
All the coroners of the county of Kildare are sessions attorneys acting as magistrates. On every occasion, [they are] taking information for assaults in consideration for the attorney general and I've never heard it being done for any other county.

In one instance, a man who was in Naas gaol for knocking down one of my police [officers] and with others disarming him (which arms have not been recovered) one of the coroners bailed him out at the last sessions by the advice of the Barrister and Bench of Magistrates. I had him retaken and committed again to gaol. After this, in open court, two of the coroners, Mr Parr and Mr Harrison, said they would bail the prisoner out again; on which our highly respectable barrister Scoles told them if they did, application would be made to the county of Kings Bench when in all probability they would be fined five hundred pounds ...

James Landy, Chief of Police, Co Kildare[46]

PS – I have the pleasure of informing you that everything goes on satisfactorily throughout my district which I entirely attribute to the vigilance of the Police. Two houses were set on fire near Dunlavin a few nights since belonging to two farmers (Protestants), one of the patrols arrived on time to save the house and property but could not discover the perpetrators.

From the evidence provided by Chief Landy, Mr Parr and Mr Harrison were using the police to arrest men for debt and assaults and were instructing the release of prisoners from gaol. Mr Parr defended himself to William Gregory, the undersecretary, and in response received a strong reminder that 'a coroner is merely a conservator of the peace ... [who] cannot administer an oath or grant a warrant' and that if Parr and Harrison were found again to exceed their authority, 'the government will direct a prosecution' against them.[47]

There was cause for local grand juries to be concerned as they could be held liable for financial damages should a coroner abuse his power. If the coroner incurred debts or was sued and did not have enough personal wealth to cover any reparations, the fines would be paid out of the local rates. This happened in 1821 in Co. Galway, where a coroner incurred many fines and much debt in the line of office. Upon the coroner's death, the plaintiff sued the government and won, and they were instructed to pay £600 out of the local rates.[48] Amid reports of misuse of power and poor behaviour, cries for changes to legislation were heard, demanding that the office be returned to its 'pristine dignity as it fell into the hands of those

---

46 James Landy to Undersecretary William Gregory, 6 Nov. 1821 (NAI, CSORP/1821/SC/1426). 47 Ibid. 48 *FJ*, 5 June 1821.

who are, in some instances, incompetent to the discharge of their even limited authority'.[49]

TENSIONS AND TRIBES: THE RELIGIOUS COMPOSITION OF CORONERS

Critical examinations of local government by the crown in the first half of the nineteenth century attempted to respond to issues of civil unrest, crises of law and order, poverty and corruption, and, specifically, to address the under-representation of the Catholic majority. The attempted repeal of the Act of Union, Catholic emancipation and the Tithe War created political and religious tensions and divisions that profoundly affected how the criminal justice system and local government operated. Acts of Parliament were passed in the first few decades of the nineteenth century to regulate local government, including reducing the powers of the sheriff, jury reform, restructuring the constabulary, introducing resident magistrates from England and prison reform, as well as legislation for coroners.[50]

The coroners in Ireland were predominately Protestant men, who shared their religion with others in local government and thereby contributed to its homogeneity. These were most often men with no professional qualifications, landowners who aspired to attain or maintain the status of 'gentleman'.[51] Some, however, had legal or medical education or experience, were civil servants, merchants, justices of the peace, land agents, gentlemen or farmers, or had a combination of these backgrounds.[52] Within the comfortable monopoly of local government, the role of the coroner posed a potential threat. A coroner, prior to 1838, was the only elected official in local government and secured the office with the support of qualified voters. Approximately one hundred men, more or less, would hold the role of coroner across Ireland at any given time in the nineteenth century, and the composition of their religious affiliation should be considered.

---

49 Sir John Jervis, *Sir John Jervis on the office and duties of coroners: with forms and precedents* (London, 1827), p. i. 50 50 Geo. III, c. 30 (18 May 1810), Coroners (Ireland) Act; 1 Geo. IV, c. 28 (17 May 1820), Coroners' Fees (Ireland) Act; 3 Geo. IV, c. 115 (1 Aug. 1822), Coroners (Ireland) Act; 10 Geo. IV, c. 37 (2 June 1829), Coroners (Ireland) Act; 6 & 7 Wm. IV, c. 89 (12 July 1836), Coroners (Ireland) Act; 50 Geo. III, c. 103 (20 June 1810), Prisons (Ireland) Act; 55 Geo. III, c. 92 (4 July 1815), Prisons (Ireland) Act; 59 Geo. III, c. 100 (12 July 1819), Prisons (Ireland) Act; 1 & 2 Geo. IV, c. 57 (1 July 1821), Prisons (Ireland) Act; 7 Geo. IV, c. 74 (31 May 1826), Prisons (Ireland) Act; 56 Geo. III, c. 87 (26 June 1816), Grand Jury (Ireland) Act; 57 Geo. III, c. 107 (11 July 1817), Grand Jury Presentments (Ireland) Act; 37 & 38 Vict., c. 35 (20 Aug. 1836), Grand Jury (Ireland) Act; 57 Geo. III, c. 68 (7 July 1817), Sheriffs (Ireland) Act; 58 Geo. III, c. 67 (3 June 1818), Grand Jury Presentments (Ireland) Act; 4 Geo. IV, c. 43 (27 June 1823), Salaries of County Officers (Ireland) Act; 7 Geo. IV, c. 62 (18 May 1826), Valuation of Lands (Ireland) Act; 3 Geo. IV, c. 103 (5 Aug. 1822), Constabulary (Ireland) Act; 6 & 7 Will. IV, c. 13 (18 Feb. 1836), Constabulary (Ireland) Act. 51 Henry Croly, *The Irish medical directory for 1843, including notes of the literary and scientific institutions of Ireland, with notes, historical biographical, and bibliographcial* (Dublin, 1843), pp 185–200; *The Irish medical directory of 1852* (London, 1852), pp 205–7. 52 *The Irish medical directory of 1852*, pp 205–7.

On 25 June 1823, radical MP Joseph Hume (1777–1855) read a list of offices and posts where Catholics were under-represented to the House of Commons. Of the 108 county coroners, only 29 were Catholics.[53] Still, the office of county coroner had the largest percentage of Catholics of any position in government, 26.9 per cent (see Table 1).

The Coroners Act (1822) made access to the office more difficult, increasing the personal wealth qualifications, and set remuneration in the form of fixed fees determined by a fixed number of inquests to be carried out in any given assizes term.[54] Men holding the office of coroner needed an estate of inheritance of the annual value of £200 or an estate of freehold for his own life.[55] This increase in property qualifications for coroners was potentially in conflict with attempting to increase the number of Catholics in the role. Throughout the 1810s, 1820s and 1830s, the emphasis on wealth as a qualification for local government officials contributed to the partisan politics in local government. There was an expectation of the country gentleman that he would contribute his time and effort to local matters as an obligation or duty. In England and Ireland, men in public office with enough property and wealth could afford to pay expenses out of pocket until they were reimbursed and this made them attractive applicants.[56] The office of coroner was intended to be a role that served the people, to find justice for the dead and the living, and it was argued that perhaps the right man for the role should not receive any remuneration.[57] Otherwise, some suspected that death investigations might take place whether there was a need for them or not, for the coroner's need to profit.

In 1829, alongside Catholic emancipation, the number of men qualified to vote in parliamentary elections was dramatically reduced when the forty-shilling freeholders were stripped of their voting rights.[58] While Catholics were given the right to vote, the qualification to vote was raised to ownership or rental of land worth £10 and upwards per annum.[59] This also restricted the persons who could vote for coroner to only those qualified to vote for a 'knight of the shire' (i.e. parliamentary voters). Political tensions became heated in the election of a coroner in Co. Cork. Catholic candidate Daniel Connellan drew the support of a group of Catholic voters, but Protestant candidate Richard Jones contested the election. A series of letters, from December 1828 through January 1829, reveals that the high sheriff of Co. Cork, Michael Creagh, wrote to Chief Secretary Francis Leveson Gower (1800–57) to explain the conflict he faced in trying to conclude the election.[60] A group of forty-two men (presumably all Catholic) were listed by name and

---

53 *Hansard 3*, ix, 25 June 1823, cc 1212–41. 54 3 Geo. IV, c. 115 (1 Aug. 1822), Coroners (Ireland) Act. 55 Ibid. 56 R.B. McDowell, *The Irish administration, 1801–1914* (London, 1964), p. 7. 57 *Hansard 1*, xxxiv, 22 May 1816, cc 681–3. 58 10 Geo. IV, c. 7 (13 Apr. 1829), Catholic Relief Act. 59 Ibid. 60 Michael Creagh, high sheriff, Co. Cork to chief secretary, 1 Dec. 1828 (NAI, CSO/RP/1828/1910/8); 10 Dec. 1828 (NAI, CSO/RP/1828/1910/7); 16 Dec. 1828 (NAI, CSO/RP/1828/1910/5); 17 Dec. 1828 (NAI, CSO/RP/1828/1910/3); 19 Dec. 1828 (NAI, CSO/RP/1828/1910/2); 6 Jan. 1829 (NAI, CSO/RP/1828/1910/1).

Table 1: Some of the offices held by Catholics in 1823

Office	Number	Catholics	%
Assistant barristers of counties	32	2	6.25
In chancery	73	0	0
Chief constables of police	350	20	5.70
Chief magistrates of Ireland	4	0	0
Clerks of the crown	12	0	0
Clerks of the peace	39	0	0
Coroners	108	29	26.9
Crown circuit court	12	0	0
Exchequer	56	2	3.50
Irish Post Office	466	25	5.30
Jailers, local inspectors and other officers of county prisons	151	0	0
King's bench	28	3	0.10
Metropolitan and consistorial courts	100	1	1
Police magistrates of Dublin	18	0	0
Royal Dublin Society	17	0	0
Total	1,466	82	5.54

Note: This is not a comprehensive list, but rather a sample taken which demonstrates the lack of Catholics in office in 1823. *Sources:* Thomas Wyse, *Historical sketch of the late Catholic Association of Ireland* (London, 1829), vol. 2, appendix xxi, p. cclxxxiii; *Hansard 3*, ix, 24 June 1823, cc 1212–41.

identified as holding common land in the mountains, paying no rent, rates or taxes and described by Creagh as 'miserable wretches'.[61] This group stated that they had 'no landlord except the Lord Almighty.'[62] The men were disqualified from voting as they had no freehold, and Jones won the election. On 15 January 1829, the conservative *Dublin Evening Packet* described how the sheriff had been harassed during this election by 'the most ignorant class in the world' and was grateful that 'where everything seems radically distempered by Popery, constitutional suffrage is at an end'.[63] The Cork election suggests that Catholics attempting to secure a role in local government, particularly that of coroner, found it difficult when the Catholic voting population was dramatically reduced due to increased property requirements.

61 Michael Creagh, high sheriff, Co. Cork to chief secretary, 16 Dec. 1828 (NAI, CSO/RP/1828/1910/5). Michael Creagh, high sheriff, Co. Cork to chief secretary, 17 Dec. 1828 (NAI, CSO/RP/1828/1910/4). 62 Michael Creagh, high sheriff, Co. Cork to chief secretary, 17 Dec. 1828 (NAI, CSO/RP/1828/1910/3). 63 *Dublin Evening Packet*, 15 Jan. 1829.

THE MEDICAL INQUEST: PARTICIPATION OF DOCTORS

Similarly to coroners, doctors were also expected to serve the public as a civic duty in the investigation of death. Up until 1846, doctors were legally required to attend inquests but many were dissatisfied with the pay, which could be inconsistent as it could be withheld by the coroner or grand jury. Meanwhile, surgeons legally were not allowed payment for their attendance at inquests within institutions. A letter written in June 1828 to the lord lieutenant, the marquess of Anglesey (1768–1854), from a surgeon and apothecary in Castlebar, Co. Mayo, John Atkinson, detailed his arrest and confinement to the county prison by Coroner Henry Moran for refusing to attend an inquest without being guaranteed his payment.[64] Surgeon Graham Acton also refused to appear without a fee but was not arrested.[65] Another letter, written in January 1830 to the chief secretary from Surgeon William Thompson, of Ballyshannon, Co. Donegal, highlights that the county treasurer refused his payment for participating in the coroner's inquest.[66] Grand juries were angered by the charges imposed by the administration. Co. Dublin grand jury foreman George Evans wrote to the chief secretary in May 1830 complaining of the high fee claims they received from county coroners who also requested reimbursement for payments made to surgeons who attended inquests.[67]

Most often, post-mortem examinations were conducted by general practitioners and local surgeons who had local private practices and worked at local medical institutions (fever hospitals, dispensaries, gaols, workhouses). In some instances, they were the doctors of the deceased and familiar with their general state of health. Few nineteenth-century Irish doctors were experts in the field of pathology or forensic medicine, but rather most were formally qualified medical practitioners. Their engagement with inquests took place when they were called to make a general observation or examination of the body.[68] The extent to which the doctor or surgeon assessed the corpse varied, whether it be an external or internal examination, based upon the nature of the wounds or its general state. The education of country doctors ranged from apprenticeship training to formal education, the latter being limited for Catholics. Trinity College did not permit the medical training of Catholics until 1845 and although the Queen's Colleges were secular, they were not supported by the Catholic hierarchy.[69]

One of the most influential drivers for improvements to the role of coroner was radical English MP and medical practitioner Thomas Wakely (1795–1862), also the founder of the *Lancet* and coroner of Middlesex Co., who campaigned for many

---

64 John Atkinson, Castlebar, Co. Mayo, to Lord Lieutenant Henry William Paget, 24 June 1828 (NAI, CSO/RP/1828/940); Virginia Crossman, 'Henry William Paget, 1st marquis of Anglesey', *DIB*. 65 John Atkinson, Castlebar, Co. Mayo to Lord Lieutenant Henry William Paget, 24 June 1828 (NAI, CSO/RP/1828/940). 66 William Thompson, Ballyshannon, Co. Donegal to Chief Secretary Sir Francis Leveson Gower, 5 Jan. 1830 (NAI, CSO/RP/1830/34). 67 George Evans, Swords, Dublin to Chief Secretary Sir Francis Leveson Gower, 25 May 1830 (NAI, CSO/RP/1830/1321). 68 McGoff-McCann, *Melancholy madness*, pp 35–6. 69 Susan Wilkinson, 'Early medical education in Ireland', *Irish Migration Studies in Latin America*, 6:3 (2008), p. 161.

years encouraging the medicalization of the modern inquest in England.[70] Wakely strove to use the inquest to evaluate death with more emphasis on the physical, scientific facts (established through the post-mortem) rather than the local knowledge that had tended to influence verdicts. He aimed to secure more doctors in the role of coroner. As a direct result of his campaigning, coroners in England saw improvements such as salaries, assistants, pensions and expenses reimbursed.[71] English coroners also formed the Coroners' Society of England and Wales in 1846, which was comprised of coroners from varying backgrounds, with some professionals from the fields of law and medicine.

Wakely's influence encouraged change in Ireland, but the coroner's office evolved much more slowly there. The men who were coroners, including those with a medical background, were elected either due to the patronage of the social elite or by qualified voters (who in many cases also supported the local elite) and who met the property requirement. Geary's study of nineteenth-century medicine in Ireland exposes how ownership of medical knowledge sat with 'Ascendancy oligarchies' and how the medical establishment and profession embodied nepotism, sectarianism and divisive politics.[72] The medical and scientific fields were dominated by Protestant elites who excluded Catholic access to education and professional employment opportunities. They also embraced policies that excluded Catholics from 'natural knowledge' as reflected by local scientific societies such as the Monaghan Literary and Scientific Society.[73] Geary's research also reveals that in the 1830s through to the 1850s, the vast majority of jobs in public hospitals were held by members of the Protestant elite, and roles were determined by politics and religion.[74] As a result, the administration had to contend with the ongoing battle of sectarianism before advancing the rights of the coroner within local government.

Catholic leaders spoke out about the need for educated and professional medical men to participate in inquests in the capacity of coroners and medical witnesses. The correspondence published in newspapers reflects some of the first demands within the burgeoning field of medical jurisprudence. On 16 November 1839, an article appearing in the *Freeman's Journal* detailed a lecture on medical jurisprudence given by Thomas Brady, esq. MD (1801–64), who addressed a theatre full of legal professionals at Dublin Law School.[75] Brady, a liberal Catholic, stated that it was impossible to find the true cause of death in cases of 'infanticide, abortion,

---

[70] David Sharp, 'Thomas Wakely (1795–1862): a biographical sketch', *Lancet*, 379:9829 (May 2012), pp 1914–21. [71] 23 & 24 Vict., c. 116 (28 Aug. 1860), County Coroners Act [Eng.] [72] Lawrence M. Geary, *Medicine and charity in Ireland, 1718–1851* (Dublin, 2004), pp 3, 128. [73] Enda Leaney, 'Vested interests: science and medicine in nineteenth-century Ireland', *Field Day Review*, 2 (2006), p. 287; the Society met locally, as reflected by their meeting notes in the *Northern Standard*. They were an evangelical organization determined to dispel superstition under the guise of the promotion of 'natural knowledge'. [74] Geary, *Medicine and charity in Ireland*, pp 130–1. [75] *FJ*, 18 Nov. 1839. Thomas Brady, *Introductory lecture on medical jurisprudence delivered in the theatre of the Royal Dublin Society on Saturday 16th November 1837 by Thomas Brady, esq MD, fellow and professor in the King and Queen's College of Physicians, Ireland* (Dublin, 1839).

murder, poisoning and lunacy' without the knowledge of how to examine and cross-examine medical witnesses. He also highlighted that the only way to do so is by using 'skilful physicians, surgeons and chemists' and stated that

> up to the present period the subject of medical jurisprudence formed but a slight portion of the study of the physicians in the United Kingdoms, and many instances might be adduced when the most serious mistakes have occurred from ignorance or inexperience of medical witnesses.[76]

A letter published in the *Freeman's Journal* on 11 September 1840 revealed the opinion on the coroners' inquest by Sir Dominic John Corrigan, physician (1802–80), a popular and leading Catholic medical professional.[77] In the letter to the attorney general on the topic of the 'disgrace of present system of coroners' inquests', he described it as 'a gross burlesque on jurisprudence'.[78] He provided two examples of suicides in which inquest participants did not provide enough expertise and knowledge of the physical evidence, which, if they had, would have led to verdicts of murder. Corrigan's statements reflect not only the need for professionalism within medical jurisprudence, but also the attempt to erode the grip of Protestant hegemony within the field.

In 1843, there were just eight medically trained coroners in Ireland out of a total of 84.[79] Varied reports appeared even as late as 1862 that Irish coroners did not always hold inquests with medical men in attendance.[80] The traditional view of the proficiency of coroners is that they may have been incompetent because of their lack of medical expertise, which led to erroneous judgments.[81] A contradictory view suggests that most coroners used trained medical men and well-known country doctors and they heeded their conclusions based on the physical evidence. In Waddell's first casebook, 271 of the 408 inquests taken by the coroner (who was not medically trained) from 1846 through 1855 included the testimony of doctors. In every single instance, the jury agreed with the doctor's medical verdict. Additionally, nearly all of the doctors who testified at inquests held by Waddell appear in medical directories as trained professionals.

Reliable knowledge of death from new scientific methods became more important and from this arose a greater need to provide answers through forensic evidence, such as in cases of homicidal poisoning.[82] Specialists in the medical profession (early chemists and pathologists) received samples of internal organs and fluids sent from local doctors conducting inquests to attempt to detect lethal substances. While increased detection of poisons did help expose the cause of some murders,

---

76 Ibid. 77 L. Perry Curtis jnr, 'Corrigan, Sir Dominic John, first baronet (1802–1880)', *ODNB*. 78 *FJ*, 11 Sept. 1840. 79 Croly, *The Irish medical directory of 1843*, pp 185–6. 80 *Dublin Medical Press*, 8 Oct. 1862. 81 McMahon, *Homicide in pre-Famine and Famine Ireland*, p. 186. 82 Ian A. Burney, 'A poisoning of no substance: the trials of medico-legal proof in mid-Victorian England' in *Journal of British Studies*, 27:1 (1999), p. 61; Victoria M. Nagy, *Nineteenth-century female poisoners: three English women who used arsenic to kill* (New York, 2015), p. 64.

suicides and botched abortions that resulted in the death of the aborting woman, a primary characteristic of an Irish inquest was how the verdict reflected the moral and social values of the jury and their decision whether to name the accused or hold them accountable. In some instances, the inquest jury determined there was no prisoner or accused to hold accountable, and they confined their verdict to the medical cause of death.[83] In these instances, the technical medical reason for death helped provide some accuracy as to the physical cause of death and coroners would rely on further investigation by constables to help identify guilty parties through further witness testimony or physical evidence.

THE TERROR OF WITNESSES: SOCIAL PRESSURE ON INQUEST JURORS

The coroner's court was an independent, public court where the local participants found a cause of death that reflected the social and moral values of their community. Coroners' juries had survived as a remnant of local independence and were known to assert themselves as the voice of the people.[84] The coroner differs from all other judicial officers in that he initiates his own proceedings, while other judicial officers must wait until the matter for their adjudication can be brought before them. It is at the coroner's discretion as to when inquests should take place and he selects his own jury. Jury members were required to be good and lawful men, not 'aliens' or 'outlaws' having a former conviction of a felony or treason, or any 'infamous' crime.[85] English juries were not always submissive and often challenged evidence and direction.[86] Examining inquest verdicts offers an opportunity to consider the characteristics of Irish coroners' juries and the relationship between the coroner and the public. The jury had a duty to review the evidence presented at the inquest to determine the cause of death of the deceased. Most often, in the Irish countryside, the jurors sitting on an inquest were local residents who knew the deceased and the witnesses. These social conditions put pressures on jurors which influenced the outcome of the verdicts.

Evidence shows that the men serving as witnesses and jurors in the coroner's court were sometimes at risk and under threat. In an impassioned speech in 1833, Prime Minister Earl Grey (1764–1845) conveyed his shock as to the many atrocities suffered by Catholic jurors and witnesses and provided insight into the pressures applied to coroners' witnesses should they participate in an inquest.[87] Grey told

---

[83] *Criminal and Judicial Statistics, 1877, Ireland, part I: police, criminal proceedings, prisons; part II: common law, equity and civil law*, 265 [C.2152] HC 1878, lxxix, 154–5. From 1873–7, only three people were tried in Ireland for administering poison to commit murder. Of those, only one was convicted. [84] W.E. Vaughan, *Murder trials in Ireland, 1836–1914* (Dublin, 2009), p. 44. [85] Edmund Hayes, *Crimes and punishments: or, a digest of the criminal statute law in Ireland, alphabetically arranged ... with notes* (2nd ed.; Dublin, 1842), p. 197. [86] J.S. Cockburn and Thomas A. Green (eds), *Twelve good men and true: the criminal trial jury in England, 1200–1800* (Princeton, 2014), pp 73–4. [87] Sir Thomas Lawrence, 'Charles Grey, second Earl Grey (1764–1845)', *ODNB*.

the story of a man who witnessed the murder of his father-in-law, but sent a message that he'd sooner 'submit to penalty of the law imposed rather than appear as a witness at the inquest, for he could not do that without eventually forfeiting his life to the vengeance of those who had murdered his relation'.[88] Witnesses and jurors in petty courts and the court of assize were also often in perilous political and social situations and many were reluctant to participate.[89] Jury reform was passed in 1833 offering protection and safe journey to witnesses and jurors when participating in petty, grand and coroners' courts, however pressure on participants continued throughout the nineteenth century.[90]

The Irish administration in pre-Famine Ireland focused its attention on reducing rural violence and local government corruption, as well as taking measures to secure more convictions in criminal trials so as to suppress and manage the use of lethal force. The low conviction rates in petty and assize trials were seen as a sign that the administration of justice was not working.[91] This resulted in a demand for more effective inquests that focused on homicide, and investigations that produced evidence and testimony that turned out verdicts either naming specific individuals or helped the constabulary to further their search for the guilty parties. Inquests that did not produce a verdict of murder were considered by the administration to be ineffective and an unnecessary burden on the tax-paying public.

The government called for coroners' returns from the years 1834 through 1839 that reported on cases of murder or manslaughter where persons known were identified. Returns included verdicts of death from gun shots, blows of a spade on the head, being beaten by stones, and being assaulted in a riot – in each instance at the hands of named individuals. One such inquest, that of Larry Meegan, included the names of several accused assailants. The inquest taken on 21 and 22 May 1838 in Dundalk, Co. Louth, reached a verdict of 'Murdered while labouring in a field by Michael McEntagart, Patrick Hanratty, Denise McCreesh, Patrick Callaghan, John, Anthony, Sylvester, Edward and David McKenna, and John Rush'.[92] The coroner and the constabulary were often working closely together, and evidence might emerge during the proceedings or afterwards upon further investigation by the constabulary.[93] At the time of Hessy Rogers' inquest on 29 June 1837, the jury found that death occurred 'by violence of strangulation by persons unknown' near the Clonfad River in Co. Monaghan. This return also contained the following note: 'Thomas, Patrick, Hugh and Mary Murphy

---

88 *Hansard 3*, xv, 15 Feb. 1833, cc 718–58, 732.   89 Niamh Howlin, '"The terror of their lives": Irish jurors' experiences', *Law and History Review*, 29:3 (2011), pp 703–61, p. 723.   90 3 & 4 Will. IV, c. 91, s. 40 (19 Feb. 1833), Juries (Ireland) Act; 3 & 4 Will. IV, c. 4 (8 Mar. 1833), Suppression of Local Disturbances and Dangerous Associations in Ireland.   91 Howlin, '"The terror of their lives": Irish jurors' experiences', p. 714.   92 *A return of all coroners inquests taken in the respective years 1835, 1836, 1837, 1838, and 1839* ... (NAI, CSO Official papers, Coroners' returns, 1839/109).   93 Vaughan, *Murder trials in Ireland, 1836–1914*, p. 45.

since arrested on further informations [*sic*] to be heard in Fermanagh'.[94] Of 133 inquests recorded in 50 months as submitted by Thomas Bourne, crown clerk of Co. Monaghan, a verdict of homicide was reached 31 times and in 10 of those cases – 7.5 per cent of the total – persons known were identified.[95]

JUSTICE AND EMOTION: THE PRISM OF BLAME

Some inquests revealed that a violent death had taken place, but identified no named suspect. Testimony given to the Select Committee of the House of Lords on Crime in 1839 by Joseph Tabeteau stated that there was 'a very great disregard' for human life among the peasantry' and that, 'even after death it is astonishing how soon the thing passes away, without leaving any remembrance, even at the very inquest there is very little feeling shown'.[96] This perception is challenged by the evidence of coroners' inquest verdicts. A contemporary evaluation of neutral verdicts in murder cases reveals an emotional and politicized community determined to seek justice. Breathnach and O'Halpin find that the emotions of the community are best examined through a 'prism of blame' when evaluating jury verdicts.[97]

This well-established approach to evaluating the verdicts of inquests was developed to evaluate early twentieth-century behaviour when coroners' juries protected mothers who had murdered their children. Farrell's study of 4,645 cases of suspected infanticide from 1850 to 1900 shows a clear trend in inquest verdicts excusing the mother of committing the crime of murder.[98] Findings show mercy and empathy was offered to the mothers in cases of infanticide, as measured by impartial or neutral verdicts which suggests they were complicit. Witness testimony and medical evidence in some instances supported and sought to decriminalize a suspect's actions. Cases of suspected infanticide often featured witnesses who did not know the mother was pregnant. In such cases, findings and verdicts included: that the mother was simply 'ignorant to tie the navel string', stillbirth, or neglect by workhouse staff.[99] All evidence attempted to shift blame away from the mother, ignoring the fact that concealment of pregnancy was a criminal act, and that she was most likely the guilty party.[100] Within these verdicts we see the moral 'good' that was sought as these were women caught in an impossible predicament, as they most often had no options for work or family support in society as a single mother.

---

94 *A return of all coroners inquests taken in the respective years 1835, 1836, 1837, 1838, and 1839* ... (NAI, CSO Official papers, Coroners' returns, 1839/109). **95** Ibid. **96** *Minutes of evidence taken before the select committee of the House of Lords appointed to enquire into the state of Ireland since the year 1835 in respect of crime and outrage* ... p. 747, HC 1839 (468) xi, xii, 1. **97** Ciara Breathnach and Eunan O'Halpin, 'Scripting blame: Irish coroners' courts and unnamed infant dead, 1916–32', *Social History*, 39:2 (2014), p. 211. **98** Elaine Farrell, *'A most diabolical deed': infanticide and Irish society, 1850–1900* (Manchester, 2013), p. 18. **99** CB1, no. 294.12, Infant Child, 22 June 1852. **100** Breathnach and O'Halpin, 'Scripting blame', pp 210–11.

This trend by which verdicts deflected blame from mothers is demonstrated in a verdict found in a King's Co. inquest led by coroner James Dillon (1788–1859) conducted at a Tullamore workhouse in 1853, which concluded that,

> on the night of the 23rd at Puttahawn Par Killride Bar, Ballycowan and King's County – Catherine Cooke was casually overlain by her mother and thereby suffocated and died – said Mother was not accountable.[101]

Using inquests taken by coroner Waddell, a separate trend emerges that women were more likely to be named in the jury's verdict as the murder suspect than men in cases of domestic murder. Damning witness and medical testimony was given during the inquest on John Mitchell against his wife, Martha, resulting in a coroner's jury verdict that stated:

> Death from effects of arsenic received into the stomach but how or by whom administered there is no evidence, but the jury however are strongly of opinion that Martha Mitchell, wife of deceased, is the guilty party.[102]

Two very different themes emerge when evaluating verdicts and applying the prism of blame to domestic murder cases within Waddell's casebooks. They can be categorized into two different spheres: a 'maternal sphere' that is inclusive of mothers and infants, when the coroner's jury took the decision to ignore evidence of murder and, as a result, there was no conviction; and a 'fraternal sphere', where men and women are involved in domestic violence resulting in murder, and regardless of the overwhelming evidence, male juries did not find the men guilty but were willing to identify women who were guilty of killing men. Evidence suggests that juries felt 'domestic privacy' should be respected, along with male authority. This priority of men's rights and social status over their wives appears on multiple occasions in the coroner's casebook. The death of Jane Gordon prompted several people to come forward and speak to Waddell, telling him that 'her death was the result of violence sustained at the hands of her husband'. As he pursued the case, Waddell could not get sworn depositions against Jane's husband, William, to justify exhuming her body or that he believed would lead to 'criminating' her husband. Waddell wrote that he 'feared the reports made were not altogether without grounds for belief in harsh if not cruel treatment', however no inquest was conducted.[103]

Similarly, in the case of Margaret Quinn, witness testimony indicated domestic abuse at the hands of her husband, however the inquest verdict concluded she died from fever.[104] Equally, the witness testimony and physical evidence presented at the

---

101 Inquest reports of James Dillon, King's Co. coroner (1846–54), no. 1054, Catherine Cooke, 24 June 1853 (Offaly Historical and Archaeological Society, Tullamore, Co. Offaly, Ireland, IE OHA OH551). 102 CB1, no. 4.153, John Mitchell, 27 July 1848. 103 CB2, inquiry, Jane Gordon, 12–19 Jan. 1867. 104 CB1, no. 10, Margaret Quinn, 29 July 1846.

inquest of Ann Cavenagh provided evidence of routine physical abuse by her husband, yet the verdict of death was from disease and natural causes.[105] Only one case stands apart. Mary Magee had provided her testimony to justice of the peace John Madden of Hilton House prior to her death, which at her inquest provided the details of her abuse by her husband Charles.[106] In this rare instance, her husband was named, and the verdict of death was stated as 'injuries caused and inflicted by her husband, Charles Magee'.[107] It is likely the reason for this unique instance where a man was named in the death of a woman in a domestic murder was the prominence of Madden and his influence in carrying out justice.

SECTARIAN MURDER: JURORS AND VERDICTS

Some historians have defined pre-Famine Ireland as a violent place where lethal violence was often used, leading government to want to convict the perpetrators of politically motivated and sectarian murders.[108] The polarized society of rural Ireland, divided between the conservative landowning elite and tenant farmers and labourers, and between Protestants and Catholics, presented significant issues when attempting to prevent crime and impose justice. If an inquest identified that murder had taken place, and if, during or after this, a suspect was named, a criminal trial by jury took place. One prominent feature of criminal trials in nineteenth-century Ireland was a lack of convictions – most accused were acquitted. Conviction rates were lowest in rural areas for two reasons: first, due to close relationships between the accused, the witnesses and the jurors; and second, because Irish society in the nineteenth century was divided due to partisanship and corruption.[109] Not all jurors might be of the class that believed in or respected the system of law in Ireland, and therefore would not consider enforcing punishment.[110] Additionally, fear of terrorization from agrarian secret societies, religious societies and other local factions was a significant problem in the countryside and this was a primary reason why jurors at trials often refused to return a verdict of guilty.[111] Similarly, there was a divide between those with power in the community, and those without power, bound together by mutual interests, shared obligations, or family bonds.[112] These persons faced social pressures and, in some cases, threats of physical violence, to reach a neutral verdict in cases involving one of their own, or one that did not name the accused.

---

105 CB1, no. 33.149, Ann Cavenagh, 27 June 1848. 106 CB2, no. 5.824, Mary Magee, 10 Sept. 1866. Magee was from Derryvolen, Co. Fermanagh. 107 Ibid. 108 McMahon, *Homicide in pre-Famine and Famine Ireland*, pp 128–9; Terence Martin Dunne, 'Cultures of resistance in pre-Famine Ireland' (PhD, NUI Maynooth, 2014); Mary Helen Thuente, 'Violence in pre-Famine Ireland: the testimony of Irish folklore and fiction', *Irish University Review*, 15:2 (1985), pp 129–47. 109 David Johnson, 'Trial by jury in Ireland 1860–1914', *Journal of Legal History*, 17:3 (1996), p. 277; Niamh Howlin, *Juries in Ireland* (Dublin, 2017), p. 216. 110 Howlin, 'Controlling jury composition in nineteenth-century Ireland', p. 227. 111 Howlin, '"The terror of their lives": Irish jurors' experiences', p. 726. 112 Hoppen, *Elections, politics and society in Ireland, 1832–1885*, p. 63.

As a result of the lack of convictions, the government constructed petty juries (or criminal trial juries) with men who met qualifications of property, residence, age and social status.[113] Most men who were qualified to perform jury duty tried to avoid it.[114] Juries could be common or special. Special juries were sought in cases with a significant public concern or inolved sectarian murder and required men considered of the highest intellect and prominent societal rank – merchants, bankers or esquires – often for the purpose of guiding justice towards a specific verdict.[115] In most cases, coroners' juries came from the same social background as assize and petty court juries, but in cases of sectarian homicide, local institutional liability or other sensitive issues, they could be composed of special jurymen or local elites. In these instances, it was said that such inquest juries were 'notorious once they were set in motion by the coroner to find one and only one verdict', and this was a similar characteristic of special juries selected in petty or assize courts.[116]

By 1842, coroners and juries were accused of costing the tax-paying public too much money and it was argued that coroners should limit themselves to conducting inquests only where murder had taken place. The report of the commissioners appointed to revise the grand jury laws in Ireland with respect to coroners found that of the 1,945 inquests submitted for the year of 1841, 'nine-tenths were unnecessary, being merely accidental deaths'.[117] Lawmakers still considered the inquest to be a function whose value was measured by the identification of murder and complained that not enough inquests were discovering murders or people guilty of them. Inquests with neutral verdicts or verdicts of death by natural causes were considered less valuable.[118]

NEW LEGISLATION: THE CORONERS' ACT OF 1846

The failure of the potato crop in 1845–6 coincided with the passing of the Coroners' Act in July 1846. Although improvements to the legislation for English coroners were championed in Parliament by Wakely, it is likely that the impending crisis in Ireland helped facilitate the passing of Irish legislation as multiple bills with proposed changes had been put forward to Parliament in the previous decade without success. The law refreshed the qualifications surrounding the office of coroner. Vaughan's assessment of the act is that it reinforced the power and status of the coroner as the only elected official in local government and gave him more power over inquests.[119] It reduced property qualifications to an estate of inheritance

---

[113] Howlin, 'Controlling jury composition in nineteenth-century Ireland', pp 227–8. [114] Howlin, 'The politics of jury trials in nineteenth-century Ireland', pp 2–3. [115] James C. Oldham, 'The origins of the special jury', *University of Chicago Law Review*, 1:1 (1983), p. 140; Howlin, 'The politics of jury trials in nineteenth-century Ireland', pp 2–3. [116] *Hansard 3*, xvi, 19 Mar. 1833, cc 827–72. [117] *Irish Examiner*, 30 May 1842. [118] Ian Burney, *Bodies of evidence: medicine and the politics of the English inquest, 1830–1926* (Baltimore, MD, 2000), p. 3; Pam Fisher, 'Getting away with murder? The suppression of coroners' inquests in early Victorian England and Wales', *Local Population Studies*, 78 (2007), pp 47–62. [119] Vaughan, *Murder trials in Ireland, 1836–1914*, pp 41–2.

valued at £50 per annum or a freehold for life of the annual value of £100 and required residence in the district where he worked.[120] However, a contradictory view highlights that after the Poor Law Act (1838) was passed to provide relief and welfare to combat Irish poverty, new local Poor Law guardians were also elected members of local government. Additionally, election procedures maintained that only those who qualified to vote in a general election could vote for the coroner.[121] So local elites were still in charge and, when combined with the limited pool of voters, the Coroners' Act of 1846 continued to prevent middle-class men of education and Catholics from applying for and securing the role of coroner.

The act did, however, attempt to address the problems that had faced coroners and participants of inquests in earlier decades. Improvements that came from the implementation of the act included a map that outlined coroners' districts for each geographical region in each county in Ireland.[122] By law, each region required an assigned coroner to investigate reported deaths, and the grand jury had to pay for his services. Qualified jurors were expected to be householders, residing in the district, who paid no less than £4 in Poor Law rates, which effectively eliminated society's poorest, the landless labourers and smallest tenant farmers as participants in the judicial process; however, the Poor Law rates requirement could be waived should people meeting it not be available to sit on a coroner's jury.[123] Additionally, an exemption from serving on a coroner's jury was no longer possible. If summoned, attendance and participation was required, and those who refused could be fined. Also, the act provided a framework of procedures for reimbursement of fees and an expenses schedule of the list of payments the coroner was authorized to make. They included payments to doctors, poor witnesses, the local public house where the inquest was conducted and for the coffin and burial (see Table 2). Overall, the act provided more structure and formality. It was a powerful piece of legislation that imposed costs on disobedient grand juries who refused to pay for services that benefited the entire community, not just the local elite.

This legislative action laid a powerful foundation for the future professionalization of the office of coroner and it made an immediate impact during the Famine. The public inquest was an important focus at the time of the humanitarian crisis and officially recorded the circumstances of death. Irish coroners were deployed as a tool of the empire as it used regulation to drive moral and social improvement through the investigation of the sudden or suspicious deaths of paupers. The number of inquests rose significantly as a result of the Famine. This increased costs for cess payers already under strain as the economy struggled, and it put coroners at odds with the local grand juries (this is covered more extensively in chapter three).

Alongside the Coroners Act of 1846 was the abolition of the deodand, the asset (or assets) liable for the death that was evaluated only by the coroner's court.[124] For

---

120 9 & 10 Vict., c. 37 (27 July 1846), Coroners (Ireland) Act. **121** Ibid. **122** Ibid. **123** Ibid. **124** 9 & 10 Vict., c. 62 (18 Aug. 1846), Act to Abolish Deodands.

Table 2: Schedule of payments coroners were authorized to make

Type of payment	£	s.	d.
To any poor witness, for each Day of Attendance at any Inquest, any Sum not exceeding, per Diem	1	1	0
To the Owner or Occupier of any private House who shall permit any dead Body to be deposited therein (if such Owner or Occupier be not related to or connected with the Deceased), any Sum not exceeding, per Diem	0	10	0
To the Owner or Occupier of any private House who shall afford Accomodation to the Coroner (or to any Two Magistrates during his Absence), Jurors and Witnesses, for the holding of an Inquest therein (in case such Owner or Occupier shall not be related to or connected with the Deceased), any Sum not exceeding, per Diem	0	3	6
To the Person or Peoples who shall, pursuant to an Order from any Coroner or of any Two Magistrates, disinter and afterwards bury any dead Body	0	5	0
To any legally qualified Medical Practitioner who, in pursuance of the Summons and Order of any Coroner or of any Two Magistrates, shall attend and examine any dead Body, and give Evidence as a Witness at any Inquest held thereon, the Sum of	1	1	0
To any legally qualified Medical Practitioner who, in obedience to the Order of any Coroner or of any Two Magistrates, shall make a Post Mortem Examination of any dead Body, and shall attend and give Evidence at the Inquest held thereon, the further Sum of	1	1	0
To any Person or Persons who shall, pursuant to an order in Writing from any Coroner or any Two Magistrates, have provided a Coffin, and buried the Body of any Stranger on which an Inquest shall have been held, the Sum of	0	10	0

Source: 9 & 10 Vict, cap. 37, schedule C.

centuries at the end of an inquest into a death, the jury had been able to declare an inanimate object or even an animal, a deodand, responsible for the death, and a cost associated with the value of that asset. Such an inquest recorded the value of a deodand prior to the implementation of the law. On 22 June 1846, an inquest taken by a King's Co. coroner, James Dillon, put the value of a scythe at £1 in the death of Bridget Feehan.[125] Feehan and her husband, William, had been attacked by dogs. While endeavouring to save himself by swinging at them with a scythe, he by misfortune struck his wife in the right leg, inflicting a mortal wound. The verdict stated 'that the scythe caused her death and that the said William is not accountable'.

The law had previously allowed the coroners' inquest juries to impose fines and collect direct compensation in fatal accidents, but no longer. The insurance industry had become a new social authority on death and offered a modern ideology and

125 Inquest reports of James Dillon, King's Co. coroner, no. 615, Bridget Feehan, Corolanty, 22 June 1846 (Offaly historical and Archaeological Society, Tullamore, Co. Offaly, Ireland, IE OHA OHS51).

solution to establishing monetary value for human life. Compensation for human life included calculation of lost salary and wages, combined with life expectancy. The abolition of the deodand and, simultaneously, the implementation of the Fatal Accidents Act (1846), which allowed for compensation claims in civil court, reflected a transformation of British legal structures towards a society better suited to liberal capitalist values.[126] Such a significant change in the law raises philosophical considerations as to how value was put on an individual life in Ireland, particularly considering that the power of the calculation of compensation was taken out of the hands of the general public in the form of an inquest. Monetary debt is a fundamental medium of capitalist social relations and, as such, traumatic events, perhaps on whole peoples in the forms of war (or Famine), must be realized in the form of monetary value.[127] However, the removal of the deodand from the coroner's court removed the previously imposed debt-collector function from the coroner. It shifted the focus from the financial gain of the coroner to the value that the inquest brought to society, albeit one that remained highly politicized.

The effectiveness of individual coroners can only be measured by how they carried out their inquests at a local level. Coroners served at the coalface of the catastrophe, inspecting corpses alongside doctors, interviewing witnesses and summoning juries, reviewing and documenting testimony and physical evidence. Holding inquests during this time would prove to be a daunting task not just based on the need to travel long distances, but because many of these deaths were a direct result of the Famine, and hence reflective of a society in distress filled with disease and desperation and a lack of resources to satisfy those in need. The reasons for excess mortality were political rather than demographic, findings that are supported by coroners' inquests.[128]

CONCLUSION

The office of coroner in the first half of the nineteenth century suffered from a poor reputation due to disruptive behaviour of coroners, lack of local government structure and poor support by grand juries and authorities, and unreliable execution of duties. Evidence shows a significant number of Catholics had taken up the role of coroner by 1823 as a means of attempting to improve their social status. As a result, they may have suffered from prejudice from the local Protestant elite. Property qualifications rose and limited the number of middle-class professionals

---

126 William Pietz, 'Death of the deodand: accursed objects and the money value of human life', *RES: Anthropology and Aesthetics*, 31 (1997), p. 107.   127 Ibid.   128 Findings of these historians have identified political factors contributing towards excess death during the Famine. Joel Mokyr, *Why Ireland starved: a quantitative and analytics history of the Irish economy, 1800–1850* (Oxford, 1983); Gray, *Famine, land and politics*; Cormac Ó Gráda, 'Mortality and the Great Famine' in Crowley et al. (eds), *Atlas of the Great Irish Famine* (New York, 2012), pp 170–98; T. McDonagh, E. Slater, and T. Boylan, 'Irish political economy before and after the Famine' in Terrence McDonough (ed.), *Was Ireland a colony? Economics, politics and culture in nineteenth-century Ireland* (Dublin, 2005), pp 212–34.

and Catholics accessing the role. A belief that political corruption existed in public inquests was in part because of ineffective fee-based compensation and inconsistent reimbursement of the coroner. Doctors also had difficulty in receiving payment for their services. Threats and intimidation of witnesses and jurors often had a negative impact, resulting in neutral verdicts and a lack of identification of murderers. Inquest verdicts reflected the social and moral environment in which the coroner operated. Changes to the office came by way of the Coroners Act of 1846, with a new framework and regulation regarding payments and an emphasis on empowering the coroner in conducting his inquests. The work of the coroner was often in direct conflict with the local grand jury who could and did refuse payment due to their reluctance to approve inquests and their associated costs based on their opinion of their 'necessity'.

2

William Charles Waddell

Orna verum [Honour the truth].
    –The motto of the Waddell family crest and coat of arms[1]

Monaghan is proverbial for the difficulty – we had almost said the impossibility – of procuring witnesses [at an inquest], so as to lead to the conviction of any atrocious criminal.
    –Newry Telegraph, 25 July 1834

On 14 August 1841, 23-year-old John Jackson Waddell of Cloverhill House, Lisnaveane, Co. Monaghan, wrote to his older brother, sea captain Alexander Stuart Waddell, who was temporarily residing in London until his next voyage returning to New South Wales, Australia. His correspondence focused on finances and the topic of emigration for himself, his younger brothers, James and Robert, as well as his father Alexander and his relative William Charles Waddell, often referred to by the family as Charles. Yet, getting away from Monaghan would require going further into debt. He wrote,

> Dear Alexander,
>   I believe this is the first time for me to sit down for the purpose of addressing you either before you left Lisnaveane, or since, nor will I now occupy much of your time by putting you to the trouble of reading a long letter; yet there are some things which I cannot help mentioning to you as I know you are strongly interested about all our welfare. You are fully aware of our having entered into an arrangement respecting emigration. What I would say to you on that subject would be in accordance with your plan of my father's staying at home for I who know my Father's bodily infirmities perhaps better than any other person do without hesitation declare that the likelihood is that if Father attempts that journey it will greatly shorten his

---

[1] John Peter Elven, *The book of family crests: comprising nearly every family bearing ... with the surnames of the bearers, their mottos, an essay on the origin of arms, crests ... a glossary of terms and an index of subjects* (London, 1840), i, p. 101.

life and make the remaining days of his life <u>bitter</u>. I know if Father stays at home, I of course must stay also and perhaps have to involve myself in some debt to enable James and Robert's getting out to NSW. Yet I would rather do anything that was possible to be done for James and Robert no matter how unpleasant than suffer Father to run the risk of embittering and shortening his (in all probability) few, very few, remaining years, and though I can with a clear conscience say that my Father's happiness is my chief reason for wanting him to stay at home yet even as it regards myself I must say I do not by any means wish to emigrate at this time.

You are, I believe My Dear Brother, aware from Father's letters in times past that I have been the only person who turned their attention towards taking care of the place or in other words keeping the remainder of Father's property out of the ravenous grasp of [future coroner William] Charles Waddell's unlimited covetousness, and although my exertions in this respect have not [been] crowned with entire secrecy and although we would still be in debt was it not for your most generous and liberal remittances, yet I believe it is acknowledged by all who know me that had it not been for my continual exertions this place would have been in other hands today and if you knew with what longing anxiety I have looked forward to the time when we would be out of everyone's power and in particular Charles Waddell's you would not wonder at my now wishing to stay at home when after so long struggling for independence I might make hope to soon arrive at that period when I could proudly say to all the world I OWE YOU NOTHING and in particular to Charles Waddell for although this farm is now reduced to something less than 12 acres (you know the rent) yet still I know that if we were once on a clear footing Father and I might yet be in a better way than we have been in for many years of his life even when he had 3 times the property he has now.

I think if Robert and James were once freed in a way to do for themselves, I would have a good chance of making a few hundreds with somebody – you know what I mean – I wish you would lay out some old London widow or other for me who has a coffer <u>well filled</u> but if old widows be scarce, I'd not refuse a young one and don't be the least afraid if I take their attention for I can tell you that I am a great Prick of a Count[2] when I get on my holiday dress.

My dear Alexander, you must excuse me for this is pressing on your time but my mind is in much suspense. I have ten thousand things to tell you about but I will not trouble you now as I trust in God to see you soon. Give my best love to my dear sister Charlotte and give each of my little nephews a kiss for me that God may bless you and all yours is the sincere prayers of your affectionate brother,

John Jackson Waddell[3]

2 'Prick of a count': grandiose, but with a sexual connotation and overtone.   3 John Jackson Waddell to Alexander Stuart Waddell, 14 Aug. 1841, State Library of New South Wales, Sydney, Australia, PXA 685/41–42.

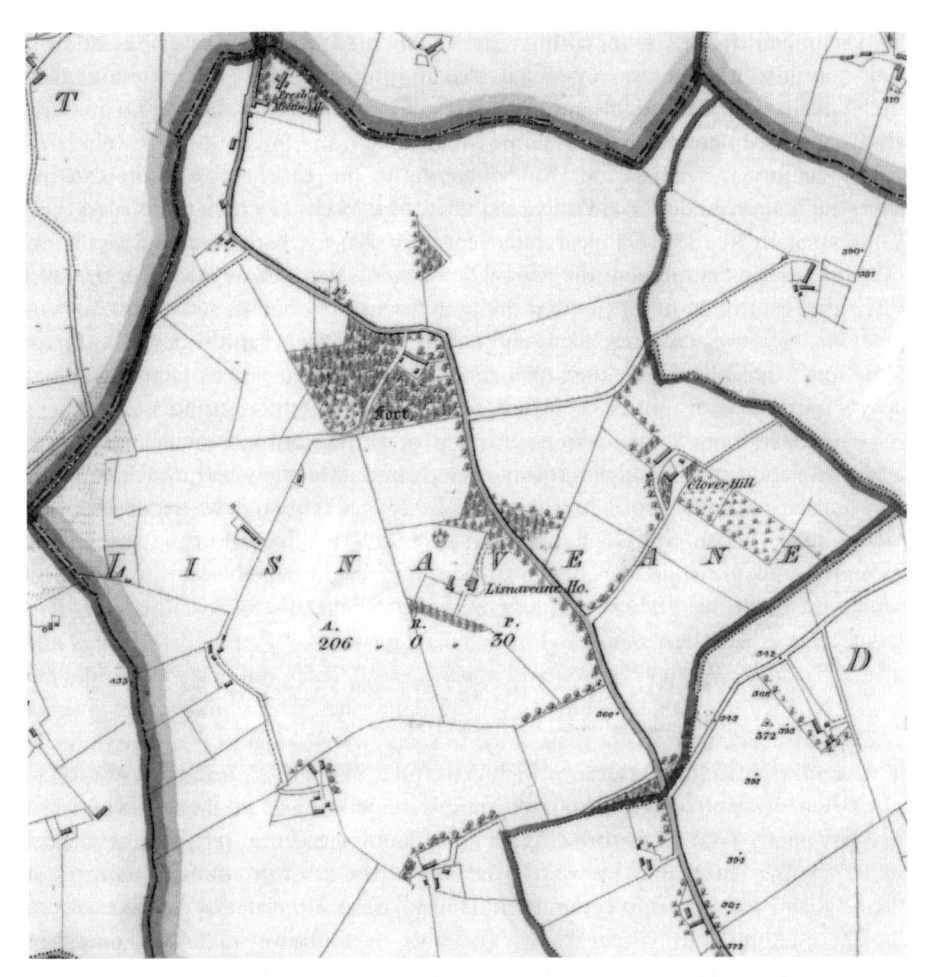

Map 2 Townland of Lisnaveane, Co. Monaghan (1836), OSi historic six-inch first edition © Ordnance Survey Ireland/ Government of Ireland, copyright permit no. MP 007322.

The Waddell family was representative of other landed families of the time who faced the difficulties of fractured relationships due to land, money disputes and emigration. Possession and lease ownership of lands willed through inheritance often involved a complex trail of covenants handed down over the generations. Multiple relatives and in-laws were named in memorials of indenture as well as marriage agreements involving subdivided plots, creating a complex web of relationships. A series of deeds provide accurate identification of landownership. From 1827 to 1855 William Charles Waddell had been paying hundreds of pounds to his uncle in order to secure the lease of over 200 acres of his land. The elderly Alexander Waddell at one time had a considerable estate but had spent his time at 'hare hunting, convivialism, spending money and not earning any' and, eventually, the estate had become reduced in value; so much so, that, as a result, he and his sons appear to have become financially reliant on his nephew.[4] For ambitious men like William Charles Waddell, the challenges of family land management would not always enhance personal relationships.

To conjure the life of the Waddell family in the 1840s, look to the existing ancestral homes, Lisnaveane House and Clover Hill House, which dominated their landscape.[5] Today the buildings retain their impressive stature, standing attentively over the rolling drumlins of the Monaghan countryside. These late Georgian and early nineteenth-century structures are large two-storey houses with classical proportions, windows, chimneystacks and rubble-walled farm buildings that enhance their quaint grandeur. A closer look reveals that the two homes face each other across the road, indicating closeness in proximity and familial support.

Understanding the man who would serve as coroner of Co. Monaghan requires an investigation into Waddell's family background, information from his personal life, and an examination of his political alliances and patronage networks as an Ulster Presbyterian. This will also help to assess how his influence shaped the community in which he lived and provide some insight into the kind of men who served the public as local officials during the Famine.

THE WADDELLS OF MONAGHAN: FAMILY HISTORY AND BACKGROUND

The Waddell pedigree traces back to Alexander Woodall, a settler in the third plantation of Scottish Presbyterians in Ulster, who obtained lands from Lord Massareene in 1698 to escape religious persecution endured by the covenanters under the later Stuarts.[6] Massareene was one of the most prominent members of the English Presbyterian community in Ireland and a supporter of dissenters from the Protestant established church. He had a strong commitment to the Monaghan Presbyterian community as demonstrated by a gift of land to establish 'ye first Presiterian [sic] congregation' in Monaghan town in 1703. In return he simply requested 'one seat nine foot long and five foot wide in ye meeting house' for his family forever.[7] Woodall lived just outside Monaghan town in the townland of Aghnasedagh and his estate comprised over 1,200 acres.[8] Public and private records

---

4 James Alexander Waddell, 'Our family history', Waddell family bible (transcription), NSW Library, Australia. The bible itself is believed to be missing or lost.   5 There are two townlands in Co. Monaghan named Lisnaveane. Lisnaveane House and Clover Hill house are located in Lisnaveane (208a. 0r. 30p.). The other townland, Lisnaveane (285a. 0r. 0p.), may have previously been called 'Lisnavany'. No historical connection has been found to connect the two townlands or the latter to the Waddell family.   6 *NS*, 11 May 1878.   7 Waddell to Graham, 1726 (ROD, deed no. 35479).   8 Tenant roll of Lord Massareene, Alexander Woddall, 23 Apr. 1698–6 Feb. 1811 (PRONI, D1739/3/9). The four tates of Shantonagh, Sheekull, Mullenveridvegg and Mullenveridmore comprised the townland of Aghnasedagh. They do not appear in any modern publication and no longer exist. Woodall also owned the three tates of Lisnaveane, Drumgavny and Cordevlis. A 'tate' is an area of land defined as 60 Irish acres in Co. Monaghan, but this varied outside the county or geographical region.

show several locations referred to by the family name including Alex Waddle's Tenements, Waddell's Lands and Waddell's Gardens, signifying his early claim and his contribution to the development of Monaghan town in the eighteenth century.[9] In addition to Woodall's influence on Monaghan town, his descendants would make their mark on their inherited lands in the Monaghan countryside, particularly in the townland of Lisnaveane, which William Charles Waddell would eventually own, and where he would live for up to fifty years on the lands and in the house of his forefathers.

Located in the barony of Cremorne in the civil parish of Tullycorbet, Lisnaveane was the location of the first Scottish Seceder church in Co. Monaghan in the early eighteenth century. It later became famous for the Cahans Exodus of 1764, whereby more than three hundred people were led to the American colonies by Minister Thomas Clarke. These Presbyterians were tenaciously independent and the lack of civil and religious freedom in Ulster contributed to their departure. The townland benefitted from the quality of the soil, which was far superior to any other part of the county in terms of fertility.[10] Leasing land to the tenantry provided the Waddell family with income as well as supplying workers for the linen trade as the Waddells obtained permits for spinning wheels.[11] The family was known to have had a close alliance to the Jacksons of Creeve, a prominent Monaghan linen-industry family to whom they leased land for the purposes of expanding the linen trade. John Jackson Waddell's name reflects a strong relationship between the families as a result of patronage and inter-marriage.

Lisnaveane's location three miles from Rockcorry, six miles from Ballybay, nine miles from Monaghan town, fourteen miles from Castleblayney, and twenty miles from Carrickmacross, provided reasonable access to local goods and services. It also served in the late eighteenth century as the headquarters for the Lisnaveane Independent Rangers, a Volunteer unit led by the Waddell family to guard the countryside against possible French invasion during the American War of Independence, and to preserve law and order. They were unusual in that they were, as a group, autonomous, self-structured, self-disciplined and, for the most part, self-equipped.[12] A few notable members of the family include Robert

---

9 *Rent roll for one year's rent, duties and agents fees due to the daughters of Colonel Murray out of their lands and tenements in the estate of Monaghan ending at and including 25th March rent 1798* (Clogher Historical Society (CHS) Collection, Monaghan). Notes include detailed descriptions of possession of leases back to the early eighteenth century. Many of Woodall's landholdings were sold off and distributed over time to other prominent families including the Cairneses, Westenras, Cunninghams, Jacksons and Waddell relations from Islandderry, Springfield House, Co. Down; *Rent rolls of Monaghan town*, p. 26 (Clones Library, Clones, Co. Monaghan). Arthur Richards Neville, *Maps of the Clermont Estate, Monaghan* (1791). 10 NAI, Valuation Office books, 1824–56, *County Monaghan: field book* (1837), pp 13–14. 11 Premiums for Sowing Flax-seed in the Year 1796 lists four spinning wheels for Alex Waddle and one for William Waddle in Murnane and Murnane, *At the ford of the birches: the history of Ballybay*, pp 272–3. 12 Pádraig Ó Snodaigh, 'Notes on the Volunteers, militia, yeomanry and Orangemen of County Monaghan', *Clogher Record*, 9:2 (1977), pp 142–66 at p. 142.

Waddell, a leader of a troop of dragoons who withdrew support for the Volunteers at the 1782 Dungannon convention in opposition to Catholic emancipation and for taking part in the boycott on imported linen through the non-importation agreement of 1779.[13] Another reputable member of the family was Captain Alexander Waddell, Robert's brother, and William Charles Waddell's grandfather. Tales of his activities include his reported association with the Jacksons of Creeve, who were considered active in the United Irishmen by 1798, and his eight-mile ride to Monaghan town that same year whereby he called for troops to head to Ballybay First Presbyterian.[14] Members of the congregation had locked out the new minister, James Morell, as they opposed him calling for declarations of loyalty to the government.[15] Morell's predecessor, John Arnold, had fled to America to escape persecution for being identified as a United Irishman, and the declaration of loyalty was undoubtedly intended as a means of protecting the congregation.[16] The United Irishmen were well organized in the county, with an estimated membership of ten thousand, but information from spies and informants resulted in numerous trials, with some men being sentenced to death. By 1798 the rebels had lost their momentum.[17]

By the time of the Act of Union in 1801, many Presbyterians in eastern and southern Ulster were withdrawing from any significant involvement in revolutionary politics, particularly as they suffered military repression during the disarming of Ulster in 1797 and were developing a new appreciation of the dangers they faced as part of a Protestant minority in a predominantly Catholic Ireland.[18] Some northern Presbyterians saw the connection to Britain as potentially less dangerous than an independent Ireland; while many Presbyterians remained liberals for most of nineteenth century. Many of those men were tenant farmers who resented the economic and political power of their landlords, most of whom belonged to the established church. Shifting away from the revolutionary politics of his elders, William Charles Waddell would learn from his early years growing up in Monaghan town, politics that supported the local Protestant gentry would help his family secure its place in the community and open opportunities for financial advancement.

---

13 Murnane and Murnane, *At the ford of the birches: the history of Ballybay*, p. 322, identifies the Lisnaveane Independent Rangers (Volunteer unit) and that Reverend Mr Rogers was the chaplain. In 1782 the Volunteers passed resolutions demanding independence for the Irish Parliament, the relaxation of trade restrictions and free importation of Irish goods into Britain, and Catholic emancipation. The Lisnaveane unit withdrew support and followed the lead of Lord Charlemont (the Volunteer Earl). David Nesbitt, *Full circle, a story of Ballybay Presbyterians* (Monaghan, 1999), p. 244. Robert was gifted a medal from his troops in 1780. The medal is located at the National Museum of Ireland, Collins Barracks, Dublin, Ireland. 14 Nesbitt, *Full circle*, pp 30–1. 15 Ibid.; Peadar Livingstone, *The Monaghan story* (Enniskillen, 1980), p. 160; Murnane and Murnane, *At the ford of the birches: the history of Ballybay*, p. 107. 16 Brian McDonald, 'Monaghan in the age of revolution', *Clogher Record*, 17:3 (2002), p. 764. 17 Livingstone, *The Monaghan story*, p. 171. 18 Sean J. Connolly, *Religion and society in nineteenth-century Ireland* (Dundalk, 1985), p. 4.

WILLIAM CHARLES WADDELL: CAREER AND PERSONAL LIFE

William Charles Waddell's life began the same year as the failed rebellion of the United Irishmen. Born in Monaghan town on 28 November 1798, he was the second son of the seven children of James Waddell, merchant, son of Alexander Waddell, and Susanna Hopes, the daughter of John Hope, grocer in the town of Maghera, Co. Londonderry.[19] As a young man, Waddell was described as a brave, resolute lad, physically hardy beyond most boys, with great strength and endurance. He had many achievements in swimming, walking and hunting and the ability to stand up for himself.[20] He also abided by the discipline and authority of his parents, who ensured that he and his siblings were off the town streets.[21] Monaghan town was a bustling marketplace with a growing population and in which there was a large Presbyterian presence.[22] One visitor stated that it was like he 'awoke in Edinburgh because the accent and manners of the people were distinctly of Scottish character,' and that it 'marked the boundary of the North'.[23] The nationalist journalist and politician Sir Charles Gavan Duffy, a native of Monaghan town, wrote about his Presbyterian schoolfellows descended from Scottish ancestors, noting how they had preserved their characteristics 'to an amazing degree ... they were thrifty, industrious, and parsimonious, and sometimes spoke a language worthy of Dumfriesshire'.[24] In fact, at the turn of the nineteenth century, more Catholics were coming to Monaghan town than Scottish Presbyterians. However, Scottish Presbyterians remained in Co. Monaghan, which made them a group whose political allegiance was attractive and valuable, particularly for their integrity, initiative and business expertise.[25]

At the turn of the nineteenth century, Co. Monaghan had the second highest population in Ulster next to Armagh, with 124,000 inhabitants in 22,500 houses, about 'six souls per house', engaged primarily in linen manufacture.[26] Monaghan was the seat of several prominent families, the five most prominent peerages being Westenra, Dawson, Leslie, Blayney and Bath; other gentry families with large estates included Anketell, Corry, Lennard, Lucas, Madden, Rose, Shirley and Templeton. The political landscape reflected a conservative majority with only Lord Cremorne (Dawson) and Lord Rossmore (Westenra) favouring Catholic relief. The county of Monaghan had lost a seat for Monaghan town in Parliament after the Act of Union in 1801 and as a result had two seats. Each family used their connections and influence on their tenants to gain votes and control. The

---

19 *Monaghan town rent rolls*, Sept. 1828 (Clones Library, Clones, Co. Monaghan). 20 *NS*, 10 May 1878. 21 James Waddell, Brooklyn, New York, US to William Charles Waddell, Lisnaveane, Co. Monaghan, Ireland, 6 Mar. 1877 (Hope Collection). 22 Lindsay T. Brown, 'The Presbyterians of County Monaghan, part I: the unfolding story', *Clogher Record*, 13:3 (1990), pp 7–54. 23 Livingstone, *The Monaghan story*, p. 479; C.W. Bingley, *The Waddells of Ireland, a genealogical resource* (Belfast, 2014), p. 266. 24 Sir Charles Gavan Duffy, *My life in two hemispheres* (London, 1898), p. 8. 25 Brown, 'The Presbyterians of County Monaghan, part I', p. 12. 26 J.H. Andrews, 'Land and people, *c*.1780' in T.W. Moody and W.F. Vaughan (eds), *A new history of Ireland, iv: Eighteenth-century Ireland, 1691–1800* (Oxford, 1984), p. 249.

Waddell family was one of many Presbyterian families well established within Co. Monaghan and their influential relationships among the Presbyterian community would have been of value to those members of the local elite interested in pursuing a political career.

William Charles' father, James Waddell, secured his place in Monaghan town as a reputable business and family man. He owned a grocery and hardware store on Dublin Street, which he started in the 1790s, and served as a committee member of the Monaghan Savings Bank.[27] James was also a member of the Monaghan Independent Club, a Liberal group of local professionals and business owners, Catholic clergy and liberal Protestants who supported Catholic emancipation and voting rights and evinced a 'spirit of independence with a duty to that cause to claim it for every man in the county'.[28] In 1826, James was one of many men of the Independent Club, including Catholic neighbour and fellow shopkeeper, John Duffy, father of Sir Charles Gavan Duffy, who supported the Honourable Henry Robert Westenra in the general election.[29] Although Westenra had voted against the Catholic relief bill in 1825, his father, Lord Rossmore, was a supporter of Catholic emancipation. Rossmore negotiated between the Catholic Association and his son, and gained the club's support.[30] Col. Charles Powell Leslie MP, who had also been a member of the Independent Club, then formed an electoral partnership with Evelyn John Shirley to try to win two seats in the election. Shirley's endorsement from Daniel O'Connell, parliamentary champion for Catholic emancipation and founder of the Catholic Association, helped secure the confidence of Catholic voters as O'Connell defined himself as a liberal.[31] However, in a letter to priests of the county, O'Connell helped split the Shirley-Leslie alliance as he wrote that both Leslie and Westenra had voted against Catholic relief measures, but Rossmore 'is one of our steady friends' and Lord Cremorne was 'a warm advocate' who was supporting Westenra.[32] Westenra and Shirley won the election, at the expense of Leslie, who had been a sitting MP.

Making different political choices to that of his father and grandfather, William Charles Waddell aligned himself to the conservative majority of the local Protestant Ascendancy. In October 1828, Waddell and his cousin Alexander attended a public gathering of several thousand men in the Diamond in Monaghan town in support of the Monaghan Brunswick Constitutional Club, which supported the doomed campaign to deny Catholics the right to enter both houses of British Parliament and other political rights promised by Catholic emancipation.[33] The Brunswick Constitutional clubs were a failed effort that mobilized across the country, led by patrician Protestants, to rally an all-class Protestant alliance. To ultra-Protestants,

---

[27] *Pigot's and Co.'s Provincial Directory of Ireland* (London, 1824), p. 405; James Waddell to Richard Wellesley, lord lieutenant of Ireland, 1 Nov. 1822 (NAI, CSO/RP/1822/2849). Waddell is endorsed by the Honourable Henry Robert Westenra and Col. Charles Powell Leslie. [28] *DEM* Supp., 19 June 1826, p. 1; Rushe, *History of Monaghan for two hundred years*, pp 185–7. [29] Ibid. [30] Rushe, *History of Monaghan for two hundred years*, pp 186–7. [31] Stephen Farrell, 'County Monaghan (1820–32)', *History of Parliament*, historyofparliamentonline.org, accessed 25 Aug. 2018. [32] Rushe, *History of Monaghan for two hundred years*, pp 186–7. [33] *Saunders's News-Letter*, 14 Oct. 1828.

Liberals were the enemy, and it was essential to fight the threat posed by them.[34] The conservative local newspaper of Co. Monaghan, the *Northern Standard*, reported that the crowd was led in a provocative speech by Lord Blayney, with others following including Sir Thomas Forster, Thomas Stewart Corry esq., Col. Leslie, and, liberal turned conservative Evelyn John Shirley, MP.[35] In 1815, when Waddell was seventeen, he served as a lieutenant in the Castleshane Yeomanry, a local infantry unit used to curb faction fighting and civil disturbances.[36] This participation in local law enforcement may have influenced Waddell's political opinions, resulting in his departure from the liberal and independent politics of his father and grandfather. It is likely that Waddell, an ambitious man, chose to support the agenda of the conservative majority in order to provide himself the opportunity to make alliances and position himself within the county elite, a move common to many of his generation of Ulster Presbyterians. To be accepted as a member of such a society, political and social standing, wealth, and, particularly, land ownership were essential to gain the respect of and the opportunity of advancement among the county elite. With an ancestry tainted by revolutionary politics, another reason for Waddell's choices may have been self-preservation and an attempt at demonstrating a political 'balance' in local social circles. As the leaseholder of more than 325 acres, Waddell secured himself the right to vote as one of only 322 men registered as £50 'freeholders' in Co. Monaghan by 1830.[37] Considering that the elimination of the 40-shilling freeholders reduced the voting population in Co. Monaghan from 12,453 registered voters to 1,148, a single member of the voting public, particularly one who could influence other voters, became much more valuable to those running for office.[38]

Waddell also had an influential patron, his uncle Charles Hopes, who provided him with work as a land agent, which gave him an advantage in gaining access to the local gentry and aristocracy.[39] Hopes was a successful independent business owner of the Stewart and Hopes legal stationary business of 3 King's Inns Quay in Dublin. Along with an impressive list of business associations, he served as chairman of the proprietors of the Royal Canal Company, as a member of the

---

34 Daragh Curran, *The Protestant community in Ulster, 1825–45: a society in transition* (Dublin, 2014), p. 132. 35 *London Evening Standard*, 16 Oct. 1828; after the 1826 general election, Shirley had begun evicting poor Catholic tenants; his politics also shifted to presenting anti-Catholic petitions in Parliament. 36 Rushe, *History of Monaghan for two hundred years*, p. 165; Bingley, *The Waddells of Ireland*, p. 268, highlights a list of Co. Monaghan yeomanry, identifying a Charles Waddell and a William Waddell, both of Tullycorbet, Lisnaveane. 37 *Return of the number of freeholders who stood registered and qualified to vote in each county in Ireland, on 1st January 1829 and 1st January 1830; distinguishing in each county the number registered in each case at each rate*, p. 2, p. 3, HC 1830 (556) xxix, 461. 38 Ibid. The term 'freeholder' was defined differently in England and Ireland. Whereas in England the true 'freeholder' was the lord or landlord, in Ireland the primary leaseholder was also called the 'freeholder'. 39 The Hopes and Hope family are of the same ancestral line and appear in original family and official documentation interchangeably; it appears that the older generation used Hopes whereas the younger used Hope. Charles Hopes was the brother of William Charles Waddell's mother, Susanna Hopes.

board of the National Insurance Company and on the committee for the National Hibernian Bank. Hopes was a large landowner, with properties throughout Co. Monaghan and other parts of Ulster; he was also a regular and significant contributor to Presbyterian churches in Dublin and Monaghan. A devout Presbyterian who served as a representative elder in the synod of Ulster, Hopes used his alliances to run for political office in later years, securing the coveted roles of Monaghan and Dublin grand jury member and high sheriff of Co. Monaghan. His generosity to his nephew came in the form of employment as land agent over several of his townlands in the parishes of Kilmore and Ballybay.[40] His interest in the young William Charles Waddell was further enhanced by Waddell's announcement of his intention to marry his own first cousin, Maria Orr Hope, Hopes' niece.[41]

By the age of 30, William Charles was employed as a land agent, working as a merchant in Monaghan town, and had enough prospects and prosperity to be considered a suitable spouse for Maria, the 26-year-old daughter of his aunt, Eliza (neé Henderson) Hope and uncle, John Hope of Maghera, Co. Londonderry.[42] The two families of Presbyterian merchants would continue to be joined as one as they had been by inter-marriages for decades. Waddell presumably made a journey to Maghera and set a wedding date, as indicated by a marriage agreement signed three days before their 8 September 1829 wedding. It provided a lease of lands to her two brothers, his first cousins – John Jnr and Charles Hope – and was witnessed by his uncle Charles Hopes.[43] Together, William Charles and Maria would have six children, who they would raise in the Monaghan countryside at Lisnaveane House.

After their marriage, Maria and William Charles were apart at various times, travelling for personal or business reasons, but had a very close and loving relationship. Letters written between couples in Irish Presbyterian marriages reveal the patriarchy, and dealing with it, to be a common theme, a constant negotiation using love, obedience and control of economic resource, which is also reflected in the contents of Maria's letters.[44] Her affections for her husband were clear and much of her correspondence included personal information – decisions taken on her confinements, the health of the children and their relationships with the rest of the family. She was active in discussions on the management of the household, farm and business matters. Maria supported William Charles by contributing

---

40 The townlands held by Charles Hopes included Mullynahinch (139*a*. 3*r*. 9*p*.), Tullybryan (151*a*. 3*r*. 9*p*.), Kilnahaltar (143*a*. 2*r*. 24*p*.), Aghalisk, also known as Coleshill (122*a*. 0*r*. 38*p*.), Annagola (44*a*. 1*r*. 17*p*.), Drumacaslan (118*a*. 1*r*. 27*p*.), Lisbane (36*a*. 3*r*. 17*p*.), Annaghervy (67*a*. 3*r*. 29*p*.) and Cordevlis South (2*a*. 1*r*. 36*p*.). 41 William Charles' mother, Susannah Hopes and Maria's father, John Hope, were brother and sister. The spellings are accurate. It appears they took on different spellings of their last name. 42 Private journal of Ina Rogers (1900), held by Henry Skeath. She remembers William Charles Waddell as the coroner and as the owner of a grocery store in Monaghan town. 43 William Charles Waddell, Maria Orr Hope, John Hope Jnr and Charles Hope, 1829 (ROD, deed No. 568807). 44 Leanne Calvert, '"Do not forget your bit wife": love, marriage and the negotiation of patriarchy in Irish Presbyterian marriages, *c*.1780–1850', *Women's History Review*, 26:3 (2017), p. 443; Hope collection, letters of Maria Orr Hope to William Charles Waddell (1829–57).

opinions about business affairs, including a strategy for leasing their vacant cottage to a potential renter without the associated 12 acres of land. It was she who was actively involved in the hands-on management of their home and farm. Maria worked in the garden tending to the potatoes, turnips, kale and cabbage and fed the pigs herself. Homes were places of hard labour and farms required daily care and management. This ambitious couple also received input and support from other members of the family in matters of business. Maria's brother, who helped run their own family shops including their uncle Charles' stationers business in Dublin, supported Waddell in offering advice regarding vendors, debtors and other merchants in trade. The collaboration of the family in promoting their own success and ambitions not only demonstrates their support network and individual roles and responsibilities, but highlights skills Waddell had that were transferable to other positions he held.

In his role as a land agent, he carried out tasks that ranged from clerical responsibilities such as keeping accounts, eliminating arrears, valuing property and managing leases, to the hands-on work of collecting rents, overseeing improvements and carrying out evictions.[45] Securing payment of rents from tenants was an often challenging task for land agents and one that could ultimately result in evicting the tenant. It required a man of strength and stamina to influence and often intimidate the tenantry.[46] In March 1839, Waddell evicted a Catholic tenant named McQuaid in the townland of Mullanahinch and placed a Protestant in possession. A group of anonymous men tore down the new tenant Francis Sommerville's cottage, left a threatening note and dug him a grave.[47] Waddell and his uncle Charles offered a reward of £100 with the support of members of the gentry to anyone willing to name or help prosecute the guilty parties. Representative of sectarian tensions of the nineteenth century, the incident sheds light on the consequences of Waddell's decision, the use of unlawful force by secret societies and the challenges presented in maintaining law and order. Waddell knew the potential repercussions and appears to have made his decision with conviction, reinforced by the offer of compensation for imposing justice.

Many land agents had formal legal training or were landed gentry with knowledge of the formalities and legalities of landownership and management taught to them by their fathers. They were men with a wide range of experience as merchants, farmers, millers, bank managers, clergymen and coroners.[48] Land agents in nineteenth-century Ireland had a generally bad reputation. They were viewed as oppressors whose activities, including joining public committees, were for the purpose of protecting their landlords' interests and their own.[49] Waddell was a committee member on a parliamentary petition to reduce 'unsupportable' county

---

[45] Terence Dooley, *The Big Houses and landed estates of Ireland: a research guide*, pp 18–19. [46] Ciarán Reilly, *The Irish land agent, 1830–60: the case of King's County* (Dublin, 2014), pp 56, 114. [47] *NS*, 9 Mar. 1839. [48] Ciaran Reilly, *The Irish land agent, 1830–60: the case of King's County* (Dublin, 2014), p. 42. [49] Dooley, *The Big Houses*; Reilly, *The Irish land agent*; Vaughan, *Landlords and tenants in mid-Victorian Ireland*; Desmond Norton, *Stewart and Kincaid: Irish land agents in the 1840s* (Dublin, 2002).

taxes, a committee member for local roads and named as part of a deputation on the Presbyterian question, debating legalizing marriage between Protestants and Presbyterians, led by Mr Charles Powell Leslie.[50] Additionally, he ran and won a seat as a Poor Law guardian in Monaghan's first election after the Poor Law Act in Ireland was passed. It was an important position as it was the de facto body in local government to make all the difficult decisions as to how to spend poor relief money and manage the impact on the tax-paying public.

The Irish Poor Law was intended to address extensive poverty through indoor relief (admittance to the workhouse) or outdoor relief (payment for public work). Relief was paid for from poor rates based on Poor Law valuations of property. Landowners were responsible for 50 per cent of the poor rates, and tenants for the other 50 per cent on tenanted land. During the Famine, these unpaid guardians, responsible for the distribution of relief to the poorest members of their community, often protected the interests of the land and property owners who they represented.[51] In fact, not all were elected. A quarter of guardians in Ireland were non-elected 'ex officios' (i.e. landed magistrates) and, after 1847, ex-officios grew to one-third of the representation of the boards of guardians.

In December 1839, following the passage of the Irish Poor Law, twenty-seven vacant seats were available to form the Monaghan board of guardians, representing the twenty-one divisions of the Monaghan Poor Law Union. Local coverage of the contests highlighted candidates by religion and party, specifically focusing on those who were Catholic and liberal, or those with liberal support. One local landlord, Mr Rose, was praised by the correspondent writing on behalf of the *Northern Standard* for nominating candidates of the people while others were chastised for not following in Mr Rose's footsteps and instead nominating men of their own choosing, indicating that they were representing their own interests. Waddell ran and won as an uncontested candidate representing the electoral division of Caddagh, but received some additional publicity in the local paper. It was reported that although 'Mr Charles Waddell was started on the first day' and it was thought that 'he was a candidate of Captain Greves ... the threats of Mr Waddle [sic] to the tenants of Mr Hope [sic] have been complained of'.[52] Other reports of his approach as a land agent described him as 'kind and considerate to honest and peaceable tenants' but to those who opposed the rules of the estate, 'he evinced a firmness and determination which were worthy of the highest admiration'.[53] Regardless of the negative disclosure in the newspaper, he was soon nominated as part of the valuation committee for the board of guardians, which would determine the rateable value of the land.

In 1841, Waddell continued to prosper, leading a funding drive towards building a new church at Cahans, which drew subscriptions from Lord Rossmore,

---

50 *NS*, 8 Jan. 1842, 3 Oct. 1846, 10 Dec. 1842.   51 Timothy W. Guinnane and Cormac Ó Gráda, 'Mortality in the North Dublin Union during the Great Famine', *Economic History Review*, 55:3 (2002), p. 488.   52 *NS*, 7 Dec. 1839.   53 *NS*, 11 May 1878.

Lord Cremorne, Lord Plunkett, Charles P. Leslie and Revd Matthew McAuley.[54] The financial investment in the church reflected not only his commitment to the Presbyterian community, but also his influence and connections in receiving support from the highest-ranking members of the local elite. In contrast, that same year, his cousin John Jackson, living at Clover House and caring for an aging father, wrote a letter to his brother Alexander Stuart living in Australia, about his resentment at being indebted to William Charles. Waddell had found prosperity, while other Waddell family members had not. The debts incurred and inherited from their father put John Jackson and his brothers at a great disadvantage. Waddell's benefactor, his uncle Charles Hopes, and the closeness of the Waddell-Hope families bolstered William Charles' opportunities. Further, his support of the local conservative elite was reciprocated and this choice in political alliances improved his status and power.

SERVING AS A JUROR: WADDELL'S POLITICS

As well as participating as a member on local government committees, Waddell also met the requirements to act as a trial juror. He was qualified by his property, social status and age (he was between twenty-one and sixty years old), and he was a local resident. An 1836 letter from his wife, Maria, referred to him being called for jury duty: 'I hope you may find being on the Jury *profitable*.'[55] There appears to be no evidence that jurors were selected to deliver a verdict for the purpose of being rewarded monetarily or with a position in return.[56] However, one might consider that jurors from the social elite, such as Waddell, would strengthen relationships and raise their profiles particularly if called upon to participate in securing the 'right' verdict in politically important cases.

From 1837 to 1843, Waddell served as a trial juror on three criminal trials, two of which were related to Sam Gray (1782–1848), one of the most infamous Orange Order leaders in pre-Famine Ireland. Gray, worshipful master of Ballybay Orange Lodge and district master of Ballybay, known for carrying two guns at all times, was a local representative of unofficial Protestant law enforcement, inciting often violent vigilante behaviour against Catholics.[57] Similar to Waddell, Gray's property holdings and work as a land agent provided him with the necessary qualifications to secure multiple positions in local government, including local loan fund officer, sub-sheriff, tithe proctor, tax collector and baronial high constable. Gray's rise as a local leader can be attributed to the political conflict of the 1820s and 1830s in Co. Monaghan where the use of extra-judicial force by Orangemen was a commonplace reaction to Catholic progression in politics and assertion of their rights.[58] Many of

---

54 Nesbitt, *Full circle*, p. 268.   55 Maria Orr Hope Waddell to William Charles Waddell, 9 Jan. 1836 (Hope Collection).   56 Howlin, 'The politics of jury trials in nineteenth-century Ireland', pp 1–2.   57 Denis Carolyn Rushe, *Historical sketches of Monaghan* (Dublin, 1895), p. 87.   58 Patrick Maume, 'Monaghan reimagined: "The Orangeman" (1915) as Ulster-American origin narrative', *New Hibernia Review/Iris Éireannach Nua*, 6:1 (2002), pp 113–14.

the Protestants in south Ulster, and particularly in Co. Monaghan, supported the Orange Order and struggled to accept changing legislation that provided emancipation for the majority Catholic population. An 1835 report found that the parish of Monaghan consisted of 7,550 Roman Catholics, 2,504 Presbyterians and 1,821 Protestants.[59] Yet, the local elite, comprised predominately of Protestants, controlled jury selection and therefore, criminal trial results.

Gray had become a nationally recognized figure and Protestant hero in September 1828 for his leadership in organizing opponents to prevent the Catholic Association leader, 'Honest Jack' Lawless, and his followers from travelling through Ballybay. As Lawless toured the country to promote Catholic emancipation, he rallied thousands of Catholics along the way. The government resented the 'disloyal' activity of the Catholic Association for, in their opinion, inciting Catholics and stirring up division, and this view was reflected in the attitudes of local law enforcement agencies and Sam Gray.[60] Gray gathered four thousand men and sent word that he would stop Lawless at Ballybay, along with any Catholics who followed him. Lawless gave a speech admonishing Orangemen who were under the command of Sam Gray, however he avoided conflict by not heading any further north. The Catholic politician Thomas Wyse believed that the incident demonstrated how close the country was to civil war at that time. As a result of the incident, Gray was portrayed as a hero of the Protestant community and was the toast of the Brunswick clubs throughout Ulster, including the one supported and attended by Waddell, making them brethren in the same cause. However, as time passed, support for Sam Gray created some unique challenges for the administration at Dublin Castle and Westminster, particularly as a real fear arose that the Orange Order could make Ulster ungovernable.[61]

After the Lawless incident, Sam Gray honoured every Twelfth of July by engaging in illegal behaviour, including shooting men and starting riots. As a result, he and his gang were regarded as posing a threat to the rule of law in Ballybay.[62] Gray was representative of other Orangemen breaking the law. This behaviour was occurring regularly and often by men who expected and continued to receive leniency from the judicial system.[63] After the Orange Order was dissolved by the government in 1836, the Party Processions Act was used to attempt to prevent July marches and arrest those who gathered.[64] In 1837, Waddell was on a jury in the trial of several Orangemen for causing disturbances in Orange

---

[59] *First report of commissioners of public instruction, Ireland, sessional papers*, p. 24a, HC 1835 (829), xxxiii, 1831–4 census figures. Note: Wesleyans/Methodists were included in the Protestant figures. [60] James H. Murnane, 'The Lawless sortie into County Monaghan: September–October 1828', *Clogher Record*, 13:3 (1990), p. 148. [61] Sean Farrell, *Rituals and riots: sectarian violaence and political culture in Ulster, 1784–1886* (Lexington, 2009), p. 95. [62] D.S. Johnson, 'The trials of Sam Gray: Monaghan politics and nineteenth-century Irish criminal procedure', *Irish Jurist*, 20:1 (1985), p. 113. [63] Daragh Curran, *The Protestant community in Ulster, 1825–45* (Dublin, 2014), p. 142. [64] 6 & 7 Will. IV, c. 118 (16 Aug. 1832), Party Processions Act.

Order processions that Twelfth of July.[65] One of the defendants was Sam's son, James. The prosecution witnesses included a stipendiary magistrate, an army captain of the cavalry regiment the Royal Scots Greys and two policemen, who all testified to witnessing a party of 1,500 with guns, drums, fifes and colours, and who then arrested the defendants. The defence argued that the men were 'merely spectators', even though one of the defence witnesses stated that 'they had to take off the sashes for fear the dragoons would tear them'.[66] Additionally, two witnesses stated that the field where the procession took place was in Co. Fermanagh, not Co. Monaghan. Sam Gray interfered in the trial, shouting out for 'the truth' as well as complimenting 'the sterling worth of the gentlemen of the jury'. Waddell and the other jury members took minutes to return a verdict in favour of the defendants not based on their actions, but because they found that the procession did not take place in Co. Monaghan and was therefore not within the legal jurisdiction of the court.[67]

Over the next several years, Sam Gray continued his blatant and flagrant disrespect for the law, and each time he went on trial he was acquitted or the charges were dropped at the assizes. Following in his footsteps was his son, James, who in 1840, was found guilty of forging the will of a friend and supporter, Moses Bradford, a fellow Orangeman, after a very long, public and expensive trial.[68] A year later, on 19 March 1841, Sam Gray was on trial for the murder of Owen Murphy, a Catholic, who had been a witness in the forgery case against James. He was accused of shooting Murphy in broad daylight in front of witnesses. The case made headlines throughout Ireland and Britain and the outcome was eagerly anticipated. The magnitude of the interest in the trial is reflected in the headlines in newspapers throughout the country and the need for an allocation of tickets to gain entry to the Monaghan courthouse in order to manage the crowds. Despite the overwhelming amount of witness testimony demonstrating his guilt, Sam was again found not guilty by a Monaghan jury.[69]

The inability of the Monaghan jury to convict Gray at the assizes widely exposed the lack of government control over the Orange Order and Monaghan local elite. Liberal newspapers carried stories of the great injustice that had taken place. On 23 March 1841, the *Freeman's Journal* published an article that described Gray's involvement in the murder of Murphy as so conspicuous that the verdict had 'created a feeling of universal surprise among all classes'.

> I do not mean to say – far be it from me – that the jury who tried the case did not consider the evidence given with impartiality, or that which was sworn by the witnesses was not perfectly true, but it does appear to me that the people of Monaghan are exceedingly incredulous, or stupid, for they affect to be thoroughly convinced that the whole defence was a farce ...[70]

---

65 The case was *The Queen v. William Johnston, William Lloyd, James Monaghan, James Gray and Brown*. 66 *Newry Examiner and Louth Advertiser*, 29 July 1837. 67 Johnson, 'The trials of Sam Gray', p. 113. 68 Ibid., p. 125. 69 *NS*, 27 Mar. 1841. 70 *FJ*, 23 Mar. 1841.

On 24 March 1841, the liberal *Vindicator* called the members of the jury 'men with whom the conviction of "a brother" was to be entirely hopeless', indicating that the jury consisted of Orangemen.[71] In contrast, the conservative Co. Monaghan newspaper, the *Northern Standard*, supported Gray. It stated,

> For years, he [Gray] has gathered round him an ocean of the most intense hatred on the part of his Roman Catholic and Liberal neighbours. Again, for some reasons, of which we are not now going to speak, he [Gray] forfeited the confidence of the Conservative party in this county and was fast sinking into oblivion, when the unfortunate circumstance of the murder of MURPHY again turned all eyes upon him and a very general, but preconceived opinion spread abroad the story of his guilt ...[72]

While the Bradford case had put Gray at odds with his fellow Orangemen, in the case of the murder of Murphy, conservatives supported Gray and defended his innocence. The article exposed the political polarization between liberals and conservatives on a local and national scale, and the injustices of the selection process of jurors in the justice system. Many were of the view that Monaghan conservatives were subverting justice by packing the jury with Orangemen in order to acquit Gray, causing much embarrassment for the government administration. This continued refusal to convict Gray for murder and other crimes may have influenced the circumstances surrounding another high-profile murder trial that same month.

On 20 March 1841, the day after the not guilty verdict of Sam Gray, the trial of Mary Anne McConkey (neé Slater) for murder was held and Waddell was once again one of twelve jurors selected. McConkey was a young woman who was held in the Monaghan county gaol for several months on a charge of killing her husband, Richard McConkey. She was accused of poisoning his dinner with a quantity of 'corrosive sublimate' (mercury), mixed in dressed greens, in July 1840.[73] It was rumoured that the 25-year-old Protestant woman from Clones had grown tired of her forty-year-old husband and was having an affair with another man.[74] Evidence supplied by her former friend, Mary Anne Johnston, not only detailed how McConkey had prepared a special set of greens for her husband's dinner, distinct from what she cooked for her father, but that she had confessed that 'George Smith was a kind good boy and if she could get £10, they would run away tomorrow.'[75] This testimony and the analysis of the stomach contents of the deceased, which found monkshood, otherwise known as blue rocket root,[76] used as a poison, provided enough evidence to convince Waddell and the rest of the jury of her guilt. The sentence ordered by Hon. Judge Robert Torrens

---

71 *Vindicator*, 24 Mar. 1841. 72 *NS*, 27 Mar. 1841. 73 Ibid. 74 Linda Stratmann, *The secret poisoner: a century of murder* (New Haven, 2016), p. 210. 75 *NS*, 27 Mar. 1841. 76 Monkshood, also known as wolfsbane, was used for medicinal purposes and also as a poison.

(1774–1856), nicknamed 'the notorious hanging judge', was unsurprising: death by hanging.[77]

Although Waddell and the other eleven members of the jury had convicted McConkey of murdering her husband, they were willing to spare her life. The jurors and over one hundred other members of the local gentry, clergy, prison authorities, merchants and traders, signed and sent a memorial to the lord lieutenant at Dublin Castle in an attempt to get McConkey's death sentence commuted.[78] It was reported that there was great sympathy for McConkey, who many felt was convicted on circumstantial evidence.[79] Research shows that McConkey found herself in a predicament: she was an uneducated woman, assigned legal counsel far too late in the process, meaning there was little or no time for communication or preparation by her lawyers, resulting in a lack of character witnesses or an alibi for her defence.[80] Other reports implied that there was a love triangle, that McConkey and a woman named McAuley both had feelings for George Smith, who did 'not care a fig for either of them'.[81] Gender politics played a part in the social and political condemnation of some murderers and the value of the lives taken, whether a man or a woman, varied greatly. It was typical of the time that while a husband murderer might be sentenced to death, very often the sentence was appealed and commuted to life in prison.

The jury in McConkey's case demonstrated empathy as they attempted to save her life by appealing for mercy to the lord lieutenant. The memorial could not attest to her good character; neither did it offer any conflicting evidence or state that they believed in her innocence. Rather, they begged that she was a woman and to take pity on her soul.[82] However, on 1 May 1841, Mary Anne McConkey was hanged by her neck in front of a large crowd in Monaghan town, and after a few convulsive struggles she was no more.[83] The Liberal Whig government's lack of intervention for the Protestant McConkey was a strong message and a reminder of government power, and their lack of support for local county conservative elites. Circumstantial evidence suggests that the inability of local jurors to convict Gray for the murder of local Catholic Murphy played a significant role in the unwillingness of government to commute McConkey's death sentence.

Edward Golding, magistrate in Co. Monaghan, once stated that it was 'almost impossible to have a fair trial in the county, say of Monaghan ... from the intimidation [of jurors] that exists', supporting findings that the government needed to intervene and pick men who could secure a conviction.[84] In 1841, the Conservatives took back control from the Whigs in the general election. And in July 1843, Gray

77 Desmond McCabe, 'Robert Torrens', *DIB*. 78 Revd Roper and Revd Henry Moffett to Lord Lieutenant Hugh Fortescue, 18 Apr. 1841 (NAI, Criminal Record Files, CRF/1841/McConkey/17). 79 *NS*, 1 May 1841. 80 Vaughan, *Murder trials in Ireland, 1836–1914*, pp 243, 249. 81 *Wexford Conservative*, 12 May 1841. 82 Ibid., pp 314–15; Revd Roper and Revd Henry Moffett to Lord Lieutenant Hugh Fortescue, 18 Apr. 1841 (CRF/1841/McConkey/17). 83 *NS*, 1 May 1841. 84 *Report from the select committee on outrages (Ireland), together with the proceedings of the committee, minutes of evidence, appendix and index*, p. 74, HC 1852 (438), xiv, 1.

was once again on trial, at the Monaghan crown court, accused of shooting at a a Presbyterian named Cunningham, with the intent to murder him.[85] This time the prosecution provided a list for a special jury, one comprised of men who were pro-establishment, with an understanding that the task at hand was to secure a conviction. As the jurors were called to be considered, the prisoner Gray challenged them:

> One of the jurors being called ... answers to his name, and the said Samuel Gray challenges the said William Charles Waddell peremptorily, and without showing any special cause why the said William Charles Waddell should not be sworn on said Jury and prays that the said peremptory challenge be allowed.[86]

William Charles Waddell, member of the local gentry, former Brunswick Club member, local land agent, merchant and Presbyterian gentleman who resided in a townland just six miles from Ballybay, was immediately rejected by Sam Gray with no explanation. Perhaps Gray knew Waddell's opinion of him and his politics, or that Waddell was a man that could be counted on by the conservative elite to gain a conviction.[87] Another view may consider the presumption of Waddell's allegiance to his fellow Presbyterians due to the attempted murder of one of their own. Yet another influence was potentially one of ancestral ties, as the Waddell and Cunningham families were connected. Of the six jurors refused by Gray and his counsel, including Waddell, none were put aside by the crown, presumably because they were special jurors who were more likely to convict.[88] Gray was found guilty of murder; his conviction finally achieved when the crown restricted the panel from which the jury was selected to the landed gentry. Even though the conviction was later overturned by the House of Lords, who found in favour of Gray on the grounds that he had been denied his right to peremptorily challenge jurors, his reputation was permanently damaged.[89] It was clear that the conservative establishment that had once protected him was no longer supporting him. The trial was captured in local folklore, that Gray 'was always acquitted by a packed jury, until he turned on one of his own. It was the British in the finish up tried to kill him'.[90] Local historian Denis Carolyn Rushe published the story that the government did what was never done before – namely, packed a jury to convict an Orangeman – and Sam Gray was found guilty.[91] The *Northern Standard* took the stance that an injustice had taken place, determining that the conviction was illegal because the

---

85 Ibid., p. 173. 86 *Irish law reports of cases around and determined in the courts of queen's bench, common pleas, and exchequer of pleas, during the years of 1843 and 1844* (Dublin, 1844), vi, p. 259; *Northern Whig*, 18 July 1843. 87 Peremptory challenges by the criminal defendant did not require a reason to be stated. 88 Howlin, *Juries in Ireland*, p. 146. 89 *Select committee on outrages 1852*, p. 173, HC 1852 (438), xiv, 1. 90 Brian Sherry (ed.), *Along the black pig's dyke* (Castleblayney, 1993), p. 185. 91 Rushe, *History of Monaghan for two hundred years*, p. 220.

Fig. 1 Daguerreotype of William Charles Waddell, *c.*1875 (Blundell Collection).

jury was not properly constituted.[92] This landmark case served as an example of the intervention that could be taken by the establishment to secure a verdict by selecting the right men for the jury.

On Friday, 15 August 1845, William Charles Waddell received the news that his uncle Alexander Waddell had died at the age of 78. He was a member of the celebrated Volunteers of '82, considered an early patriot of respectable character, and one of the three last survivors of that well-known body in Co. Monaghan.[93] The

92 *NS*, 5 Oct. 1844.   93 *NS*, 23 Aug. 1845.

death represented the passing of a generation of men of purpose and principles who sought to protect the country at a time of potential invasion, some of whom evolved to embrace radical ideologies that led to the United Irishmen rebellion, which left them dead or at odds with the administration. In November 1845, at forty-eight years old, William Charles might have reflected that he too had established himself as a man of purpose. He owned and resided in his family's ancestral home, worked as a land agent and merchant, as well as serving as an elected Poor Law guardian and working on various local committees. He had aligned himself with the local conservative elite on matters of justice to which some of his success and popularity could be attributed. He was a member of a new generation of middle-class professionals who used their patronage, social networks, determination and hard work to improve their social status. In April 1846, Waddell would secure himself the role of county coroner, one that no doubt he set out to attain using his patronage networks, just as Ireland was about to endure the treacherous years of the Great Irish Famine.

CONCLUSION

William Charles Waddell, a descendant of planted Scottish Presbyterians, following in the footsteps of his ancestors, made a significant contribution to the history of the social, political and economic landscape in Co. Monaghan. Contributing land, buildings and funds towards the protection and expansion of the Presbyterian community, Waddell and his family supported the local economy and themselves, working as landlords, farmers and merchants and contributing to the growth of the linen trade. Waddell benefited from the financial security of his established family, but cultivated his own career as a landlord, land agent and local government representative, joining multiple committees and serving as a petty juror. Politically conservative, Waddell is reflective of other men of his generation who moved away from the radical and liberal Presbyterian politics of previous generations in order to further establish himself within the Protestant community. His marriage to his first cousin and close family ties helped retain tacit knowledge and experience in business as well as prosperity within the immediate family.

Waddell's politics and reputation can be best evaluated by his work as a land agent, as well as in his associations and political alliances, with special emphasis on his early association with the Brunswick Clubs and later his involvement as a juror in the trials of Sam Gray. He transformed himself over nearly two decades from a man supporting conservatives in opposing O'Connell's government agenda of Catholic emancipation in 1828, to helping to convict an Orangeman who was a killer and felon, thereby imposing law and order and supporting the government's agenda. Waddell's political commitment to the establishment likely contributed to his appointment as coroner, and it is used as a foundation and framework to examine his decision making in his work as the coroner of north Monaghan.

PART II
During the Famine

3

The Famine and moral ambiguity

The man, indeed, over whose dead body the coroner holds an inquest, has been murdered, but no one killed him. There is no external wound, there is no symptom of internal disease. Society guarded him against all outward violence – it merely encircled him around in order to keep up what is termed the regular current of trade, and then political economy, with an invisible hand, applied the air-pump to the narrow limits within which he was confined, and exhausted the atmosphere of his physical life. Who did it? No one did it, and yet it was done.[1]

—John Hughes, March 1847

How is it that the GRAND INQUEST of the nation has made no inquiry as to the death of thousands of people?[2]

—Isaac Butt, April 1847

In 1841, the population of Co. Monaghan was over 200,000 and it had a rural density of 370 persons per square mile, most of whom were landless labourers.[3] By 1851, the county had experienced an exodus, with a reduction in population to 141,000 and a loss of over 10,000 homes, which significantly and dramatically changed the landscape.[4] Co. Monaghan suffered greater losses in the Great Famine, when compared with the rest of Ulster, due to the density of its population, poverty and a landholding crisis arising from extensive subdivision.[5] While it had a history and long-standing tradition of seasonal migration and emigration, both used through difficult times as methods of 'disaster relief', many also died.[6]

1 John Hughes, *A lecture on the antecedent causes of the Irish Famine in 1847, delivered under the auspices of the general committee for the relief of the suffering poor of Ireland, by the Right Rev. John Hughes, D.D., bishop of New York, at the Broadway Tabernacle, March 20, 1847* (2nd ed.; New York, 1847). 2 Isaac Butt, 'The Famine in the land: what has been done, and what is to be done', *Dublin University Magazine*, 29:172 (Apr. 1847), p. 514. 3 *Report of the commissioners appointed to take the census of Ireland, for the year 1841*, 1 [504], HC 1843, xxiv, 452–7; Duffy, 'Mapping the Famine in Monaghan', p. 443. 4 *Census of Ireland for the year 1851, part I, showing the area, population and number of houses, by townlands & electoral divisions, County Monaghan*, 259 [1575], HC 1852–3, xcii, 1–34. 5 Duffy, 'Mapping the Famine in Monaghan', p. 440. 6 Cullen, 'Economic development, 1750–1800', p. 170; Patrick Duffy, 'Placing migration in history: geographies of Irish population movements' in *Migration and myth: Ulster's revolving door* (Belfast, 2006), p. 28.

When excluding the towns, Monaghan experienced the third heaviest rural decline in Ireland at almost 30 per cent between 1841 and 1851.[7]

The Famine-related deaths investigated by William Charles Waddell in his first fifteen months as coroner of Co. Monaghan reveal how government legislation and the actions of the local elite played a role in the deaths of the poor. The available evidence in his casebook highlights the often ambiguous role of the inquest as a political and moral barometer. Public opinion varied as to the usefulness and value of the coroner during the Famine. The local and national press publicized the work of coroners, and the exposure of such cases (or lack thereof) reflected the interests and politics of their readership. Coroners, as authority figures, were agents of the colonial administration making a significant contribution to the modernization of Ireland, yet their authority was often undermined.

WADDELL: A FAMINE CORONER

William Charles Waddell was elected, without opposition, as the coroner of Co. Monaghan in April 1846. Identified by the conservative unionist *Northern Standard* as 'an uncontested, popular candidate', Waddell was listed that same year in the *National Commercial Directory* as a member of the gentry.[8] Coroners were elected by the residents in the district who were entitled to vote for the election of members of Parliament for the county, however no election took place as he had no opponent.[9] Given this, one might wonder whether election tactics outside the realm of normal procedure may have been used to deter potential liberal opponents. Just like he had no opponent for his election to the board of guardians for the electoral division of Caddagh.

There is no evidence to prove any local electoral management by the elite, yet corruption and bribery were common in local elections, as stated by Curran and Hoppen.[10] Instead, perhaps it was simply that he was the preferred candidate of his party and the grand jury and, therefore, other candidates were discouraged. He had the right qualifications, after all. He was a local resident, with an historical pedigree in the county, with local knowledge and experience, and a track record of supporting and being supported by the conservative local elite who had similar political and socio-economic outlooks to his own. As outlined in chapter two, Waddell's skills as a land agent and Poor Law guardian emphasized his ability to lead as well as to perform the tasks involved. Lastly, his financial experience while serving in public office was presumably an appealing quality to those who elected him county coroner.

---

7 Duffy, 'Mapping the Famine in Monaghan', p. 443; Livingstone, *The Monaghan story*, p. 211.   8 *Slaters National Commercial Directory of Ireland*, 1846 (Manchester, 1846), p. 497; *NS*, 18 Apr. 1846, 25 Apr. 1846.   9 9 & 10 Vict., c. 37 (27 July 1846), Coroners (Ireland) Act; also *Hansard 3*, cclx, 5 Apr. 1881, cc 751–2.   10 Curran, *The Protestant community in Ulster, 1825–45*, pp 87–9; K.Theodore Hoppen, 'Roads to democracy: electioneering and corruption in nineteenth-century England and Ireland', *History*, 81:264 (1996), pp 558–9.

Once elected, Waddell served as coroner during one of the most deadly and challenging times as Ireland experienced the worst humanitarian crisis in its history. In his first fifteen months, he conducted 91 inquests in 21 of the 23 civil parishes in Co. Monaghan, an area of almost 1,300 square kilometers or 800 square miles.[11] He worked alongside coroner Dr Robert Murray (1790–1858) for nearly a year after his initial posting.[12] Murray, a landlord with an MA from Trinity College Dublin and an MD from the University of Edinburgh, was a member of the Royal College of Surgeons in London.[13] He had served as coroner in Monaghan for many years prior to Waddell and his presence would have provided some continuity.[14] It was not until the election of Hugh Swanzy, a solicitor from Castleblayney, in 1848 were the county's two divisions of north and south adequately covered, with Swanzy appointed to a southern and Waddell to a northern district.[15] This left a gap of more than a year where Waddell served as the only coroner for the entire county.

The type of inquests investigated by the coroner fell under categories such as: accidental death (including drowning, burning, road accidents, farming and industrial accidents and misadventure), sudden death (cardiac causes, stroke, acts of God and natural causes), chronic disease and illness (internal diseases), infant death (nearly all of these children were murdered), murder (a known or unknown person hastened the death of the deceased) and suicide (drowning, self-inflicted knife wounds, hanging, gunshot wounds) (see Table 3). Inquests during the Famine revealed a greatly augmented or 'excess' level of mortality. According to Mokyr and Ó Gráda, the causes of excess Famine death can be grouped into two additional broad categories: first, the change in personal circumstances or living conditions arising from abnormality of the operation of society; and second, nutrition-related death as a result of starvation.[16] They maintain that most people during the Irish Famine died from infectious diseases and that pure starvation was relatively uncommon as a direct cause of death.[17] At least 48 of Waddell's inquests from May 1846 to July 1847, 53 per cent of the total inquests taken in that period, identify exceptional changes in circumstances leading to starvation and Famine-related death.

Identifying deaths in the casebook as Famine-related or non-Famine related included a reappraisal of the contemporary evaluation and the application of categories, not those of Waddell. Using the criteria outlined by Mokyr and Ó Gráda, Famine-related deaths included those where there was evidence of starvation,

11 *NS*, 20 Feb. 1847. 12 *NS*, 6 Feb. 1858. 13 Croly, *The Irish medical directory, for 1843*, p. 280. 14 Murray would announce his retirement in February 1847, so from then until autumn 1848, Waddell was the only coroner in the county. 15 There is no official documentation to support the exact day and month when Swanzy became the coroner for the district of South Monaghan. He first appears in the *Northern Standard* alongside Waddell on 16 Sept. 1848. They both submitted their expenses for mileage, and the grand jury finance committee reduced the amount they were due. 16 Joel Mokyr and Cormac Ó Gráda, 'Famine disease and Famine mortality: lessons from the Irish experience, 1845–50' in Tim Dyson and Cormac Ó Gráda (eds), *Famine demography: perspectives from the past and present* (Oxford, 2002), pp 19–43. 17 Ibid.

Table 3: Inquests taken from May 1846 to July 1847

Type of death	No. inquests	% of total
Famine-related	48	52.7
Accidental	24	26.4
Infant	8	8.8
Chronic disease/illness	3	3.3
Murder	3	3.3
Sudden death	3	3.3
Suicide	2	2.2
Totals	91	100

Source: CB1.

poor diet or dietary changes, change in circumstances as a result of the Famine, or death from disease but with evidence of Famine-related circumstances. Deaths that resulted from want, destitution, or exposure were categorized as Famine-related, as well as those of persons living on the charity of neighbours or relatives. Inquests that identified the deceased as a beggar, wandering stranger, or pauper, were also included. Some Famine-related deaths were more difficult to define such as the circumstances surrounding death due to disease in gaol or the workhouse. These deaths were categorized as Famine-related, due to the epidemic of Famine-related diseases that were prevalent in both institutions at that time. Additionally, the inmate populace at both institutions were largely committed and admitted as a result of the lack of employment and food throughout the county. Other deaths, such as suicide or murder, are included in this study only if the circumstances surrounding the death provided evidence of circumstances that were Famine-related and, thus, are categorized as such.

WADDELL'S FAMINE INQUESTS

Waddell's first inquest was on 7 May 1846, into the death of a young servant boy who had the appearance of a person who had been badly injured by an explosion of gunpowder, but in fact had been killed by lightning.[18]

> [Inquest no. 1]
> No. 1
> Held in the townland of Drummond. Parish of Magheracloone. Barony of Farney on view of the body of Patrick Boyland who was killed being stroke by Lightening; Held on 7 May 1846.

18 CB1, no.1, Patrick Boyland, 7 May 1846.

Witness Examined. Simon Larkin was deposed to having see[n] deceased lying on the door on which he had been carried in from the field. Lifted up his head [and] saw the hair on back of it burned. Shirt on his back burned. Face black and dirtied. His mouth full of mud and dirt on which he had fallen down.

Patt Cambell. Saw body of deceased about ½ an hour after decease. There had been an awful storm of rain thunder and lightning. When he saw deceased, his mouth was full of mud and dirt on which he had fallen down. Hair on back of head burned.

Thomas Fleming, M.D. was called in by Mr William Kelly to see a boy of his who had been found dead in his field about 3 o'clock afternoon of Tuesday 5 May 1846 has no hesitation in saying from appearance presented by the body that the deceased was killed by Lightening.

Medical Witness Examined Thomas Fleming M.D. and Surgeon to whom I gave an order on the County Treasurer for £1.1.0 for his evidence on the Inquest.

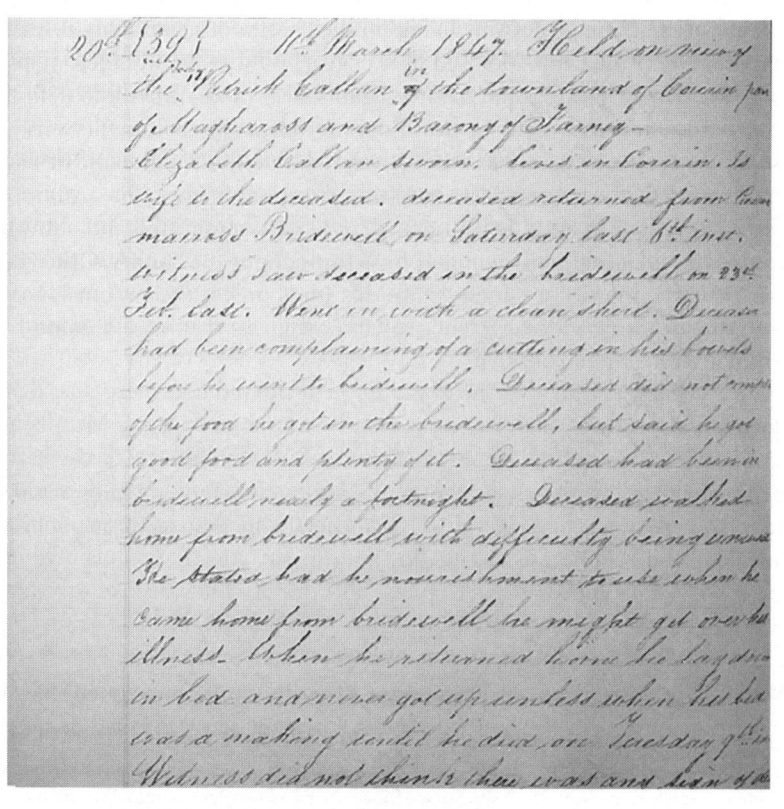

Fig. 2 A page from William Charles Waddell's casebook.

Waddell conducted his first inquest at a time when Prime Minister Sir Robert Peel's administration (1841–6) had been labouring under the weight of the Great Famine for several months.[19] Reports of the failure of the potato crop in Ireland began in the autumn of 1845, which triggered Peel's administration to attempt to thwart a catastrophe by secretly purchasing Indian corn to feed the poor, as a substitute for the potato, and abolishing the UK Corn Laws and thereby removing tax on imported food. They established a Relief Commission for Ireland to administer temporary relief supplementary (and separately) to that provided under the Poor Relief Act (Ireland) of 1838, and they also initiated public works policies, offering jobs to able-bodied men (and sometimes women) involving building roads, digging drains and other hard labour for low wages. The Relief Commission was the primary body overseeing the funding and distribution of relief and the public works, with its Irish Board of Works responsible specifically for works relief. Funding for public works was granted by the Treasury and was intended to be equal to the sums offered by local ratepayers.[20]

Relief in the form of food was delivered in several ways: first, through the grinding and storage of maize in depots managed by the Army Commissariat, led by the chairman of the Relief Commission, Sir Randolph Routh, to eventually be sold at subsidized prices through local relief committees. Second, government loans and grants were offered to local relief committees, staffed primarily by private individuals and clergy, whereby government funding matched local subscriptions in order to purchase and distribute food. Third, county grand juries were offered the option of loans with matching grants to undertake extensive public works, including grants for half the costs of road works.[21]

Two of the three government initiatives were implemented in Co. Monaghan. Maize depots and local relief committees managed by local clergy and private individuals were put into operation to support the poor. As for the third initiative, on 9 April 1846, the Co. Monaghan grand jury unanimously decided not to avail of the loans and grants to fund employment for the poor.[22] A news report published in the *Northern Standard* reveals that the grand jury considered that there was 'plenty of employment at present'; this was supported by grand juror Mr J. Murdoch, who stated that there was no lack of employment in his neighbourhood, the barony of Trough.[23] Reported in an article entitled, 'The Famine Panic', the decision taken reflected the interests of conservative landowners who were at this time reluctant to admit that the Famine was a crisis on the scale the government claimed it to be and refused to take on financial responsibility for it. They also mostly opposed the repeal of the Corn Laws and argued that a drop in the price of grain that was expected to follow was not the right solution. Their primary concerns were the predicted reduction of their profits and the undermining of their political power.

19 *Newry Examiner and Louth Advertiser*, 9 May 1846. 20 A.R.G. Griffiths, 'The Irish Board of Works in the Famine years', *Historical Journal*, 13:4 (1970), p. 635. 21 Gray, *Famine, land and politics*, p. 132. 22 *NS*, 11 Apr. 1846; Fr John Mullen to Rt Hon. Sir Thomas Freemantle, MP or Richard Pennefather, 1 Apr. 1846 (NAI, Distress papers, 1402/D.332). 23 *NS*, 11 Apr. 1846.

Reflective of these attitudes, the founder and editor of the *Northern Standard* and secretary of the Co. Monaghan Orange Lodge, Arthur Wellington Holmes, bitterly and regularly complained about liberalism, Sir Robert Peel and the threat of the Corn Laws being repealed throughout the first half of 1846.[24] On 18 April 1846, in his weekly editorial column, Holmes reported that potato prices in Monaghan had increased in one year by 50–100 per cent, while wages remained the same.[25] Representative of the view of the local elite, the editor's position remained firmly against the repeal of the Corn Laws. He criticized the policy as 'unpatriotic' and believed it would take purchasing power away from the poor and offer less profit for the landed class:[26]

> The great fallacy of the politico-economic cheapness of produce – a vulgar faction which Sir R. Peel in his old days had been foolish enough to join – is that they do not take into their calculation the effect upon income and active purchasing power, which high prices produce ... No doubt the cheapening of food would be a great boon to the labourer, his income remaining the same. But that is impossible if his employment is taken away from him.[27]

Holmes recommended that the government offer employment to the 'surplus population' in the form of railway jobs throughout Ireland, rather than reduce the purchasing power (or investment power) of the Irish landowner.[28]

Another factor to consider, as highlighted by Richard Butler, was that the Monaghan grand jury, along with other grand juries such as those of counties Dublin, Carlow and Cork, embodied a sectarian ideology of Protestant supremacy termed 'Orangeism', and their lack of accountability for taxation and governance led to accusations of political bias, jobbery and waste.[29] The decision not to avail of a loan to offer employment to society's poorest, when evidence indicated there was need to fund and create employment opportunities, might suggest that a bias existed in the politics of Monaghan local elites. Writing one week earlier to Richard Pennefather, undersecretary for Ireland, the Catholic priest Fr John Mullen, who resided in the electoral division of Emyvale in the barony of Trough, the same barony as grand juror Murdoch, gave a sharp contrast to Murdoch's statement. Fr Mullen said Emyvale had lost 50 per cent of its potato crop and 50 per cent of its labourers had no work, stating that,

> hundreds of families have not provisions sufficient for one day and many others have not provisions for one month, nor the means of providing it.

---

24 Aiken McClelland, 'Orangeism in County Monaghan', *Clogher Record*, 9:3 (1978), p. 403.   25 *NS*, 18 Apr. 1846.   26 Ibid.   27 Ibid.   28 Ibid.   29 Richard J. Butler, '"The radicals in these reform times": politics, grand juries, and Ireland's unbuilt assize courthouses, 1800–50', *Architectural History: Journal of the Society of Architectural Historians of Great Britain*, 58 (2015), p. 110.

The parish lies 10 miles north of Monaghan, where no public business [n]or works are carried on that would give the people employment ...[30]

On 15 April 1846, Fr Mullen again wrote to Pennefather,

> I find to my astonishment that the grand jury postponed the consideration of the question and I therefore have no means of making any of these acts available to the alleviation of the very general and appalling distress in this parish.[31]

Using Waddell's inquests as an indicator of the impact of policy and local decision making, none of the nine inquests in May and June 1846 were Famine related. The deaths comprised of accidents such as Patrick Boyland being struck by lightning, accidental drownings and burnings, and pre-existing conditions that led to sudden death. This correlates with the findings of Ó Gráda, Boyle and Mokyr that normal mortality prevailed in Ireland in 1845–6.[32] However, the situation took a turn when a new government was put in place and along with it a very different approach to managing and implementing Famine support for Ireland in the face of a second and more devastating potato crop failure.

THE IMPACT OF FAMINE POLICY IN MONAGHAN: RUSSELL'S GOVERNMENT

In July 1846 the Whig-Liberal administration, led by Lord John Russell (1846–52), was formed as a minority government after the Conservative party split as a result of the repeal of the Corn Laws. Peel resigned in June 1846, and Russell became prime minister and dramatically changed the policies put in place in Ireland by his predecessor with immediate effect. He accused the former Conservative administration of over-generosity to Irish landlords and peasants, and took the advice of his assistant secretary to the Treasury, Charles Trevelyan (1807–86), and discontinued the Relief Commission. The government adhered to their strict belief in not interfering with the markets and food pricing. They allowed the food depots to run until they were empty and cut grants to aid in relief. Reports described the worsening conditions around the country and word spread that local gentry and landlords were still not contributing to support the effort to feed and employ the

---

30 *Further return showing the progress of disease in the potatoes, the complaints of the scarcity which have been made, the applications for relief for the week ending the 4th day of April 1846*, p. 1, HC 1846 (213) xxxvii, 459; Fr John Mullen to Rt Hon. Sir Thomas Freemantle, MP or Richard Pennefather, 1 Apr. 1846 (NAI, Distress papers, 1402/D.123).   31 Fr John Mullen to Rt Hon. Sir Thomas Freemantle, MP, 15 Apr. 1846 (NAI, Distress papers, 1403/D.431).   32 Joel Mokyr, *Why Ireland starved: a quantitative and analytical history of the Irish economy, 1800–1850* (Oxford, 1983), pp 263–4; Phelim P. Boyle and Cormac Ó Gráda, 'Fertility trends, excess mortality and the Great Irish Famine', *Demography*, 23:4 (1986), p. 543.

poor. One such report was written on 12 July 1846, by the chairman of the relief committee for the barony of Ross, Co. Galway, Alexander Clendining Lambert, to the chairman of the Relief Commission, begging for information about his recent application for public works, stating:

> I regret to inform you that I have just heard that a coroner's inquest has within the last few days, returned a verdict of death by starvation within a few miles ... [This] county is ... the poorest district perhaps in Ireland and I regret to say its state has met with but little consideration and attention but one small public works being granted in it.[33]

At the same time, Catholic clerical engagement with the state was crucial to Russell as he hoped the church would help his administration to try to restore balance to society and stabilize Ireland.[34] On 29 July 1846, Fr Paul McCusker of Trough, Co. Monaghan, wrote to the new undersecretary, Thomas Redington, a Catholic, that 1,500 Catholic families were without food or means of procuring it:

> There is comparatively little employment for the numbers able and willing to work, no public works except those carried on by the ordinary grand jury assessments, no sympathy on the part of the landlords or local gentry – not one of whom has subscribed a single shilling, with the exception of Lord Cremorne who gave some meal to his tenantry.[35]

McCusker pleaded for aid from the government, claiming that he could hear the 'cries of hunger' which is what compelled him to make the appeal and hoped that the government would act quickly with funds.[36] McCusker's appeal was successful but soon after, further requests were denied. On 20 August 1846, James Warner, secretary for the Monaghan relief committee, reported 'the potatoes in this district are entirely gone', yet received a reply just a few days later that explained he had missed the deadline for applications by two days, and that grants were no longer available.[37]

MIGRATION AND EMIGRATION: A SURVIVAL STRATEGY

With resources and employment unavailable, migration and emigration were used as social and economic 'safety valves'. South Ulster had a long-standing tradition and history of seasonal migration to Scotland and England, referred to in the early poetry of Séamus Dall Mac Cuarta (1647–1733) with references to Ulster

33 Lambert to Labouchere, 12 July 1846 (NAI, FRC, RLFC3/1/4261). 34 Donal Kerr, 'A nation of beggars'? Priests, people and politics in Famine Ireland, 1846–1852 (Oxford, 1994), p. 28. 35 Fr Paul McCusker to Undersecretary Thomas Redington, 29 July 1846 (NAI, FRC, RLFC 3/1/5011). 36 Ibid. 37 James Warner to Relief Commission, 12 Aug. 1846 (NAI, FRC, RLFC 3/1/5363).

'spalpeens' or migratory labourers.[38] This was later supplemented by long-distance emigration, primarily to North America.[39] References to emigration feature in an inquest taken by Waddell on 29 July 1846, the same day as Fr McCusker's letter to the undersecretary. This revealed the sad story of the suffering of Margaret Quinn, a woman who had received a beating from her husband John in her third trimester of pregnancy. A rare note made by Waddell in the margin of his casebook said, 'A general impression that the deceased's death was brought on by abuse sustained from her husband. Caused a doctor being called to examine the body posthumously internally.'[40] This was also the first Famine-related death in Waddell's career. Although the verdict of her death concluded she died of fever, this was not the focus of this examination. Instead, the analysis of this inquest is focused on witness testimony that revealed the options and use of migration and emigration. Terance Whelen testified he had helped Quinn 'burn fires while her husband was away in Scotland' prior to her death, suggesting that Quinn was a migratory worker and local employment was not available.[41]

The option or threat of emigration was another pressure facing the Quinn family, as was captured in the testimony of witness Catherine Kairns, Cooldarragh, who stated that,

> About 16 April last, John Quinn came to her house stating that his father-in-law's family were going to America and he feared they would persuade his wife to go with them, leaving her children with him.[42]

This inquest shows how migration and emigration were used for survival by those who could avail of those options, as well as being potentially dangerous when applied to unique personal circumstances, placing stress on familial relationships.

THE FAILURE OF THE SECOND POTATO CROP

In August 1846, a major shift took place when it became clear that the potato crop had failed again and reports throughout Co. Monaghan highlighted the great devastation. On 1 August 1846, the *Northern Standard* published a short news report saying accounts of the seasonal potato crop harvest were frightful as the blight had returned.[43] It questioned whether it was a sign of providence or science or if the government could produce a remedy. As part of the continuing theme in conservative reporting, it identified the government as the responsible party required to provide solutions or the people would starve. Absent from the article was any acknowledgment of local elites having a responsibility to support the poor. The facts as to the state of the crop were reported by county inspector James

---

38 Anne O'Dowd, *Spalpeens and tattie hokers: history and folklore of the Irish migratory agricultural worker in Ireland and Britain* (Dublin, 1991), p. 9. 39 Cullen, 'Economic development, 1750–1800', p. 170. 40 CB1, no. 10, Margaret Quinn, 29 July 1846. 41 Ibid. 42 Ibid. 43 *NS*, 1 Aug. 1846.

J. Sanderson on 24 August 1846 to the Relief Commission. He stated that the whole crop throughout the county had been affected by the blight. The districts of Carrickmacross, Castleblayney, Clones and Glasslough consisted of 'fields [that are] perfectly withered and black and vegetation has to all appearance ceased'.[44] With both the early and late crop affected, Sanderson reported that the people suffered from 'great anxiety' as they faced the future without their primary food source and the means to support themselves.[45]

That same month, Russell's government rushed through the Labour Rate Act. The plan was to massively expand public works employment, with strict adherence to offering the lowest wages in the locale for non-permanent improvement work, so as not to compete with private business. However, first one had to qualify for the work. Local relief committees were meant to interview and consider petitioners who qualified as destitute to receive the benefit of employment. The committee then supplied the list of persons requiring relief by employment to the officer of the Board of Works. Emyvale Catholic priests Frs Mullin, McCusker and McQuaide wrote to the lord lieutenant, John William Ponsonby, earl of Bessborough, pleading for his intervention in the local management of the process. A single local commissioner had interviewed hundreds of destitute applicants who were 'in a state of actual starvation' and 'only 70 were returned for employment'.[46] Local interpretation of the government instruction was executed with a lack of urgency as well as a rigid evaluation of destitution. Similarly, in the civil parish of Tydavnet, Co. Monaghan, a memorial was sent to the undersecretary from Catholic priests Frs James Duffy, P. Carolan and J. Rooney, stating that no money had been sent to provide for the population of 12,000 human souls. Regardless of how destitute and numerous a family, the local committees' interpretation of the process involved the selection of only one member of a family as an eligible candidate for employment on the public works. The priests desperately pleaded,

> What then must become of the other two, four, six, eight, ten or twelve starving members of the family? Delay is already doing the work of death ... for Christ's sake send immediate relief.[47]

Under the new Public Works Act of 1846, the lord lieutenant now had the power to compel grand juries to hold presentment sessions and enforce their vote for public works where and when he believed them necessary. In October 1846, baronial presentment sessions were held where 'large sums' were voted to be allocated towards various public works.[48] Monaghan baronial sessions, attended by William Charles

---

44 NAI, FRC, RLFC 5/23. His report includes reports from the districts of Carrickmacross, Castleblayney, Clones and Glasslough carried out by Sub-Inspectors T.R. Barry, Samuel Smith, Robert Faussett and Charles McKelvey, respectively; Charles McKelvey's report from Glasslough, 26 Aug. 1846. 45 Ibid. 46 NAI, Distress papers, 1411/D.6438. 47 NAI, Distress papers, 1411/D.6711. 48 *Dublin Evening Packet and Correspondent*, 6 Oct. 1846.

Table 4: Grain prices in Co. Monaghan in Oct. 1845 and Oct. 1846

Food	October 1845	October 1846
Oats (per stone)	1s. 1d.	1s. 4d.
Barley (per stone)	1s. 1d.	1s. 2d.
Oatmeal (per cwt/112 lbs)	16s.	19s. 6d.

Sources: NS, 25 Oct. 1845; NS, 24 Oct. 1846.

Waddell, Lord Rossmore and various members of the local elite, agreed on a sum of £6,000. It was reported by the *Dublin Evening Packet and Correspondent* that thousands of people had assembled outside the courthouse in Monaghan town that day, and that they had cheered and thanked the gentry for their attention to the wants of the poor.[49] In contrast, it was highlighted that the Cremorne baronial sessions also agreed a sum of £6,000, but Lord Cremorne concluded that it would not be enough to fund work for the thousands who needed it and predicted the money would last only one month.[50] Given that labourers in the county were reported to receive an average wage of 10d. per day, £6,000 would allow 5,000 people to work for 28.8 days, but this does not factor in the cost of materials and overseers, so the number of people supported by employment would likely be much less. McDonald identified that the public works would be executed over a period of four months in six separate districts, thus further reducing the resources needed to make an immediate impact.[51] This support for the poor would not be enough to satisfy the increasing number of starving and destitute people. Additionally, food prices, specifically grains that served as a substitute for potatoes, continued to rise (see Table 4). As it grew in severity, the crisis would increasingly impact the poor.

By November 1846, the landed proprietors of Co. Monaghan, including Lords Rossmore, Blayney, Cremorne, members of the grand jury and clerics, as well as Lord Cremorne's son, Vesey Dawson, MP, succumbed to the new law that required 'Irish property to pay for Irish poverty', and finally appealed for a loan for further public works to the lord lieutenant, Earl Bessborough. It is important to highlight that E.J. Shirley, MP of Farney, did not sign the memorial – the behaviour of Shirley towards his tenants will feature later in this chapter. The group clarified the provisions outlined in the law regarding the taxation of those proprietors willing to offer works on their property, and negotiated the adoption of townlands rather than electoral divisions as a way of allocating funds and labour.[52] Lord Rossmore also asked for 'labourers on public works to be paid twice in the week in place of once' as it would 'assist greatly in preserving the peaceable demeanour of the suffering workmen and their families'.[53] The tardiness of the formal request

49 Ibid. 50 *NS*, 3 Oct. 1846. 51 McDonald, *A time of desolation* (Clones, 2001), p. 42. 52 Monaghan grand jury, clerics and MP to Lord Lieutenant Bessborough, 27 Nov. 1846 (NAI, Distress papers, 1414/D.8819). 53 Ibid.

for funding demonstrates a lack of commitment to the poor by the local elite. As the winter of 1846–7 began, the death toll increased as a direct result of the new government policies and the reluctance of local landowners to enact them. The work of the coroner at the coalface captured the impact of their delayed behaviour and the ensuing crisis.

THE PUBLIC WORKS

British public opinion embodied a belief that the Irish peasant was morally deficient and inferior, which influenced government policy during the Famine. Gray states that Trevelyan's opposition to interfering in food trade, combined with a belief in divine providence, and the government's heavy reliance on his guidance also impacted the programmes of Irish relief.[54] In the belief that restricting relief would bring moral improvement to the Irish poor, the Labour Rate Act (1846) imposed new restrictions and regulations that shifted payment of a day's wage for public works, a flat rate, to payment by how much work a labourer could carry out.[55] This would severely discriminate against men who were ill, or with pre-existing conditions, and older men, who experienced more difficulty doing the hard labour of breaking rocks on the road as compared to healthy, younger men. These younger men, who needed money for food for themselves and their families, might not have demonstrated much sympathy for older, sick men who were not able to pull their own weight. The weather during the winter of 1846–7 was particularly harsh and many days were lost for those engaged in the public works; as a result many workers only received half-pay. In addition to lower wages, grain prices continued to rise from October 1846 to December 1846 (see Table 5). With the average public works wage at 10*d.* per day, half-pay at 5*d.* would make purchasing any food source that would sustain life difficult if not impossible.[56] This contributed to many deaths, particularly those most vulnerable, including the physically weak, the elderly and children.

Deaths from want from around the country were being reported by clergymen; furthermore, reports were sent by coroners to the inspector general of the Constabulary, which highlighted inquests with verdicts of death from want and starvation. On 4 December 1846, Sligo Constabulary Sub-Inspector John Grant wrote to Constabulary Inspector General Col. Duncan McGregor regarding the verdict of death of Bryan Waters.[57] A coroner's jury in Ballynakill returned a verdict that stated, 'the deceased ... came to his death by absolute want of food to support life'.[58]

---

[54] Peter Gray, 'British relief measures' in John Crowley, William J. Smyth and Mike Murphy (eds), *Atlas of the Great Irish Famine* (New York, 2012), p. 85. [55] 9 & 10 Vict., c. 1 (Aug. 1846), Labour Rate Act. [56] *NS*, 19 Dec. 1846; 1 shilling = 12*d*. [57] McGregor was appointed inspector general in 1838 and was knighted in 1848. He retired in 1858 having served in the role for twenty years. [58] Grant to McGregor, 4 Dec. 1846 (NAI, FRC, RLFC3/2/26/42).

Table 5: Grain prices in Co. Monaghan in Oct. and Dec. 1846

Food	October 1846	December 1846
Oats (per stone)	1s. 4d.	1s. 9d.
Barley (per stone)	1s. 2d.	1s. 4d.
Oatmeal (per cwt/112 lbs)	19s. 6d.	24s.
Indian Meal (per stone)	2s.	2s. 6d.

Source: NS, 26 Oct. 1845; 24 Oct., 19 Dec., 26 Dec. 1846.

A series of inquests beginning in December 1846 conducted by Waddell exposed the failure of relief policy and its direct contribution to deaths in Co. Monaghan. On 9 December 1846, John Caraher of Drumanan, a labourer taking part in the public works, was found by neighbour Mary McMahon dead where he had fallen on his way to work on the road. Witness Ruth Murphy explained that McMahon came running back from having found Caraher dead and 'saw none of the men coming'.[59] He had in the past suffered pains in his chest if walking particularly fast or uphill, indicating that outdoor, physical work would prove detrimental to his state of health. It was noted that he had a supply of wheaten bread in his pocket which when found was given back to his wife. Elisabeth Caraher, wife of the deceased, provided testimony that she 'often heard her husband say he did not think he would live long'.[60] Dr Thomas Reed provided evidence of heart attack which the jury also found as the cause of death.[61] Another inquest taken that same month, this one on John Cambell, relayed the tale of how he, his wife and children were released from the poorhouse and had found shelter at the house of Hugh Gault. Gault said out of feelings of compassion for Cambell and his family he allowed them to stay at his house, where the deceased had eaten three meals a day. Cambell acquired a position on the public works, where it was said 'he was treated kindly and put to easy work'.[62] However, after three days, he arrived home each night with complaints of great chilliness and swelling in his legs. On the fourth morning, he was found dead in his bed. Dr Reed, previously acquainted with Cambell, found his death was caused by cold and a diet unsuited to the deceased's broken and diseased constitution.[63]

THE INQUEST AS 'THE VOICE OF THE PEOPLE'

National and regional Irish newspapers published verdicts of inquests that reflected negative public opinion of government policy and show how the inquest was used as a platform for 'the voice of the people'.[64] In January 1847, the *Limerick and*

[59] CB1. no. 17, John Caraher, 9 Dec. 1846. [60] Ibid. [61] Ibid. [62] CB1, no. 2.21, John Cambell, 19 Dec. 1846. [63] Ibid. [64] Vaughan, *Murder trials in Ireland*, p. 52.

Clare Examiner, a nationalist newspaper, reported a coroner's inquest taken at the Galway workhouse,

> We find that the deceased Mary Commons, died from the effects of starvation and destitution, caused by a want of the common necessities of life; and as Lord John Russell, the head of her Majesty's government, has combined with Sir Randolph Routh, to starve the Irish people, by not, as was their duty, taking measures to prevent the present truly awful condition of the country, WE FIND THAT THE SAID LORD JOHN RUSSELL AND THE SAID SIR RANDOLPH ROUTH, ARE GUILTY OF THE WILFUL MURDER OF SAID MARY COMMONS.[65]

The Galway city inquest jury, comprised of urban middle-class Catholic men, was not fearful of delivering a nationalist anti-government position that policy was killing the people. However, the coroner refused to receive the finding and the jury was forced to return the verdict in a modified form of,

> We find that the deceased, Mary Commons, died of the effects of destitution and starvation. And we further find, that the policy adopted by the present Government, in reference to the supply of food, has been such as to raise to an extraordinary high rate the price of provisions, thus placing food beyond the reach of persons in the rank of life of the deceased, and causing innumerable deaths throughout the country.[66]

Just a few weeks later, Dublin City Coroner Dr Kirwin led a jury through an inquest on the bodies of husband and wife, John and Ellen Mulgerin, who died of starvation in their home. Kirwin stated that he hoped the case would arouse the authorities to a sense of their duty and hoped the government would dispense with their cold 'political economy' and come forward to save the people.[67] With less condemnation than the Galway jury and in a rather pleading tone, a Dublin inquest jury verdict begged the government, on behalf of their fellow citizens, to adopt immediate measures and modify their policies to stop the effects of the Famine.[68] That same month, a coroner for King's Co., Mr Midgley, reported a death from want and starvation of a man who worked on the public works for three successive days and was supplied with only a quart of broth each day. The *Freeman's Journal*'s reporter highlighted that there were numberless families prolonging a miserable existence on the same scanty allowance of food as the deceased.[69] But while other juries' verdicts of deaths due to starvation were reported in local newspapers, Waddell's inquests were only infrequently published in the *Northern Standard* or other publications and were in sharp contrast to the rhetoric of the Galway city,

---

65 *Limerick and Clare Examiner*, 20 Jan. 1847. 66 Ibid. 67 *FJ*, 16 Feb. 1847. 68 Ibid. 69 *FJ*, 20 Feb. 1847.

Table 6: Grain prices in Co. Monaghan in Dec. 1846 and Feb. 1847		
Food	December 1846	February 1847
Oats (per stone)	1s. 9d.	1s. 11d.
Barley (per stone)	1s. 4d.	1s. 8d.
Oatmeal (per cwt/112 lbs)	24s.	25s.
Indian meal (per stone)	2s. 6d.	3s.

Sources: *NS*, 26 Dec. 1846; *NS*, 6 Feb. 1847; *NS*, 20 Feb. 1847; MacDonald, *A time of desolation*, pp 52–3.

Dublin city and King's Co. inquest verdicts and news coverage. This suggests political agency was exerted by Co. Monaghan's conservative leadership, the local elite and local government agents, of which Waddell was a member, over the majority Catholic populace and society's poorest. It is also reflective of the conflicting ideologies of local conservatives towards the poor at that time.

While coroners' inquests from around the country reported on Famine deaths, clergymen continued to write to the government directly to inform them of the local crisis. In Monaghan, with no supply of potatoes, work unavailable for many, a widespread inability to purchase food due to high prices and no other relief, emotional correspondence was sent to the administration from the religious leaders. On 25 January 1847, Revd Roper, Protestant rector of Monaghan, wrote to Sir Randolph Routh,

> I lately visited about 90 families of all denominations in a limited district ... I have no reason to doubt that for two days previous some of the inmates had not tasted food!!! And, at the last meeting held for giving employment under the Labour Act, of which I was chairman, one man fell down from exhaustion and tho' food was immediately given, he was a corpse in two days!!![70]

In February 1847, Monaghan market food prices continued to rise (see Table 6), yet wages were reported as low as 6d. per day.[71]

Additionally, that same month, the extraordinary presentment sessions were held for a second time throughout the county to vote on the amount of funding needed to offer further public works. This time the local elite voted on sums twice as large as at the first presentment sessions in November 1846. A total of £35,540 was voted upon to continue funding in four of the five baronies: Trough, Cremorne, Dartrey and Monaghan. Many of those struggling without employment, adequate wages or food began to feature in Waddell's inquests. Just one

---

70 Revd Roper to Sir Randolph Routh, 25 Jan. 1847 (NAI, Distress papers, 1472/D.969) 71 In Monaghan, oral tradition states a day's wage was 6d. for public works. Duchas, Schools Collection, Corvoy, Co. Monaghan, vol. 951, p. 9.

month later, in March 1847, he would record the highest number of famine deaths in his casebook in a single month.

On 20 February 1847, Waddell investigated the death of Pat Murphy of Drumcrew, a cottier, who had 'nothing of work save an odd day with Paddy Byrne from whom he held his house and garden' since harvest of 1846.[72] He had some money saved from harvest work in Co. Dublin and had recently sold a pig, but other than this, he had no means of support. The state he was living in was described by his brother, Terence Murphy,

> Witness always considers deceased got a sufficiency of food which consisted of oatmeal stirabout, occasionally with milk to them but oftener with raw sowens as a substitute commonly called Bull-milk. The food that for some time past deceased partook was unsuitable to his state of health. The bed clothes of deceased was an old single blanket and when the weather was wet, the rain fell on them, when lying in bed from the very deficient state of the thatching of the house. In addition to the old blanket, deceased also had an old quilt or sack, but not under clothes whatever to the bed. The sufficiency of food which deceased had arose from his not being able in three meals to eat what would have made one for a man in good health.[73]

Murphy's daughter, Alley, who lived with her father, was also questioned,

> They had not near sufficiency [*sic*] of food, had no fleshmeat but a little at Christmas and one pound got a few days since, but the deceased was unable to eat ... Sometimes the deceased was able to get one stone of meal for the week for the use of three persons and sometimes but half a stone ... Often their diet was broth made of boiled turnips with meal and water. There were two days which they had one meal of food but repeatedly they had but two meals of food and then not a sufficiency of it. When there was much down rain deceased would lie on some straw on the floor. Witness sometimes lay by herself on a little straw but had no bed clothes or other covering save her daily clothing.[74]

Dr Reed found that dysentery was the cause of death but also that Murphy's stomach was absolutely void of the slightest appearance of food.[75] The verdict was 'death from dysentery terminating in inflammation of the stomach and bowels which was brought on from unsuitable and insufficient food, combined with a wretched dwelling and miserable bed clothing'.[76] The inquest reveals that the family used all their resources to feed themselves to survive, but to no avail. In contrast, the *Northern Standard* published a very different version. On 13 February 1847, a very brief report praised the 'efficient coroner and respectable jury' for

72 CB1, no. 10.29. Patt Murphy, 8 Feb. 1847. 73 Ibid. 74 Ibid. 75 Ibid. 76 Ibid.

returning a verdict of dysentery brought on from insufficient and 'injudicious diet' implying such a diet was the poor judgement of the dying man.[77]

That same month, seventy-year-old Mary Sherry was found dead in her house, a dwelling 'so miserable of a kind that when any rain fell, it poured into the house'.[78] Unable to leave, she had been visited by several neighbours bearing food to keep her alive. A post-mortem examination found the body greatly emaciated, feet swollen, chronic ulcers on the front of both tibias, the stomach greatly contracted and empty and the doctor and jury concluded that her death arose from extreme cold, combined with want of sufficient and nourishing food.[79] A cord had been tied around the door on the outside of her house, which may have indicated that she was deliberately kept in the room, and was perhaps the catalyst for the coroner's investigation. No additional evidence was produced that could prove foul play.

The increase in starvation deaths of beggars and 'vagrants' (the mobile poor) in Waddell's casebook throughout the spring of 1847 exposes a break in the pre-Famine cultural narrative in Co. Monaghan, when charity was offered to strangers. Famine conditions interrupted the traditional moral obligation towards the poor and eroded sentiments of empathy. The inquests reveal changed attitudes towards the local versus wandering beggars, the former were seen as deserving of support and compassion, while the latter were increasingly feared and associated with criminality and vice as resources to survive decreased.[80] On 19 February 1847, Waddell investigated the discovery of the body of a stranger, identified as James McKierney, who was believed to be using a form of 'trickery' when he repeatedly fell down in the road and needed assistance in being picked up.[81] James Carrigan said upon seeing a young boy supporting the man to walk, that he 'laughed on them thinking it was but rougeuing [sic] of deceased'.[82] The next day, there was another inquest, this one on the body of a very elderly man not from the area, identified as Daroley. Returning from visiting his daughters in Scotland, he attempted the journey supported by charity along the way, but 'received very little of it'.[83] One might consider that a man of great age and experience had travelled by such means on many occasions, but his death revealed that it was no longer possible. He died from 'over-fatigue combined with a severe and protracted attack of dysentery, working on an old and emaciated constitution'.[84]

Another inquest a week later recorded the activities of 'a strange man' who had attempted to secure lodging, including at the gate lodge of Mr Johnson of Errigal, only to be refused.[85] He was found in the graveyard near death, and taken to Reverend Hurst's house. There, he was given some light, warm food and a little tea with a spoon, and his feet were bathed in warm water. The nameless man died from the effects of want of nourishment combined with extreme cold. The post-mortem examination revealed that there was no food in his body whatsoever

---

77 *NS*, 13 Feb. 1847. 78 CB1, no. 12.31, Mary Sherry, 13 Feb. 1847. 79 Ibid. 80 Virginia Crossman, *Poverty and the Poor Law in Ireland, 1850–1914* (Oxford, 2013), pp 199–200. 81 CB1, no. 14.33, James McKierney, 19 Feb. 1847. 82 Ibid. 83 CB1, no. 15.34, _____ Daroley, 20 Feb. 1847. 84 Ibid. 85 CB1, no. 16.35, the body of a strange man, 27 Feb. 1847.

and noted that the deceased's pockets had 'neither money nor bread ... except of few horse beans and crumbs of bread'.[86] Being a vagrant was viewed as a lifestyle choice rather than a necessity, and people categorized this way provoked a negative response from the public.[87] Additionally, during times of crisis, such as Famine or epidemic disease, the charity and generosity of the lower classes was conditional and vagrants might be unwelcome everywhere.[88] On 13 March 1847, the *Northern Standard* reported that an inquest was held on a stranger who came to his death by starvation and placed emphasis on the charity of the Revd J. and Mrs Hurst of Errigle Trough.[89] The report also stated that two other cases of starvation had occurred within the past few days in the neighbourhoods of Ballybay and Castleblayney.

Accounts of women travelling long distances at great hardship to find food to feed their hungry children are recorded in the oral tradition, as well as being captured in Waddell's casebook.[90] The sad tales include recollections of their poor treatment by others, their need to survive by begging, the beatings they endured at the hands of others, the robbery of the food they needed to feed their children and the devastation the political economics of the time had on them and their children in the procurement of food.[91] At one such inquest, that of Mary Ann McDermot in March 1847, the views and voice of the people featured prominently represent an indictment on society and government policy. McDermot was a beggar woman with two children to feed and was without a male partner. Evidence from her eleven-year-old daughter, Catherine, contributed to the following special verdict of death:

> Mary Ann McDermot lived for the last 4 months (in the village of Killeevan) by begging but refused to go into the poor house and charged her children never to do so. She supported herself and two children with meal which she spent the whole day collecting 1/2 cup (of Indian meal) in small quantities throughout the country bringing home at night what she collected during the day and making gruel of it for herself and her 2 children. She got a few pence also by begging with which she paid her house rent 2*d*. twice a week and to give herself and children 2 meals on Sunday. On Friday 12th inst. deceased walked from Killeevan to Clones [eight miles] on an errand for which she received a loan of a cup full of meal which she divided among herself and children and made into gruel – being a tea cup full to each. On Thursday, deceased got a quart of soup from the soup kitchen and was told to call each day after for it. On Friday, deceased's child went for the soup while her mother was in Clones, the 2

86 Ibid.   87 Laurence M. Geary, '"The whole country was in motion": mendicancy and vagrancy in pre-Famine Ireland' in Jacqueline Hill and Colm Lennon (eds), *Luxury and austerity* (Dublin, 1999), p. 126.   88 Ibid.   89 CB1, no. 16.35, the body of a strange man, 27 Feb. 1847; *NS*, 13 Mar. 1847.   90 Patricia Lysaght, 'Perspectives on women during the Great Irish Famine from the oral tradition', *Béaloideas*, 64:5 (1996/7), pp 63–130.   91 Ibid.

children each took a porringer full of it, leaving one for their Mother for her return. On deceased's return, she became weak and sat down about 2 miles from Killeevan and close to the house of Bernard Greenan whose sister went and asked deceased was she ill and would she like any food who on deceased's saying, she would return into the house and warmed some stirrabout and milk, and put it into the mouth of the deceased as if she would feeding an infant ... deceased could not swallow it and commenced struggling violently with her arms for about 20 minutes when she died. It appeared upon examination of the body, deceased had some greens of a bad quality in her stomach and a small quantity of raw turnips in her bowels insufficient to sustain life. The Jury find the death arose from want of proper and nourishing food.[92]

This special verdict was one that reflected the outcry of the jury as to the injustice done to McDermot and had the endorsement of the coroner. Special verdicts required no particular form of words, but every fact and circumstance necessary to constitute the offence was required to be positively stated.[93] These were cases referred to a judge for further evaluation to establish any liability.[94] This special verdict was the only one of its kind in Waddell's thirty-two years as coroner. No evidence exists that a follow up action identifying accountability for McDermot's death ever took place and it was not published in the *Northern Standard*. The inquest and verdict reflect the effects of the Russell administration's inadequate relief support to feed those most in need. Although the Temporary Relief Act (also known as the Soup Kitchen Act) was passed in February 1847, for the purpose of implementing soup kitchens throughout Ireland, this effort was slow to get started before May as evidenced by the death of McDermot.

Complicated and slow-moving bureaucracy was a salient feature of local committees' relief efforts and the actions taken by boards of guardians. The consequences are captured in the death of Patrick McCabe in March 1847, demonstrating the extent to which local government officials in Co. Monaghan prioritized policy and procedure over timeliness for a family in great distress. The Catholic curate of Magheross, Fr Edward McGovern, summoned Captain Barry of the police. Barry immediately wrote to coroner Waddell, who then travelled over 45 miles round trip to the townland of Greaghlatacapple, located in the southern half of the county. The parish of Magheross, south Monaghan, had been experiencing a high death rate from want and destitution varying from seven or eight deaths per day to as high as fourteen as reported by Charles MacNally, bishop of Clogher, and Fr McGovern.[95] McCabe, a recently evicted cottier, was taking shelter in a ditch with his wife and child. Fr Thomas McEnally and Fr McGovern went to the boardroom of the Carrickmacross poorhouse to plead with the board of guardians,

---

92 CB1, no. 21.40, Mary Ann McDermot, 13 Mar. 1847.   93 Hayes, *Crimes and punishments*, p. 630.   94 Ibid.   95 Kerr, *'A nation of beggars'?*, p. 40; CB1, no. 19.38, Patrick McCabe, 10 Mar. 1847.

who happened to be in session, to get admission for McCabe.[96] The guardians told the clergy that they had no power to approve McCabe's admission but rather it was the warden of the division who must investigate. Both men then proceeded to the warden's home, where they procured the ticket of admission for all three members of the family as well as a horse and cart to take them to the poorhouse. Finally, they then proceeded six miles from the town to the townland of Greaghlatacapple where they found,

> The body of deceased lying in an open field with no covering except his usual tattered dress. At a short distance from the body of deceased sat deceased's wife, with her child exposed to the inclemency of weather, having no other covering but their clothes which were of the worst description.[97]

Fr McGovern took great care to build a fire and instruct the neighbours to take turns alternately watching the body, whereby he proceeded to inform the police captain and coroner to ask for further investigation. Fr McGovern also tried but failed to get admittance to the home of Mr George Morant, the nearest magistrate and the agent of the estate on which the deceased was found, that of Mr Evelyn J. Shirley, the county's largest landowner, whose estate in Co. Monaghan comprised of 26,000 acres with a population in excess of 20,000. Although a Pat McCabe did appear in Shirley's estate records in which the names of cottiers and their families were listed, his identity cannot be confirmed as one and the same.[98] Fr McGovern's demand for the coroner demonstrates the strength of feeling that an official recording of certain starvation deaths was important and necessary in order to expose the injustice of deaths such as these, which were occurring across the country. Circumstantial evidence suggests that Catholic clergy around the country believed in the institution of the coroner as a means of obtaining some justice for the dead. The verdict in the case of McCabe was death 'in consequence of the combined effects of want of a sufficiency of food and exposure to the inclemency of the weather'.[99]

Elsewhere in Ireland, the pressure of the crisis and high levels of excess death also brought a reluctance to request the coroner. In March 1847, in Omagh, Co. Tyrone, it was considered pointless to order the coroner to act. Revd Henry Lucas St George, rector of the parish of Dromore, told the relief commissioners that many in his parish had died from actual want; that parents were unable to feed their children more than a drink of gruel once a day; that mothers with infants at their breasts were themselves starving; and that 'coroners were not applied to for

---

96 Inquest testimony from tenants on the Shirley estate identified a Patrick McGuffy [McCaffrey] as McCabe's former employer. McCaffrey is listed as the lessor of land and houses in Greaghlatacapple in Griffith's Valuation (1847–64). **97** CB1, no. 19.38, Patrick McCabe, 10 Mar. 1847. **98** Shirley estate papers 1840–7 (PRONI, Shirley estate papers, D3531/M/1–2). **99** CB1, no. 19.38, Patrick McCabe, 10 Mar. 1847.

the neighbours said there was no use to do so'.[100] However, in Monaghan that same month, Waddell's inquests captured several examples of hostility towards society's poorest, which appeared to illustrate the fear and diminished humanity of the countryside. Elderly blind beggar Laurence Daily became very weak and was cared for overnight in the home of cottier, Terry Hughes.[101] When tenant farmer Peter Coogan was informed of Daily's presence, Coogan told him to get out of the bed, took him by the wrist and arm and removed him from the house. Coogan 'took him on his back and carried him up the road, laid him down in a ditch on the side of the road where he lay on the broad of his back'.[102] Daily died from want of proper food, exposure to the weather and neglect of the state of his bowels. Waddell took a note that reflected the feelings of the jury:

> The jury at the same time expressing their disapprobation of the conduct of Peter Coogan as being void of humanity towards the poor, dying old man.[103]

Another case that same month exposed the cruelty of Patrick Coogan, who fired and evicted his man servant, Charles Coyle, leaving him without work or home, or any means to provide for himself.[104] When Patrick Traynor of Cornanure tried to intervene on behalf of Coyle, asking Coogan to take the poor man back into his home, Coogan 'threatened to shoot him if he did not be gone about his business'.[105] Coyle spent his last days lying on a bed of straw by the side of the road in the cold without food. His death was determined to have arrived as a result of the combined effects of cold and want of food acting on a weak and debilitated constitution.[106] At this crucial point in time the Monaghan coroner was still being utilized in the administration of justice, capturing the horrors of the crisis.

YOUR MONEY, YOUR LAND AND YOUR LIFE: KEY SURVIVAL STRATEGIES

In a desperate effort to stay alive, the poor faced difficult choices as to how to utilize their few remaining assets while risking starvation in a fight for survival. The following inquests reflect those who had some means to protect themselves, but equally allocate a level of blame as to the victims' contribution towards their own death via the lack of practical utilization of their monies or property. In March 1847, James Williamson was gathering and selling rags and old iron, but died from great want of nourishing food and exposure to inclemency of the weather as he had been living in an open outhouse. The verdict of death captured by Waddell reflects

---

100 Henry Lucas St George, rector of the parish of Dromore, Co. Tyrone to the Relief Commission Office, 16 Mar. 1847 (NAI, FRC, RLFC3/2/28/32). 101 CB1, no. 26.45, Laurence Daily, 25 Mar. 1847. 102 Ibid. 103 Ibid. 104 CB1, no. 17.36, Charles Coyle, 2 Mar. 1847. 105 Ibid. 106 Ibid.

inequitable attitudes towards the poor, as it specified that Williamson was found with £5 16s. 1¼ d. silver and copper money on his person therefore 'his destitution was so far voluntary'.[107] He was probably seeking to save enough money to secure the means to emigrate, while trying to feed himself; yet, the verdict reflects a lack of understanding of his choices and plight. A similar paradox existed for small tenant farmers, many of whom had to decide whether to keep their land or sell. Ulster tenant right, a security of tenure whereby the tenant was due the monies from improvements made to the houses and the land from the incoming tenant or landlord, gave the tenant the right to sell his interest to a third party with agreement of the landlord. However, with landlords burdened with increasing costs most would be more likely to evict than pay, and small holders with money were scarce as they struggled to survive and keep their own holdings. The inquest of Patt Banagan revealed that 'about November last, deceased could have sold his holding (i.e. tenant right) of two and a half acres ... and knew him to be in great want of food for himself and his family'.[108] Banagan died after a fall into the roadside grip filled with water while on the way to Carrickmacross to get a relief ticket for meal to feed his family. Similarly, the inquest of Francis Mulligan identified that Mulligan 'had a small farm of two acres that he could have sold [his tenant right] for £22 but his wife was averse to selling it'.[109] He died on the way to find a priest to obtain a relief ticket. The value placed upon Mulligan's land may indicate a pre-Famine estimate. The actual value of the land during the Famine was much less.

The death of Michael Hughes, in May 1847, reveals that he, like Banagan and Mulligan, also had a small holding of just two-and-a-half acres of land, and had been 'without employment since the public works ceased'.[110] He had sought to be put on the list for relief, but was refused. Hughes, his sister-in-law and wife had gathered nettles and the leaves of young cabbage plants just planted, boiled them together and ate them, without either meal or salt. Hughes persisted in trying to obtain relief, was finally given a ticket post-dated one week, but he died before it came due.

While relief was provided to many, those who availed of the outdoor relief of the soup kitchen in Monaghan were for some time suffering from restrictive portions of food. It was reported in May 1847 that the relief officers in Monaghan town were only providing 3 quarts of soup for every seven adult persons, resulting in death from dysentery and fever.[111] Two inquests represent both working and non-working persons with no assets, each of whom died as a result of the inadequate food available. An inquest was held on the body of Rose Sweeny, a widow whose husband had died two years earlier. She had four children to feed and no means of support other than the charity of her neighbours who held her in high esteem. She was receiving two rations per day at the soup kitchen, although her

107 CB1, no. 27.26, James Williamson, 31 Mar. 1847. 108 CB1, no. 59.40, Patt Banagan, 4 May 1847. 109 CB1, no. 41.60, Francis Mulligan, 6 May 1847. 110 CB1, no. 47.66, Michael Hughes, 18 May 1847. 111 *NS*, 22 May 1847.

name was on the list for three, but she died from 'great destitution' before her third ticket was released.[112] Under the Soup Kitchen Act, Sweeny was entitled to three rations: one for herself, and a half-ration for each of her children per day.[113] This would indicate why the inquest was held as Waddell would have suspected mismanagement or potential corruption on the part of the local committee managing the soup kitchen. Additionally, the inquest of Isaiah Moore in May 1847, who was the sole supporter of his family, revealed that although he was receiving meal from the relief fund at Rockcorry, it was not enough to sustain his life.[114] Both inquests supported the predominant belief that relief policy was fundamentally flawed, and emphasized and exposed the fatalities that resulted. They both contribute additions to a growing body of evidence that Co. Monaghan authorities were restrictive when distributing relief to the poor.

THE 'BARBAROUS' MURDERS OF VULNERABLE WOMEN

On 20 March 1847, the government reported the average daily number of persons employed on relief works in Ireland was 685,932.[115] Monaghan had a daily average of 10,448 and while it was the third largest number of people employed in such works in Ulster, relief work only supported 5 per cent of the county's population.[116] The gap in employment needed to be filled by Irish landlords, but in most cases this did not happen. Men acquired public works employment more often than women, leaving many women with little or no options to generate income. The linen trade had gone into decline decades prior to the Famine and of those still earning a living by spinning, a stark statistic reflects how much further it declined. In 1841, Monaghan still had 22,574 registered licensed spinners and spinsters, but by 1851, only 2,223 remained.[117] With no prospects of being paid for their labour or the goods they could create, those 20,351 skilled workers either died or emigrated, and disappeared from the landscape of south Ulster.

The groups that were most vulnerable during the Famine were those with the least amount of resources, such as income or property, to secure their survival. The gender labour divide in rural Ireland involved men providing the labour and being responsible for the production of the food while women managed the home, including the task of preserving the food supply.[118] Women's roles changed during the Famine – they now had to procure funds or provide food, often in the form of relief, roles that were vital for family survival through the crisis.[119] Reilly's study of Strokestown loan fund accounts in Co. Roscommon indicates that 90 per cent of

---

112 CBI, no. 51.70, Rose Sweeny, 26 May 1847. 113 9 & 10 Vict., c. 107 (26 Feb. 1847), Temporary Relief Act (also known as the Soup Kitchen Act). 114 CBI, no. 44.63, Isaiah Moore, 13 May 1847. 115 *Northern Whig*, 6 Apr. 1847. 116 Ibid. Donegal had 21,078 persons employed on relief works and Cavan had 18,543. Ulster had the least number of persons employed in relief works. 117 *Northern Whig*, 6 Apr. 1847. 118 Patricia Lysaght, 'Perspectives on women during the Great Irish Famine from the oral tradition', *Béaloideas, Iml.* 64/5 (1996/7), pp 63–130, p. 77. 119 Ibid.

applicants for relief were women, with a high number listed as 'widows' suggesting that men were more susceptible to death in the early stages of the Famine – or too proud to apply for relief.[120] However, many of the stories include how women were subjected to having their food stolen and raises questions about how often they were victims of theft, violence or murder.[121] The records reveal that men were more likely to avail of loan funds to supplement their income and close the gap until gainful employment was once again possible.[122] Witness statements in Waddell's casebook show that both men and women were identified as having sought relief in the form of meal or a place in the local workhouse in equal measure.[123] The abandonment of traditional male behaviour may reflect the degree of hardship in Co. Monaghan.

The working activities of women identified in inquests reveal that most women carried out domestic chores in and around the home, including cooking, housekeeping and caring for children and sick family members, and outdoor tasks such as gathering creels of sods, hanging dried dung leaves to repair cottage roofs, drowning flax, keeping fowl for eggs, and field work. Yet, one inquest captured by Waddell in April 1847 identifies Ally Reed, a woman employed in breaking stones on the road, indicating that women were also engaged in public works employment when it was available.[124] Women in Waddell's inquests were also employed as beggars, prostitutes, servant maids in private residences or institutions such as the bridewells, workhouses or hospitals, barkeeps, or, in rarer instances, as shopkeepers. Women who had the ability to financially support themselves, particularly single or marriageable women, were in an unusual marginal social position and the evidence in Waddell's inquests indicate they were extremely vulnerable.

On 9 April 1847, Waddell conducted inquests on the bodies of two elderly women, Ann and Catherine Collen, who had been murdered in their own home in the townland of Mullaghcroghery, on the Shirley estate. The *Northern Standard* reported,

> The barbarous murder of ... two very inoffensive and respected old women who supported themselves by a little hucksters shop, aided by their neighbours, by whom they were generally esteemed, and also frequent contributions from Mr Shirley, who was so much concerned on hearing of their murder, that he has offered £200 of a reward for the discovery of the perpetrators of the horrid deed ... they survived on selling a few cakes and small quantities of tobacco.[125]

---

120 Ciarán Reilly, '"Nearly starved to death": the female petition during the Great Hunger' in Christine Kinealy, Jason King and Ciarán Reilly (eds), *Women and the Great Hunger* (Hamden, 2016), pp 47–56, p. 50. 121 Ibid. 122 Ibid. 123 The casebook recorded 10 men and 7 women, who applied for or received relief, and 17 men and 16 women who were inmates of a local workhouse during the years of the Famine. 124 Inquest no. 56.37, Peter Reed, 26 Apr. 1847. 125 *NS*, 17 Apr. 1847.

Their house had been ransacked and the two sisters found inside. Ann Collen's body was lying in a pool of blood on the floor, her 'arms blackened and her whole person bloody down to her ankles'.[126] She had suffered blunt-force trauma to her face and head as if hit with the sharp end of a pointed hammer multiple times; her hair covered her face, 'stuck to it from hardened blood'.[127] Five of the seven severe blows to her head had broken her skull, each one sufficient to have caused her death. Ann also suffered a severe deep cut from behind her ear halfway across her neck. Defence wounds were found on her arms matching a strap of leather found at the doorstep believed to be a belt commonly worn by male labourers. Catherine Collen's body lay halfway off her bed, and she was 'perfectly naked'.[128] Of two severe blows to the head, one had fractured her skull and was determined to be the cause of death.

The murders appeared in newspapers around the country, in articles calling the crime 'barbarous', a word used when a murder was perpetrated on the vulnerable and when the act was of a particularly brutal nature. It was also a term used by conservative newspapers to illustrate the savagery of the Catholic Irish in their native countryside. Several interpretations of the term may be considered, but stigma and shame are common to all of them. The *Louth Advertiser* described the women as 'maiden sisters', indicating that they were unmarried, and therefore probably virgins.[129] The murders were called 'an inhuman act', 'one of the most hideous outrages that ever disgraced humanity' and the perpetrators considered 'inhuman wretches'.[130] Catherine's body was found naked, which may indicate that the crime was sexual in nature and, applying modern forensic evaluation of crime scenes, the removal of her clothing may indicate the perpetrator's or perpetrators' desire to humiliate. While the inquest identified that Catherine had a large fracture of the skull over the right temple that was fatal, the *Nenagh Guardian* published that the blow was 'in addition to other injuries'.[131] However, no other injuries were documented by Waddell.

A similar lack of documentation was captured in the reporting of the rape and murder of Margaret Smith that took place the same month. Newspapers reported that 'a lone woman of 60 years of age' underwent 'a most barbarous and revolting outrage'.[132] A drunk 22-year-old labourer named James Robb broke into Smith's cottage and 'so maltreated and shamefully abused' her so as to cause her death.[133] 'When apprehended Robb's face was found marked and scratched so to further provide evidence of the altercation with the deceased.'[134] While a sexual assault had taken place, as was documented in court records, those details were omitted from the newspaper article. Over the thirty-one years of Waddell's inquests, only three mentioned 'abuse', which indicated a suspected crime of sexual assault. The absence of any details requires further examination into the language used to describe the victims and their assailants, as well as the social conditions of the

---

126 Inquest no. 32.51 Catherine Collen, 9 Apr. 1847; inquest no. 33.52, Ann Collen, 9 Apr. 1847. 127 *Nenagh Guardian*, 21 Apr. 1847. 128 Inquest no. 33.52, Ann Collen, 9 Apr. 1847. The detail of how Catherine's body was found was documented in the inquest of her sister Ann. 129 *Louth Advertiser*, 17 Apr. 1847. 130 Ibid. 131 *Nenagh Guardian*, 21 Apr. 1847 132 *Morning Post*, 20 Apr. 1849; *Aberdeen Press and Journal*, 18 Apr. 1849. 133 Ibid. 134 Ibid.

communities where the murders took place. The most common victims of sexual assault were children, elderly women, servants and adult women who were alone or without male protection.[135]

The Collen sisters had been robbed. Missing property included blankets from the two beds, two new cloaks, a new flannel petticoat and their shoes; however, a purse found hidden in a barrel contained 17 shillings, a significant sum of money.[136] Constabulary Sub-Inspector Barry carried out a search for the plunder in houses nearby but found none of the missing items. The women appeared to have been doing well for themselves, particularly at a time of great hardship for many. The identities of the culprits were debated in the newspapers. The *Louth Examiner* stated that the prevalent opinion was that 'the inhuman wretches who committed this outrage are inhabitants of a distant county', while the *Northern Standard* reported a different view:

> The general impression of the jury, who were all neighbours [of the deceased], was that the deed was committed by some person or persons well acquainted with their habits and residing not very far distant.[137]

An examination of the evidence lends some clues as to why the jury had such suspicions. Two of the Collens' closest neighbours from the same townland provided testimony at the inquest. Neighbour James Lundy, a large landholder on the Shirley estate, was the first witness to find the sisters dead. He was putting his cows out on the morning of 8 April, saw the Collens' cottage door partly opened and pushed it open to find the gruesome scene. Lundy alerted neighbours of his findings, including James and Mary Bell, who then returned to the house with him. He then sent word to the authorities to notify them and request an investigation. Mary Bell had been at the sisters' house the evening before their death to repay them 6*d*. that she had borrowed. She told the coroner and the jury that both women were in 'good health and spirits sitting at the fire'. The next morning, when Mary heard about the murders from Lundy, she returned to their cottage, saw them dead, and threw an old gown over the naked body of Catherine Collen.[138]

The jury's concerns were likely raised by the testimony of several male witnesses, who claimed to have seen a 'stranger woman' in the neighbourhood. George Jones and Pat Hill told the jury that having quit their work on the evening of 7 April 1847, they were asked by a strange woman where she could get some tobacco to buy, having been denied it by other dealers. The men provided directions to the Collens' house and parted ways. The physical description of the stranger offered that 'she was a stout, hearty woman, rather tall than otherwise'.[139] Witness James

---

135 James Kelly, '"A most inhuman and barbarous piece of villainy": an exploration of the crime of rape in eighteenth-century Ireland', *Eighteenth-Century Ireland*, 10 (1995), pp 78–107, p. 90. 136 CB1, no. 33.52, Ann Collen, 9 Apr. 1847. 137 *NS*, 19 Apr. 1847. 138 CB1, no. 33.52, Ann Collen, 9 Apr. 1847. 139 Ibid.

McCullen stated that he'd been at the Collens' house at 8 p.m. that evening for just a few minutes to buy some tobacco. He saw the strange woman there, 'stout and hearty looking, who was smoking strongly and appeared as if she was going to stop there for the night'.[140] Both accounts of the strange woman identify her as 'hearty' implying strong, healthy, well-fed and therefore potentially capable enough to carry out the murders with the physical force required. However, the descriptions were in conflict as to whether she was stout (short) or tall. No further details about the stranger's appearance were captured in the inquest transcript such as her state of dress, accent, hair and eye colour. While the absence of more specific details about the primary suspect may indicate poor investigation procedure by the authorities, it may also suggest a lack of belief in the credibility of the witnesses. None of the newspapers covering the story of the murders published the suspicions of the men that the culprit was a strange woman.

Further examination of the testimony reveals that witness McCullen was the only person providing a statement who required an alibi. McCullen's brother and sister-in-law swore that he had stopped at their house that same evening for a short-time and corroborated his statement. Additionally, he may have been the last person to see the women alive as his statement was the only one that had a timestamp documented by Waddell.

A motive for the murders may reside with the nature of the Collen sisters' means of generating an income during the Famine. Some local shopkeepers (or hucksters) supplied food on credit and lent money to the poor at extortionate rates, which offered some a potential solution to staying alive. Anyone seen by some members of the community to have prospered through the misfortunes of the poor was known as a gombeen. These persons were known to grab the land of those who had been evicted, emigrated or died, buying it at far below its actual value or taking it in lieu of unpaid debts that were run up with them. It was also documented that interest rates charged by local shopkeepers in heavily populated districts were reported to range 10–15 per cent.[141] Mary Bell was one of the last people to see the sisters alive the night before their death as she'd visited them to pay back a loan. While circumstantial evidence suggests that the women may have been usurers, there is no direct evidence that the women were taking advantage of others in their community. Ann and Catherine had a significant sum of money and had recently purchased new clothes at a time when others were starving. The prosperity of two single, independent women, at such a desperate time may have triggered the resentment of those aware of their financial gain and comfort.

The Collens had the support of the landlord, Shirley, and middleman, James Lundy, two men with notorious reputations, disliked by at least some tenants and cottiers under their management. Shirley was well known as a difficult landlord and those supported by his generosity may have themselves been scorned. In 1847, the Shirley estate was the largest in Co. Monaghan, with over 3,284 cottiers who

---

140 Ibid.   141 Cormac Ó Gráda, *Ireland: a new economic history, 1780–1939* (Oxford, 1995), p. 124.

were struggling for survival. Records from the estate and newspaper reports show that the majority of inmates at the Carrickmacross workhouse were previously Shirley's cottiers or tenants.[142] According to the records of the deputy keeper, rules were imposed on tenants that prevented subletting and subdivision. Lundy was a middleman on the estate with four holdings comprised of just over 25 acres. In May 1847, just one month after the murders, Lundy evicted a large cottier family of seven known as the Keenans. Mr Bashford, one of the Carrickmacross Poor Law guardians, defined Lundy's behaviour as an 'inhumane act'.[143] The board of guardians (of which Shirley and his agent, George Morant, were members) did not allow the Keenan family entry to the workhouse. The Keenans were instructed to go to a local relief committee, which meant they would simply receive a meal and whatever supplies may be available, but no shelter in this crucial and dangerous month of the Famine. Evidence suggests that the Collens' association with such men, and their having prospered from this patronage, may have made them unpopular with others in their neighbourhood.

The study of death during the years of the Famine often focuses on the horrors of starvation, the apathy of local officials and the inability of the administration to facilitate the survival of the poorest members of the population. Yet, murders, particularly those carried out on single women, raise questions as to the social and political factors that contributed to their deaths. They reflect the acute moral and social decay in the communities that correlate with poor government legislation and local implementation of relief. Using coroners' inquests as official documentation of such atrocious crimes can provide a more accurate history about the Famine crisis in specific geographical regions and privately owned estates where murders took place.

THE VALUE OF THE CORONER'S WORK

While the results of the coroner's work exposed life-threatening government policy and local practice in the delivery of relief, how the inquests were valued and measured depended upon the political and social environment in which they were carried out. Coroners were required to submit formal reports back to the lord lieutenant's office annually, including their number of inquests. In cases of homicide, further documentation was required: the name of the deceased, the verdict of death, whether the killer was known, and, if known, their name. The value placed upon the role of the coroner and the function of the inquest relied heavily on their ability to identify guilty parties and help raise awareness and accountability.

By mid-April 1847, Cork city coroners had declared their determination not to hold inquests on the bodies of persons dying in the streets from want and fever, to 'avoid the great expense which the innumerable inquests from the causes would

142 *NS*, 14 June 1847. 143 Lorraine O'Reilly, 'The Shirley estate 1814–1906: the development and demise of a landed estate in County Monaghan' (PhD, Trinity College Dublin, 2014), p. 141.

bring upon the city'.[144] The *Evening Chronicle* also published an article that same month saying that in Sligo the grand jury asked the coroners not to hold inquests on those who died of starvation.[145] The liberal *Fermanagh Reporter* stated that same month,

> where causes of death were self-evident the services of the coroner are now dispensed with in most places, otherwise the counties which are already too heavily taxed, would be put to an enormous deal of unnecessary expense. Death by starvation, more than any other cause, excites scarcely any emotion at the present time: there are so many instances of it occurring day after day that the people have grown as familiar to it as to feel no sensation more than they would if old age, or any other of the most natural causes had brought it about.[146]

In contrast to reports of attitudes regarding paying for the costs of inquests, the *Cork Examiner*, a nationalist newspaper, published an article with a reminder of the coroners' inquests which brought in a verdict of 'wilful murder' against Lord John Russell, and reported that Fr Maginn and the Catholic clergy of Londonderry would record their own findings. The registries of their diocese recording death would bear an inscription, which included,

> The records of the murders of the Irish Peasantry, perpetrated in A.D. 1846–7, in the 9th and 10th Victoria, under the name of economy, during the administration of a professedly Liberal Whig Government of which Lord John Russell was the Premier.[147]

In June 1847, it was reported in the *Northern Standard* that the corpse of an old itinerant beggar, a man not known to the Clones neighbourhood, was found lying dead in a pigsty nearby in the townland of Clonfad, Co. Fermanagh, after eight days unnoticed. The local paper reported that the cause of death was so obviously starvation that 'the authorities did not deem it necessary to have an inquest on the body'.[148] This may indicate that the Co. Fermanagh coroner refused to take an inquest not seeing the value or importance for such an investigation. It reflects a shift in the attitudes of the middle-class public in Co. Monaghan, and potentially Co. Fermanagh, whereby they purportedly became desensitized to excess deaths or Famine-linked deaths of society's poorest. This attitude was reflected in the lack of local press coverage of the formal investigations into Famine-related deaths in Co. Monaghan recorded by Waddell.

Of inquests carried out by Waddell in his first fifteen months as coroner, only a handful of those deaths appeared in the *Northern Standard*. On 20 February 1847,

---

144 *Cork Examiner*, 16 Apr. 1847.   145 *Evening Chronicle*, 7 Apr. 1847.   146 *Fermanagh Reporter*, 29 Apr. 1847.   147 *Cork Examiner*, 26 Apr. 1847.   148 *NS*, 12 June 1847.

the newspaper reported the inquest taken on the body of a 5-year-old child who was found frozen and left dead in the snow. The inquest found that the carcass had been mutilated by dogs, but deemed it 'an affair shrouded in mystery' as to whom the child belonged.[149] No explicit reference was made connecting the death to the local Famine crisis. The newspaper incorrectly reported that there had been no medical examination of the body, while insisting that it would have been necessary, but Waddell's casebook recorded the doctor's payment.[150] Only two articles identifying local deaths as a result of starvation were published by the *Northern Standard* in February and March 1847; the first blamed the victim and the second praised the efforts of those trying to save the victim.

Other inquests published focused on accidental deaths, those that might be considered public-interest stories. These included deaths that resulted from accidental gunshot wounds, a fall from a horse, drunkenness, a visitation of God, and an accidental drowning. One such case was the inquest on 7 May 1847 of Elizabeth Grimes, a servant of William Calvert, a tenant of Waddell in the townland of Drumgavny.[151] She was found to have accidentally drowned in the roadside grip on the way home at night. A letter to the editor was also published outlining the need for improvements to the road for the sake of public safety.[152] Besides reflecting Waddell's self-interest in improving the roads in his own townland, can an assumption be made that these non-Famine related inquests reported in the *Northern Standard* reflect the type of inquests that were of importance to the Protestant middle-class public, as opposed to the Famine-related deaths of the poor? The lack of local stories published on local Famine-related death up to this point in time may reflect the suppression of evidence by the local elite to quell the frustration of the populace. Evidence suggests that local news of the crisis was not of 'value' to the local elite and the grand jury, and the work of the coroner investigating dead paupers was viewed as a cost imposed by the administration.

On 17 July 1847 Waddell submitted his expenses to the grand jury for approval and payment, a claim that included sixty-five inquests conducted over six months, payment for his fees per inquest at £1 10s. each, eighteen different doctors for post-mortem examinations at £3 4s. 1d., mileage for 1,440 miles travelled, along with payments for coffins, witness expenses and rental for space to conduct inquests. Like all those in his profession, Waddell paid for all expenses out of pocket, which came to a total of £8 8s. 6d.[153] The coroners' fees and expenses were to be repaid out of the county rates. Grand jury member Edward Golding, agent of Lord Blayney, highlighted that the law indicated that a coroner would not receive more than £50 per half-year regardless of the number of inquests they conducted.[154] With a deficit of £60, one might consider if Waddell would thereafter do fewer inquests. Being paid per inquest, rather than being paid a salary, undermined the

149 *NS*, 20 Feb. 1847. 150 CB1, no. 13.32, an unknown child, 15 Feb. 1847. 151 CB1, no. 42.61, Elizabeth Grimes, 7 May 1847. 152 *NS*, 15 May 1847. 153 CB1, Summary of preceding inquests, June 1847. 154 *NS*, 17 July 1847.

authority of the coroner. The threat of non-payment might condition a coroner to question whether a 'needs-based decision' came before fiscal considerations, and both views purported to be driven by civic responsibility.

The Coroners Act of 1846 stipulated the need for mapping coroners' districts throughout Ireland to ensure proper coverage, and as a result, Co. Monaghan had been split into two divisions, north and south in February 1847.[155] It was determined that the northern district would be comprised of the baronies of Monaghan, Dartrey and Trough, and part of the parish of Tullycorbet, in the barony of Cremorne; the south district took on the other half of the Tullycorbet parish, and the baronies of Cremorne and Farney.[156] That same month, coroner Dr Robert Murray resigned. Although this created the need for a new coroner and election, one did not take place. By July 1847, this lack of action was presented by Waddell's attorney, William Wright, as evidence that 'he was doing the job of two men' and should be compensated commensurately.[157] A letter written by Waddell to the editor of the *Londonderry Standard* in May 1856 states,

> I recall with pleasure your strictures on the conduct of the grand jury in your county in forbidding *post mortem* examinations, except on the requisition of the jury. You might have gone farther in your condemnation of the course they have adopted, and also pronounced it illegal, the Legislature having given them no such power. The 9 & 10 Vic., cap. 37, sec. 33, places the power of ordering *post mortem* examinations wholly in the hands of the coroner, and on no account should any person or party be permitted to interfere in the exercise of it.
>
> As a senior coroner of this county, I have had to resist many attempts to interfere with the discharge of my duties, as well from the grand jury as individual justices. The latter I have dealt with myself and effectively; with respect to the former, I always appealed from their decisions to the Judge of Assize, employing the best counsel this circuit could produce. The consequence is, I in every instance defeated them, and *I now have peace*. One of my subjects of appeal was respecting employment of doctors, when Chief Baron-Pigot told the jury the exercising of the right of calling in doctors, and judging as to the necessity of doing so, rested alone with the coroner.[158]

This suggests that Waddell was paid the excess above the £50 agreed upon by the grand jury that year.

The office of coroner was wrought with conflict reflected by not only the fee-based payment structure, but the fiscal restrictions as to number and types of inquests. However, the usage of the press in publicizing inquest findings reflected

---

155 *NS*, 13 Feb. 1847; Coroners' Districts, Jan. 1846–Mar. 1846 (NAI, CSO/OPMA/1015 (2)); coroners' districts also included boroughs in urban areas. 156 *NS*, 13 Mar. 1847. 157 Ibid. 158 *LS*, 15 May 1857.

nationalist political views and provided a voice for the poor. Nally states that government regulation and control over the means of survival does not support the radical nationalist view that the Famine was a calculated genocide, but rather that the experiments with relief strategies resulted in a class of people being exterminated.[159] Gray outlines the failures of the administration, and argues that policies that embodied providentialism were ostensibly intended to improve the social and moral condition of the Irish through free trade and emigration, but ignored the human costs involved.[160] Both views can be applied to question the accountability of the coroner as an agent abiding by the administration's policies, but offer a lens through which to examine the moral ambiguity surrounding the lack of reports of Famine-related inquests in the local press to educate and inform the public. As the coroner was both an elected public official and an agent of the administration, were individual coroners ethically and politically bound to expose or hide the public crisis? The closely related politics of an individual coroner and the local elite may have impacted the number of Famine-related inquests exposed locally.

CONCLUSION

The Irish coroner served in a role of authority carrying out public inquests during the humanitarian crisis of the Great Famine in Ireland. However, the coroner's authority was challenged by local grand juries who did not want to pay for their services or what they deemed unnecessary costs, thereby undermining the important work of identifying unusual and unnatural death. The coroner's procedure, practice and documentation were tools used to capture evidence to evaluate the cause of death, but they also reflected the dynamics of complex, divisive relief policies, meant to provide support for the destitute. During the years of the Famine, public inquests uncovered unnecessary, preventable deaths and revealed inadequate relief policies for society's poorest. The inquests taken included some of those who had become victims of political economy, however, the coroners' inquests are limited by the exceptional circumstances that they captured. The deaths in Waddell's casebook are not typical and are a relatively small sample of the vast majority of deaths that took place in his district during the Famine. The great majority of deaths during the Famine were not investigated by coroners. Although the coroners' inquests are interesting, those deaths were investigated for additional reasons and the circumstances surrounding them. The work of the coroner further exposed the moral ambiguity that surrounded the government and local authorities' ideology of improving Irish behaviour through regulation by reporting deaths that directly resulted from its policies and legislation.

---

[159] David P. Nally, *Human encumbrances, political violence and the Great Irish Famine* (Notre Dame, IN, 2011), p. 172. [160] Gray, *Famine, land and politics*, p. 337.

4

Managing and investigating pauper death

> We shall be equally blamed for keeping [the Irish] alive or letting them die and we have only to select between the censure of the economists or the philanthropists – which do you prefer?
> –Lord Clarendon, August 1847[1]

In 1848, Universalist preacher William Stevens Balch (1806–87) travelled from America to Ireland with the intention of capturing his impressions of the Famine crisis for historical and humanitarian purposes. He travelled the country throughout the spring and arrived in Carrickmacross, Co. Monaghan, on 29 May 1848, a fair day. Balch found a bustling market with a mixture of abundance and want, food sellers and buyers, prosperous punters and starving beggars.

> Carrickmacross is the first town in Ulster. To us it was rendered attractive by the vast assemblage of people. It was a Fair-day, and the street, for a mile, was crowded with people, horses, hogs, cows, asses, sheep, and goats, young and old; dry goods, groceries, books, boots, dried fruit, green vegetables, grain, potatoes, butter, cheese – all sorts of things, jumbled together helter-skelter. Auctioneers were bawling, pedlars hawking, babies crying, women scolding, men drinking, smoking and quarrelling; the young folks chatting, laughing, dancing, frolicking.
> Beggars of all descriptions haunting us from one end of the town to the other. It was judged 5000 people, 500 head of cattle, as many sheep, and hogs without number were there, and goods enough to clothe, and provisions enough to feed the whole. But alas, few were permitted to do more than look at them. It was sort of a beggars' fair. The lame, the halt, the blind, the sick, the decrepit, were there, begging of whom they could, and exhibiting their deformities to excite sympathy and secure a penny. Of course, decently clad strangers, able to ride in a coach, could not pass unbegged. We were importuned at every step. Here a mother thrust her skeleton child into our faces; another exposed her cancer breast; a little girl

---

1 Letter from Lord Clarendon, the lord lieutenant, to Prime Minister Lord John Russell, 10 Aug. 1847, Letterbox I (Clarendon Deposit, Bodleian Library, Oxford).

led her blind father to us; a fourth exhibited a fractured leg. The most hideous being I ever saw in mortal shape was an old man, a complete skeleton doubled together, his chin resting on his knees, with his fleshless legs and arms exposed to view. As we passed him, he turned upon us a deathly stare and stretched out his long thin arm muttering a prayer in the name of the Almighty and the Holy Virgin, that we would give him something to keep him from starving. His hollow cheeks, projecting jaws, eyeballs sunken deep in their sockets – oh, horror, I can not describe him – the image of Death, doubled together![2]

Balch visited Monaghan at a peak time of crisis when many of society's most vulnerable were without food or shelter. Local institutions such as the gaols and workhouses were overcrowded and filled with disease. His recording of the beggars at the market supports the evidence captured in inquests as to the difficult conditions in Monaghan. The impact of Lord John Russell's legislative changes and the local mismanagement of paupers as well as the flawed ideology and approach to managing them were captured by the work of the coroner.

Similar to England, the nineteenth-century coroner's court in Ireland was a site of conflict for local officials who were responsible for the management of the poor, and coroners, who had a legal obligation to investigate deaths reported to them, including specifically at gaols.[3] Waddell's casebook of inquests helps to identify the correlation between the verdicts of death and the quality of the management at local institutions, the gaol and the workhouses, where death occurred. In addition to the inquests, the annual reports of the inspectors general of Irish prisons, the expenditure of the Co. Monaghan grand jury and the activities and decisions taken by the guardians of the Monaghan and Clones Poor Law unions, offer a new history of the Monaghan gaol and workhouses in this period.

Following an examination of the gaols, this chapter reviews the politics and policy surrounding the county's workhouses, including the effects of local politics on pauper deaths in Monaghan and the impact of the increasingly restrictive criteria for relief for those attempting to gain entry. Monaghan paupers suffered as a direct impact of Russell's policies after the third potato crop failure in September 1848. There was distress in workhouses, which peaked in June 1849, and in the gaols in December 1849, as well as suffering for those outside these local institutions. Trends in the behaviour of those who left the workhouse are revealed, as well as the process of Waddell's decision making when holding an inquest for the public welfare.

A second violent double homicide of two financially independent women investigated by Waddell is examined, and reflects the further social decay, and lack of

---

2 William Stevens Balch, *Ireland, as I saw it: the character, condition and prospects of the people* (New York, 1850), p. 411.   3 Joe Sim and Tony Ward, 'The magistrate of the poor? Coroners and deaths in custody in nineteenth-century England' in Michael Clark and Catherine Crawford (eds), *Legal medicine in history* (Cambridge, 1994), p. 249.

resources, and again emphasizes the vulnerability of these women as a marginal group. Lastly, the chapter evaluates a call for the abolition of the coroner's office that took place in August 1848 and reveals the moral ambiguity surrounding the priorities and fiscal decision making of conservative local gentry in respect to the examination of the deaths of local paupers.

CONDITIONS IN MONAGHAN: JUNE 1847

When the government abandoned the expensive public works in March 1847, many small tenant farmers and labourers were without work, and unable to pay their rents. With no employment and food prices still critically high, there were few options available for survival. The repercussions of the government's decision included diminished income for Irish landlords who were already burdened with paying for the workhouses and loans from the previous year for public works, exacerbated by the surge in the need for indoor relief. Landlords were resentful of the government's lack of support and the imposition of further levies under the Poor Law, and evictions followed, along with a soaring death rate. In Co. Monaghan, from March through June 1847, the numbers of inquests taken by Waddell were the highest per month over a four-month period of all the Famine years (see Figure 2). Out of 53 inquests taken by Waddell during this period, 35 were deaths directly attributed to the Famine.

These difficult few months filled the Monaghan institutions with inmates. On 8 June 1847, Monaghan Poor Law Union's board of guardians, of which Waddell was a member, temporarily closed the workhouse and the fever hospital for new admissions. While Monaghan did not have an asylum until 1869, both the 'lunatic' and general pauper populace were suffering from fever at the local workhouse and gaol. In fact, one-fifth of the inmates of the Monaghan poorhouse, upwards of 200 persons, were reported to be in hospital and 140 suffered from fever. The *Northern Standard* reported on 12 June 1847 that for the 28 beds at the Monaghan fever hospital there were 45 patients, 'some lying two and even three in a bed'. The editorial also stated that the Monaghan gaol was full, 'but not so much with crime as with poverty' and described the gaol at that time as a 'haven of rest for the free citizen' that offered food and shelter.[4]

On 29 June 1847 an inquest taken by Waddell describes how Bernard Kelly, a weak and infirm man, 'extremely filthy, swarming with vermin' and considered 'ill with yellow fever', had broken the panes of glass in the house of James Welsh.[5] Kelly was said to be in a state of great destitution and 'anxious to get into jail as a means of support, but Welsh would not press charges'.[6] A bed of straw on the side of the road was made for the dying man, and he was fed by neighbours but soon expired. The verdict of death was 'from filth and extreme destitution'.[7] Two

---

4 *NS*, 12 June 1847.   5 CB1, no. 4.87, Bernard Kelly, 29 June 1847. Kelly was a tenant of Charles Hopes living in the townland of Coleshill.   6 Ibid.   7 Ibid.

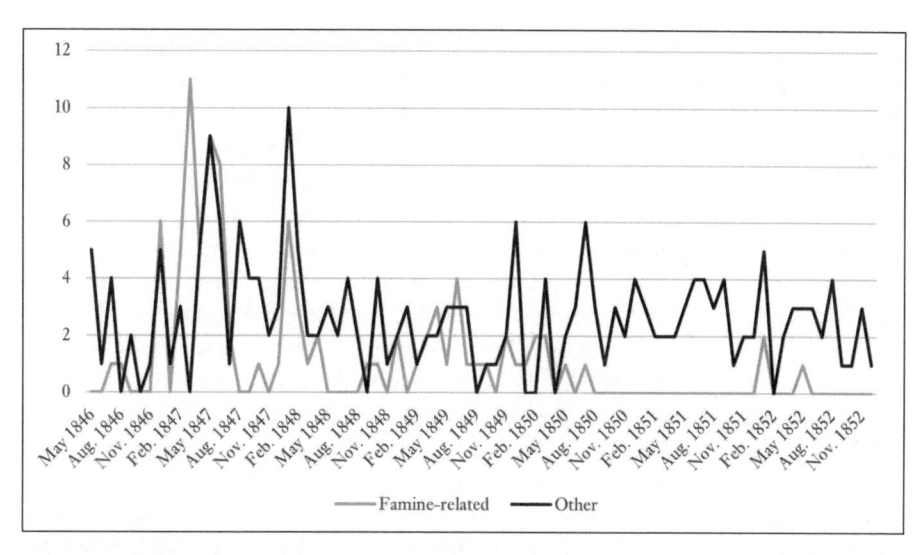

Fig. 3 Inquests taken May 1846 to Nov. 1852. Source: CB1.

other inquests Waddell held that same month revealed persons dying in the open, starving and destitute, and were representative of the weak local economy and infrastructure.[8] The inquests of two children who had recently left the workhouse are worthy of further consideration. Thomas and Margaret Chessar, brother and sister, children of Henry Chessar of Coleshill, had left the poorhouse by choice.[9] They were given permission to use the barn of Mrs Anne Hamilton of Tullaghan for shelter, but died just a few days later, emaciated and filled with sickness and disease. The deceased children's relatives had promised to come to get Margaret's remains and bring a coffin to Kilmore church, but they never appeared. The Chessar children's death draws attention to the conditions within the workhouse and their desire to leave it, and the grim result of their decision. An examination of the conditions inside the institutions of Co. Monaghan using Waddell's inquests and official government reports reveals the overcrowding and disease first hand, and the challenge for local authorities in managing the needs of inmates.

8 CB1, no. 60.79, James Gillespie, 7 June 1847; ibid., no. 61.80, Ann Gray, 10 June 1847. 9 CB1, no. 63.82, Thomas Chessar, 11 June 1847; ibid., no. 64.83, Margaret Chessar, 12 June 1847; Coleshill, as a place-name or townland, does not appear in any modern publication and no longer exists. Waddell appears to have had first-hand knowledge of the family as they were tenants at Coleshill, a property he managed for his uncle, Charles Hopes. Coleshill is now the townland of Aghalisk. A personal note in the casebook stated, 'These were the children of Henry Chessar.' Additionally, Mr Waddell is referred to in inquest no. 287.5, Jane Hanna of Coleshill, which took place on 23 Apr. 1852. He was acquainted with the deceased as part of his duties as a land agent. Waddell had instructed the deceased to stop crossing through the field of Hu Marron, another tenant, who had taken Hanna's house and land, for which she resented him. The inquest captures the disharmony between the two families, the Hannas and the Marrons, resulting from eviction.

RUSSELL'S GOVERNMENT: IMPACT OF POLICY CHANGES

By July 1847, a difficult phase of the Famine had come to an end. The Temporary Relief (Soup Kitchen) Act (1847) had cost lives due to delays; however, once implemented it brought at its peak three million daily rations distributed to the Irish poor paid for by government loans to be repaid via the Poor Law rates. Soup kitchens fed those outside the workhouse and the recovering market brought with it lower prices for food for those who had income to afford it. The uptake of those availing of meals offered by soup kitchens varied by region. Some areas of Ulster saw less than 10 per cent, whereas Connaught would see the highest numbers, of over 80 per cent of the population.[10] In Co. Monaghan, the percentage of the populace that took relief from soup kitchens in the summer of 1847 ranged, in different Poor Law unions, between 20.1 per cent and 40 per cent.[11]

As the Irish struggle for survival continued, British public attention turned inwards due to the start of their own recession, which began in 1847. With growing concerns about the British economy, the opposition to Irish aid became stronger, particularly as a result of regular reports of corruption, administrative inefficiency and lack of cooperation from local Irish elites.[12] By August 1847, the work of the harvest brought employment for many and there was also a belief that the potato blight was over and would not return.[13] Within this context, in September 1847 Russell dissolved the Relief Commission and passed on all responsibility for the poor and Famine relief to the Irish Poor Law Commission.[14] Most significantly, implementation of the Poor Law Extension Act began that same month and placed virtually the entire financial responsibility of Poor Law relief on angry Irish landowners and ratepayers.[15] Further measures included the government abandonment of soup kitchen relief, closure of food depots and no new public works policies. Russell's approach to managing the Irish economy sought to focus on the country's long-term socio-economic health rather than short-term support.[16] Qualifications for relief became more restrictive and small tenant farmers were now required to give up possession of everything above a quarter acre of their holdings to get even temporary relief under the Poor Law. These families now faced permanent poverty and the loss of even their remaining quarter acre and cottage. They needed to 'prove destitution' even when some were in fact homeless as well as starving. The implementation of such restrictions by the board of guardians when evaluating the needs of those most vulnerable not only ran against the spirit of the law but contributed towards a catastrophic rise in inmates at local gaols and workhouses. This corresponded with an increase in deaths, leading to inquests taken by coroners involving those institutions. For some, gaining entry into a local institution was their last hope for survival, and for many it meant their death.

---

10 Smyth, 'The story of the Great Irish Famine', p. 9.   11 Ibid.   12 Gray, *Famine, land and politics*, pp 289–90.   13 Ibid., p. 285.   14 Ibid., p. 291.   15 *The Nation*, 18 Sept. 1847.   16 James S. Donnelly Jnr, 'The administration of relief, 1847–51' in W.E. Vaughan (ed.), *A new history of Ireland*, v: *Ireland under the Union, 1801–70* (Oxford, 2013), p. 316.

A SHORT HISTORY OF THE COUNTY GAOL

After the Act of Union prison reform established a pattern of centralization and nationalization by government paid for by the county landholding elite.[17] Influenced by the English philosopher and social theorist Jeremy Bentham (1748–1842) in the eighteenth century, modernization of the institutions introduced humane management that was reformatory, rather than punitive (see Figure 3).[18] Reform included the institution of an annual report by two government-appointed inspectors, the inspectors general of prisons, who visited every prison in the country.[19] Prison Acts in 1810 and 1826 introduced the segregation of classes of prisoners for specific application of treatment, improved diet, clothing, furniture and linens, and encouragement to report ill treatment by gaol officers, including the gaoler (or governor) and his subordinates.[20] The costs for these improvements were borne by the county grand juries, which were responsible for prison administration. A board of superintendence was formed, half the members of which were local justices of the peace, and half the grand jury. It was responsible for decisions on the general management, operations and improvements of the gaol.[21] However McDowell and MacDonagh assert that most local authorities were reluctant to adopt the new penal philosophy because of the high costs for such treatment and modern facilities.[22]

Irish prisons needed to be replaced, and while older buildings were upgraded and improved at great expense, new gaols were built that were often the most impressive architectural institutions in Irish towns.[23] The new buildings were designed to incorporate Bentham's model of the 'panopticon', whereby the subjects are controlled by the knowledge that they are being watched.[24] While not all new prisons had a single universally adopted architecture like that of the Irish workhouses, the pre-Poor Law ethos upon which they were constructed embodied reform, education and philanthropy. By 1824, eight of the new gaols were built on a semi-circular plan, including Monaghan's, while the prison in Londonderry was a 'panoptic' attached to the governor's house.[25] The intention of modern gaol management was to instil a uniform system offering adequate accommodation for the purpose of the improvement of its inmates. This was a departure from the tyranny and oppression seen in prisons in Ireland prior to the 1820s. Analogous to workhouses, the construction and costs of Irish gaols were imposed by government onto the local elite and intended as much for them as for the reform of the inmates.

---

17 MacDonagh, 'Ideas and institutions, 1830–45', p. 211. **18** James E. Crimmins, 'Jeremy Bentham', *Stanford encyclopedia of philosophy*, plato.stanford.edu, accessed 28 Dec. 2017. **19** 3 Geo. IV, c. 64 (16 Jan. 1822), Prisons Act. **20** 50 Geo. III, c. 103 (20 June 1810), Prisons Act; 7 Geo IV, c. 74 (31 May 1826), Irish Prisons Act; MacDonagh, 'Ideas and institutions, 1830–45', p. 211. **21** McDowell, 'Administration and the public services', p. 544; 7 Geo. IV, c. 74 (31 May 1826), Irish Prisons Act. **22** MacDonagh, 'Ideas and institutions, 1830–45', p. 211; McDowell, 'Administration and the public services', p. 545. **23** McDowell, 'Administration and the public services', p. 546. **24** Crimmins, 'Jeremy Bentham'. **25** McDowell, *The Irish administration, 1801–1914*, p. 152. The new gaols built on the semi-circular plan were in Ennis, Galway, Roscommon, Sligo, Louth, Longford, Limerick and Monaghan.

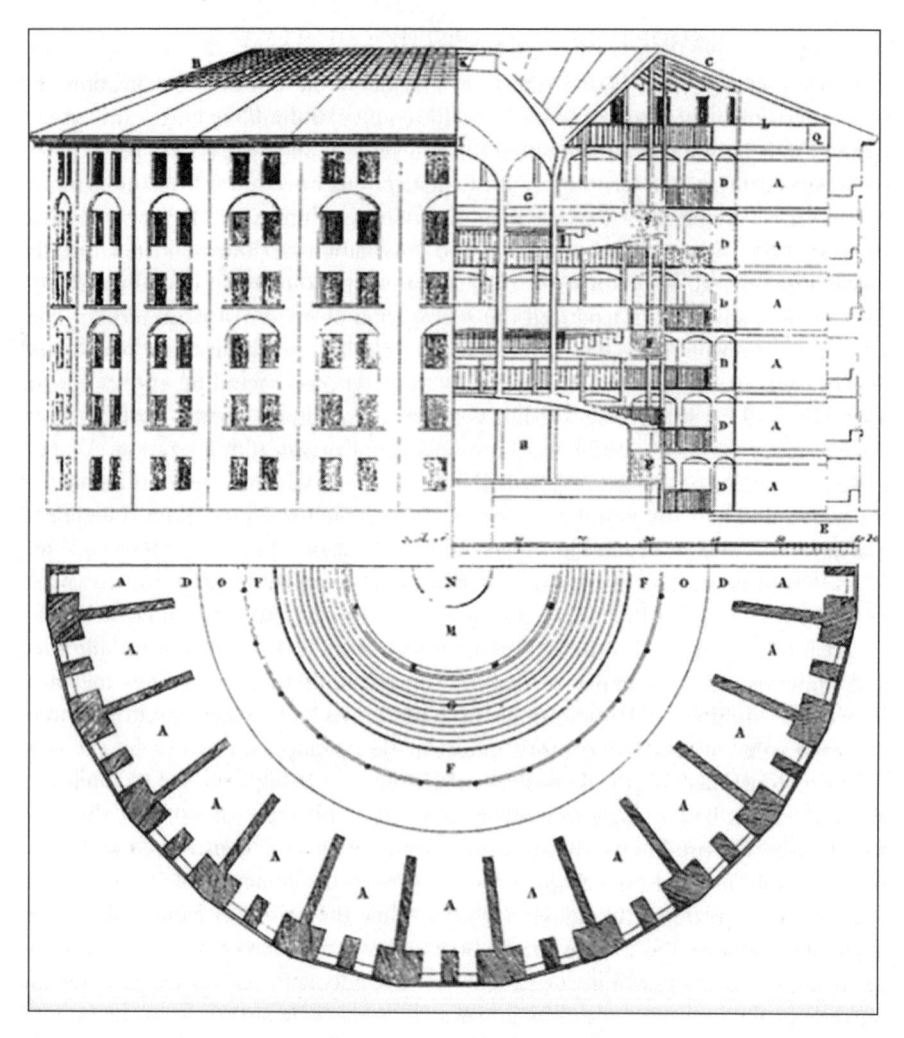

Fig. 4 Panopticon architecture of Victorian gaols. Sections A indicate the cells where inmates lived; Section N is the watchtower from where the officers could observe inmates and all behaviour. Source: Jeremy Bentham, *The works of Jeremy Bentham* (Edinburgh, 1843), iv, pp 172–3.

While the prison itself was a physical manifestation of government control and ideology on the landscape, the central state failed to ensure that the daily operation and management of the institution would reflect the values it was founded upon. Gray states that the adoption of the laws, the architecture and the institutional template were not only imposed to overawe and inflict moral discipline on inmates, as Foucauldian ideology implies when used in examining nineteenth-century institutional reform, but was also intended as a form of social conditioning for the landed class.[26] This theoretical approach can be used to examine the adoption or rejection of legislation and costs by the local elite, and the work of Waddell as coroner at the Monaghan gaol can be employed as supporting evidence.

Coroners were required to inquire on all deaths at the gaol reported to them, with costs covered by the county grand jury. If they failed to do so, they would incur a fine. The coroner's first duty upon deciding to hold an inquest was to prepare a precept to a constable and the gaoler requiring the attendance of a jury to proceed, on any day but a Sunday.[27] Jury composition guidance for Irish coroners said that 'in inquests on a deceased prisoner, it is not competent for any other prisoner of the gaol to serve as a juror'.[28] In contrast, English law outlined that half the coroner's jury ought to be prisoners of the gaol upon inquests taken in that institution.[29] Burney stated that reformers of the modern administrative state sought to establish the coroners' inquests in English gaols as a necessary component of reform to protect the public against authoritarian abuse by the state.[30] Of all the duties of the coroner in the nineteenth century, what stood out more than any other was the duty to hold an inquest into the death of a prisoner.[31] The objective was to find the true cause of death because while gaolers and officers were under special protection as ministers of justice, 'the law watches with great jealousy' the conduct of such persons and the gaoler was required to notify the coroner to investigate all deaths at the gaol.[32] As such, the composition of coroners' juries in Ireland, with non-inmates brought in to establish a verdict of death, may have caused distrust in the verdicts.

Coroner's inquests taken at the gaol were brought to the attention of the inspectors general of prisons, who then could carry out their own examinations of the evidence. This was demonstrated by the inquest of Mary Byrne, a prisoner who had died in the Carrickmacross bridewell. Waddell and his jury reached a verdict that the immediate cause of death on 2 December 1846 was due to an inflammation of the stomach, aggravated by the extreme cold.[33] Inspector General Edward Cottingham inquired into the death, read the notes from the foreman of the coroner's jury, examined some of the jury and concluded there was no blame attached to the bridewell keeper, Mr Armstrong.[34]

The Monaghan grand jury was one of the first to vote to build a new gaol, and in the spring of 1824, after three architects and nine long years of delays, the new Co. Monaghan gaol was ready to accept inmates.[35] The new building was located

26 Peter Gray, 'Conceiving and constructing the Irish workhouse, 1836–45', *Irish Historical Studies*, 38:149 (2012), pp 23–4. 27 Edmund Hayes, *Crimes and punishments: or, an analytical digest of the criminal statue of law of Ireland* (Dublin, 1837), p. 406. 28 Ibid., p. 197. 29 Ibid., p. 407. 30 Burney, *Bodies of evidence*, p. 20. 31 Ibid. 32 John Jervis, *On the office and duties of coroners: with forms and precedents* (3rd ed.; London, 1866), p. 183. 33 CB1, no. 16, Mary Byrne, 3 Dec. 1846. 34 POI, *Twenty-fifth report of inspectors general on the general state of the prisons of Ireland, 1846*, p. 64 [805], HC 1847 xxix, 151. 35 Architect and builder John Behan, originally from Galway, worked on the construction of the Co. Monaghan gaol until he was dismissed in 1820. He was replaced by John Bowden of Dublin in 1821, who subsequently died in 1822. Bowden was replaced by Joseph Welland of Cork

on the west side of Monaghan town, perched high on a hill, 'a fine building, in a healthy elevated position, commanding a view of the whole town and cost £20,000' to build.[36] In 1830, the inspectors general complimented it as being one of the

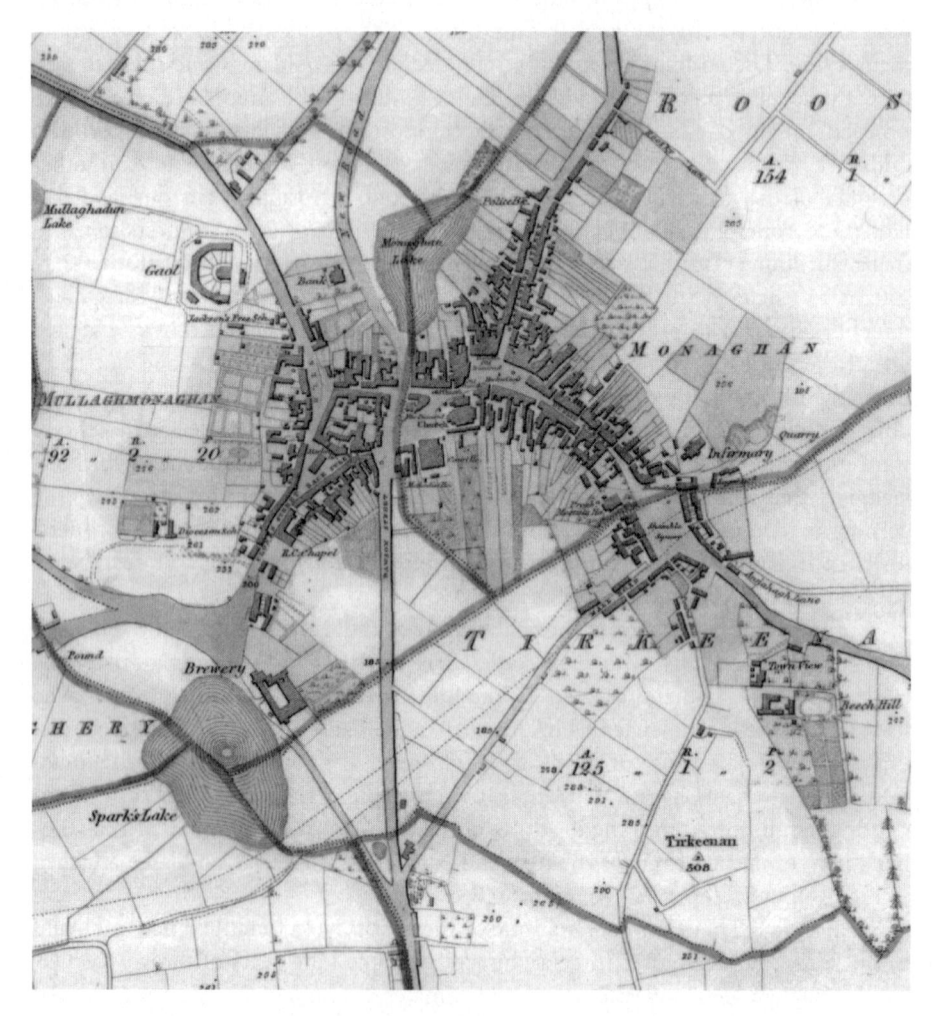

Map 3 Monaghan town and gaol (1836). OSi historic six-inch first edition enhanced by author © Ordnance Survey Ireland/Government of Ireland, copyright permit, no. MP 007322.

and completed the construction of the gaol in 1824 (cited in Irish Architectural Archive, 'John Behan', *Dictionary of Irish architects*, dia.ie); *Inspectors general report: state of prisons of Ireland, 1818, with appendix*, pp 22–3, HC 1819 (534) xii, 453; *Report of the inspectors general on the general state of the prisons of Ireland, 1824*, p. 5, HC 1824 (294) xxii, 269. **36** *Pigot's and Co.'s directory of Monaghan town, 1826*, pp 404–5; POI, *Report of inspectors general, 1823 with abstract from appendix of general observations on each prison in the several districts &c.*, p. 5, HC 1823 (342) x, 291.

most 'distinguished amongst the best regulated gaols in Ireland'; however, the Co. Monaghan gaol's management, like many other gaols', had a legacy of issues.[37]

In 1807, the inspectors general described the Monaghan gaol at that time as 'very dirty and in great disorder ... in a ruinous state'.[38] The gaoler was absent and the local inspector, Mr Brickie, was confined to bed and resigned from his post.[39] It also had experienced epidemic breakouts of disease. In 1817, the second of two years of famine, the deaths in the gaol were considered 'very great' when 27 inmates died from typhus.[40] The fever had started in the gaol and spread through the town and to the country making 'sad havoc among all classes'.[41] Just three years after the excellent 1830 inspection, the inspectors general report of 1833 highlighted an alarming rate of cholera in Monaghan town.[42] There was concern for an outbreak of the disease in the new gaol because new arrivals remained in their own clothing. Under the authority of the Prison Acts, the inspectors general ordered clothing for prisoners 'as the poor prisoners needed and were entitled to receive', the costs of which were paid for by the county.[43] In addition to reports of disease and a lack of clothing, Monaghan gaol governor, John Rowland, appointed by the local grand jury, was criticized by the inspectors general during the years between 1831 and 1834 for his 'lack of zeal and skill' in carrying out his duties and for not being 'an efficient or active governor'.[44] Evidence suggests that the criticism of Rowland was reflective of the opinion of central government as to the decisions taken by the Board of Superintendence and their management of the institution. Annual reports on Monaghan gaol after 1834 varied but showed gradual improvement in the management, training and education of its inmates.[45] By 1845, the year

---

37 POI, *Eighth report of the inspectors general on the general state of the prisons of Ireland*, 1830, p. 41, HC 1830 (48) xxiv, 719.   38 *Inspectors general report on general state of prisons of Ireland for the year 1807*, p. 15, HC 1808 (239) ix, 351.   39 Ibid.   40 *Report of prisons in Ireland, 1818*, p. 21; Livingstone, *The Monaghan story*, p. 177.   41 *Report of prisons in Ireland, 1818*, p. 21.   42 POI, *Twelfth report of the inspectors general on the general state of the prisons of Ireland, 1834*, p. 48, HC 1834 (63) xl, 69.   43 Ibid., p. 13.   44 POI, *Ninth report of the inspectors general on the general state of the prisons of Ireland, 1831*, p. 30, HC 1831 (172) iv, 269; POI, *Tenth report of the inspectors general on the general state of the prisons of Ireland, 1832*, pp 30–1, HC 1832 (152) xxiii, 451; POI, *Eleventh report of the inspectors general on the general state of prisons in Ireland, 1833*, p. 43, HC 1833 (67) xvii, 307; POI, *Twelfth report of prisons of Ireland, 1834*, p. 48.   45 An annual evaluation of the performance of the Monaghan gaol was included in the annual inspectors general reports from 1835 through 1844; POI, *Thirteenth report of the inspectors general on the general state of the prisons of Ireland, 1835*, pp 30–1, HC 1835 (114) xxxvi, 381; POI, *Fourteenth report of the inspectors general on the general state of the prisons of Ireland, 1836: with an appendix*, p. 29, HC 1836 (118) xxxv, 431; POI, *Fifteenth report of the inspectors general on the general state of the prisons of Ireland, 1836: with appendixes*, p. 28, HC 1837 (123) xxxi, 605; POI, *Sixteenth report of the inspectors general on the general state of the prisons of Ireland 1837: with appendixes*, pp 33–4, HC 1838 (186) xxix, 475; POI, *Seventeenth report of the inspectors general on the general state of the prisons of Ireland, 1838: with appendixes*, p. 34, HC 1839 (91) xx, 403; POI, *Eighteenth report of the inspectors general on the general state of the prisons of Ireland, 1839: with appendixes*, p. 37, HC 1840 (240) xxvi, 165; POI, *Nineteenth report of the inspectors general on the general state of the prisons of Ireland, 1840: with appendixes*, p. 38, HC 1841 (299) xi, 759; POI, *Twentieth report of the inspectors general on the general state of the prisons of Ireland, 1841: with appendixes*, p. 84, HC

of Rowland's retirement after twenty-two years as governor, the inspectors general concluded that the gaol should be remodelled.[46] There was concern that there was not enough space for proper separation of inmates by class. That year the average daily gaol population was ninety inmates.[47]

THE FAMINE AND THE COUNTY GAOL

The inspectors general report on prisons for 1847 outlined three reasons for a recent increase in the population at Irish gaols: the distress from the Famine, the cessation of transportation to Van Diemen's Land (Tasmania), and the passing of the Vagrant Act (1847), which outlawed beggars and mendicants (wandering poor) and led to many being incarcerated.[48] Of the latter, the law compelled magistrates to commit all persons found begging to gaol, and as a result, 'an immense mass of destitution, filth and disease was forced into prisons, never in their original construction had they been calculated to receive'.[49] There was a lack of room within the prisons, bedding and clothing were limited, and the fiscal pressure which all counties of Ireland were under meant that money and supplies were not capable of meeting demand.[50] In January 1848, Kilmainham gaol in Dublin reported a 30 per cent increase in inmates who were classified beggars and vagrants (37 men and 8 women, in a total population of 146), as well as many young boys incarcerated for 'food-related' crimes.[51] In December 1847, the Cavan gaol reported 'the immense evil' of the number of paupers in the gaol (40 men and 2 women, comprising 22 per cent of a population of 187), some of whom had been detained for over-holding land, and of whom it was said 'in justice ... they should not be obliged to feed'.[52] This opinion reflects the view of many at the time that those who had equity in their Ulster tenant right should cash it in, rather than receive any form of relief. However, this view ignores the sharp fall in the value of tenant right due to the pressures of the Famine. That same month, Inspector General Clement Johnson stated, upon investigating the Enniskillen gaol, that

> The debtors' class, as usual, containing 55 individuals in very inadequate accommodation, is that for which least can be done. The presence of the

---

1842 (377) xxii, 117; POI, *Twenty-first report of the inspectors general on the general state of the prisons of Ireland, 1842: with appendixes*, p. 47, HC 1843 (462) xxvii, 83; POI, *Twenty-second report of the inspectors general on the general state of the prisons of Ireland, 1843: with appendixes*, p. 57, HC 1844 (535) xxviii, 329.   46 POI, *Twenty-third report of the inspectors general on the general state of the prisons of Ireland, 1844: with appendices*, pp 31–2, HC 1845 (620) xxv, 231.   47 POI, *Twenty-fourth report of the inspectors general on the general state of the prisons of Ireland, 1845: with appendices*, pp 48–50, HC 1846 (697) xx, 257.   48 POI, *Twenty-sixth report of the inspectors general on the general state of the prisons in Ireland, 1847; with appendices*, p. 5, HC 1848 (952) xxxiv, 253. Transportation to Van Diemen's Land was stopped in 1847. This resulted in the government leaving large numbers of inmates in county gaols temporarily, until they could find other locations, including Bermuda as well as Spike Island, to relocate them to.   49 Ibid.   50 Ibid., p. 7.   51 Ibid., p. 30.   52 Ibid., p. 51.

convicts, also, is another great but unavoidable evil. Including, with these two classes, the lunatics, there are upwards of 80 persons in the gaol whose presence must be considered in a degree a grievance, and an obstacle in the way of improvement in discipline or instruction.[53]

There were two types of debtors, master and pauper. Master debtors were those who had debts of over £10 or were chronically in debt. Pauper debtors were those inmates whose food, clothing, and health were paid for by the county cess, and who were put to work in return. These were not criminals, but persons who were confined for debts of less than £10, most of them detained for owing rents but refusing to surrender their holdings. If they chose to surrender, they were discharged and the debt was cleared. Gaol could serve to some as a survival strategy that ensured retention of land, as opposed to the workhouse, where, by law, the inmate upon committal must forfeit their tenancy and land above a quarter acre. Tristram Kennedy, land agent for the Bath estate in Co. Monaghan, documented his observations on the unwillingness of tenants to pay. He found that,

> [it] was not in all instances consequent on the inability to pay, as was evinced by the comparatively few cases in which proceedings were permitted by tenants to go to extremes, but was induced in many instances by their fear of another season's failure in the potato crop ... and this was probably induced by the disorganised state of society and in the hope of being released from some portion of the rent in consequence of the previous year's losses in crop.[54]

Kennedy highlighted that out of 794 civil bill processes he initiated, as documented in his year-end report in July 1848, 'in 550 instances proceedings were attended with very considerable trouble', but only 12 resulted in tenants being imprisoned for not paying rent.[55] Of these, ten were discharged and of the remaining two, one paid a portion of their rent.[56]

On 22 December 1847, Monaghan gaol, which was meant to accommodate 97 persons, instead held 180 inmates, of which 29 per cent were pauper debtors (see Table 7). The 52 pauper debtors were living in four small rooms and one dayroom, the latter being 'quite impossible to keep clean as many of the debtors being old, ill and feeble'.[57] Pauper debtors were brought to the prison from other county bridewells, such as Carrickmacross, where inmates were living in dangerous conditions. The sewer at the Carrickmacross bridewell was overflowing and inspectors warned that 'the lives of many persons might be sacrificed'.[58] The new arrivals to

---

53 Ibid., p. 57. 54 Tristram Kennedy's 'Observations accompanying the accounts of the agents of the Bath estate in Ireland', year ending 1 July 1848 (Longleat House, Bath estate (Irish) papers. Irish Papers Box III, bundle 2). 55 Ibid. 56 Ibid. 57 *Twenty-sixth report on prisons in Ireland, 1847*, pp 71, 112. 58 Ibid.

Table 7: Inmate population and available accommodation at Monaghan gaol in Dec. 1847

Population by class of inmate	Males	Females
Master debtors	3	0
Pauper debtors	49	3
Felons convicted	41	8
Misdemeanants convicted	5	0
Felons untried	19	16
Misdemeanants untried	5	3
Revenue prisoners	8	0
Summary convictions	12	5
Lunatics	3	0
Totals	145	35
Total inmate population	180	
Available accommodation		
Single cells	68	
Solitary cells	7	
Rooms with beds (including five in hospital)	13	
Day rooms	9	
Total	97	

Source: POI, *Twenty-sixth report of the inspectors general on the general state of prisons in Ireland, 1847; with appendices*, p. 71, HC 1848 (952) xxxiv, 253.

Monaghan gaol were not given new clothing, as that was only provided for convicted felons, and there was a lack of washing arrangements. Disease among the population would follow.[59]

According to the inspectors general report in 1847, a total of 81 inmates died in Irish gaols in 1845; 131 died in 1846; and 1,315 died in 1847, the largest number ever recorded.[60] By comparison, one death occurred each year in Monaghan gaol in 1845 and 1846, respectively, until a catastrophic rise in death took place in 1847 when 33 deaths were reported (see Table 8). This rise in deaths was consistent with neighbouring Ulster counties such as Armagh, Cavan, Fermanagh and Tyrone, where gaol populations had also soared, as well as deaths. Waddell recorded 13 inquests at the Monaghan gaol from June 1847 through December 1847. The remaining 20 deaths that year went without inquests, which indicates

59 Ibid.   60 Ibid., p. 6.

Table 8: Deaths reported at Ulster gaols, 1845–52

County	1845	1846	1847	1848	1849	1850	1851	1852
Antrim	1	3	9	3	3	6	9	12
Armagh	2	4	33	15	5	7	5	4
Cavan	1	4	27	13	12	1	1	2
Donegal	0	1	5	8	8	4	2	3
Down	2	3	16	4	14	4	8	0
Fermanagh	4	0	46	21	7	4	7	5
Londonderry	1	0	8	3	8	3	1	4
Monaghan	1	1	33	11	8	11	1	1
Tyrone	2	2	21	28	2	7	7	5
Totals	14	18	198	106	67	47	41	36

Sources: POI, Twenty-sixth through thirty-first reports of the Inspectors General on the general state of the prisons in Ireland: HC 1848 (952) xxxiv, 253; HC 1849 (1069), xxvi 373; HC 1850 (1229) xxix, 305; HC 1851 (1364) xxviii, 357; HC 1852 (1531) xxv, 251; HC 1853 (1657) liii, 1.

that Waddell's attendance was not requested; in cases he attended but declined an inquest, and instead conducted an enquiry, he documented that in his casebook. The greatest number of inquests taken at the gaol in any given two-month time frame from 1847 to 1852 was in December 1847 and January 1848, with a total of 11 inquests in two months. The verdicts of death revealed gaol fever, typhus, cholera, bronchitis, yellow fever and dysentery.[61] Many were ill with pre-existing conditions upon arrival.

An inquest was taken on 9 December 1847 on inmate Brian Martin, who, when admitted to the gaol just one week earlier, had complained of being unwell. Monaghan gaol governor Thomas Mayne and hospital nurse Francis Woods served as witnesses, confirming that Martin's death was a result of bronchitis and pain in the chest.[62] Less than two weeks later, Waddell conducted an inquest on Owen McGarrell. On 24 December 1847, Dr McDowell, Monaghan

---

61 CB1, no. 25.108, Brian Martin, 9 Dec. 1847; CB1, no. 26.109, Owen McGarrell, 24 Dec. 1847; CB1, no. 27.110, Patt Maginn, 28 Dec. 1847; CB1, no. 28.111, Francis Woods, 30 Dec. 1847; CB1, no. 29.112, Phillip Mayne, 1 Jan. 1848; CB1, 3 Jan. 1848, Entry of potential inquest at Monaghan gaol on John Quinn, but as the body had been removed, and notes of the illness captured by Dr McDowell, Waddell did not consider the inquest necessary; CB1, no. 33.116, John McPhillips, 6 Jan. 1848; CB1, no. 1.117, Bernard Carr, 6 Jan. 1848; CB1, no. 2.118, James McCarron, 10 Jan. 1848; CB1, no. 4.120, John Smith, 12 Jan. 1848; CB1, no. 5.121, Dan Finley, 12 Jan. 1848.   62 CB1, no. 25.108, Brian Martin, 9 Dec. 1847; Thomas Mayne esq. took the office of governor of the Monaghan gaol on 19 Mar. 1845, as published in the *Northern Standard* on 22 Mar. 1845.

gaol's physician, described the deceased as having been 'admitted to the gaol just 16 days earlier, in a very weak and sickly state with all the appearance of want and destitution' and said he 'considered his death to have arisen from old age and destitution'.[63] Fever was rife in the gaol and not only the inmates were susceptible. On 30 December 1847, Francis Woods, the hospital nurse who had testified at the inquest of Brian Martin just three weeks previously, died at the gaol from low typhus fever.[64] He was described by Dr McDowell as 'a person of great humanity'.[65]

Inquests taken by Waddell in January 1848 reveal the deaths of elderly men with pre-existing conditions among the prison population. Such a case was investigated on 6 January 1848. Dr McDowell testified that 80-year-old inmate of Monaghan gaol, Bernard Carr, died from the effects of want and extreme poverty as this was his condition upon arrival at the gaol six or seven weeks prior.[66] Witness testimony was taken from other inmates that Carr was 'indulged by his fellow prisoners at the fire' but was delicate upon his arrival at the gaol and his health had been steadily declining. Reflective of the population of the gaol at the time, many of the witnesses and the dead were identified in Waddell's casebook as debtors.[67] In February 1848, Monaghan gaol had the fifth largest debtor inmate population in Ireland: 82 men and women.[68]

In addition to the debtor population in the prison, a great number of male prisoners under sentence for transportation were left in county gaols, paid for by local rates, while the government made arrangements for their removal. Prior to the Famine, these inmates could have counted on their swift removal from the gaol, effectively emigrating to Australia, paid for by the government. Inmates sentenced to transportation were felons and dangerous, with habits that required a significant amount of vigilant attention and who obstructed the progress and potential prosperity of the other prisoners. Among Monaghan gaol's prisoners awaiting transportation was a colourful and notably notorious local character, Michael Dawley, who had been sentenced in 1844 to transportation to New South Wales for cattle theft and for a series of highway robberies that took place in Co. Monaghan. This included stealing an iron plough that belonged to coroner William Charles Waddell.[69] Comparing him to famous English highwayman Dick Turpin (1705–39), the *Northern Standard* described Dawley as a leader of a local Catholic

---

63 CB1, no. 26.109, Owen McGarrell, 24 Dec. 1847. 64 CB1, no. 28.111, Francis Woods, 30 Dec. 1847. 65 Ibid. 66 CB1, no. 1.117, Bernard Carr, 6 Jan. 1848. 67 CB1, no. 57.76, James McEneny, 1 June 1847; CB1, no. 29.145, James Clark, 16 May 1848; CB1, no. 32.148, James Duffy, 15 June 1848; CB1, no. 3.172, Mathew Cassidy, 24 Mar. 1849. Witness Peter Clark is identified as a debtor in the gaol; CB1, no. 5.196, George Smith, 1 Sept. 1849. Witness William Elliott is identified as a debtor in prison; CB1, no.12.203, John Armstrong, 11 Dec. 1849. Witness George Armstrong is identified as a debtor in gaol; CB1, no. 18.209, John Reidy, 29 Dec. 1849. Witness George Armstrong is identified as a debtor in the gaol; CB1, no. 14.237, Michael Gartland, 14 Oct. 1850. Witness Sylvester McMahon is identified as a debtor in gaol; CB1, no. 329.15, Thomas Riddle, 28 May 1853. 68 *Twenty-sixth report on prisons in Ireland, 1847*, p. 6. 69 *NS*, 30 Dec. 1843.

gang of Ribbonmen, who had managed to return back to Monaghan before the end of his sentence in autumn of 1847 but was recaptured and put in gaol.[70] In December 1847, a group of conspirators consisting of convicts awaiting transportation, headed up by Dawley, made plans to gag, bind and potentially murder the governor, Mr Mayne, and the turnkeys in an attempt to escape. The plot was found out and failed. Given the consequences, the evidence indicates that the overcrowding at the gaol combined with disease, and significant increase in excess death, influenced Dawley and his followers' decision to coordinate a prison break. While this concern was absent from the February 1848 *Northern Standard* coverage of the trial, circumstantial evidence might suggest that the conditions in the gaol would spark healthier inmates to try to flee the disease.

While going to gaol served for some as a survival strategy, for others, healthy and fit men like Dawley, it was the opposite. Dawley, a 42-year-old widower, stood five foot nine inches tall, with grey hair, blue eyes and a fresh complexion.[71] He explained that he only returned to take his children to America, stating, 'I would not stop in the country if I could not help it. It was not to live in it I came. No man should live in it that who could help it.'[72] Dawley was sentenced by Judge Torres for returning from transportation without authority. He was sent from the Kilmainham convict depot in March 1848 to Richmond gaol in August 1848, and then to Spike Island in November 1848.[73] He was considered 'a most determined person of former bad character and wholly concerned of his fate should he not gain permission from the government to go to America to join his children'.[74]

THE COUNTY WORKHOUSES

While the county gaols struggled with the pressure of surging inmate populations from June 1847 through to January 1848, the workhouses also faced the crisis, with an infrastructure unable to meet the demands of a public in critical need. The Irish Poor Law Act, passed in 1838, had been imposed by government to address Irish poverty and rural inequality, as well as provide moral regulation, reformation and social stability. Some opposed the system, saying the cost was too difficult to bear even in pre-Famine Ireland, and was too restrictive as it did not include outdoor relief and employment.[75] Workhouse construction throughout the country was funded by government loans that were to be paid back using local rates. Workhouses

70 *NS*, 30 Oct. 1847; Born in 1806, Michael Dawley was convicted of cow stealing and sentenced to 10 years in Van Diemen's Land. 71 NAI, Prison registers, Dublin-Smithfield prison general register, 1844–9, book no. 1/14/1, 6. 72 *NS*, 26 Feb. 1848. 73 NAI, Prison registers, Dublin-Kilmainham prison general register, 1840–50, book no. 1/10/31, 4; ibid., Dublin-Bridewell, Richmond prison general register, 1847–83, book no. 1/13/42, 3; ibid., Dublin-Smithfield prison general register, 1844–9, book no. 1/14/1, 6. 74 NAI, Prison registers, Dublin-Smithfield prison general register, 1844–9, book no. 1/14/1, 6. 75 William J. Smyth, 'The creation of the workhouse system' in John Crowley, William J. Smyth and Mike Murphy (eds), *Atlas of the Great Irish Famine* (New York, 2012), pp 121, 124.

were different than gaols as landowners and ratepayers were forced to meet the costs of poverty and they were managed by elected boards, rather than self-appointed grand juries; however, they were comparable in ideology and architectural framework. Gray asserts that the workhouse system was part of the social reform designed to infuse social equity into a society whose rural inequalities were considered the root of its political and social problems.[76] Legislation surrounding the workhouse and its management imposed strict discipline on inmates through diet, work and the separation of men and women, and 'idiots' and children. However, it was also intended as a form of social conditioning for the Irish social elite as they bore the costs of the workhouse as imposed by government.[77] This theoretical approach can be used to examine the behaviour and decision making of local elites through their adoption or rejection of legislation and costs, as well as their roles in evictions and assisted emigration arrangements during the crisis of the Famine. The work of Waddell as coroner can be employed as supporting evidence.

Unlike prison legislation, which encouraged holding inquests, workhouse legislation did not require coroners to hold inquests on deaths in the workhouse (see Table 9). Deaths at the workhouses were considered commonplace, and so few inquests were taken there. Investigations by the coroner at workhouses most often involved accidental or sudden deaths (including of recent arrivals who died shortly after their committal or were brought to the workhouse by police), but they could expose mismanagement within the institution. In the latter type of cases, inquests can unveil the importance of the work of the coroner as a potential champion of the interests of the poor. Other workhouse-related inquests during the Famine (taken on persons outside the workhouse) can be viewed as exposing societal and political changes that contributed to so many people becoming 'pauperized' across the countryside, and the horrors of the legislation that contributed to their death.

Ireland's workhouses were built in two phases, the first from 1839–45 and the second in the early 1850s, to an institutional design by British architect George Wilkinson (1814–90), which was adopted universally with few exceptions (Figure 5).[78] Within the boundaries of Co. Monaghan there were four workhouses that opened their doors to paupers between May 1842 and February 1843, each at the centre of a Poor Law union. The workhouses in the towns of Clones, Monaghan, Castleblayney and Carrickmacross were funded by the Poor Law rates on local property collected from electoral divisions within each Poor Law union. Clones and Castleblayney Poor Law unions included several electoral districts in Fermanagh and Armagh respectively. The electoral district of Inniskeen was in the Dundalk Poor Law Union, Co. Louth. Cootehill Poor Law Union, located in Co. Cavan, incorporated four electoral divisions located in Co. Monaghan, including Aghabog, Cormeen, Dawson's Grove and Drum. Waddell conducted inquests in those areas, such as the Drum auxiliary workhouse (also referred to as Drum dispensary). Each

---

76 Peter Gray, 'Conceiving and constructing the Irish workhouse, 1836–45', *Irish Historical Studies*, 38:149 (2012), p. 25. 77 Ibid., pp 23–4. 78 Ibid.

Table 9: Inquests at the workhouses supporting Co. Monaghan, 1848–50

1848

Workhouse	HC No.	Date	Waddell No.	Date
Carrickmacross	0		0	
Castleblayney	0		0	
Clones	0		2	24 Jan., 26 Oct.
Cootehill	1	2 Mar.	0	
Monaghan	0		0	
Total	1		2	

1849

Workhouse	HC No.	Date	Waddell No.	Date
Carrickmacross	0		0	
Castleblayney	0		0	
Clones	1	13 June	1	12 June
Cootehill	1	17 July	0	
Monaghan	1	2 Sept.	1	2 Sept.
Total	3		2	

1850

Workhouse	HC No.	Date	Waddell No.	Date
Carrickmacross	2	31 Jan., 12 Sept.	0	
Castleblayney	1	18 Sept.	0	
Clones	1	3 Apr.	0	
Cootehill	1	18 Feb.	1	19 Feb.
Monaghan	0		0	
Total	5		1	

Note: The official number of inquests reported to the House of Commons is inaccurate, when compared to Waddell's casebook. The inquests in CB1 were taken at the workhouse and do not include inquests on inmates who left, and died hours or days later. Sources: CB1; *Return of the number and dates of any coroners' inquests ...* HC 21 June 1851.

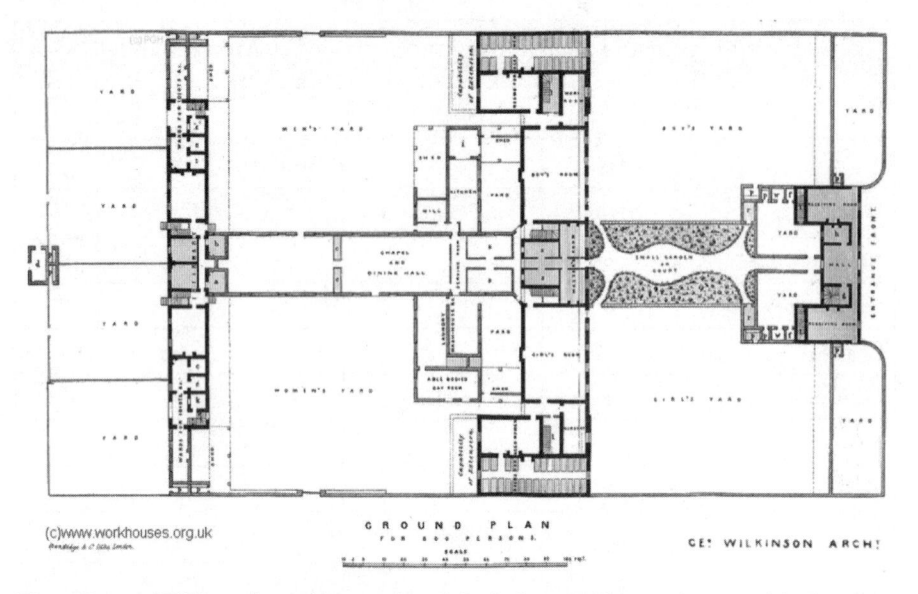

Fig. 5 George Wilkinson's workhouse plans (1839), from *Fifth annual report of the Poor Law Commissioners*, 1839, p. 98 (239), HC 1839, xx, 1.

Poor Law union was governed by a board of guardians made up of elected and ex-officio guardians, who were responsible for the financial decisions. The boards of guardians were known for protecting their own interests in many rural unions and were often exclusively composed of the local elite. With the ability to accommodate just 2,600 inmates in all the Co. Monaghan workhouses in 1843, the local landowning elite decided how to best to utilize their resources and keep costs down.[79]

LOCAL POLITICS AND PAUPER DEATH: MONAGHAN 1848

The aftermath of the Poor Law Extension Act inspired some of the local elite to increasingly constrict the scope of relief to the poor. While in theory, all qualified paupers had a right to relief, in reality, local criteria and eligibility became more restrictive and evidence suggests a defiance of the spirit of the law existed within some of the local elite. Donnelly asserts that administrative decisions about relief during the Famine years were focused primarily on costs.[80] Social and regional variations of conditions existed that resulted in differing instances of Famine-related destitution, death and emigration.[81] The performance of the Monaghan board of guardians has been identified in the work of Ó Gráda and reflects the prioritization

---

[79] *Abstract of the census of Ireland for the year 1841*, p. 2, HC 1843 (459) li, 319. The census states that the population of Co. Monaghan in 1841 was 200,442. [80] James S. Donnelly Jnr, *The Great Irish Potato Famine* (Stroud, 2010), p. 107. [81] Ibid., p. 169.

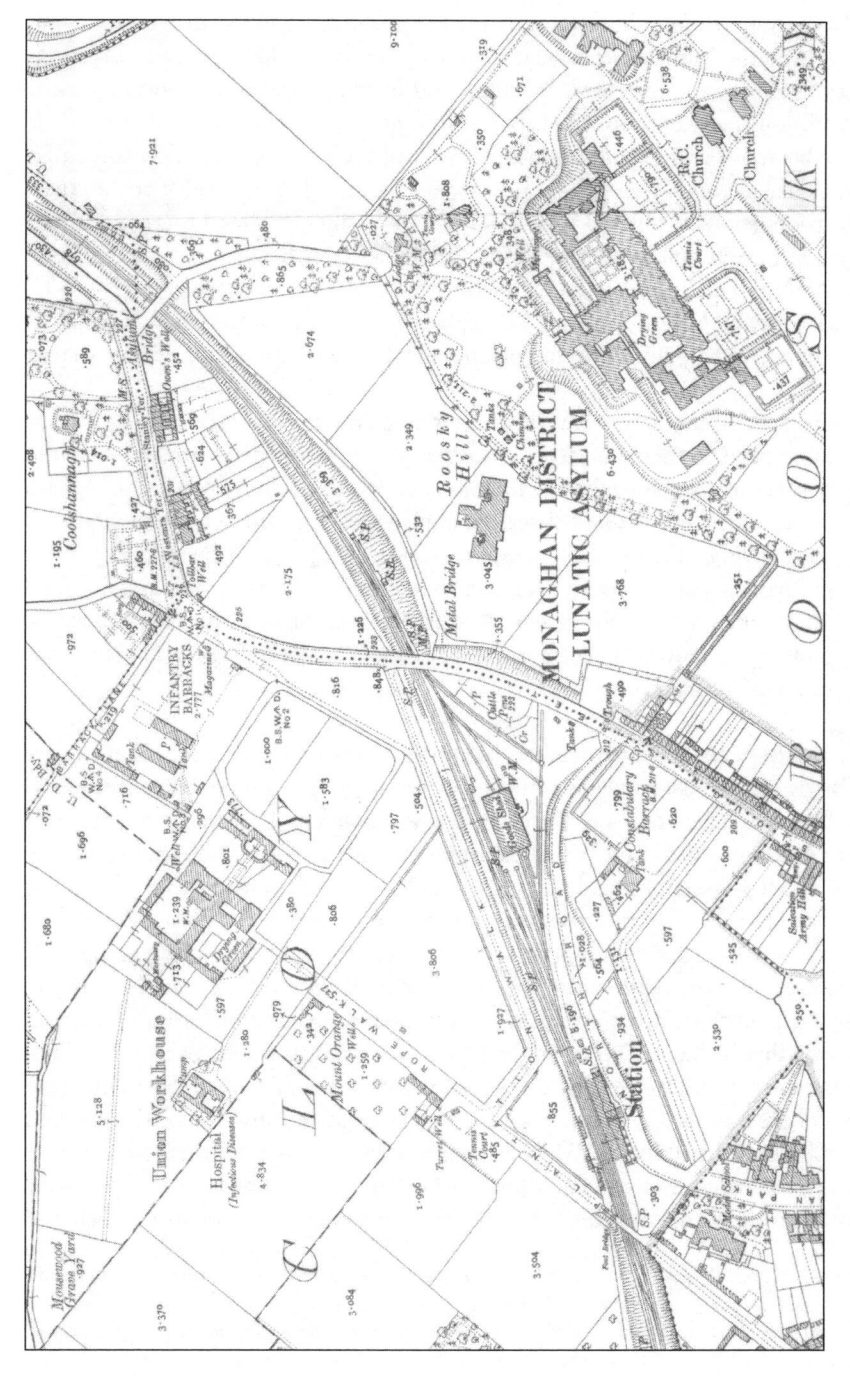

Map 4 Monaghan town, and workhouse and hospital (1908). OSi historic 25-inch map © Ordnance Survey Ireland/Government of Ireland, copyright permit no. MP 07322.

of cost-savings over care. Using two measures, his findings revealed the Monaghan Poor Law Union to have been the third worst performing union in Ireland. First, it had one of the highest percentages of death in the workhouse from infectious diseases (malnutrition, marasmus, dropsy and outright starvation), and second, it was the union that went into the least amount of debt, ranked at number one.[82] It appears the union underspent despite evidence of high rates of Famine-related disease, the level of which should have necessitated a much higher level of spending so as to be proportionally aligned with that of other Ulster counties. Offering outdoor relief could have been a way of reducing the high rate of death.

On 1 January 1848, a letter to the editor of the *Northern Standard* written by a Clones guardian asked why the Monaghan board of guardians had refused or neglected to adopt a policy of outdoor relief for the pauper populace. He wrote that

> the board cannot be aware of the terrible amount of destitution and want unrelieved in their districts ... because all, unfortunately, situated near the borders of the Monaghan Union are worried to death by hordes of beggars crowding in upon them, because unprovided for and starved at home ... after paying a high tax, and supporting a large number of our own poor, and not having a single pauper (known to be such) unrelieved, it is unfair, if we are to be swamped altogether by the hundreds of poor starving creatures, pouring in on us from the divisions of Clones, Drumhillagh, and Drumsnat in the Monaghan Union.[83]

Under the 1847 act, the guardians were empowered to offer outdoor relief to certain classes of paupers when the workhouse was full but could not be compelled to do so. The Poor Law unions of Carrickmacross, Clones and Castleblayney were all offering outdoor relief while Monaghan was the only one that did not.[84] Evidence from Waddell's casebook highlighted the deaths of paupers from need within the Monaghan Poor Law Union that same month and supported the Clones guardians' position as to the need for outdoor relief. On 24 January 1848, Pat Connolly, ill, filthy and having been exposed to the inclemency of the weather, was taken to the Monaghan poorhouse where he died within a day of admission. An inquest witness stated that he 'never saw a person in such a horrible state with vermin'.[85] That same day another inquest was held on a pauper in Monaghan town. Sub-constable Timothy Scanlin told the coroner's jury he arrived at the shambles in Monaghan town and found the deceased, Mary Lambert, lying at the door of lodgings where she had been refused entry. Pat Coony, who had known Lambert, explained to the coroner's jury that he had 'advised her to go into the poorhouse which she

---

82 Cormac Ó Gráda, 'Yardsticks for workhouses during the Great Famine' in Virginia Crossman and Peter Gray (eds), *Poverty and welfare in Ireland, 1838–1948* (Dublin, 2011), pp 88, 92, 93. 83 *NS*, 1 Jan. 1848. 84 *First annual report of the commissioners for administering the laws of relief for the poor in Ireland, with appendices*, 563, HC 1847–8, xxxiii, 166. 85 CB1, no. 10.126, Pat Connolly, 24 Jan. 1848. The vermin referred to was likely human body louse.

positively refused doing'.[86] Outdoor relief could have perhaps saved Lambert and others like her. The verdict was death from sickness, exposure to the inclemency of the weather and destitution.[87] Just one week later, two other inquests were held on people who might have survived if outdoor relief was offered. Thomas Clements tried to make his way to Monaghan town to attempt to gain admittance to the poorhouse. He suffered from dysentery, was too weak to walk upright, and could not continue. At his inquest, Dr Moorhead determined that his death had been caused by disease, destitution and exposure to cold from want of proper clothing.[88] The inquest of John Casey showed he was an elderly man in 'very distressed circumstances', who 'had no means of support but depended on occasional charity amongst the neighbours'.[89] He was found in the fields, dead, with a few heads of cabbage beside him. Dr Moorhead found him to have had a concussion but believed it to have been caused by a fall and considered that, combined with destitution and exposure to the severity of the weather, as a cause of death.[90]

The local conservative view on the implementation of the Poor Law was shared by the editor of the *Northern Standard*, Arthur Wellington Holmes. In his weekly editorial column in February 1848, he argued that the way the board of guardians was managing paupers and the interests of ratepayers and landowners was correct. The editor questioned the integrity of liberal Poor Law guardians who neglected their own interests as advocates of the poor and were the type that laid heavy burdens upon the ratepayer.[91] He stated,

> We think it always suspicious when we see a man neglect his own business to attend to that of others. When we see a shop-keeper leave his counter, where he can make money, to spend his time at a board of guardians, we are inclined to think that his business is not worth attending to, or that he wants to make himself popular by some particular course of conduct, either by forcing the poor upon his division, that those who are less poor may deal with him, or by sinister means he may attract the attention of the ratepayers, which in the end may pay.[92]

Holmes, who was secretary to the Monaghan Local Relief committee, remained firm that the administration of the Poor Law required 'merely common sense' and that speech makers, popularity hunters and talking busybodies retarded the real business of a board of guardians, which was simply a business transaction.[93] This might suggest that local landed conservatives were critical of middle-class ratepaying Catholics who were elected guardians. Holmes further described the composition of the Monaghan and Clones boards of guardians (Waddell belonged to the former) as being exempt from liberal 'intruders' and congratulated them

86 CB1, no. 9.125, Mary Lambert, 24 Jan. 1848. 87 Ibid. 88 CB1, no. 13.129, Thomas Clements, 4 Feb. 1848. 89 CB1, no. 12.128, John Casey, 2 Feb. 1848. 90 Ibid. 91 *NS*, 5, 26 Feb. 1848. 92 *NS*, 5 Feb. 1848. 93 Ibid.; *NS*, 6 Mar. 1847.

on the 'great unanimity which prevails at their meetings'.[94] The members of these boards were presumably conservative Protestants. They were a group of like-minded men who placed their own economic interests over those of the poor and subscribed to a belief that in doing so, they helped save and support the rate paying community.

In the same February edition of the *Northern Standard*, reports on the inquests taken by Waddell on Casey and Clements appeared. According to the paper, Casey was found dead and 'the poor creature had collected some cabbages, and bits of the vegetables were in his mouth'.[95] It also identified Clements and 'a man named Little' as being found dead from 'sheer want and starvation'.[96] Considering the last phase of the Famine was well underway and Russell's government had placed the entire financial burden of supporting paupers and managing the Famine on the local Irish elite, this curious appearance of starvation inquests might suggest a possible change in local attitudes towards pauper death.

RESTRICTIVE CRITERIA AND RELIEF DENIED

The aftermath of the Poor Law Extension Act inspired some local guardians and relief officers to become increasingly restrictive as to their interpretation of the law in relation to the eligibility of paupers to gain access to relief. In their attempts to keep costs down, their questionable judgment resulted in the deaths of paupers who needed support to survive. A series of inquests starting in February 1848 conducted by Waddell expose the legislative changes, combined with restrictive criteria and decision making that directly contributed to deaths in Co. Monaghan. On 28 February 1848 an inquest on Terance Conolly revealed the destitute circumstances in which he had been living.[97] Conolly was a labouring man who had had no means of support since Christmas 1847 except the compassion of Margaret Pickens of Drum. Ill from dysentery, he sought the help of Dr Taylor at the Drum dispensary two weeks before his death. Conolly applied for and got a ticket for outdoor relief and medicine, but testimony from Pickens indicates that he only got relief occasionally from the relieving officer of the united division of Drum and Aghabog, which was part of the Cootehill Poor Law Union. What he received was not enough to support life.

Another inquest reflecting a clear case of injustice was taken on 27 February 1848, as Bernard Rudden was found drowned in the water in the townland of Killark, blue in the face, mouth hanging open. He was a beggar who the neighbours often provided with breakfast and supper. Witnesses told the coroner's jury that Rudden had often attempted to gain entry into Clones workhouse, but was repeatedly denied. He was able to purchase relief at a private soup kitchen and for this reason the Clones board of guardians were 'impressed that he had some money'.[98] Rudden had no bedclothes, nor shoes or stockings that winter, but the

94 *NS*, 26 Feb. 1848. 95 Ibid. 96 Ibid. 97 CB1, no. 18.134, Terance Conolly, 28 Feb. 1848 98 CB1, no. 17.133, Bernard Rudden, 27 Feb. 1848.

board declared him (legally) not destitute. The verdict was death from destitution, want of food and exposure to the cold of the season.[99]

While money prevented entry to the workhouse, so did possession of property. The Gregory clause demanded that only tenants in possession of less than a quarter acre were eligible for relief and it contributed to many deaths including those investigated by Waddell. One inquest taken shows how the Gregory clause was directly responsible for a small farmer's death. On the evening of 31 March 1848, a little girl appeared at the door of Thomas Higgins of Derrydorraghy, who cried that her father, Owen Treanor, had taken very ill and asked for help. Higgins followed to where Treanor was lying against a ditch on the roadside with his wife and a little girl beside him. Although Higgins also sought the help of Revd Rooney, they could not get the support of neighbours to admit Treanor into their homes. Higgins built a fire to keep Treanor and the family warm but during the night, at approximately 4 a.m., he died. Higgins testified that the deceased had been suffering from destitution for some time and that Treanor and his family were in great want, sometimes without a meal for an entire day. Treanor had once been a small tenant farmer. But he had disposed of some of his five acres and then, after some time, the remainder. Three or four months earlier, Treanor had applied for a ticket to the poorhouse, declaring himself to be in great want. He was declined by Richard Hewlett, relieving officer of the united districts of Killylough and Tedavnet, part of the Monaghan Poor Law Union, on 'account of having a farm'.[100] Families like the Treanors were failed by the Poor Law and the restrictive criteria applied by local officials that prevented their survival.

DEPARTING THE WORKHOUSE

Workhouse operations and the business of the Poor Law union were reviewed by the board of guardians, and workhouse daily functions managed by the master and matron, who were appointed by the board. The execution of their duties was reviewed weekly, and admissions, departures, births and deaths of inmates were published regularly in local newspapers. Workhouse rules stated that any pauper could leave after giving the master three hours' notice, and after quitting the workhouse must return his workhouse clothes or other articles belonging to the board of guardians unless he had express permission to keep them.[101] Additionally, any pauper who had a family dependent upon him, if he chose to quit the workhouse, would have to take his family.[102] While not highlighted in any official report, Waddell's inquests reveal there was an observable phenomenon throughout the years of the Famine that elderly inmates left the workhouse, returned to the townlands where they had once lived looking for support from former neighbours,

---

99 Ibid.   100 CB1, no. 24.140, Owen Treanor, 3 Apr. 1848.   101 *Irish workhouse rulebook, 1844* (Dublin, 1844).   102 Ibid.

friends and family, and soon died.[103] They appear to have had a desire to leave the workhouse as quickly as possible, and to have done so with ease. In the majority of cases, these inmates were diseased and starving which indicated unhealthy conditions at the workhouse. Circumstantial evidence suggests they may also have suffered from a variety of mental illnesses.

Two such inquests were taken by Waddell in 1848. On 21 March, witnesses stated that William Quigley, former inmate of Clones workhouse, appeared at the Clones police barracks at midnight asking for food and lodging. He was taken to the residence of Hugh McKenna, who refused Quigley entrance as he believed him to be drunk and filthy. Quigley was found the next morning lying on a dung hill and died soon afterwards. The verdict was that he had died from the effects of cold, debility and destitution.[104] One of the effects of starvation includes disorientation, staggering and a loss of balance and equilibrium. No evidence was produced that indicated Quigley had consumed alcohol. Andrew Dickson, relieving officer of Newbliss and Currin united district, stated that he did not know why Quigley had left the Clones workhouse after receiving a ticket for admission just one month earlier.[105]

By contrast, former Monaghan workhouse inmate Joseph Abraham made his motives clear upon departure, having spent two months in the institution. He told workhouse Master Mr Williams that he was leaving to spend Easter at Mr Cochrane's of Leek. Abraham had done work for Mr Cochrane in the past and had been treated with kindness. An elderly man, Abraham was described as a person 'weak of mind and regarded as a fool'.[106] On that day of severe rain, he attempted the journey of eight miles from Monaghan to Leek, but was found lying on the road leading from Glaslough to Caledon. He was removed to the house of Mr Alexander Pringle, where he died.[107] The request for investigations by the coroner indicates there were concerns in the community as to the treatment of these men, as well as many others who left the local workhouse.

'MY DUTY TO THE PUBLIC': THE POLITICS OF THE CORONER

The process by which a coroner was called to duty began when a writ of enquiry was delivered to him from the constabulary or a magistrate. He would consider the circumstances and needs of the case, and then begin the journey to where the body lay, form a jury, recruit a doctor to examine the body, gather witnesses and conduct the inquest. Although transparency was available via public inquests, and

---

103 CB1, no. 22.138, William Quigley, 21 Mar. 1848; CB1, no. 27.143, Joseph Abraham, 20 Apr. 1848; CB1, no. 13.162, Alice Connolly, 14 Dec. 1848; CB1, no. 6.175, Mary Boyland; CB1, 3 Apr. 1849; CB1, no. 8.199, Ann Treanor, 2 Nov. 1849; CB1, no. 19.210, Bernard Cosgrove, 13 Jan. 1850; CB1, no. 20.211, John McGorman, 8 Feb. 1850; CB1, no. 4.215, Ann Magaghy, 19 Mar. 1850; CB1, no. 276.17, Ann Fee, 2 Jan. 1852; CB1, no. 305.11, Sarah McGarvey, 27 Nov. 1852. 104 CB1, no. 22.138, William Quigley, 21 Mar. 1848. 105 Ibid. 106 CB1, no. 27.143, Joseph Abraham, 20 Apr. 1848. 107 Ibid.

reports of inquests presented to the grand jury and to the Chief Secretary's Office were available, the Monaghan grand jury often challenged Waddell's decision making in order to attempt to reduce their costs, questioning why he undertook so many inquests. One inquest capturing an instance of domestic abuse stands out in Waddell's casebook. Ann Cavenagh was regularly beaten by her husband, Philip, and on the day of her death, 27 June 1848, she was reported to have been lying on her back on the ground exclaiming 'Good God am I going to be murdered' while her husband was standing over her. She made it back to her home but died just an hour later. Multiple witnesses testified that Cavenagh had been subject to abuse from her husband, receiving beatings, black eyes and cuts to her mouth. While this had occurred on the day of her death, her post-mortem returned some unusual results. Drs McClean and Finley returned similar reports that Cavenagh had a cancerous ulcerated opening near one of the natural orifices of her body, as well as a disease of the liver and spleen, and ascribed her death to natural causes.[108] McMahon states that women were considered inferior and therefore many murders of women in the home went unpunished.[109] It is likely Cavenagh died as a result of abuse from her husband. Waddell made a special note explaining his intentions and process:

> From the high degree of excitement that prevailed and general strong impression that the death of deceased arose from abuse sustained from her husband and from the degree of decomposition that had set in Dr Finley considered the assistance of another Dr absolutely necessary. I therefore called in Dr McClean of Ballibay [sic] to assist in the post-mortem examination of the body. After having been some time engaged in the Inquest collecting and empanneling [sic] the jury I discovered the case lay within Mr Swanzy's district on which I would have retired and let the case be reported to him but that the body would not keep, decomposition having made considerable progress having been near 4 days doubt – being up 1 o'clock and about 11 miles from Mr S., he could not have held it that evening as the Jury would disperse that day being the one preceding the Grand Sessions. Considered Mr S would not either that on for 2 or 3 hold the inquest on account of the sessions. I therefore held it under such circumstances considering I would not be doing my duty to the public to have declined in holding it.[110]

Although the verdict of death by natural causes may be disagreeable, specifically the failure to find culpability of Philip Cavenagh, the corpse was given the utmost attention that Waddell could provide. He carried out the investigation into the death upholding his duties while he demonstrated his concern for the public interest in the case.

108 CB1, no. 33.149, Ann Cavenagh, 27 June 1848. 109 McMahon, *Homicide in pre-Famine and Famine Ireland*, p. 34. 110 CB1, Notes taken by Waddell on no. 33.149, Ann Cavenagh, 27 June 1848.

THE THIRD POTATO CROP FAILURE

In September 1848, the potato crop again had disease and as the Famine worsened, it reflected all the failures of Russell's policy. All remaining food depots were closed at the end of 1848, and while prices of food remained low, without any public works or employment policy, those outside the workhouse were unable to support themselves and were threatened with starvation. Tenants' inability to pay rent rendered many landlords and tenants incapable of paying rates for poor relief.[111] By December 1848, the populations of local institutions such as the gaol and the workhouse again began to rise and a cholera epidemic swept through the country. Chief Poor Law Commissioner Edward Twisleton and Trevelyan fought publicly about how to handle the crisis. Twisleton resigned in March 1849 after the government's refusal to provide additional funding rendered him powerless to help preserve the lives of the Irish people. Russell sought to devise new legislation to address the crisis.

In Co. Monaghan, through the winter of 1848–9, the Monaghan Poor Law Union still refused to offer outdoor relief, insisting on only indoor relief (i.e., the workhouse) to support the poor.[112] Their actions continued to put pressure on neighbouring Poor Law unions and, evidence suggests, contributed to an increase in deaths. Waddell held inquests on bodies found in fields and on roadsides, demonstrating how the Poor Law and Monaghan local elites continued to fail those they were meant to support. Alice Connolly left the Clones workhouse in December 1848 to return to her former neighbourhood, where she was found lying dead in a field, identified by neighbours who had known her for years.[113] Starving and homeless, Mick Smith was found dead on the roadside having been seen earlier appearing very weak and speaking indistinctly. The jury's verdict was death from exposure due to the severity of the weather.[114] Pat Keenan, with no means of support but what he received from his neighbours, was found lying dead on the roadside on 21 February 1849.[115] The inquest revealed that Keenan was hungry, had asked for bread from the neighbours and had died from weakness and exposure to the cold of night.[116]

In the spring of 1849, inquests revealed that some people were determined to support themselves at a time when there was little or no employment to do so, refused to enter the workhouse and died of want and starvation.[117] In April 1849, the son of Bernard Rorc, who had died, told the coroner's jury that his father had had very little food, having only occasional work. During the preceding fortnight,

---

111 Gray, *Famine, land and politics*, p. 305. 112 *First report from the select committee of the House of Lords appointed to inquire into the operation of the Irish Poor Law, and the expediency of making any amendment in its enactments, and to report thereon to the house; together with the minutes of evidence*, p. 8, HL 1849 (192) xvi, 4. 113 CB1, no. 13.162, Alice Connolly, 14 Dec. 1848. 114 CB1, no. 14.163, Mick Smith, 23 Dec. 1848. 115 CB1, no. 20.169, Pat Keenan, 21 Feb. 1849. 116 Ibid. 117 CB1, no. 14.163, Mick Smith, 23 Dec. 1848; CB1, no. 20.169, Pat Keenan, 21 Feb. 1849; CB1, no. 9.178, Bernard Rorc, 26 Apr. 1849; CB1, no. 10.179, Mick Cuningham, 26 Apr. 1849; CB1, no. 17.186, Thomas McCarvle, 10 June 1849; CB1, no. 19.188, Thomas Madill, 17 June 1849.

their meals had consisted of broughin, meal and water mixed into gruel and thickened with boiled nettles.[118] The verdict was death from 'general dropsy', hastened by want and destitution. In another inquest, Sarah, the proud wife of deceased labourer Mick Burk, told the coroner's jury that he ate well, generally three meals a day, and that he would have gone to the poorhouse when he had nothing left to sell, but not sooner.[119] A note in Waddell's casebook refutes these facts and states,

> This witness was told by the jury she was not swearing the truth as they all [k]new deceased was in a starving state for some time past but would not be persuaded to go into the poorhouse but begged amongst the neighbours.[120]

The revelation that Sarah Burk was lying about having enough food available to keep her husband alive reflects her shame. In June 1849, a similar inquest revealed a widow and her two children had been living in wretched hovels among the rocks at the quarry of Carricknabrock on Slievebeagh mountain.[121] Although making besoms to sell at local fairs and begging for many months, Alice Madill was unable to provide enough for her family to survive. According to witness Bernard Murry, 'she was urged to go into the poorhouse with her family but would not. Nor did she allow her late husband when he wanted and her young son Thomas, died of want, sickness and exposure to the weather.'[122] This decision indicates there was a deep shame felt if one were to enter the poorhouse and some would rather risk death. With no other choice but life on the outside, options were limited; and the lack of sufficient employment and outdoor relief directly contributed to the deaths of both father and son.

A SECOND 'BARBAROUS AND REVOLTING OUTRAGE': INSTITUTIONAL FAILURE

Waddell's work as the coroner during the Famine captured the deaths of people who died from exposure and starvation as a result of a lack of resources and support at times of peak distress. The inquests also reflect the failures of institutions to protect and care for their inmates, including in the administration of justice. Several murders captured in Waddell's casebook show a pattern of violent acts that correlate with peaks in the local crisis.

McMahon's study on homicide reveals that murders during the famine weren't unusual, and those that took place against vulnerable groups bore similar characteristics. He found that murders of women often went unpunished, as they were considered inferior.[123] While cases of premeditated murder were rare, they were predominantly committed by men.[124] McMahon found that in cases where

---

118 CB1, no. 9.178, Bernard Rorc, 26 Apr. 1849. 119 CB1, no.16.185, Mick Burk, 8 June 1849. 120 Ibid. 121 CB1, no. 19.188, Thomas Madill, 17 June 1849. 122 Ibid. 123 McMahon, *Homicide in pre-Famine and Famine Ireland*, p. 60. 124 Ibid., pp 81–2.

murders were perpetrated by family members, they were most often carried out by male relatives, with money at the root of the conflict.[125] These relatives fought over property, land and economic resources.[126] Such murders were often condemned, but when men murdered women and children, Waddell's inquests show they generally went unpunished. Social norms protected men and considered their family matters private.

From June 1846 through December 1852, Waddell conducted 306 inquests, which included 11 suicides, 23 instances of infanticide and 7 suspected murders (the inquest lacked evidence or the jury returned a neutral verdict). There were six inquests with a clear verdict of homicide; two men and four women were violently murdered.[127] The female victims were killed in two separate crimes; the murder of the Collen sisters in April 1847 and the murders of Catherine McCourt and Catherine Trainor in May 1849.[128] Murders during the Famine weren't unusual and the two cases share similar characteristics.[129] The women's homes were broken into by assailants in the middle of the night. Robbery was considered the primary motive. None of the four women had a husband or the protection of a man living in the house. In both instances the women were known to have money and had means to provide for themselves. Additionally, both sets of murders were described by newspapers of the time as 'barbarous', particularly violent and savage, and rewards were offered for information that would lead to the conviction of the assailants.

On 3 May 1849, Waddell held the inquests for McCourt and Trainor. Dr Andrew K. Young, surgeon to the Co. Monaghan infirmary, examined the bodies and established that the women were attacked with a hatchet or similar instrument, which was used to smash their skulls. McCourt was strangled. A modern analysis of the act of strangulation indicates that the attacker often has a close personal or intimate relationship with their victim.[130] Additionally, McCourt and Trainor's bodies were burned and the inquest details as to the state of their bodies were published in newspapers with great detail.[131] Trainor's legs were burnt up to the

---

125 Ibid. 126 Ibid. 127 CB1, no. 28.47, James Henry, 2 Apr. 1847; CB1, no. 33.51, Catherine Collen, 9 Apr. 1847; CB1, no. 33.52, Ann Collen, 9 Apr. 1847; CB1, no. 309.15, Hamilton Clark, 8 Jan. 1853; CB1, no. 12.181, Catherine McCourt, 3 May 1849; CB1, no. 13.182, Catherine Trainor, 3 May 1849. 128 CB1, no. 12.181, Catherine McCourt, 3 May 1849; CB1, no. 13.182, Catherine Trainor, 3 May 1849. 129 McMahon, *Homicide in pre-Famine and Famine Ireland*, p. 60. 130 Sara Vehling, 'Taking your breath away – why strangulation in domestic violence is a huge red flag', MobileODT, mobileodt.com, accessed on 30 Oct. 2020. 131 The announcement of the murder appeared in *NS*, 5 May 1849; *NS*, 12 May 1849; *Bell's New Weekly Messenger*, 13 May 1849; *Bristol Times and Mirror*, 12 May 1849; *Newry Telegraph*, 8 May 1849; *Banner of Ulster*, 8 May 1849; *Sligo Champion*, 19 May 1849; *Hampshire Advertiser*, 12 May 1849; *Southern Reporter and Cork Commercial Courier*, 8 May 1849; *Mayo Constitution*, 8 May 1849; *Cork Examiner*, 9 May 1849; *Dublin Evening Post*, 5 May 1849; *King's County Chronicle*, 9 May 1849; *FJ*, 7 May 1849; *London Evening Standard*, 7 May 1849; *Kentish Independent*, 12 May 1849; *Belfast News-Letter*, 8 May 1849; *Standard of Freedom*, 12 May 1849; *Monmouth Merlin*, 12 May 1849; *Manchester Times*, 8 May 1849; *Oxford Chronicle and Reading Gazette*, 12 May 1849; *Limerick and Clare Examiner*, 9 May 1849.

knee as if placed into the fire. Also, a resin candle was placed in the waist of her petticoat, burning the upper part of her torso and arms. McCourt's 'abdomen' was burnt completely, while her feet and legs were only severely blistered, and mysteriously the straw underneath her body was not burned.[132] The abdomen was likely a general term for female genitalia. An evaluation of her body revealed that she had been burned while still alive. She was then sat down on the dry straw in front of the hearth. Lastly, the women's bodies were propped up against either side of the fireside, 'face to face as if in social converse'.[133]

Neighbours and relatives told Waddell and the inquest jury they believed the women were murdered for 'on account of they had money'.[134] McCourt's uncle Peter had lived 'a long life of extreme poverty' in a 'wretched hovel built in a gully of the mountain water course' and over his lifetime, he saved £30.[135] Upon his death, he gave more than £20 to his niece, the young, unmarried McCourt, who had taken care of him and been his companion, while other nephews and nieces received significantly smaller sums by comparison. As a result, McCourt suffered the jealousy and ill-will of other family members.[136] She remained living in her 16-foot by 9-foot labourer's cabin and took on a companion, 65-year-old widow 'Kitty' Trainor (neé McKenna). A day before the murders, on 2 May 1849, McCourt had visited the executor of her trust, Brian McKenna, and instructed him to buy flax seed at the Aughnacloy fair, which was to be used for sowing her conacre. She had also expressed interest in the purchase of a cow.

On 5 May 1849, the *Northern Standard* reported,

> Barbarous and Revolting Murders
> We have a most disagreeable duty to perform that of recording the particulars of a double murder perpetrated in the county of Monaghan, more familiar in its details to the savage atrocities of the Greenacres or Goods of the sister island than to the vengeful sacrifices of human life that have unfortunately stained the history of Ireland. A murder, the incentives to which were not the accumulated wrongs of the years, nor yet that obedience which has unfortunately been blind yielded to a bloody and vengeful code of man-made retributive laws; but a cold-blooded, revolting atrocity done upon the bodies of two wretched unprotected women, for the filthy sum of a few paltry pounds – a murder so atrocious, it is marked by sheer calculating villainy, and attended by so many revolting circumstances, that we weep for the country that gave birth to the perpetrators.[137]

In 1837, English grocer James Greenacre (1785–1837) dismembered the body of his fiancée, Hannah Brown, with the help of his mistress, taking her money and

132 CBI, no. 12.181, Catherine McCourt, 3 May 1849. 133 *NS*, 5 May 1849. 134 CBI, no. 12.181, Catherine McCourt, 3 May 1849. 135 *NS*, 5 May 1849. 136 Ibid. 137 Ibid.

intending to emigrate to America.[138] In 1842, Daniel Good, an Irish coachman, dismembered and burned the remains of English woman Jane Jones, with whom he was having an affair; he was believed to have killed her after discovering she was pregnant.[139] Reporters in the mid-nineteenth century often made reference to crimes of the past in order to sensationalize news.[140] However, the comparisons of the murders to those of Greenacre and Good and 'so many revolting circumstances' may indicate a more intimate connection, potentially a motive of a sexual nature to the assailant or assailants.[141]

The *Northern Standard* did not make any connection between the murders and the desperate conditions in Co. Monaghan at that time. Rather, the focus was on the details of the murder and the inquest jury verdict naming Peter and Ellen McKenna, cousins of the deceased McCourt, as the killers. This verdict would have been a positive outcome for Waddell, as any coroner's inquest that resulted in a verdict naming the suspects in a murder case was considered a success, per the demands of the office to do so. The naming of suspects validated the authority of the coroner's work and its value to the community. However, the outcome of the McCourt-Trainor criminal trial reveals how national and local politics could undermine the verdict of the coroner's jury.

On 9 March 1849, the Monaghan *Northern Standard* newspaper announced that Lord Lieutenant Bessborough was offering a reward of £80 to any person or persons who would provide information leading to the arrest of those who committed 'the Drumfernasky murders'.[142] Editor Andrew Holmes wrote that the reward appeared to undermine the coroner's verdict naming the McKennas as the killers, perhaps giving the impression that the suspects were either wrongfully accused or that the government needed further evidence to convict them in a criminal trial.[143] However, he concluded that as the government had set an example, the magistrates and gentlemen of the barony of Trough should also initiate a local reward towards ensuring the suspect or suspects were found, identified and convicted.[144] Letters to the editor and editorial commentary published in the *Northern Standard* revealed that there were only three magistrates in the barony of Trough and none had been available to attend the inquest. Comparisons were made to the number of magistrates in the barony of Monaghan. There were 'so many [magistrates] thickly placed' that they 'could whistle to one another from their hall-doors'.[145] The government's reward, combined with local attitudes about the lack of governance and responsibility taken by the local elites in Trough may have exposed and shamed them. The gruesome nature of the murders increased the need to prosecute and convict the assailants. Without intervention or immediate action, the gentlemen of Trough looked apathetic and incompetent, having ignored their responsibility to

---

138 J. Gilliand, 'James Greenacre', *ODNB*. 139 *London Evening Standard*, 18 Apr. 1842, 13 May 1842. 140 Alice Smalley, 'Representations of crime, justice and punishment in the popular press: a study of the *Illustrated Police News*, 1864–1938 (PhD, 2017, Open University). 141 *NS*, 5 May 1849. 142 *NS*, 12 May 1849. 143 Ibid. 144 Ibid. 145 Ibid.

enforce the law as was their duty. Another perspective considers that the crime and lack of magisterial control was a collective embarrassment for all of Co. Monaghan's local elite, because such a violent and disturbing crime had taken place under their jurisdiction. A pattern of behaviour existed whereby Monaghan local elites often defied the instructions of the government's administration as these were considered an interference in their own local matters.

Ten months later, on 3 March 1850, the criminal trial of 19-year-old Peter McKenna took place at the Monaghan assizes. Charges against his sister Ellen had been dropped. Another relative, Patrick McCourt, had been named but charges were also dropped as he had a witness provide him with an alibi. McKenna's trial began with the testimony of informant James Trainor, witness for the prosecution. Trainor, the son-in-law of the murdered widow Catherine McKenna, testified that he had travelled with Peter McKenna and Patrick McCourt to the home of the two women the night of the murders.[146] The men intended to rob Catherine McCourt of money, and Trainor was promised a cwt.[147] of Indian meal (112 lbs) for his participation as the lookout. After entering the women's cabin, Trainor saw McKenna strike Catherine McCourt on the head with the flat end of a hatchet, while Patrick McCourt looked for the money they believed was in the house. The informant claimed that after seeing the initial attack on the women, he immediately left the premises and returned home. It was Trainor's wife, Ellen (neé Trainor), who was the first at the crime scene in the morning and discovered the bodies of her mother and Catherine McCourt. Circumstantial evidence suggests that Trainor told his wife what happened at the house the night before and she arrived in the morning to investigate.

The legal defence for Peter McKenna put their efforts into attacking Trainor's character, to discredit him. They accused him of only serving as a witness to secure the £80 reward money. Shortly after the murders, in May 1849, Trainor gained entry into the workhouse. It was during his time there he became an informant for the prosecution and provided testimony as to his, Peter McKenna's and Patrick McCourt's involvement in the crime. At the trial, he was mocked by McKenna's barrister, who asked him, 'Were you a besom-maker [at the workhouse], making "Castleblayney Besoms, besoms fine and new?"', a reference to a local rhyme.[148] His previous status as a pauper diminished the credibility of his testimony to the local gentry who served on the jury, regardless of the detailed eyewitness testimony he provided.

Another blow to the prosecution was the testimony of Dr Young, the medical expert, who examined the bodies at the inquest. He was called upon by Sergeant McKelvey, investigator, to provide his opinion as to the source of the hairs and fibres on the presumed murder weapon, a hatchet, and on a man's coat that was taken from Peter McKenna's home. Using a microscope, Dr Young found that the hairs on the hatchet were from an ox and the red marks on the man's coat (believed

---

146 *NS*, 9 Mar. 1850. 147 Cwt. = hundredweight = 112 lbs. 148 *NS*, 9 Mar. 1850. Duchas, Schools Collection, Killybrone, Co. Monaghan, vol. 1798, p. 232. A fragment of the local rhyme remains, 'Castleblayney besoms, sold in Mullacrew/ If I can get them two a penny, what is that to you.'

to be McKenna's) were not blood, but rather paint. The use of microscopic examination of the hairs was widely publicized in newspapers around the country as a new scientific achievement for medical jurisprudence.[149] Several prominent members of the Trough community, including two parish priests and justice of the peace Thomas Anketell, a prominent figure of the landed gentry in the local area and member of the grand jury, testified to McKenna's 'excellent moral character'.[150] Peter McKenna was found not guilty by the all-male jury.

No further evidence exists revealing any person or persons convicted for the murder of Catherine McCourt and Catherine Trainor in May 1849. The case adds to the growing body of evidence that Monaghan juries, comprised of local elites, rarely secured convictions in murder cases against women and other marginal groups. It also reveals the social attitudes and possible collusion of Co. Monaghan authorities in fighting government intervention into what they considered local matters. Additionally, the lack of murder convictions at the assizes undermined the authority of the coroner and inquest juries who often had first-hand knowledge of the circumstances surrounding the crime.

PEAK DISTRESS IN THE WORKHOUSES: JUNE 1849

While the inquests held outside Monaghan institutions revealed the vulnerable conditions for those greatest in need and marginal groups at risk, the Monaghan workhouses saw significant increases in inmates each month from January through to June 1849. In June 1849, the Monaghan workhouse had 1,784 inmates, a record number. Carrickmacross was reported to have 1,581 inmates, Clones, 1,601 and Castleblayney 2,000 (see Table 10). With the overcrowding came fear of disease. On 20 June 1849, the Clones workhouse master William Montgomery and his daughter, Elizabeth, who served as matron, resigned from fear of becoming ill, as disease was running rampant within the institution.[151]

In June 1849, the Rate in Aid Act was enacted in order to raise the money to pay to relieve distress in unfunded, failing unions. The regional tax was levied on the north and east of Ireland to pay for the distress in the south and west. While counties like Monaghan had been restrictive in their relief spending, they now incurred an additional bill whereby local taxation became part of a national relief fund. Rate in aid and the Poor Law rates kept costs high for land agents and landlords who were looking to reduce costs. A letter from John Hope, brother-in-law (and first cousin) of Waddell, written to him that year on the topic of the Poor Law rate and the changes to the law stated:

> There is some change I understand in the mode of dividing the poor rate by an act of the last session that throws more of the rate on the

---

149 *NS*, 9 Mar. 1850; *Armagh Guardian*, 25 Mar. 1850; *Weekly Vindicator*, 30 Mar. 1850. **150** *NS*, 9 Mar. 1850. **151** *Newry Examiner and Louth Advertiser*, 20 June 1849.

Table 10: Populations of workhouses supporting Co. Monaghan, Dec. 1846–Dec. 1849

Workhouse	Monaghan	Castleblayney	Carrickmacross	Clones	Cootehill[152]
First admissions*	May 1842	Dec. 1842	Feb. 1843	Feb. 1843	Dec. 1842
Initial inmate capacity*	900	600	500	600	800
Add. Famine capacity	300		240	220	
December 1846	764		508	772	1,099
January 1847	689	767	535	799	1,094
February 1847	809	802		811	1,040
December 1847	786		583		860
January 1848	936	1,091	558	862	
February 1848	892	1,017	642	867	
January 1849			1,070		
February 1849	1,185	1,462	1,083	1,314	2,479
March 1849	1,172	1,312	1,152	1,362	2,365
April 1849	1,224		1,342	1,338	
May 1849	1,268	1,746	1,533	1,365	2,948
June 1849	1,784	2,000	1,581	1,601	2,979
July 1849	1,689			1,589	
August 1849	1,447	961	1,568	1,410	
September 1849	955	868	1,367	995	
October 1849	870	791	1,424	891	1,189
November 1849	885	954	1,492	871	
December 1849	962	996	1,675	910	1,478

Sources: John O'Connor, *The workhouses of Ireland* (Dublin, 1995), pp 233–6, 259–60. *Returns of the numbers of paupers in workhouses in Ireland ... transmitted to the Home Office in pursuance of Sir William Somerville's letter ... 5th December 1846. Newry Examiner and Louth Advertiser*: 30 Dec. 1846, 16 Jan. 1847, 4 Dec. 1847, 22 Jan. 1848, 1 Sept. 1849. *Anglo-Celt*: 17 Dec. 1847. NS: 26 Dec. 1846; 23 Jan., 6 Feb., 25 Dec. 1847; 16 Jan., 5 Feb. 1848; 17 Feb., 10 Mar., 24 Mar., 5 May 1849; 2, 9, 23, 30 June 1849; 7, 14, 21 July 1849; 11 Aug. 1849; 15, 29 Sept. 1849; 6, 27 Oct. 1849; 3 Nov. 1849; 15, 29 Dec. 1849. Carrickmacross workhouse minute books, 4 Nov. 1848–23 June 1849; 4 Aug. 1849–23 Mar. 1850.

tenant who cannot now claim more from the landlord than the half of the amount he pays instead of as formerly half the rate on every pound of rent he paid.[153]

152 The Cootehill board of guardians was dissolved by order of the commissioners for failing to carry out the provisions of the Irish Poor Law. *Drogheda Argus and Leinster Journal*, 19 Feb. 1848. **153** John Hope to William Charles Waddell, 9 Dec. 1849 (Hope Collection).

Half of the rates were paid by the landowner for most holdings, but all the rates on holdings worth less than £4 each year. In Co. Monaghan farms that were valued at less than £4 were 5 acres or less.[154] Between 25–33 per cent of the population of the Clones and Carrickmacross unions held farms valued at less than £4 as compared to the Monaghan union where that population was just over 10 per cent.[155]

CLEARING THE LAND: EVICTION

The financial burden encouraged landlords to evict their smallest tenants. As the Famine continued, landowners began to shift the use of their land from tillage to cattle, as grazing cattle helped them recover losses when rental incomes collapsed.[156] The removal of tenants became important to them, in order to create larger grassland farms. The conversion from tillage to meat production started before the Famine but began to increase during the crisis.[157] This resulted in even further pressure to remove the local landless labourers and cottiers, and forced them to choose the workhouse, emigration or starvation.

The lack of local news surrounding evictions in Co. Monaghan was similar to the absence of local starvation inquests in the *Northern Standard*. Evictions did take place and various sources reveal how landlords used all means necessary to clear the land of cottiers, labourers and small tenant farmers. A government report in February 1849 stated that 12,859 evictions had taken place under the Evicted Poor Protection Act (1848); of those, 2,284 were in Ulster and 156 in Monaghan.[158] The report states that each recorded eviction was of either an individual or a family. This indicates that the actual number of people evicted is much higher than 156. In Co. Monaghan, the Poor Law unions reported 33 evictions in the union of Castleblayney, 20 in the union of Clones, 16 in the union of Cootehill, 6 in the union of Dundalk and 81 in the union of Monaghan. Curiously, no evictions were reported from the union of Carrickmacross, although the populations of the Shirley and Bath estates were the largest in the county. It appears no return was sent. Waddell's inquests prove there were indeed evictions in the union of Carrickmacross and the lack of transparent reporting suggests there may have been an unwillingness by the landlords or land agents in that district to provide the numbers of individuals and families they removed from their land.[159]

---

154 Duffy, 'Mapping the Famine in Monaghan', p. 445.   **155** Ibid.   **156** Enda Delaney and Breandán Mac Suibne (eds), *Ireland's Great Famine and popular politics* (Abingdon, 2016).   **157** Anne Kane, *Constructing national identity, discourse and ritual during the Land War, 1879–1882* (New York, 2011), p. 102.   **158** *Evicted Destitute Poor (Ireland) Act: Abstract of return to an order of the honourable House of Commons dated 19 February 1849, for Return 'of all notices served upon relieving officers of Poor Law districts in Ireland by landowners and others, under the Act of last session, 11 & 12 Vict., c.47, intituled "An Act for the Protection and Relief of the Destitute Poor evicted from their Dwellings"'*, p. 35, HC 1849 (517) xlix, 412.   **159** CB1, no. 19.38, Patrick McCabe, 10 Mar. 1847.

On the list of evictions in the union of Monaghan, one name is immediately recognizable. Waddell's uncle, grand jury member Charles Hopes, was listed in the report as having instructed William Hanna as his agent to evict two families from his townlands of Coleshill and Kilnahaltar.[160] While no further information is furnished, Waddell's inquests captured earlier in this chapter, those of Bernard Kelly and the Chessar children, show that all died of starvation.[161]

The Evicted Poor Protection Act was intended to assist the victims of Famine clearances by enabling local guardians to grant outdoor relief for one month to those evicted.[162] The inmate populations at local workhouses indicate that evictions contributed to the increase in admissions. One of the few mass evictions publicized during the Famine was that of landlord E.P. Shirley and his agent George Morant, which took place in September 1849. They reportedly made 1,225 men, women and children homeless in what were referred to as 'monster evictions'.[163] The series of evictions, removing people from their land and homes, contributed to the continous rise in the inmate population of the Carrickmacross workhouse from September 1849 onwards (see Table 10).[164] One inquest taken in November 1849 reflects the emotional impact and repercussions of eviction. Rose Treanor deposed that the deceased, her mother Ann Treanor, had been 'served with a notice to quit by her Landlady Mrs Foster which prayed much on her mind'.[165] Ann Treanor had recently returned home after having spent six months as an inmate in the Clones poorhouse. The dread of 'being put out of her place played so much on her mind' that she put an end to her life by cutting her own throat.[166] As a consequence of the quarter-acre clause, presumably all Treanor had left was her cottage and up to a quarter of an acre of land, which was not enough to live on.

PEAK DISTRESS IN THE GAOLS: DECEMBER 1849

While the populations of some of the Monaghan workhouses began to wane after July 1849, the Monaghan gaol saw a significant increase in inmates throughout the year. Inquests at the gaol captured deaths from the spread of disease on otherwise healthy inmates, and elderly pauper debtors with pre-existing conditions.[167]

---

160 Ibid., p. 26. Waddell was Hopes' land agent but Hanna was employed as well to manage evictions. **161** CB1, no. 4.87, Bernard Kelly, 29 June 1847. Kelly was a tenant of Charles Hopes living in the townland of Coleshill; CB1, no. 63.82, Thomas Chessar, 11 June 1847; CB1, no. 64.83, Margaret Chessar, 12 June 1847; CB1, no. 287.5, Jane Hanna, Coleshill 23 Apr. 1852. The inquest documented that the discord between the Hanna and Marron families was as a result of the former being evicted. **162** Crossman, *Politics, pauperism and power*, p. 72. **163** *NS*, 15 Sept. 1849. **164** *Dublin Weekly Nation*, 22 Sept. 1849. **165** CB1, no. 8.199, Ann Treanor, 2 Nov. 1849. **166** Ibid. **167** CB1, no. 2.170, Mary Hughes, 16 Mar. 1849; CB1, no. 3.172, Mathew Cassidy, 24 Mar. 1849; CB1, no. 21.190, William Barker, 25 June 1849; CB1, no. 5.196, George Smith, 1 Sept. 1849; CB1, no. 7.198, Ann Martin, 4 Oct. 1849; CB1, no. 17.298, Andrew English, 18 Dec. 1849; CB1, no. 18.209, John Reidy, 19 Dec. 1849; CB1, no. 6.217, Silvester Gartland, 27 Mar. 1850; CB1, George McMeighan, 2 July 1850.

By October 1849, the inspectors general report stated that although the gaol was built to accommodate 97 inmates, there were 39 more inmates since the last inspection, bringing the population to a total of 213; however, the number had reached a high point of 319 earlier that year.[168] The number of pauper debtor inmates had decreased from 29 per cent to 10 per cent of the total prison population. In 1849, the largest class in the gaol population were 146 convicted and accused felons.[169] While the population of the gaol remained high throughout 1850, the reduction in the number of paupers at the gaol reflected the start of the end of the crisis. The changing composition of the inmates in gaol also provided some indication of potential social changes to come.

DEATH INSIDE THE WORKHOUSE

Despite the high excess mortality in Irish workhouses during the Famine, relatively few coroners' inquests were conducted inside workhouses. During a parliamentary debate on a coroners bill in the House of Commons on 28 May 1851, Dublin MP John Reynolds stated that there were over a thousand persons dying from want of food within the walls of the workhouses each week but,

> no inquests were held because those who had the government of the workhouse did not wish ... to put the union to the expense, and they did not wish to expose the malpractices that occurred, lest they be censured by the public.[170]

A government report from 84 Poor Law unions stated that only 225 inquests were conducted on workhouse inmates from 1848 to 1850.[171] Waddell conducted just seven inquests on workhouse inmates in those years. Evidence suggests that because death in the workhouses was considered 'normal', newspapers and government reports provided public transparency, and only the most unusual circumstances would require investigation by the coroner. Using Waddell's casebook, the circumstances surrounding such deaths are examined, some which cannot be directly linked to Famine conditions. One such inquest captured the death of an inmate at the Clones poorhouse, Darby Ferguson, who was shot by Robert Little, a collector of poor rates who was part of a hunting party that included Mr William

---

168 POI, *Twenty-seventh report on the general state of prisons in Ireland 1848, with appendices*, pp 62–4, HC 1849 (1069) xxvi, 373; POI, *Twenty-eighth report of the inspectors general on the general state of prisons of Ireland 1849, with appendices*, p. 7, p. 60, HC 1850 (1229) xxix, 305. 169 Ibid. 170 Hansard 3, cxvii, 28 May 1851, cc 100–13. 171 *A return of the number and dates of any coroners' inquests that have been held on the bodies of any paupers that have died in the workhouses of any of the Unions in Ireland, in the years 1848, 1849 and 1850*, p. 1, p. 2, HC 1851 (448) l, 387. Just 84 unions participated in the return. The total number of inquests per year was as follows: 61 (1848), 73 (1849) and 91 (1850). Two inquests in Clones, conducted by Waddell on 24 Jan. and 26 Oct. 1848, did not appear in the government report and have been added to the total for Co. Monaghan.

Shegog, clerk of the Poor Law guardians.[172] The coroner's inquest found that the gun was accidentally fired within the hallway of the lodge on the workhouse premises.[173] Other inquests included a person who died shortly after his arrival, a young man who drowned while cleaning the workhouse cesspool, and an investigation of infanticide at Clones workhouse that resulted in finding the mother, Elizabeth Boyland, guilty of manslaughter.[174] Witness testimony revealed that while the healthy child was just 12 days old, Boyland had shared with a fellow inmate that, 'if it weren't for the child, she would be in America'.[175] Of the remains in one of Clones workhouse's burial yards, 18.6 per cent were of juveniles (under the age of 17) and none were of infants.[176] The absence of infants' remains suggests that such deaths may have been rare, and correlates with the findings of Waddell's casebook.

Another one of the rare inquests taken by Waddell inside a workhouse during the Famine revealed the inadequate medical treatment available to inmates and the poor conditions behind its walls. The Cootehill Poor Law Union, located in Co. Cavan, supported four Monaghan electoral districts – Aghabog, Cormeen, Dawson's Grove and Drum – that were a part of the northern coroner's district covered by Waddell. In February 1850, at the Cootehill auxiliary workhouse in Drum, inmate Catherine Connolly had woken up in the middle of the night complaining of a great pain in her head accompanied with vomiting from her mouth and nose, and a few hours later, her face turned black and she died.[177] Waddell noted in his casebook that the quantity of food she had been getting was sufficient, even describing it as 'excellent and sufficient to maintain health and strength'; yet, the format in which he captured the inquest was unusual.[178] Each witness provided their mark or signed their name next to their testimony inside the casebook. The testimony of the matron of the workhouse, Miss Letitia Thompson, included her statement that there was no medical attendant or nurse, nor even a messenger onsite to send for a medical attendant at the Cootehill workhouse which was four miles away.[179] She proceeded to explain the over-complicated and inefficient bureaucracy. A messenger was sent daily from the Cootehill workhouse to the Drum auxiliary to record the number of inmates at Drum. Should an inmate need medical attention, the messenger then returned to the workhouse to gain permission to bring an inmate from Drum. If approved, he would be sent back to Drum to retrieve the inmate and bring them back to Cootehill, where they would receive treatment. The testimony of Dr John Taylor provided further condemning evidence about the failings of the Drum workhouse. Waddell asked Dr Taylor, 'Do you consider the inmates of Drum auxiliary workhouse receive sufficient care and attention?'[180]

172 CB1, no. 18.187, Darby Ferguson, 12 June 1849; NS, 23 June 1849. 173 Ibid. 174 CB1, no. 10.126, Pat Connolly, 24 Jan. 1848; CB1, no. 6.197, Patrick Calaghan, 2 Sept. 1849; CB1, no. 11.160, Thomas Wright, 26 Oct. 1848. 175 Ibid. 176 Linda G. Lynch, 'Death and burial in the Poor Law union workhouses in Ireland', *Journal of Irish Archaeology*, 23 (2014), p. 193. 'A mass burial site, the Clones Famine (workhouse) graveyard is believed to hold up to 5,000 unidentified bodies, therefore these findings are only a sample from which to draw conclusions.' 177 CB1, no. 21.212, Catherine Connolly, 19 Feb. 1850. 178 Ibid. 179 Ibid. 180 Ibid.

Taylor replied that since his services had been discontinued on 31 December 1849, neither he nor any other medical man had attended there, so there were 200 to 300 inmates in the workhouse who had received no medical attention.[181]

Catherine Connolly's inquest exposes the inadequate conditions in at least some workhouses and provides evidence that may explain the deaths of other inmates of the workhouse, as detailed in Waddell's inquests. The Connolly inquest, one of the last related to Famine conditions taken by Waddell, is also representative of the power of the investigation by the coroner and jury. It is a significant addition to the body of evidence that negligence and poor decision making of the local landed elite contributed to paupers' deaths during the Famine.

THE ABOLITION OF THE CORONER'S OFFICE: THE POLITICS OF THE GRAND JURY

While the financial pressures on the local elite and landowning classes to pay for the Famine continued to increase, and at a time when the death rates remained high, a suggestion was made to abolish the coroner's office. On 10 August 1848, the English Catholic Co. Cork Liberal MP Thomas Chisholm Anstey (1816–73) submitted two petitions to the House of Commons – on behalf of the high sheriff of Cork and the grand jury of Sligo, respectively.[182] The first petition prayed for an amendment to the Irish Poor Law stating that 'they viewed with great alarm the increase of able bodied paupers'.[183] The appeal for Poor Law reform indicated their claimed inability to fund the relief of the poor. The second petition prayed for the abolition of the office of coroner in Ireland.[184] They claimed that eliminating it would save the cess payers of Ireland £25,000 per annum.[185] This suggests that the overwhelmingly conservative Protestant landholders on the grand juries of Cork and Sligo were looking to reduce costs and the increase in inquests held on paupers was viewed as unnecessary.

Several conservative newspapers throughout the country carried the story, including the *Dublin Evening Mail*, which declared that in this 'present stage of society, [the coroner] is a supernumary and useless functionary'.[186] The article proposed that the coroner's duties could be left to the discretion of the country gentlemen, local justices, resident magistrates or constabulary officers and encouraged every county in Ireland to adopt the petition.[187] Referring to the coroner's office with contempt, the newspaper quoted Shakespeare's *Hamlet*, with hopes that soon they might celebrate the finale of the 'Crowner's Quest Law'.[188] In Act 5, Scene 1 of *Hamlet*, two gravediggers are in a conversation about the recent suicide of Ophelia, a wealthy woman.[189] Religious doctrine dictated that suicides not

---

181 Ibid. 182 Sidney Lee, revised by K.D. Reynolds, 'Anstey, Thomas Chisholm (1816–1873)', *ODNB*. 183 *Hansard 3*, ci, 10 Aug. 1848, cc 54–5; *FJ*, 12 Aug. 1848. 184 Ibid. 185 Ibid. 186 *DEM*, 21 Aug. 1848; *Kerry Evening Post*, 23 Aug. 1848; *Mayo Constitution*, 29 Aug. 1848; *Sligo Journal*, 1 Sept. 1848. 187 Ibid. 188 *DEM*, 21 Aug. 1848. 189 Johnathan Bate and Eric Rasmussen (eds), *William Shakespeare: Hamlet* (Hampshire, 2008), p. 121.

receive a Christian burial. Although suicide is also against the law, the king insisted she be buried in consecrated ground in the church graveyard. The comparison of the scene from Hamlet to the Irish coroner highlights the paradox of the legalities of the coroner's duties and social inequality. One might consider that the conservative Irish elite saw the role of the coroner as an English office, one imposed upon them, and one which represented British law and authority.

The view of the *Dublin Evening Mail* was shared also by a grand juror and landowner from Kildare, the Hon. E. Lawless. He wrote a letter to the editor of the *Leinster Express*, supporting the claims of the Sligo grand jury as well as acknowledging that the Dublin grand jury had called for abolition of the office. However, the liberal editor of the paper, Michael Carey, convincingly argued against the petitions to amend the Poor Law and abolish coroners. While 81 coroners received average payments of £100 per year, their expenses (costs for running an inquest) would still have to be spent by the local magistrate or person assigned such duties. The national savings of £8,100 a year from eliminating coroners was negligible. Carey stated that it was an injustice to the freeholders of the country to recommend the abolition of 'the only paid officer to which they still have right of presentation'.[190] Additionally, as for the qualifications and background of coroners, he stated that conservatives were too anxious to have the office filled by 'gentlemen' and said,

> Our contemporary seems to forget, that the present law requires a qualification of considerable extent of freehold or fee-simple inheritance, thereby providing ... for the election of candidates for the office *sans peur et reproche*; and it is only in places [like] ... Sligo, [that] the electors, by a misuse of their discretion, returned an improper person ...[191]

It was revealed that the Sligo coroner had recently been charged of defrauding the grand jury by billing for fictitious inquests and fees for a deceased medical practitioner. He was convicted and transported.[192] Additionally, the persuasive and convincing arguments of a *Leinster Express* article (which was republished in the *King's County Chronicle*) were shared by the King's Co. grand jury, who declined to support the petition to abolish the coroner's office.[193] In a separate article, the *King's County Chronicle* published a short piece of its own on the matter, stating that they agreed fully with the views put forward in the *Leinster Express*, and were convinced that 'the more the question is scrutinized, the stronger the reasons will appear for maintaining this ancient and useful office'.[194]

By contrast, on 16 September 1848, the *Northern Standard* published a report on a meeting of the Monaghan grand jury's finance committee, which announced its alignment with the Dublin grand jury and called for the abolition of the office

---

190 *Leinster Express*, 2 Sept. 1848.   191 Ibid. *Sans peur et reproche*: without fear and reproach.   192 *King's County Chronicle*, 6 Sept. 1848.   193 Ibid., 13 Sept. 1848.   194 Ibid.

of coroner.[195] They evaluated the mileage fees submitted by the coroners and, with no explanation, imposed a reduction in the reimbursement of mileage due to Waddell and Swanzy of £3 3s. and £1 11s. 3d., respectively.[196] When considering both men were from the local elite and fitted the ideal qualifications for gentlemen coroners, refusing payment of their full bill again demonstrates how the values of the Monaghan conservatives undermined their authority as coroners. It also made a political statement as to the Monaghan grand jury's resentment of the imposition of the coroner's office on them by the government.

CONCLUSION

The work of the coroner exposed the exceptional circumstances of paupers who died inside and outside local county gaols and workhouses, directly as a result of government legislation, specifically the Gregory clause and the £4 clause. Overcrowding and disease contributed towards the deaths of many inside the institutions. The inquests identified in Waddell's casebook show that persons unable (due to restrictive criteria) or unwilling to gain entry into the workhouse died directly as a result of not having access to outdoor relief as well as a lack of proper employment. That Co. Monaghan conservatives sitting on the grand jury, the board of superintendents and the boards of guardians often made decisions based on cost-saving rather than life-saving is supported by the evidence in individual inquests. The inquests, when reviewed collectively and sequentially, expose how the Poor Law failed to support those who it was meant to keep alive.

---

195 *NS*, 16 Sept. 1848. The finance committee was comprised of two former high sheriffs of Monaghan, George Forster, second baronet of Coolderry, and landlord F.D. Lucas of Castleshane, land agent for the Bath estate; Tristram Kennedy; Lieutenant Colonel Arthur Gambell Lewis of Scotstown; and Kilkenny and Monaghan magistrate Edward Golding of Gowran Castle, Kilkenny.   **196** Ibid.

PART III
After the Famine

5

Public welfare and justice

> Liberalism is trust of the people tempered by prudence. Conservatism is distrust of the people tempered by fear.[1]
> —William Ewart Gladstone, 1866

> Persons that belonged to societies that were the curse of this land ought not to be in the position of sub-sheriffs to empanel jurors ... Men whose every feeling was poisoned with prejudice and with hatred of their fellow men, and who lived as foreigners in a land which they should love as their native land, were unfit for such positions.[2]
> —Denis Caulfield Heron, 1869

After the Famine, Waddell's inquests reflected the behaviours and circumstances of a society no longer suffering through a humanitarian crisis. Instead, these deaths reveal abuses of authority and power. They are examined within the national political landscape of Ireland and reflect the social and political climate in Co. Monaghan. Waddell's personal and professional circumstances are used to gain a deeper understanding of his and his family's influence and social standing in the community. His work as coroner put him in conflict with members of the local elite, as it sometimes required him to reveal injustices and wrong-doing, which was directly opposed to their political and social interests, and in some instances, his own. The great majority of inquests captured by Waddell in the 1850s and 1860s are accidental deaths or those with a medical cause, unconnected to crime; but the focus of this chapter is to explore a sample of cases where a death had taken place and institutional power contributed to it. The composition and behaviour of the judiciary and trial juries are examined, as well as the impact, if any, of coroners' inquests on convictions or acquittals in cases of politically motivated murder. The investigation of familial and sectarian murders in Co. Monaghan provides an opportunity to determine whether the work of the coroner influenced the outcome of criminal murder trials.

---

[1] *Merthyr Telegraph and General Advertiser for the Iron Districts of South Wales*, 7 Apr. 1866. [2] *Evening Freeman*, 8 Mar. 1869.

POST-FAMINE IRELAND: A NEW LANDSCAPE

Post-Famine Ireland experienced significant social changes, including within the family unit. The age of those engaging in marriage had risen, and fewer marriages and births were taking place than in the pre-Famine years. A static death rate once again resumed and high levels of emigration continued.[3] Subdivision and inheritance of land for all sons declined, with usually only the eldest son taking possession of the parents' land.[4] As for management of the land, farmers invested in livestock more than grain and they responded to changes in the economy with more commercial awareness.[5] The social landscape had changed dramatically for small landholding tenants in rural society who had been of a higher social standing than the majority of agricultural labourers prior to the Famine but who now found themselves at the 'bottom of the landholding hierarchy'.[6] The relationships between remaining landlords and tenants after the Famine were often a struggle. Post-Famine society was measured by numbers of evictions and levels of rents, observation of the custom of – and redemption value of – tenant right, estate expenditure and investment, and agrarian outrages. The general tenant population in Ireland was still not represented fairly in local government or in the administration of justice, which reinforced a sense of oppression and unfairness.

Exacerbating feelings of uncertainty, several changes in government took place in the years after the Famine. Russell's Liberal Whig government was replaced by the Conservative earl of Derby (1799–1869) for ten months from February 1852 to December 1852, and then the government changed again, resting for just two years until January 1855 with the Peelite Conservative earl of Aberdeen (1784–1860) serving as prime minister in a coalition administration.[7] The premiership again changed hands to Whig Liberal Lord Palmerston (1784–1865), who helped bring some political stability and economic recovery to Ireland for the next three years.[8] Unfortunately, Palmerston, who had inherited an Irish estate of 10,000 acres in Sligo, did not support tenant right and while he had been a supporter of Catholic emancipation, his views pivoted around British interests that he felt would naturally have priority over those of Ireland.[9] The changes in government leadership continued for the next two decades, but the governments regularly implemented new legislation, which at times exacerbated the tensions of inequality in Irish society.

Partisan antagonisms of Orangemen and Ribbonmen during the Famine had been heightened by two significant events, the battle at Dolly's Brae in Co. Down in 1849, with reports of up to thirty men killed, and the reaction of government to the conflict that resulted in the Party Processions Act (1850). The act was one of

---

3 Lee, *The modernisation of Irish society*, p. 1.   4 Ibid., p. 3.   5 Ibid., p. 11.   6 Vaughan, *Landlords and tenants in mid-Victorian Ireland*, p. 29.   7 Martin McElroy, 'Stanley, Edward George Geoffrey Smith 14th earl of Derby', *DIB*.   8 David Steele, 'Temple, Henry John, third Viscount Palmerston (1784–1865)', *ODNB*.   9 Roland Quinault, 'Victorian prime ministers and Ireland' in Roger Swift and Christine Kinealy (eds), *Politics and power in Victorian Ireland* (Dublin, 2006), p. 57.

the last major pieces of legislation implemented and passed by Russell before he left office in February 1852. It banned Orange marching, and the Orange Order were no longer allowed to manifest themselves as a group publicly. The resentments that followed contributed to uncertainty about land reform and significant anxiety about the future of the landed Protestant interest, while concerns regarding Palmerston's policy towards the Catholic church increased tensions within most local communities that were already polarized. These sectarian tensions fuelled agrarian violence in many parts of the county.

A wave of agrarian crime that took place in south-east Ulster between 1849 and 1852 was followed by several hangings for attempted murder.[10] In July 1853 in Co. Monaghan, Thomas Hodgins and Patrick Breen were found guilty and given a sentence of hanging for conspiracy to murder the Bath estate bailiffs McArdle and McMahon.[11] The murder of Templetown land agent Thomas Douglas Bateson in December 1851, which made national headlines, resulted in the hanging of three men in March 1854.[12] Death by hanging was imposed when the crime of attempted murder or wilful murder was believed to have been committed by men who were part of the Ribbon conspiracy. Evidence of jury-packing suggests that the hangings were a result of the political power of the conservative landlords who used their influence over procedures to attempt to construct justice. While the Protestant local elite retained the role of high sheriff and places on grand juries, appointments to jury membership and participation of laymen in criminal trials also continued to discriminate against Catholics and small-holding tenants. Juries composed of a selection of the Protestant elite did not always make decisions based on the sentiment of the general public, something which led to failures in civil justice, corruption and disillusionment.[13]

Land agent, magistrate and Monaghan grand juror Edward Golding testified before the Select Committee on Outrages in Ireland in 1852. He stated,

> It is exceedingly difficult to convey to you how that [jury trials] operates in Ireland. I do not think that they look upon trial by jury in Ireland so much as the administration of justice, as that it is rather a lottery. A man gets off because somebody is on the jury; or he gets off because some important witness has got out of the way; or a man gets off because a good alibi case has been set up. They do not look upon the institution in Ireland of trial by jury as they do in England; they do not think it is the palladium of their liberties.[14]

Golding's testimony reflects the attitudes of the local elite, who found it too difficult to convict people and so implemented measures in order to impose convictions.

10 Hoppen, *Elections, politics and society in Ireland, 1832–1885*, p. 370; Vaughan, *Landlords and tenants in mid-Victorian Ireland*, p. 138; Vaughan, *Murder trials in Ireland, 1836–1914*, pp 22, 58. 11 *Dublin Weekly Nation*, 23 July 1853. 12 Vaughan, *Murder trials in Ireland, 1836–1914*, p. 58; *NS*, 13 Aug. 1853. 13 Howlin, *Juries in Ireland*, p. 5. 14 *Report from the select committee on outrages (Ireland)*, p. 91, HC 1852 (438) xiv, 1.

His knowledge of jury-packing and witness tampering provides further evidence of politicized jury trials. The grip that the conservative elite had on the justice system in Monaghan (Hoppen referred to them as 'a Tory monopoly') implies collusion not simply on the part of Ribbonmen from the county.[15] The Orange Order and many members of the local elite in Monaghan were, in fact, one in the same.

The Orange lodges in Co. Monaghan remained independent from the Grand Orange Lodge of Ireland from the turn of the century until June 1849. The evidence suggests that the Orange members of Co. Monaghan supported their own interests in their local communities and county government and shared their own ideals of justice. In July 1848, the *Northern Standard* reported on the Twelfth of July celebrations and identified several members of the local elite who were 'sterling friends of Orangeism', highlighting by name grand jury member and Templetown land agent Thomas Douglas Bateson; local landowner, magistrate Thomas Lucas; solicitor E.P. Morphy; 'and many more gentry of the neighbourhood'.[16] The grand secretary of the Monaghan Orange Lodge, and editor of the *Northern Standard*, Arthur W. Holmes, was also named.[17] Reports also stated that while they were not authorized to print the names of recent converts to the Monaghan Orange Order, they were comprised of thirteen members of the Monaghan grand jury and five clergymen from the established church.[18] Additional description included the information that they were 'men of the highest rank, the greatest extent of property, the most enlarged and refined views, and the greatest talent in the county of Monaghan'.[19]

Co. Monaghan Grand Orange Lodge minutes were not made public but identified those who joined the society on 14 July 1848.[20] They included County Monaghan MPs Sir George Forster and Charles Powell Leslie, along with grand jury members James Hamilton, Thomas Coote, Thomas Douglas Bateson, André Allan Murray, Edward Golding, Richard Mayne and William Murray, as well as landowners Henry Mitchell, Fitzherbert Dacre Lucas and Thomas Lucas.[21] This group supposedly had been operating in the shadows for many years. However, their public image and the reported activity in the local paper contradicts this belief.[22] Rather, it indicates a high degree of transparency as to their support of the organization and political beliefs, as well as their opposition to tenant and Catholic rights and liberal politics. It is likely that the 'shadows' are a belief or reference to influencing justice or other activities that undermined liberal contemporaries. The evidence suggests that those men publicly recognized as Orangemen, such as Bateson, accepted the risk of personal harm and the threat of murder.

In opposition to the Protestant landowning elite control, the Tenant League in Monaghan was formed to put forward demands for fair rents, the free sale of tenant interest in their landholdings (also known as the 'Ulster custom'), and fixity

---

[15] Hoppen, *Elections, politics and society in Ireland, 1832–1885*, p. 281. [16] *NS*, 15 July 1848. [17] Ibid. [18] *NS*, 22 July 1848. [19] *NS*, 15 July 1848. [20] *County Monaghan Grand Orange Lodge minute book*, 14 July 1848 (Schomberg House, Belfast). [21] Ibid.; *Newry Telegraph*, 18 July 1848; *NS*, 15 July 1848. [22] McClelland, 'Orangeism in County Monaghan', p. 393.

of tenure.[23] Founded in August 1850, nationally the group was comprised of and represented all creeds of tenants. However, in Monaghan it was dominated by Catholics and Presbyterians.[24] They held several large gatherings in Co. Monaghan, the largest of which was reported in Ballybay in October 1850 and had more than 12,000 attendees.[25] While the Tenant League had a significant number of members and was supported by leading liberal politicians including Charles Gavan Duffy (1816–1903) and William Sharman Crawford (1781–1861), local landowners and agents were believed to have discouraged tenants from membership.[26] Livingstone stated that landlords and agents used tactics that included terror and bribes in the form of rent reduction.[27] Bath estate agent William Steuart Trench told Lord Bath that he dispossessed those tenants on the estate who were guilty of conspiracies, 'but whom the ordinary channels of law could not reach'.[28]

In 1852, the political landscape in Monaghan was dominated by the Protestant local elite, and the Conservative MPs Charles Powell Leslie and Sir George Forster defeated the Tenant League supporter and owner of the *Freeman's Journal* Dr John Gray in the general election that year.[29] Conservatives collaborated to secure their position. Minutes of the Orange Order meeting in Monaghan town captured the commitment of the members to the cause of supporting their candidates for election,

> That this Grand Lodge is of [the] opinion that every effort should be made by every Orangeman in this County to secure the triumphant return of Col. Leslie and Sir George Forster, and that it is the bonded duty of our Brethren throughout the County to do everything in their power to attain this object.
>
> Approved, H.S. Johnston[30]

The local elite known to have pressured their tenants to vote for Leslie and Forster included Edward Lucas, Captain Richardson, Charles French, Lord Rossmore and Matthew Anketel.[31] After the election several reports were published in national newspapers about the retribution of landlords on tenants who had voted for Gray against their instructions. In August 1852, a letter from Henry de Burgh of Clones to his tenant, John Murphy, was published in the *Dublin Evening Post* and carried in newspapers across Ireland. De Burgh wrote to Murphy that he had not voted per his wishes, and so he wanted the rent immediately, in full.[32] Other victims

---

23 Ibid. 24 Livingstone, *The Monaghan story*, p. 226. 25 *NS*, 5 Oct. 1850; *FJ*, 3 Oct. 1850. 26 *FJ*, 3 Oct. 1850. 27 Livingstone, *The Monaghan story*, p. 227. 28 Longleat, Bath estate papers, Report accounts and rental of the estate of the most noble, the marquis of Bath situate in the barony of Farney and County of Monaghan for the year ending 1 Mar. 1855 drawn up by the agent William Steuart Trench (1 Mar. 1855), p. 1. 29 B.M. Walker (ed.), *Parliamentary election results in Ireland, 1801–1922* (Dublin, 1978), p. 85. 30 County Monaghan Grand Orange Lodge minute book, 1852 (Schomberg House, Belfast). 31 *FJ*, 2 Feb. 1852. 32 *Dublin Evening Post*, 21 Aug. 1852.

of retribution included two tenants on the Leslie estate who also voted for the tenant right candidate: Presbyterian minister and friend of Maria and William Charles Waddell, Revd John Rankin and a Mr Joseph Glass.[33] It was reported in the *Freeman's Journal* that Leslie demanded Rankin and Glass pay their half-yearly rent immediately or be evicted.[34] These men dared not to vote for Protestant landholding interests, and the response from Leslie shows how support for the Tenant League from some Presbyterians, men like Waddell, would have posed a problem. Land agent of the Shirley estate George Morant was said to have stolen 180 cattle in total from all the electors who voted for Dr Gray and bragged that he did it to make the point that 'priests are political vampires' (supporters of Gray).[35] Gray's defeat not only ended the Tenant League in Monaghan, but also reinforced the fact that neither middle-class Catholics nor the tenantry had any power or representation in local government.[36] The chasm between the landlords and tenants in regards to their respective rights became more pronounced.[37] It would be more than a decade before liberal opposition again formally challenged the Protestant elite at election.

WADDELL'S LIFE: 1853–5

With the Famine over, the 1851 census revealed a loss of nearly 60,000 inhabitants in Co. Monaghan, which had seen a decline in population from 200,442 in 1841 to 141,758 and a decrease in the number of houses from 35,072 to 25,742.[38] Unsurprisingly, the townlands owned by the Waddell families showed dramatic population declines. These were located within the Poor Law electoral division of Caddagh, an area that had been heavily invested in the linen trade in years past and would have retained a generous number of landless labourers and cottiers. It lost 32 per cent of its inhabitants, its population declining from 3,057 to 2,060.[39] Circumstantial evidence suggests that these persons were swept from the land by eviction and emigration, or death. Waddell saw a significant number of people disappear from his land and that of his family. By 1851, the townland of Lisnaveane, the location of Waddell's residence, saw the number of inhabitants decrease from 105 to 50. Cordevlis South saw a decline from 71 to 45, and Drumgavny from 85 to 56.[40]

There were winners and losers from the Famine, and one group who could be classed as winners were those who could afford to purchase the land of

---

33 Letters of correspondence from Maria to William Charles refer to John Rankin and members of the Rankin family on several occasions: Maria to William Charles, 19 July 1830; Maria to William Charles, 25 July 1830; Maria to William Charles, 28 Aug. 1830; Maria to William Charles, 21 Jan. 1836; Maria to William Charles, 15 Sept. 1837; Maria to William Charles, 26 June 1839; Maria to William Charles, 3 Dec. 1849; James Waddell to William Charles, 3 Aug. 1877 (Hope Collection). 34 *FJ*, 5 Oct. 1852. 35 *FJ*, 28 Aug. 1852. 36 Livingstone, *The Monaghan story*, pp 229, 234. 37 Rushe, *History of Monaghan for two hundred years*, p. 285. 38 *Census of Ireland for the year 1851*, 259 [1575] HC 1852–3, xcii, 285. 39 Ibid. 40 Ibid.

neighbours or family members to enhance the size of their farms.[41] Sales under the Encumbered Estates Act after 1849 were compared to Darwin's survival of the fittest in that the land sold was purchased by those who were in a strong financial position and who believed a bright prosperous future lay ahead of them.[42] Of five thousand property buyers under the act, 95 per cent were the younger sons of the Irish elite, along with solicitors and shopkeepers who had done well for themselves during the Famine.[43] Landlordism became stronger (at least temporarily) for those with the means to persevere and avail of the opportunity that presented itself.

While the inability of tenants to pay rents and the impotence of landlords to collect them led to the bankruptcy of over 10 per cent of Irish landlords between 1845 and 1849, Waddell seems to have been relatively debt-free and financially stable. He appears to have been one of the 'winners' during the Famine, as demonstrated by the actions taken to improve his property portfolio through private negotiation. In June 1852, Waddell renewed the 1698 lease on the three family townlands, or tates, known as Drumgavny, Cordevlis and Lisnaveane, held by Viscount Massereene of Antrim Castle, which gave him practical ownership and managerial supervision. The following year, in October 1853, his cousin John Jackson Waddell (1817–99) of Clover Hill House, Lisnaveane, sold his rights to twelve acres of land and the house to his cousin Alexander Waddell, for £225.[44] By July 1855, Alexander had died and his rights were then passed on to his heir, William Waddell, who maintained a residence at Clover Hill House with the twelve acres adjoining, paying William Charles Waddell the rent in arrears, plus an annual £13 19s. 11d. to be split into two payments on two separate gale days.[45] The Waddell families of Lisnaveane did not offer to sell land through the encumbered estates court, which suggests that their lands were unencumbered, and they stayed financially stable through this difficult period. They engaged in transfers and purchases of lands and homesteads within the family, from which Waddell himself benefited.

While Waddell continued to increase his property portfolio, his political and social status was enhanced by his uncle Charles Hopes, who remained a key figure in Monaghan throughout the 1850s. His position reflects the exceptional social status of the Hopes and Waddell Presbyterian families, as they were able to move between the communities of south Ulster and the elite of the city of Dublin. Although Charles Hopes' primary residence prior to 1855 was in Dublin, he was a member of the Monaghan grand jury and he was also the lessor of nearly 700 acres in Monaghan. He lived at South Hill Demense, a most desirable residence on 11 acres and 36 perches with an extensive lawn, grounds and sizable house, located

41 R.V. Comerford, 'Ireland 1850–70: post-Famine and mid-Victorian' in Vaughan (ed.), *A new history of Ireland*, v, p. 385. 42 K. Theodore Hoppen, *Ireland since 1800, conflict and conformity* (2nd ed.; London, 2013), p. 94. 43 Lee, *The modernisation of Irish society*, p. 37. 44 Massareene to Waddell, 1852 (ROD, deed no. 29/269/768); Massareene to Waddell, 1852 (ROD, deed no. 29/268/767); Waddell to Waddell, 1853 (ROD, deed no. 27/238). 45 Waddell to Waddell, 1855 (ROD, deed no. 25/29/635). Gale day was the day the rent was due. The deed states that William Waddell will pay William Charles Waddell half the rent on 1 May and half on 1 November each year.

between Merrion Avenue and Booterstown Lane, Rathdown in Dublin, which he rented at £150 per annum from Mrs Elizabeth Pittar.[46] The Hopes and Waddell families' conservative Presbyterian politics led them to support the local Protestant elite, a characteristic of Presbyterian communities of south Ulster that differentiated them from the less powerful Presbyterians in other parts of rural Ulster. Hopes was rewarded for his power and wealth with positions including grand jury member in Monaghan in 1847, 1849, 1851–6 and 1859–62.[47] He was also appointed high sheriff in 1853.[48] With such influence, Hopes' alliances would be shared by the wider family circle and their contribution to the stable gentry community demonstrated through their political patronage.

JURISDICTIONAL AUTHORITY: CONSTRUCTING JUSTICE

When Templetown land agent, Monaghan grand jury member and Orangeman Thomas Douglas Bateson was murdered in December 1851 it dominated headlines throughout the United Kingdom, captured the attention of the queen and government and instilled fear in grand juries, landowners and upholders of the status quo. The Bateson murder was one of the most widely publicized and controversial of its time, due to reports that it was the result of a Ribbon conspiracy. While no evidence was offered that indicated the killing had a sectarian motive, the Monaghan grand jury, and local and national media reported that it was the result of actions of secret societies circulating in the area. The land agent had been severely beaten and left to die on the side of a road on the estate and a £3,000 reward was offered for the capture of his murderers.[49]

At the assizes in March 1852, four months after the murder, Judge Louis Perrin (1782–1864) requested to speak to the grand jury. The liberal Catholic Perrin, former sergeant-at-law and Dublin lawyer, had knowledge of Co. Monaghan and a strong opinion of the management and practices of Monaghan conservative elite. He had served as a Whig MP for Monaghan in 1832–5, having won his election with support from the Monaghan Independent Club (of which Waddell's father was a member) and had faced great opposition from local conservatives during a very personally expensive race.[50] Having returned to Monaghan as a crown court circuit judge in the Bateson case twenty years later, Perrin spoke out against unjust and illegal local practices. His viewpoint and political position were representative of similar criticisms from judges across Ireland. Perrin had two objectives, the first of which was to expose the lack of evidence to support the rumours and accusations that a secret society was in operation in the county. He highlighted four cases he tried in Co. Monaghan where charges were pressed as committed under

---

46 NAI, Landed Estates Court Rentals 1850–85, xxxiv, 80. Hopes lived at Rockville, Mount Merrion Avenue, Dublin, after 1855.   47 *Vindicator*, 27 Feb. 1847; *BN*, 6 Mar. 1849; *LS*, 6 Mar. 1851; *Belfast Mercury*, 28 Feb. 1852; *Longford Journal*, 4 Mar. 1854; *Evening Freeman*, 2 Mar. 1855; *NS*, 1 Mar. 1856, 12 Mar. 1859, 2 Mar. 1861, 2 Mar. 1862; *Saunders's News-Letter*, 1 Mar. 1860.   48 *NS*, 12 Feb. 1853.   49 Outrage papers (NAI, Monaghan, 1851/244).   50 Desmond McCabe, 'Louis Perrin', *DIB*.

the Whiteboy Act, yet none showed evidence of such an organized group.[51] The liberal *Dundalk Democrat* supported Perrin's argument that there was no evidence of secret societies in Monaghan and that aspersions had been cast and 'imposed by vile slanderers of the people', the Monaghan grand jury and the prosecution.[52] His second objective was to expose the illegal and unacceptable list of potential jurors for the Bateson trial. The editor of the *Northern Standard* highlighted that only a thousand names were submitted when there were over four thousand qualified and eligible jurors.[53] Perrin severely reprimanded the magistrates and barony cess collectors for panel-packing and jury-packing but his efforts proved futile,[54] as Monaghan local elites still ordered the executions of men suspected of being 'ribbonmen'. The relationships between the Monaghan local elite and the Orange Order became much more intertwined over the next two decades, which led to further instances of corruption and tampering of trial juries.

The real motive for Bateson's murder was most likely the oppression and anger of a few of the tenantry.[55] Bateson was an unsympathetic land agent, who worked for an unsympathetic landlord who did not reduce rents during the Famine and ordered evictions.[56] Many of the tenants on the Templetown estate were behind on their rent, some up to three years in arrears.[57] Authorities were determined to secure a conviction by any means necessary and their practices were questionable, particularly around collecting evidence and finding credible witnesses.[58] Although there were many arrested, the most notable results were the prosecutions of Owen and Francis Kelly, who were put on trial three times, concluding with Owen's acquittal in July 1852. Francis was held for seven more months, defended by the famous barrister and MP Issac Butt, and was finally released in February 1853. Convictions were secured for Bryan Grant and Neal Quin for Bateson's murder, and Patrick Coomey for being an accessory to the murder in March 1854.[59] The popular belief was that innocent men were charged, but the Monaghan grand juror, prosecutor and resident magistrate Charles Hunt, and other local conservatives, were determined to secure a conviction. Several others were arrested and released in March 1854 – just weeks before the hanging deaths of Grant, Quin and Coomey at Monaghan gaol – only after serving over two years in gaol awaiting trial.

Jury-packing, which was attempting to create a jury with sympathizers for one side, involved local officials revising the county jurors books, and in extreme circumstances, in divisive political trials, hand-picking jurors.[60] Panel-packing involved the high sheriff creating a list of preferred or 'competent' potential jurors to choose from.[61] The Bateson defendants at trial in March 1854 were allowed to challenge seventy-eight potential jurors, forty of whom were challenged

51 *NS*, 6 Mar. 1852. 52 *DD*, 6 Mar. 1852; *FJ*, 17 Dec. 1832. 53 *NS*, 6 Mar. 1852. 54 Livingstone, *The Monaghan story*, p. 234. 55 Michael McMahon, *The murder of Thomas Douglas Bateson, County Monaghan, 1851* (Dublin, 2016), p. 60. 56 Ibid., p. 60. 57 Ibid., p. 58. 58 Ibid., p. 62. 59 Ibid., p. 50; *FJ*, 29 Jan. 1852, 3 Feb. 1852, 30 Apr. 1852, 6 May 1852, 12 July 1852, 13 July 1853, 14 July 1853, 9 Mar. 1854, 10 Mar. 1854, 13 Apr. 1854. 60 Howlin, *Juries in Ireland*, pp 150–1. 61 Ibid., pp 26–7.

peremptorily (without cause), before a jury of twelve was finally selected.[62] The primary purpose for such a large number of rejections was to try to remove the jurors prioritized by the sheriff and the crown. However, one of the men on the jury who convicted Grant, Quin and Coomey was John Jackson Waddell, first cousin of Coroner Waddell and valued relation of High Sheriff Charles Hopes. John Jackson fitted the profile of the 'right type' of juror. To try to secure a conviction in an agrarian trial required members of respectable Protestant middle-class families, which in Monaghan could include Presbyterians. However, some men feared reprisals for their participation. John Jackson Waddell, who had just six months earlier sold his property and presumably cleared the family debt owed to his cousin William Charles, emigrated with his family that same year, after the trial concluded, to New South Wales, where he worked as a local magistrate.[63]

Although William Charles Waddell was aligned to the conservative politics of the grand jury and those of his cousin, John Jackson Waddell, he nevertheless carried out his duty and conducted investigations that exposed abuses of local power. Waddell's work as the coroner contributed to the Bateson case file as it exposed the injustice of the administration in pursuing convictions against men with little or no evidence. One man arrested and charged with Bateson's murder was 82-year-old Bernard Rooney, a feeble man, and a tenant of the Templetown estate. Resident Magistrate Hunt alleged that Rooney was part of a gang of Ribbonmen, along with others who were held under suspicion. Upon his incarceration in November 1852, defence council Peter McEvoy Gartlan, speaking at a hearing at the Monaghan gaol, argued that there was no evidence on which a grand jury could find a bill, and that keeping Rooney in custody defeated the ends of justice.[64] He added that should Rooney die in gaol, he would demand a coroner's inquest.[65] Hunt refused to release the prisoner, regardless of the absence of evidence.

Waddell's casebook contains Rooney's inquest taken at Monaghan gaol in October 1853. It says he had spent over a year incarcerated, having been charged with conspiracy to murder the late Thomas Douglas Bateson.[66] Although he was treated for gravel (kidney stones) his health declined rapidly over three weeks, and he died. The verdict of death was from advanced age and general debility accompanied with disease of the bladder.[67] The account of Rooney's death was not publicized in any local or national newspaper, perhaps deliberately so as not to expose the injustice of his imprisonment and stir up further tensions among the tenantry. The lack of transparency in the press as to Rooney's fate suggests a complicit relationship by which Waddell and the *Northern Standard* functioned to support the local elite. The trials and hangings for the Bateson murder contributed to the continuing disharmony within the social and political landscape of Co. Monaghan as well as the rise in both Orangeism and Ribbonism in primary areas of the county including Monaghan, Glaslough, Castleblayney and Farney.[68]

62 *NS*, 11 Mar. 1854. 63 *Sydney Morning Herald*, 21 Sept. 1899. 64 *DD*, 20 Nov. 1852. 65 Ibid. 66 CB1, no. 342.12, Brian Rooney, 5 Oct. 1853. He is listed as Brian, rather than Bernard, in the casebook. 67 Ibid. 68 Livingstone, *The Monaghan story*, pp 236–7.

MISMANAGEMENT EXPOSED: INFANT DEATH AT THE GAOL AND WORKHOUSE

The workhouse and gaol inmate numbers were reduced but a heavy burden still rested upon the landed class and ratepayers to fund their continual maintenance, including the employment of supporting staff (see Tables 11 and 12). As a result, local institutions were under continuous scrutiny for mismanagement and corruption as the government continued to impose regulation and legislation to ensure proper care of the inmate populace. Waddell's inquests revealing deaths that were

Table 11: Populations of workhouses supporting Co. Monaghan, 1853–5

Workhouse	Monaghan	Castleblayney	Carrickmacross	Clones	Cootehill
Initial capacity	900	600	500	600	800
June 1849	1784	2,000	1,581	1,601	2,979
January 1853	322	528	702	290	531
April 1853	315	473	619	259	495
July 1853	288	349		202	385
October 1853	176	223	206	131	236
January 1854	217	285	321	159	311
April 1854	216	243		168	257
July 1854	252	249	244	166	224
October 1854		169		110	163
January 1855	211	284		136	258
April 1855	205	267		158	
July 1855	195	225		143	
October 1855	224				

Sources: NS, 15 Jan., 16 Apr., 2 July, 19 Oct. 1853; 7 Jan., 29 Apr., 15 July, 7 Oct. 1854; 27 Jan., 21 Apr., 28 Apr., 21 July, 20 Oct. 1855; *DD*, 29 Jan., 30 Apr., 15 Oct. 1853; 14 Jan., 29 July 1854. Carrickmacross workhouse minute books, 1849 and 1853.

Table 12: Population of inmates, Co. Monaghan gaol, 1849–55

	Capacity	1849	1850	1851	1852	1853	1854	1855
Monaghan gaol	97	319	218	167	119	111	93	57

Sources: Thirty-second to thirty-fourth reports of the inspectors general on the general state of prisons of Ireland (1853–5).

a direct result of mismanagement raised questions as to the moral and social culpability of local leaders. This created a tension between the duties that required Waddell to expose the truths around a death and the authority of the local elite, despite his political patronage.

The officers in charge of local institutions were expected to be upstanding citizens, with zeal and commitment to their management, while also embracing the correct ethos and ideology in terms of the treatment of its inmates. Qualifications, for example, that were considered essential for a gaol governor included,

> daily acquiring in public estimation increased importance and respectability ... [H]is station is honourable, the nature of his charge arduous and responsible. To him is delegated a peculiar trust, and the upright performance of his duties entitle him to the esteem and gratitude of the community ... [H]e is a moral functionary, in whose exertions are involved the interests of society and the welfare of the most wretched of mankind.[69]

Co. Monaghan gaol governor Thomas Mayne, a gentleman who was 'highly connected in the county', had served the institution from March 1845, managing disease and over-population during the Famine, and had positive reviews each year in the inspectors general reports.[70] The *Northern Standard* printed an excerpt from the inspectors general report of 1847 that praised him for being a 'most zealous and active officer, his books particularly well kept and checks upon the expenditure judiciously managed'.[71] A report two years later, written by Inspector General Frederic B. Long after an inspection on 4 October 1849, complimented Mayne for his thorough nightly inspections, stating that even though there were no night watch in the passages, 'the governor ... made a practice of going round to all parts of the prison at uncertain hours during the night'.[72] The reputation of Mr Mayne was considered a credit to the local authorities.

On 12 August 1853, Waddell was called to hold an inquest on a death at the Monaghan gaol. The death reported was not that of an inmate, but rather that of an infant who had been born alive to Mr Mayne's servant, Maria Leonard. Testimony from Leonard's mother, Sally Leonard, and midwife Jane Barber reported that the child had convulsions and Surgeon Lepper had advised to give it castor oil. Still, the baby turned black and died.[73] However, witnesses provided evidence that suggested there may have been a motive for killing the child. Surgeon Lepper told the coroner and jury that Mr Mayne had informed him that he believed the child was his, and that in consequence of a child of his by the late Mrs Mayne

---

[69] *Report of the prisons of Ireland, 1824*, p. 13.   [70] *NS*, 22 Feb. 1845, 22 Mar. 1845. There were several prominent Mayne men in Co. Monaghan with significant influence, including the Revd Charles Mayne and Colburn Mayne, with 1,810 and 1,640 acres, respectively, as well as Richard Mayne, land agent, magistrate, freemason and prominent Orangeman from Newbliss who had married into the Coote family of Bellamont Forest.   [71] *NS*, 2 Jan. 1847.   [72] *Twenty-eighth report of prisons in Ireland, 1849*, p. 60.   [73] CB1, no. 332.2, infant child, 12 Aug. 1853.

having died of convulsions, he felt uneasy about the illness of the present one.[74] Additionally, conflicting evidence was given by Leonard's mother, Sally, and Fr James Hughes. While Sally Leonard told the jury she was not aware of any wish to conceal the birth of the child, Fr Hughes revealed that he had been called upon by Sally Leonard just two weeks earlier. On 30 July 1853, she spoke to the priest after Sunday Mass and asked him to contradict a report that her daughter Maria was in the family way, as 'there was no truth in it'.[75] The jury returned a verdict of death from natural causes.[76] The story never appeared in the *Northern Standard*. There is a strong likelihood that as a result of the embarrassment, Mayne resigned or was fired. In the thirty-third annual inspectors general report, conducted ten months after the infant's death, John Temple is named as the new governor of Monaghan gaol. A former officer at the gaol, Temple was described as one who 'appears to be very painstaking, efficient, and attentive to his duties'.[77]

The Poor Law Act (1838) outlined that unmarried mothers were wholly responsible for the care of their children, while the father was not legally liable.[78] This accounts for the high number of unmarried pregnant women entering the workhouse, as they had no other support. One of the primary issues facing Poor Law commissioners in the 1850s was their concern regarding the high level of orphan infant mortality in the workhouses.[79] The minding of foundling children was the least desirable of all occupations and the task was considered lower than washing the dead or cleaning workhouse toilets.[80] While women outside the workhouse were paid well as wet nurses, those inside the workhouse had to be persuaded with a daily jug of porter.[81] This implies that children with a mother inside the workhouse had a much higher chance of survival. There were rules as to how mothers and children could maintain their relationships, including on the physical space provided to them, and on the amount of time they were permitted together. Children under the age of 2 were allowed to remain with their mothers. Mothers with children between ages 2 and 7 were given access to them at all reasonable times (when they were not in school).[82]

To further support the relationship between mother and child, the duties of the matron of the house outlined that, with the assistance of the nurses, she was required to take care of the children and the sick paupers, to provide the proper diet for them and to furnish them with such changes of clothes and linen as may be necessary.[83] The medical attendant was required to 'give all necessary directions as to the diet of the children', as well as ensure their vaccinations.[84] Overall, these

---

74 Ibid. 75 Ibid. 76 Ibid. 77 *Thirty-third report of the inspectors general of the general state of the prisons of Ireland, 1854*, p. 92, HC 1854–5 (1956) xxvi, 307. The inspectors general visited Co. Monaghan on 13 May 1854. 78 NAI, *Irish workhouse rules, 1844* (Dublin, 1844). 79 Caroline Skehill, 'The origins of child welfare under the Poor Law and the emergence of the institutional versus family care debate' in Virginia Crossman and Peter Gray (eds), *Poverty and welfare in Ireland, 1838–1948* (Dublin, 2011), p. 116. 80 Dympna McLoughlin, 'Workhouses and Irish female paupers 1840–70' in Maria Luddy and Cliona Murphy (eds), *Woman surviving* (Dublin, 1989), p. 142. 81 Ibid. 82 *Irish workhouse rulebook, 1844* (Dublin, 1844). 83 Ibid., article 63, no. 11. 84 Ibid., article 66, no. 6.

vulnerable women and children were at the mercy of the authorities of the institution to ensure for their well-being and care.

In August 1855, the *Northern Standard* reported that plans were being made to take all the children in the Clones workhouse to the Monaghan workhouse, as the latter had become a depot for the different unions of the county to send children to, and doing so would reduce the expense to the Clones union.[85] This meant moving orphans, deserted children and some children who had parents inside and outside of the workhouse. Moving children in this way was meant to deter the parent (mother) from being in the workhouse; however, this meant she would have to beg to survive.[86] In order to further reduce costs, the master and matron of the Clones workhouse, John and Catherine Kirkpatrick, had taken on additional duties for the union at additional salaries.[87] Mr Kirkpatrick would serve not only as the master, but also as the clerk and returning officer of the union, while Mrs Kirkpatrick served as a paid nurse to the infirmary as well as matron.[88]

In October 1855, directly as a consequence of a coroner's inquest, two deaths involving infants were investigated at the Clones workhouse, and similar to the death at the Monaghan gaol, they revealed the injustice of abuse of power by management. On 19 October 1855, Waddell conducted inquests on two pauper children, five-month-old Robert Gillespie and two-month-old Jane Armstrong, both workhouse inmates who died from a lack of proper care. Robert Gillespie's mother, Elizabeth Rennocks, had nursed him for four months but was then taken to nurse the matron's child instead. Gillespie was then passed to several women for suckling, lastly being given to Ellen Armstrong, who 'though without suck took good care of him'.[89] Dr Hoskins had seen Gillespie ten to twelve days after his birth, stating that he was a healthy child, but a month prior to his death, he treated him for a minor skin ailment, and he no longer looked healthy. He further stated that had Gillespie's own mother been nursing him rather than the matron's child, 'he would have been in better health, he did not get it and his death was the consequence'.[90] Dr Hoskins' testimony included that he had repeatedly drawn the master and matron's attention to the children of the workhouse, saying that they were not getting sufficient nourishment. Dr Hoskins and the Kirkpatricks all knew that a child had died from want of care but never reported the information to the board of guardians.[91] The verdict was death from natural causes, accelerated by the culpable neglect of the nurses in charge, and that several officers of the house did not discharge their duties in the vigilant manner they should have.[92]

The second inquest held that day was that of infant Jane Armstrong. Dr Hoskins testified that Armstrong had been a healthy child, but her mother was subject to epileptic fits so had asked the matron to select a woman from the workhouse as a wet nurse.[93] As it appears there were only two women available, and

---

85 *NS*, 4 Aug. 1855. 86 *Tenth annual report of the commissioners for adminsitering the laws for relief of the poor in Ireland* (Dublin, 1857), pp 61–9. 87 Ibid. 88 Ibid. 89 CB1, no. 13.401, Robert Gillespie, 19 Oct. 1855. 90 Ibid. 91 Ibid. 92 Ibid. 93 CB1, no. 14.402, Jane Armstrong, 19 Oct. 1855.

both were suckling the matron's child, Armstrong was spoonfed. It appears that all the child was receiving was bread and milk at nine o'clock each morning. A week before her death, her diet was improved: she began to have feeds at six o'clock each morning and seven o'clock each evening. However, it was too late and the child died. Dr Hoskins testified that the food the child received was insufficient in quantity and quality, and believed destitution was the cause of death. Dr Henry performed a post mortem and concluded that while he found the child emaciated, he also found enlarged mesenteric glands and that internal disease may have contributed towards her death.[94] The verdict reached by the jury stated that death had come from great neglect on the part of the nurse from not administering food in proper time, and in connection with internal disease. The jury stated, 'We consider more strict attention on the part of the officers of the house to their duties would be most desirable.'[95]

A report in the *Northern Standard* a week later claimed that based on Dr Henry's evidence the rumours travelling abroad of children dying at the workhouse of starvation were unfounded and that both children died from natural causes, as concluded by Waddell's jury.[96] Interestingly, it highlights that the Poor Law inspector, Henry Robinson, had visited the workhouse just a few days earlier and had held an inquiry into the conduct of the medical attendant, master and matron, which the *Northern Standard* reporter had attended.[97] It claims that Rennocks, Gillespie's mother, declared that she 'entirely volunteered' to nurse the matron's child and believed all the possible care had been given to her child.[98] Other nurses and inmates of the house deposed to the attention bestowed on children and that they could not possibly have died from either starvation or neglect.[99]

In the following week, on 3 November 1855, the *Northern Standard* published a letter to the editor from Waddell's jury foreman and some jury members contradicting the previous week's report of the infant deaths. These men highlighted that they did not return a verdict of natural causes, but rather found the nurses guilty of culpable neglect and cited the actual verdicts.[100] They also pointed out a fact not included in Waddell's casebook, that,

> you make Dr Henry to say that the children did not die from starvation or neglect. This is incorrect, for he stated distinctly that the child, Jane Armstrong, presented a very emaciated appearance, but would not take upon him to say what it died of; while, on the other hand we have Dr Hoskins's testimony that this child died from insufficient and improper food.[101]

Such damning evidence shows the moral and civic responsibility taken by the jury foreman and some members of the jury, and how they went public to ensure that

94 Ibid. 95 Ibid. 96 *NS*, 27 Oct. 1855. 97 Ibid. Poor Law inspectors conducted investigations as to the conditions at the workhouse and were required to report back to the Poor Law commissioners. An annual report of their findings was published. 98 Ibid. 99 Ibid. 100 *NS*, 3 Nov. 1855. 101 Ibid.

the truth was revealed. The jury's public response is even more powerful when contrasted with Waddell's silence. Editor John Holmes (brother of Andrew, who took over the newspaper after his death on 13 July 1851) defended the paper's original news article by reiterating that they only made their observations based upon the evidence given before the Poor Law inspector.[102] While Holmes did not admit having made an error, his rebuttal indicates that prejudiced and false evidence was officially delivered during the investigation of the infants' deaths to the Poor Law inspector. Further, Holmes failed to pose questions as to the responsibilities of those managing the institution. This indicates that he was significantly tied to the politics of protecting the local elite.

Master Kirkpatrick continued to hold the office of clerk and returning officer, but evidence indicates that he and Mrs Kirkpatrick either resigned or were dismissed from their duties as matron and master.[103] In September 1856, Mr William Graham was appointed master of the Clones workhouse, and his wife Amelia became matron.[104] Mr Elliott, presumably a temporary master in between Kirkpatrick and Graham, resigned upon Graham's election.[105] It is likely that Waddell's investigation exposed the injustice of the matron's mismanagement of the infants of the workhouse, embarrassing local leaders.

WADDELL: PROFESSIONAL AND PERSONAL POLITICS

On 15 May 1856, a letter written by Waddell to the editor of the *Londonderry Standard* was published that addressed an incident involving the Londonderry coroner, Minchin Lloyd. Lloyd had not carried out a post-mortem examination on an infant who died as he wrongly believed he needed the approval of the grand jury. Waddell cited the legislation of 9 & 10 Vic., cap. 37, sec. 33, which placed the power of ordering post-mortem examinations wholly in the hands of the coroner. He wrote,

> As senior coroner of this county [Monaghan], I have had to resist many attempts to interfere with the discharge of my duties, as well from the grand jury as individual justices. The latter I have dealt with myself, and effectively; with respect to the former, I always appealed from their decisions to the judge of Assize, employing the best counsel this circuit could produce. The consequence is, I in every instance defeated them, and I now have peace.[106]

Waddell criticized Lloyd for being too cautious and pointing out that his role was to challenge the local magistrates and grand jury in carrying out his duties.

In addition to his censure of Lloyd, in his letter Waddell also posed a rhetorical question to the editor, asking whether he was the owner of a property in

---

102 Ibid.   103 *NS*, 27 Oct. 1855   104 *NS*, 13 Sept. 1856; Adam Bisset Thom, *Thom's Directory for 1857* (Dublin, 1857), p. 914.   105 *Thom's Directory for 1857*, p. 914.   106 *LS*, 15 May 1856.

Londonderry that yielded £10 per year, which would entitle him to a vote for a representative of Parliament.[107] He took the opportunity to then answer his own question to demonstrate his political alliances to the Presbyterian community in Londonderry. He stated that if he could indeed exercise his right to vote, it would be for a 'member of the Presbyterian church coming forward as a candidate for the suffrages of the county'.[108] Surprisingly, it is likely Waddell was referring to Samuel MacCurdy Greer (1810–80), a liberal Presbyterian, co-founder of the Tenant League (alongside Charles Gavan Duffy), who had lost the contest in the general election of 1852, but went on to win a seat in April 1857.[109]

Waddell owned a dwelling in Maghera town alongside neighbour, historian and Presbyterian leader Revd Thomas Witherow (1824–90), with whom he shared correspondence.[110] Witherow was a supporter of MacCurdy Greer. This admiration and support was representative of the Presbyterian politics that Waddell followed and supported in Londonderry.[111] Circumstantial evidence from a letter between Waddell and Witherow indicates that Waddell's loyalty to Presbyterian alliances was a part of his politics. In a December 1857 letter, Witherow shared his best wishes at the return of Waddell's brother, the minister Hope Masterson Waddell (1804–95), who had founded missions in Jamaica and Nigeria, and extended the same sentiment to Revd Matthew McAuley, minister of Cahans church, Lisnaveane, from 1829 to 1876.[112] Witherow also highlighted his famous work, 'Historical Sketch of the Presbyterian Church in Ireland', how he was hoping it would be published for popular use, how he was reading it anywhere he could in neighbouring congregations and how he thought Waddell 'would be pleased with the warm Presbyterian love of it'.[113] He said he was disappointed that Co. Monaghan was so far away and wished the congregations there knew more about 'Presbyterian principles and values and history as perhaps they would love their church better than many of them do'.[114] The influence and friendship of a well-known and prominent Presbyterian leader indicates that Waddell shared at least some of his liberal beliefs and offered his political support when needed.

Waddell's political and personal alliances were comprised of both local conservative elites and liberal Presbyterian clergy, family and friends. When executing his duties in the role of coroner, which were often politicized, he was frequently in direct conflict with both groups. While his work required a fight for his fees, it also exposed local corrupt figures of authority which proved embarrassing for the local elite, while at the same time, neutral verdicts were perceived as a failure by

107 Ibid. In Griffith's Valuation (1859), Waddell is listed as owning three houses on Coleraine Road, Maghera town, Londonderry and renting them to tenants James Connor, Nicholas Cassidy and Catherine Kane. The total rateable value of the three properties was £8 5s. 108 Ibid. 109 Walker, *Parliamentary election results*, pp 84, 91; David Murphy, 'Samuel McCurdy Greer', *DIB*. 110 Thomas Witherow rented a house, offices and a garden from Revd Bellingham Mauleverer, while renting out a shop and room of his own to a tenant. 111 Linda Lunney, 'Thomas Witherow', *DIB*. 112 Nesbitt, *Full circle*, pp 267, 285. 113 Thomas Witherow to William Charles Waddell, 6 Dec. 1857 (Hope Collection). 114 Ibid.

the coroner to fulfil his duties. Some cases required evidence that was impossible to obtain due to political polarization of witnesses and jury members. Exacerbating this dilemma, political tensions in the 1850s and 1860s increased in Monaghan between the landed class and tenantry, and Protestants and Catholics. Violence increasingly became a part of the democratic electoral process, along with sectarian murder, which threatened not just Waddell's authority, but the foundation and stability of local government and rural society.

SECTARIAN ORGANIZATIONS AND POLITICS: 1857–68

The rise of the Ribbon movement and foundation of Fenianism in the 1850s and 1860s was perpetuated as nationalists and Catholics engaged in the formation of underground military organizations. It developed out of the need to fight corruption within a political system that did not allow for fair representation. Orangeism was immune to economic changes and determined to fight equality for Catholics.[115] From these opposing forces, polarization of society into factions continued to intensify, especially at election time with anticipated changes in political power. National politics shifted from the Conservative government led by the earl of Derby (1858–9) to the Liberals led by Palmerston (1859–65) and Earl Russell (1865–6) and brought with it potential empowerment for Catholics, and violent opposition from Conservatives and Orangemen.

Monaghan Conservatives had kept a foothold in local government. After the defeat of tenant right and Liberal candidate John Gray in 1852, the general elections of 1857 and 1859 returned both Colonel Leslie and Sir George Forster, who served two consecutive terms together.[116] Both had run unopposed. Orangeism appeared to remain strong in the region, with reports of Co. Monaghan Grand Orange Lodge meetings with record attendance numbers taking place.[117] Even while they fought for the legality of their organization in Parliament, they remained a powerful local force. With both county MPs, grand jurors and many large landowners as Orange members, partisan representation in local government continued.

On 26 August 1857, a man was shot and killed after he attended the twenty-first birthday of John Madden esq., eldest son of Captain William Wolseley Madden, at Hilton Park. The party was held for the tenants of the estate and reported to have had five hundred attendees who were treated to a seated meal, and who engaged in various activities such as dancing, donkey-racing, foot-racing, and pole climbing while the music of a military band played throughout the grounds.[118] The *Northern Standard* reported that Michael Muldoon, an inoffensive young Catholic man, had been shot and killed on the walk home from the party with his friend, who was a Protestant.[119] The newspaper was quick to refute the idea that the murder was sectarian in nature, highlighting that the shot easily could have killed anyone and that

---

115 Lee, *The modernisation of Irish society*, p. 171. 116 Walker, *Parliamentary election results*, p. 92. 117 *NS*, 31 Oct. 1857. 118 *NS*, 29 Aug. 1857. 119 Ibid.

the homicide was not 'in any way attributed to maliciousness or intent to kill'.[120] An investigation was held immediately afterwards by justice of the peace John Brady, Madden's land agent, and constabulary Sub-Inspector Henry Kirwin esq. They discovered the pistol used and identified a man named John McGowan, a journeyman baker, living in Clones, as its owner. Passionately, the reporter stated,

> a few remarks on the conduct of a class of men, calling themselves Protestants – Orangemen, if you will – who think that the chief qualification to belong to the faith of a Protestant, or the society of Orangemen, is to cry to hell with the Pope, and carry a loaded pistol, even within the most peaceful society. Whomever may be the man who shot Muldoon, we cannot help thinking he belongs to the class we have named. These men we denounce, as a disgrace to their faith, and injurious to the welfare of the Orange Society, should they be members of that body.[121]

Waddell held an inquest on the body of Michael Muldoon on 27 August 1857.[122] Testimony from four witnesses denied hearing a cry of 'No surrender!' before the gunshot, discounting the claim of a sectarian motive for the murder, while four other witnesses testified they did hear it; however, they did not identify the man who shouted and then shot.[123] The night of the shooting, Sub-Inspector Kirwin went to the canal bridge where the incident had occurred and found a pistol on the road that had recently been discharged. It had the name of the maker of the gun, who was located in Clones, who in turn identified the gun as belonging to McGowan.[124] Two other men – who had sold the gun to McGowan, and repaired it for him – also testified, and while one man could not recollect if it was the same gun, the other one claimed it was.[125] The inquest verdict stated that 'Michael Muldoon came to his death from a gunshot wound inflicted maliciously by some person yet unknown on the night of 26 on the morning of 27 August 1857.'[126]

The *Dundalk Democrat* reported that McGowan was arrested, and 'although the jury at the coroner's inquest decided upon their oaths that this was a foul and malicious murder' and identified him as the owner of the gun, he was liberated.[127] One week later, on 1 September 1857, several magistrates held an investigation at the courthouse and ordered McGowan to be arrested and sent to Monaghan county gaol to be tried at the next assizes.[128] He was released on bail on 16 November 1857.[129] McGowan was reported as on trial at the February 1858 assizes for manslaughter but further reports do not provide the outcome. The absence of evidence

---

120 Ibid. 121 Ibid. 122 CB2, no. 6.470, Michael Muldoon, 27 Aug. 1857. 123 Ibid. Witnesses named who denied hearing the cry of 'No surrender!' were George Rennock, Robert Kirkpatrick, James Cross and John Wigans. Those witnesses who acknowledged hearing the cry were Ann McAree, Mary Ann McDermot, Alexander McCleland and John McCleland. 124 Ibid. 125 Ibid. The witnesses were David Andrews and James Hooks. 126 Ibid. 127 *DD*, 5 Sept. 1857. 128 Ibid. 129 *FJ*, 21 Nov. 1857.

in local and national newspapers that he was convicted suggests that McGowan was acquitted or the charges were dropped.

The general election of 1865 reflected a shift in the power dynamic in Co. Monaghan when the conservatives lost Forster's seat, which left Leslie to serve alongside a new Liberal MP, Hon. Vesey Dawson (later Viscount Cremorne).[130] While Orangemen had petitioned and focused their efforts on returning Leslie and Forster yet again, Dawson was supported by Liberal Catholics. Several factors contributed towards securing the Liberal win, the first in Monaghan in eighteen years. Catholic voters made up half of the eligible voters in the county and they plumped their votes (each voter gave both their votes to a single candidate) for the Liberal candidate. Another factor was the withdrawal of Lord Bath's support from the Conservatives.[131] Additionally, support for Dawson from the Catholic clergy was matched by several Presbyterian ministers who nominated him as a candidate.[132] McGimpsey highlights that the Liberal candidate won, however, 'without the aid of liberal Presbyterians'.[133] If Co. Monaghan Liberal Presbyterians were intimidated and repressed, it was by the knowledge that to vote against Conservative Protestants would result in their social expulsion.

Mobs formed in each town in Co. Monaghan on the day of the election. Conservatives blamed Catholic priests for driving the electors to the polls carrying muskets, blunderbusses, pistols, sticks with knives on the end, bayonets and scythes.[134] Opposing reports claimed that Orangemen kept up a 'murderous fusillade' on crowds.[135] Riots took place and a Catholic man, Peter Shevlin, was killed when shooting broke out in Castleblayney.[136] The inquest was held by the south district coroner, Hugh Swanzy, and his jury found three Orangemen guilty of murder: John Glenn, John Steen and Edward Warren Gray, son of the notorious Sam Gray.[137] They were arrested but not held, tried at the March 1866 assizes for murder and acquitted.[138]

SECTARIAN MURDER IN MONAGHAN: 1868

By 1868, it was anticipated that should the Liberals win the general election of that year, and Gladstone become prime minister, they would disestablish the Church of Ireland.[139] This did, indeed, come to pass, and it was a remarkable event – one of the most significant in nineteenth-century Irish history due to the acceptance in Westminster that Irish majority opinion should decide a constitutional issue.[140] The year 1868 also saw the last general election in Ulster and Ireland with only two

---

130 Walker, *Parliamentary election results*, p. 104. 131 Hoppen, *Elections, politics and society in Ireland, 1832–1885*, p. 153. 132 Frank Wright, *Two lands on one soil: Ulster politics before home rule* (Dublin, 1996), p. 271. 133 Callan to Donnelly [undated] (PRONI, Dio (RC) 1/11A/9); McGimpsey, '"To raise the banner in the remote north"', p. 121. 134 *Cork Constitution*, 29 July 1865. 135 *Newry Examiner and Louth Advertiser*, 26 July 1865. 136 *BN*, 27 July 1865. 137 Ibid.; *DEM*, 26 July 1865. 138 *NS*, 10 Mar. 1866. 139 *FJ*, 8 May 1867. 140 R.V. Comerford, 'Gladstone's first Irish enterprise, 1864–70' in Vaughan (ed.), *A new history of Ireland*, v, p. 443.

parties, Liberal and Conservative, and the first election that provided an indication of division within the conservative social and political order.[141] In a situation specific to Ulster, the conservative local landowning elite held the power over local interests and concerns, but the 1868 election was the final election where they dominated parliamentary representation.[142]

In response to the upcoming threat, in Co. Monaghan, conservatives initiated a new county branch of the Ulster Protestant Defence Association, formed with the support of nearly two thousand members.[143] The deputy grand master of the Orange Order of Co. Monaghan, Captain William Wolseley Madden, called for action to defend and support Protestantism.[144] In the tenant and Catholic community, Ribbonism and Fenianism were building momentum. The townland of Leitrim in the parish of Tyholland was the birthplace and home of James Blayney Rice (1830–1908), a prominent Ribbonman and leader of the Co. Monaghan Fenians.[145] He was believed to be actively collecting an arsenal of guns for protection and attack, and was involved in recruiting members to carry out sectarian activities.[146] When the Twelfth of July marches came, violence predictably followed.

On 13 July 1868, Co. Monaghan Orangemen gathered for their annual Boyne victory celebrations on the grounds of Brandrum House, the home of John Lindsay (formerly the home of county Orange Order deputy master Thomas Coote), located just two miles outside Monaghan town. After the event was over, fourteen Orangemen walked back through the town and were ambushed by an angry mob of close to one hundred persons.[147] Some fought their way to their lodge on Dublin Street, and others were taken in by pub owner David Baird, who shot at the mob hurling stones from the street.[148] When the affray was over and the street cleared, several people lay wounded and one young man from Crumlin, Tyholland parish, Thomas Hughes, a Catholic, was dead from a shotgun wound.[149] Tyholland was considered a centre for Fenianism and it was believed that men from that background were involved in the attack.[150] Waddell asked to conduct an inquest. As a result of Hughes' murder, riots had broken out in Monaghan town and a hundred men from the 72nd Highlanders were sent from Armagh to support the local constabulary, who could not maintain order on their own.[151]

On 14 July 1868, Waddell initiated the inquest but this was only to allow the family to identify the body and take it for burial. Once completed, the proceedings were adjourned until 16 July 1868 at 9 a.m. in the morning.[152] The Hughes family

---

141 Brian M. Walker, *Ulster politics, the formative years, 1868–86* (Belfast, 1989), p. 47. **142** Ibid. **143** *Tyrone Constitution*, 12 June 1868. **144** Christopher D. McGimpsey, 'Border ballads and sectarian affrays' in *Clogher Record*, 11:1 (1982), p. 8; McClelland, 'Orangeism in County Monaghan', p. 403. **145** Charles T. Rice, 'Fenianism in Monaghan: memoir of James Blayney Rice: personalities of the Fenian movement and interesting details of activities in Monaghan, 1865–1885', *Clogher Record*, 1:4 (1956), p. 30; Breandán Mac Giolla Choille, 'Fenians, Rice and Ribbonmen in County Monaghan, 1864–67', *Clogher Record*, 6:2 (1967), p. 222. **146** Ibid. **147** McGoff-McCann, *Melancholy madness*, p. 298. **148** Ibid. **149** Ibid. **150** McGimpsey, '"To raise the banner in the remote north"', p. 151. **151** *LS*, 18 July 1868. **152** CB2, no. 1.892, Thomas Hughes, 14 July 1868.

placed the corpse in a coffin and proceeded through the streets of Monaghan town followed by a crowd of three thousand, who set the coffin in front of Baird's pub where Hughes had been shot. The *Cork Examiner* reported that the crowd shouted 'murder', 'to hell with the heretics', and prayed aloud asking the Virgin Mary 'to have vengeance poured down' on their heads.[153] The crowd then made their way with the body to Leitrim graveyard in Tyholland and laid Hughes to rest.[154]

The inquest reconvened at the courthouse in Monaghan town on 16 July 1868 as planned. Unusually, the names of the jurors were made public. The *Belfast Morning News* sent a reporter to Monaghan, who provided a detailed account of the day including listing the names of twenty-two inquest jurors. They were Samuel Burnside (foreman), John Rafferty, Richard Clarke, John McCready, Benjamin Skelton, Bernard Geraghty, Bernard Kearan, Thomas Kelly, George Mulligan, Patrick McGurk, George Blackburn, Francis McCleary, Joseph Blackburn, Peter Deeghan, John Loughran, John Woods, John Jebb, James Cinnemond, George Steenson, James Watkins, Patrick Gormally and Charles Lowry.[155] Also in attendance were Monaghan resident magistrate Lucas Alexander Treston esq., county inspector of the constabulary Richard Singleton, crown solicitor Parkinson, solicitors Mitchell and Cochrane representing the Orange party, solicitor Reilly as a representative of the next of kin and parish priest Fr O'Neill.[156] Witnesses who testified included five local law enforcement officers, two Dublin Street merchants, a police constable from Manchester and Dr William Temple.[157] Eyewitnesses identified Baird as the shooter.[158] While evidence indicated Baird was responsible for Hughes' death, a verdict was not agreed among the jury and with Waddell, and Waddell adjourned the inquest.[159]

Several newspapers reported that the jury was split down the middle, eleven versus eleven, one side prepared to find Baird guilty of wilful murder.[160] The diary of Bishop James Donnelly (1822–93) states that the inquest jury actually had twenty-three members, though, including nine Protestants and fourteen Catholics.[161] He claimed that the reason Waddell adjourned the inquest was that the jury wanted to return a verdict of wilful murder, which the coroner refused to accept. Further, he stated that the jury was split down the middle (eleven versus eleven) in naming Baird for wilful murder because the twenty-third juror abstained from voting.[162] The *Dundalk Democrat* and *Northern Standard* reported that Waddell had refused to accept the verdict from the jury of wilful murder as he believed it was against the weight of the evidence, yet he would have accepted a verdict of manslaughter.[163] The reporter for the *Belfast Morning News* captured a statement from Waddell,

---

153 *Cork Examiner*, 18 July 1868; *BMN*, 17 July 1868. 154 *BMN*, 17 July 1868; *Yorkshire Post and Leeds Intelligencer*, 18 July 1868. 155 *BMN*, 17 July 1868. 156 Ibid. 157 CB2, no. 1.892, Thomas Hughes, 14 July 1868. 158 Ibid. 159 *Liverpool Daily Post*, 18 July 1868; *LS*, 18 July 1868; *BMN*, 17 July 1868; *DEM*, 17 July 1868. 160 *Halifax Courier*, 25 July 1868; *Pall Mall Gazette*, 18 July 1868; *Leeds Mercury*, 20 July 1868; *NS*, 18 July 1848. 161 Bishop Donnelly's Diary (PRONI, Dio (RC) 1/11B/11); Kate Newmann, 'James Donnelly (1822–1893): Bishop, Roman Catholic', *DUB*. 162 Ibid. 163 *DD*, 15 July 1868; *NS*, 18 July 1868.

He [the coroner] would not occupy time in speaking of any alleged discrepancies in the evidence, inasmuch as the jury would have all the depositions before them. He was of opinion that the parties inside the house had fired in self-defence; and very high authorities had stated that it was perfectly legal for persons to defend themselves when attacked.[164]

Waddell was reluctant to allow the jury to return a verdict of wilful murder because it undermined the position of the conservative local elite and Orange Order and the long-standing Protestant proclaimed right to self-defence.[165] While Protestants serving on juries supported the use of weapons under the circumstances of self-defence, the reality was that the conservative landowning elite used the Orangemen to help them confront and fight Catholics.[166]

The jury refused to comply with Waddell. Later that evening after the adjournment, Waddell recalled the jury. Just twelve of the jurors returned to the court and, defying Waddell's original position and guidance on the verdict, they found a verdict of wilful murder committed by David Baird.[167] Waddell then issued a coroner's warrant for the arrest of David Baird, his father John Baird and his cousin John Clarke.[168]

On 21 July 1868, the conservative *Dublin Daily Express* published a column discussing the case, using it as a platform to complain about the 'absurdity of the present system of coroners' inquests'.[169] It stated that the case was a mockery of judicial investigations and,

> The Monaghan proceedings present a new aspect of the ludicrous. We have seen verdicts of manslaughter returned by coroners' juries against Lord John Russell in cases where persons died of destitution, and other instances where the findings were scarcely less repugnant to law and reason, but the peculiarity of the verdict in Monaghan is that it was found without a jury.[170]

Claiming that there was no legally constituted jury when the verdict was handed in, the report blamed Waddell for calling them back by irregular summons. It further stated that Protestant inhabitants were indignant at the conduct of the coroner and demanded an investigation, and they declared the verdict 'illegal'.[171] On 25 July, the indignation of the Protestants of Monaghan was reflected in the editorial column of the *Northern Standard*. Editor John Holmes emotively reacted, stating that 'Irish verdicts are the laugh of the whole civilized world. Coroners' juries are

---

164 *BMN*, 17 July 1868. **165** Thomas Bartlett, '"This famous island set in a Virginian sea": Ireland in the British empire' in Peter James Marshall (ed.), *The Oxford history of the British empire: the eighteenth century* (Oxford, 1998), pp 253–75; R.B. McDowell, 'The age of United Irishmen: reform and reaction' in W.E. Vaughan (ed.), *A new history of Ireland*, v, pp 289–338. **166** Wright, *Two lands on one soil*, p. 273. **167** Ibid.; CB2, no. 1.892, Thomas Hughes, 14 July 1868. **168** *Dublin Daily Express*, 22 Aug. 1868. **169** Ibid., 21 July 1868. **170** Ibid. **171** Ibid.

rather celebrated for their literary feats ... but this [the Hughes inquest] distances anything ever effected before by these eccentric bodies.'[172]

> The little game about the discharge of the jury recalled, and not resworn, the [Waddell's] acceptance of a verdict really different from that which the 'eleven' endeavoured to get passed when their fellow journeymen were in consultation: all this will be enquired into: so we say nothing about it.[173]

Holmes' insinuation that Waddell was insincere or covert in his approach to managing the inquest further exemplifies the social risks for those who did not serve and protect the interest of the conservative local elite. Demonstrating support for the cause manifested itself through the collection of funds for the defence, led by Orange Order deputy master William Wolseley Madden. One donation of £30 came from Br J. Waddell in Australia.[174] Circumstantial evidence suggests that the contribution came from a member of the Waddell family, who originally hailed from Lisnaveane. This endowment not only reflected solidarity for the Orange cause, but was a gesture made to reinforce the patronage of the Waddell family and support Waddell, the controversial coroner at the centre of the case.

On 20 July 1868, news of the peculiar procedures and requests for investigation had reached Parliament. Conservative MP John Vance asked the chief secretary, the earl of Mayo, if he had any information as to the irregularity of the proceedings of Waddell's inquest in Monaghan town and in regards to the affray itself, as he was keen to understand who were reported as the aggressors.[175] The earl of Mayo stated that a report on the proceedings had not yet reached him and he would not 'express any opinion upon the subject, seeing that it was likely to be made the subject of judicial investigation'.[176] The magisterial investigation into the case began in August 1868 and was published in newspapers nationwide.[177] Its purpose was to review the procedure and witness testimony from the original inquest. Well-known Belfast solicitor John Rea (1822–81) was hired to defend Baird and paid with donations from the Orange Order.[178] Rea appealed to have Waddell's inquest verdict and warrants dismissed based on the irregularities. On 17 September 1868, after several weeks, and a total of twenty days of re-examining inquest witnesses on the stand, the magisterial inquiry was terminated. The justices returned their decision to the attorney general.[179] Waddell's warrant was upheld.[180] Baird was committed for trial, and held in custody, without bail.[181]

While Baird remained in Monaghan gaol awaiting trial, public attention shifted to the anticipated November 1868 general election. It brought with it considerable

172 *NS*, 25 July 1868.   173 Ibid.   174 Monaghan Orange Lodge minute book, p. 148 (Schomberg House, Belfast). Bishop Donnelly and a number of prominent Catholics were also involved in raising funds – in order to defend any Catholics who might be charged with offences arising out of the riot. PRONI, Dio (RC) I/IIBII, Donnelly's Diary, 16 July 1868.   175 *Hansard 3*, cxclll, 20 July 1868, c. 1482.   176 Ibid.   177 *Ulster Gazette*, 12 Aug. 1868; *Belfast Weekly News*, 22 Aug. 1868.   178 Bridget Hourican, 'John Rea', *DIB*.   179 *Bristol Mercury*, 26 Sept. 1868.   180 Ibid.   181 *BMN*, 18 Sept. 1868.

tensions for landholding conservatives as they faced the threat of disestablishment of the church and a liberal government led by Gladstone. Landlords had the greatest influence on a county's governance when a small number of them together owned a large share of that county's land.[182] In Co. Monaghan, figures for 1873–4 show that the top ten landlords owned 46.3 per cent of the land in the county, second in Ireland after Longford.[183] However, a shift in the Liberal county leadership took place on 10 October 1868, when MP Lord Cremorne announced his withdrawal from his seat and that he would not run again. While he had planned to run on the Liberal ticket, he did not support the disestablishment of the church. Cremorne lacked the backing of Bishop Donnelly and the support of Catholic voters he needed to secure a win. Co. Monaghan had the only contested seat in Ulster, and Monaghan Liberals lacked a local leader.

William Gray, an Orangeman, son of the notorious Sam Gray and brother of Edward Warren Gray who was accused and acquitted of the murder of a Catholic during the 1865 election, attempted to secure a liberal seat in the 1868 general election. Gray's stand against the official conservative establishment was a bold move, one that reflected a brief moment in reformist Orange politics. It was an important sign of political diversity and unrest within the Conservative party, and the start of the decline of the social position and influence of landlords. Although from a family of ultra-Protestants and infamous Orangemen, evidence suggests that William was a supporter of tenant rights. Gray requested a public meeting in September 1850 along with more than three hundred Catholic and Presbyterian clergymen and tenants from all over the county supporting tenant rights.[184] Ballybay was considered the stronghold of the Tenant League and their gathering in October was reported to have had an attendence in excess of ten thousand.[185] An argument reportedly took place between two tenant right leaders in 1851 as to which Gray family establishment in Ballybay to hold a tenant right meeting in.[186] This suggests that Gray, the owner of the Duke of York Hotel in Ballybay, had been tolerant or, more probably, a sympathizer in the cause of tenant right.

In 1868, Gray's platform was grounded on 'fair and equitable value of land', fair rents and fixity of tenure and compensation for improvement for tenants; he called for landlords to pay half of the county cess and declared his support for the disestablishment of the church.[187] That same year, another conservative Orangeman and ultra-Protestant, William Johnston (1829–1902) from Ballykilbeg, Londonderry, ran as a liberal in the 1868 election in Belfast. Johnston, like Gray, represented the working-class and advocated for land reform but, at the same time, was a staunch Orangeman and supporter of Protestant rights.[188] He had decided to run against local Conservative MPs as he believed they had not sufficiently

---

182 Hoppen, *Elections, politics and society in Ireland, 1832–1885*, p. 152. 183 Ibid. 184 *NS*, 28 Sept. 1850. 185 *NS*, 5 Oct. 1850 186 Livingstone, *The Monaghan story*, p. 228. 187 *NS*, 21 Nov. 1868; Brian M. Walker, 'The land question and elections in Ulster' in Samuel Clark and James S. Donnelly Jnr (eds), *Irish peasants, violence and political unrest, 1780–1914* (Oxford, 1983), p. 233. 188 Walker, *Parliamentary election results*, p. 60; Brian Walker, 'Johnston, William', *DIB*.

objected to the Party Processions Act, which prohibited marching and parades of a sectarian nature.[189] By comparison, Gray also needed the votes of the 'lower orders' of Monaghan, the tenantry and Catholics, and liberals eager to move away from the oligarchy, and the self-serving interests of the landed gentry.

Due to a lack of Catholic support, a lack of clergy championing his efforts and the vast majority of tenants continuing to support the wishes of their landlords, Gray lost the election with just 960 votes, to Leslie's 3,130 votes and Shirley's 2,785 votes. The Conservatives regained control of Co. Monaghan's second seat.[190] However, Gray captured nearly 14 per cent of the vote, which showed green shoots of local cooperation and support, and willingness to oppose the landowning class. Gray's withdrawal of political support for the landed elite marked the start of changes to come, both nationally and locally.

A REVENGE KILLING

On 23 November 1868, election night, at Campbell's Hotel, the Orange Order's electoral headquarters in Monaghan town, another politically motivated murder connected to the July 1868 killing of Thomas Hughes took place. Catholic John McKenna from Emyvale, in the parish of Tyholland, shot and killed Protestant and Orangeman James Clarke, David Baird's first cousin, in a premeditated act. Waddell held the inquest over several days.[191] Testimony from witnesses proved beyond a reasonable doubt that the murder had been planned and Clarke targeted. Samuel Clarke, father of the deceased, testified that McKenna had said to James earlier the day of the murder, 'he [James] was a great man today but would be killed before he went home'.[192] Witness Mary Catherine Tailor, a servant at the hotel, had heard McKenna identify James, stating 'the boy is here that he wanted'.[193] Several witnesses, including David Baird's brother, John Baird Jnr, testified that they saw McKenna shoot Clarke. As for the inquest jury members, in another rare occurrence, their names were published in the *Northern Standard*.[194] Although a breakdown of their religious persuasion was not published, at least three of the same men from the inquest jury of Thomas Hughes were chosen again, indicating that Waddell selected jurors with a perspective he found applicable or helpful in evaluating such cases.[195] The inquest jury reached a verdict on 9 December 1868,

---

189 Walker, *Ulster politics, the formative years*, p. 59; Brian Walker, 'William Johnston', *DIB*. 190 Walker, *Parliamentary election results*, p. 110. 191 CB2, no. 17.900, James Clarke, 26 Nov. 1868. 192 Ibid. 193 Ibid. 194 *NS*, 5 Dec. 1868. Patt Gormley, Joseph Blackburne and Benjamin Skelton were also on the inquest jury for the Thomas Hughes inquest. There may have been more as the last names match, but not the first names, thus 'at least three' jurors served on both inquests. On the James Clarke inquest, the twenty-three jurors were Robert Graham, Edward Murphy, Thomas Little, Bernard Murphy, Edward Blackburne, John Treanor, William Swan, Thomas Naughton, William Hennessey, Patt Gormley, Joseph Blackburne, John Woods, H. Breakey, Bernard McCready, Robert Whitla, William Lough, B. Kearns, Thomas Mitchell, Charles Slowey, John Irwin, Patt Woods, Benjamin Skelton and James Connolly. 195 Ibid.

concluding that 'James Clarke met his death on the night of 23 November 1868 in Cambell's Hotel, Monaghan, from a wound inflicted by a pistol shot fired wilfully by John McKenna.'[196]

The Monaghan spring assizes took place over three days starting on 4 March 1869, with testimony from multiple witnesses for both the defence and prosecution presented before crown court magistrate Hon. Justice William O'Connor Morris (1824–1904).[197] By the next day, the criminal trial of David Baird, along with his father John Baird, and cousin John Clarke concluded. The jury returned with a verdict. All three were acquitted.[198] The *Northern Standard* reported that while no attempt was made to applaud the verdict in court, it was announced outside to a supportive crowd that cheered loudly.[199]

The enthusiasm of Orange Baird supporters and the conservative local elite would be short lived. Immediately following the conclusion of Baird's trial, the assizes heard the case against John McKenna, for the murder of James Clarke. McKenna was defended by special counsel including QC Isaac Butt and Catholic lawyer and politician Denis Caulfield Heron (1824–81), both of whom immediately challenged the array of the jury constructed by High Sheriff Major Thomas Coote, and Sub-Sheriff William Mitchell.[200] They argued that there were 1,200 eligible jurors in Co. Monaghan, 800 Protestants and 400 Catholics, however, the jury panel had consisted of 250 men but only 40 were Catholics.[201] They also accused Coote and Mitchell of being members of the Orange Order, 'subscribers to its funds' used to support the prosecution and part of a conspiracy to design a jury of Protestants to direct justice in the cases of Baird and McKenna.[202] In an emotive speech addressing the court, Heron stated,

> Persons that belonged to societies that were the curse of this land ought not to be in the position of sub-sheriffs to empanel jurors ... Men whose every feeling was poisoned with prejudice and with hatred of their fellow men, and who lived as foreigners in a land which they should love as their native land, were unfit for such positions.[203]

Co. Monaghan was 'the most extreme example of overt elite pan-Protestantism' having abused the legal system in order to bolster conservative control and undermine Catholic rights and interests.[204] The local imbalance of power in Co. Monaghan was such that out of 192 county officials, only 6 were Catholic, which contributed to conspiratorial abuse of justice.[205] Judge Morris ordered the jury panel in the McKenna trial to be quashed. The spring assizes concluded and, as

---

196 CB2, no. 17.900, James Clarke, 26 Nov. 1868. 197 Patrick M. Geoghegan, 'William O'Connor Morris', *DIB*. 198 *NS*, 6 Mar. 1869. 199 Ibid. 200 Bridget Hourican, 'Denis Caulfield Heron', *DIB*. 201 *Saunders's News-Letter*, 8 Mar. 1869; *NS*, 6 Mar. 1869. The figures as to the number of jurors vary per publication. 202 *Saunders's News-Letter*, 8 Mar. 1869. 203 *The Evening Freeman*, 8 Mar. 1869. 204 Wright, *Two lands on one soil*, pp 273–4. 205 Ibid.

a result of having no jury, over one hundred Catholic prisoners and 13 Protestant prisoners were released without trial, and the venue for McKenna's trial was ordered to be changed.[206] It took place in July 1869 in Dundalk, Co. Louth. He was acquitted.[207]

The government took action and continued its investigation surrounding the allegations against Coote and Mitchell of jury-packing. On 3 July 1869, at the Monaghan summer assizes Coote was ordered to remove Mitchell as sub-sheriff. When he refused, he was dismissed from office.[208] Four years later, in June 1873, a select committee working on the Irish jury system heard further testimony on the case.[209] It was demonstrated that Sheriff Thomas Coote and Sub-Sheriff William Mitchell had tampered with the jury, excluded Catholics and inserted the names of Protestants.[210] Mitchell had drawn up a panel of which the first 48 names included only 2 Catholics.[211] It was also proven that of the 250 names on the jury panel, 84 were Orangemen.[212] While Coote had denied his membership of the Orange Order (although his father was deputy master of the Monaghan Grand Orange Lodge for many years) and any wrongdoing, Mitchell admitted his membership.[213] Mitchell also confessed his knowledge of the funds to defend Baird and to secure the conviction of McKenna.[214]

The McKenna case became a legal landmark that successfully outlined and proved jury-packing. It embarrassed and angered the government and resulted in significant legislative change.[215] Lord Chancellor Thomas O'Hagan (1812–85), a Catholic, used the case to push for reform of the jury system, resulting in the Juries Act (Ireland) 1871.[216] The act abolished the sheriff's power to select jurors, expanded the qualifications to widen the jury pool and implemented a system of name rotation.[217] The Juries Act was implemented as a direct result of the corruption of the local elite in Monaghan and throughout the country, and was a signal that the government would not tolerate corruption in jury selection. It was also an indication of further change to come in moving towards fair and balanced representation in Irish society.

CONCLUSION

Waddell's work as the coroner revealed abuses of power and authority in north Monaghan during a time when the county was controlled by a landowning, conservative elite. The inquests that he conducted at local institutions, such as the gaol and workhouse, emphasize how the work of the coroner helped reveal injustice

---

206 *DD*, 10 July 1869.   207 Ibid.   208 Ibid.   209 *First, second and special reports from the select committee on juries (Ireland); together with the proceedings of the committee, minutes of evidence, and appendix*, pp 258–61, HC 1873 (283) xv, 389.   210 Ibid., p. 342.   211 Ibid.   212 Ibid., p. 82.   213 Ibid., p. 276.   214 Ibid.   215 John F. McEldowney, 'The case of the Queen v. McKenna (1869) and jury-packing in Ireland', *Irish Jurist*, n.s., 12 (1977), pp 339–53.   216 Patrick M. Geoghegan, 'Thomas O'Hagan', *DIB*; 34 & 35 Vict., c. 25 (21 Aug. 1871), Juries Act (Ireland).   217 McEldowney, 'The case of the Queen v. McKenna (1869)', p. 347.

and corruption to the public. They also show how Waddell's professional commitments put him in direct conflict with his social and political alignment to local elites and, in some instances, they clashed with his own commitment to his fellow Presbyterians. While little evidence exists to examine the political composition of coroners' juries, their behaviours, particularly in sectarian murders, revealed an ability to return verdicts that held perpetrators accountable. Evidence shows that convictions in criminal court were difficult, if not impossible to achieve due to the imbalance of power within the local justice system. Although the inquests conducted by Waddell failed to result in convictions in murder cases in criminal court, they did reflect the voice of the people in a politically polarized society that often struggled to provide equal justice.

6

The value of a life: the emergence of the modern Irish coroner

Modernisation is defined as the growth of equality of opportunity ... that merit supersedes birthright as the primary criteria for the distribution of income, status, power, and this involves the creation of political consciousness among the masses, the decline of deference based on inherited status, and the growth of functional specialisation without which merit can hardly begin to be measured.
  —Joseph Lee, *The modernisation of Irish society, 1848–1918*[1]

THE CHALLENGE OF LIBERALISM

Gladstone's first administration (1868–74) saw the implementation of legislative measures that were meant to pacify Ireland and heal the nation yet alienated both conservatives and liberals as they fought each other and the government. The Land Act of 1870 enforced fixity of tenure and free sale as the Ulster custom of tenant right became the law, and gave tenants, for the first time, legal rights over their land; at the same time, it denied the landlord unrestrained freedoms over the land he owned.[2] However, the act fell short of giving tenants the security of rent control. The unforeseen results included an increase in evictions for non-payment of rent, a further breakdown in tenant-landlord relations, a rise in reported violence in some areas and a lack of trust of authorities.[3] The disestablishment of the Church of Ireland in January 1871 was primarily a symbolic gesture, but it meant Catholic farmers no longer had to pay tithes to the church – and it resulted in alienating many Protestant elites from the government.[4] Another significant piece of legislation was the Irish university bill (1873) which was intended to expand the university system to include a Catholic institution, yet refused to offer an endowment to the Catholic University.[5] The bill was defeated.[6] It had

---

[1] Lee, *The modernization of Irish society*, pp i, ii. [2] 33 & 34 Vict., c. 46 (1 Aug. 1870), Landlord and Tenant (Ireland) Act; MacDonagh, *Ireland: the Union and its aftermath*, p. 48. [3] MacDonagh, *Ireland: the Union and its aftermath*, p. 48. [4] 32 & 33 Vict., c. 42 (26 July 1869), Irish Church Act; R.B. McDowell, 'Administration and the public services, 1870–1921' in Vaughan (ed.), *A new history of Ireland*, v, p. 574; W.E. Vaughan, 'Ireland c.1870' in Vaughan (ed.), *A new history of Ireland*, v, p. 726. [5] Bruce L. Kinzer, 'John Stuart Mill and the Irish university question', *Victorian Studies*, 31:1 (1987), p. 76. [6] *Hansard 3*, ccxiv, 11 Mar. 1873, cc 1739–1868.

angered the Catholic church and turned them against the Liberal party, which cost Gladstone the 1874 general election.[7] Perhaps even more important than the university bill was the Secret Ballot Act (1872).[8] It removed tenant farmers from the political control of landlords and agents and allowed, for the first time, the freedom of political choice. Overall, the Gladstonian liberal state, according to Kinzer, 'managed to offend Anglicans, who felt disenfranchised, nonconformists, employers, trade unions, the drink interest and temperance movement' as well as the burgeoning middle-class, liberals and Catholics.[9] These reforms would lead to an unpredictable political climate with changeable conditions over the duration of the administration.

In 1871, the population of Co. Monaghan was 114,269, 12,000 fewer than it had been a decade earlier, and the number of inhabited houses had declined by 1,744 to 22,420.[10] Those who could emigrate did so. The population was 73.4 per cent Catholic, 13.6 per cent Protestant and 12.1 per cent Presbyterian. The grand jury was still controlled by the local elite, and conservative Anglican Protestants still held most of the professional and civil service jobs in the county and controlled commercial life.[11] The rural density of the county was 36 persons per square mile, a drop of more than 1,000 per cent compared to 1841 when in some areas it had been 360.[12] In 1870, 90.4 per cent of agricultural tenants on holdings valued at under £15 were tenants at will, and while the Ulster custom still operated in the county it was 'far weaker' compared to in Antrim and Down, and 'subject to much greater control and restriction than in the more northern counties'.[13] The 1870 reports from the Poor Law inspectors quoted an unnamed land agent from an extensive estate in south Monaghan, saying that the Ulster custom was 'confined to yearly tenants ... in the cases of leases it has been claimed but not granted'.[14] Agriculture remained the primary source of survival for many, and while interest in tenant right grew, tenants would remain compromised by their relationship with the politics of their landlords.

The home rule movement initiated by Isaac Butt in 1870, promoting Irish domestic self-government, faced growing pressure from Gladstone's liberal administration. It was supported by a mix of independent Orangemen and Catholics who desired the freedom to govern over their own domestic issues, and opposed by conservatives who did not want to break with the United Kingdom

---

7 *South London Chronicle*, 14 Feb. 1874; Susan M. Parkes, 'Higher Education, 1793–1908' in Vaughan (ed.), *A new history of Ireland*, vi, p. 558.   8 35 & 36 Vict., c. 33 (18 July 1872), Ballot Act.   9 Kinzer, 'John Stuart Mill and the Irish university question', p. 77.   10 *Census of Ireland, 1871, Part III: general report with illustrative maps and diagrams, summary tables and appendix*, 1 [C.1377], C1 1876, lxxxi, 35, 111.   11 Ibid.; Livingstone, *The Monaghan story*, p. 330.   12 *Census of Ireland, 1871, Part III: general report with illustrative maps and diagrams, summary tables and appendix*, 1 [C.1377], C1 1876, lxxxi, 35, 111.   13 *Reports from Poor Law inspectors as to the existing relations between landlord and tenant in respect of improvements on farms, drainage, reclamation of land, fencing, planting, and also as to the existence (and to what extent) of the Ulster tenant-right in their respective districts, &c.*, 37 [C.31], HC 1870, xiv, 101; *Return of number of agricultural holdings in Ireland, and tenure held by occupiers*, 5, 6 [C.32], C1.1870, lvi, 737.   14 Ibid., p. 102.

and face Dublin Castle's control of the country. It also encountered resistance from the Irish Republican Brotherhood, who wanted a complete separation from the Union. Butt sought a platform to insert himself and home rule into the political landscape and found his opportunity in the by-election in Monaghan in July 1871.

The Conservative MP and Monaghan Orangeman Charles Powell Leslie III had died suddenly in June 1871 and a by-election was held the following month.[15] Leslie's death was so sudden that Waddell enquired if an inquest was required. Head Constable Pollock of Glaslough confirmed that an inquest was not necessary, but Waddell recorded a memo in his casebook of his inquiry.[16] The deceased had been reported in good health on Saturday walking out through his demesne. He was at church on the Sunday and that evening he had a party of friends to dinner. Leslie took ill in the middle of the night and Dr Stewart of Glaslough and Surgeon Young of Monaghan were telegraphed but were too late to be of any service, as he died two hours after the illness began. The *Northern Standard* reported that he died, 51 years of age, from inflammation of the windpipe.[17]

The Conservative John Leslie, brother of the former MP, committed to run in the July 1871 by-election to represent the Conservatives and the union, while local landlord, Orangeman and Home Government Association member John Madden dropped out of the race as he lacked the backing of Catholics due to his Orange Order membership.[18] Upon Madden's withdrawal, Butt, leader of the home rule movement, put himself forward and positioned himself as a protector of tenant right.[19] McGimpsey states that as Butt had in March 1869 accused High Sheriff Coote and Sub-Sheriff Mitchell of being directly involved in jury-packing in the trial of John McKenna, it appears he lacked support from local conservative Protestants.[20] Equally, he was a former member of the Grand Orange Order of Ireland and without the strong support from Clogher Bishop Donnelly, he would not receive the Catholic vote either. While his position on home rule led to some co-operation between Catholics and Orangemen during the election, Butt lost to Leslie by nearly two to one, with Leslie securing 2,538 votes and Butt only 1,451.[21] Notably, there was no liberal candidate. The Liberal party had had no leader in the county since Viscount Cremorne stood down at the 1868 election. The conservative win put Monaghan on a 'political periphery' that reinforced its position as the 'bulwark of the Protestant North'.[22] Although conservatives secured their seats in Parliament and kept their stronghold of political power, their security would continue to be threatened by the liberals, Catholics and the home rule movement.

15 *NS*, 1 July 1871. 16 CB2, Inquiry, C.P. Leslie, 27 June 1871. 17 *NS*, 1 July 1871. 18 Walker, *Ulster politics: the formative years*, p. 80. 19 Ibid. 20 McGimpsey, '"To raise the banner in the remote north"', pp 238, 246. 21 Walker, *Parliamentary election results in Ireland*, p. 114; Hoppen, *Elections, politics and society in Ireland, 1832–1885*, p. 327. 22 McGimpsey, '"To raise the banner in the remote north"', p. 181.

POLITICS IN CO. MONAGHAN AND THE UNDER-CURRENT OF LIBERALISM (1874–80)

While Monaghan conservatives remained fixed within local government, shifts in support for the local Conservative party began to reveal themselves. The 1874 general election returned Shirley (2,417) and Leslie (2,481) over home rule candidate Madden (2,105), who lost the contest as a result of a lack of support from Farney and the overall lack of Catholic support.[23] Again, the Liberal party had no candidate. This is likely due to liberal disorganization. Madden's brother, then county grand master of the Orange Order, William Wolseley Madden, had also contributed towards his brother's election defeat by calling on Orangemen and the Hilton estate tenants not to vote for him.[24] W.W. Madden did the same again at a meeting of the Co. Monaghan Orange Lodge at Carlisle's Hotel in Monaghan on 3 February 1874.[25] He advised the Orangemen in attendance 'not to vote for any home rule candidate' and read a statement that said,

> We therefore pledge ourselves to return to the Imperial Parliament men who will fully represent us in supporting such measures as will be conducive to the interests of Protestantism and that we shall to the utmost of our power not only resist the encroachments of Popery either in the form of 'Home Rule' as laid down by the 'Home Rule' association or in denominational education and that we shall continue to support and maintain the Constitution of 1688 against all foes foreign or domestic.[26]

Such rhetoric illustrates the emergence of fracture within Conservative party dominance and reflected the fear and anger felt by some Orangemen, representative of many Anglican Protestants, at the fragmentation of support from their brethren. Most significantly, this was the last general election in the century in which the Conservatives held both seats and the Protestant elite managed Co. Monaghan.

Liberal political interests and support in Monaghan were reflected by the appointment as high sheriff of Sir William Tyrone Power (1819–1911) of Annaghmakerrig, Newbliss, Co. Monaghan, in January 1874.[27] He had arrived in Monaghan shortly before his appointment, after his wife, Martha Moorhead, inherited her father's estate. Identified as 'a Gladstone candidate', Power, a Presbyterian, had demonstrated interest in running for MP that year but without a replacement for him as high sheriff, he was unable to do so.[28] Speculation exists that the local Anglican Protestant elite believed Power would win the Catholic vote and thus the election, and therefore did not help him in his quest for a

---

23 Walker, *Ulster politics, the formative years*, p. 103; Walker, *Parliamentary election results in Ireland*, p. 118. 24 *NS*, 7 Feb. 1874. 25 County Monaghan Orange Lodge minute book, 3 Feb. 1874 (Schomberg House, Belfast). 26 Ibid. 27 *FJ*, 21 Jan. 1874; *Northern Whig*, 4 Feb. 1874; *BN*, 3 Feb. 1874. 28 *NS*, 7 Feb. 1874.

successor for high sheriff.[29] Power relied on local knowledge and political influence in his failed attempts to secure the position of MP in 1874 and in 1880. One of his advocates with local connections was Isabella Tod (1836–96), who was regarded as the most prominent feminist in nineteenth-century Ireland.[30] She had campaigned for legislation to protect women's lives, property, health and political rights. In 1866, she signed the first female suffrage petition that was sent to the House of Commons and was the author of a private pamphlet sent in 1884 to Ulster's MPs entitled *Women and the new franchise bill: a letter to an Ulster member of Parliament, complaining of the lack of educational and other facilities for women*.[31]

Tod was also Waddell's niece, his sister Maria Isabella's daughter, which suggests that both women and men in the Waddell family were educated and allowed free and individual thought. Waddell was aware of Tod's progress and successes with her causes. His sister-in-law Jessie Waddell wrote to him from Dublin in June 1874 and referred to Isabella, complimenting her as 'very clever and active' and stating, 'I believe [she] is doing much good.'[32] Tod had spent time in London that summer speaking at the annual meeting of the National Society for Women's Suffrage at Westminster Palace Hotel in July 1874.[33] Circumstantial evidence suggests that Isabella's knowledge of Monaghan local affairs would have come from her family living in Lisnaveane who had a deep understanding of local government matters, and an indication that at least some of her liberal Presbyterian politics may have been shared within the family. While Power did not secure a place in Parliament, his leadership and relationship with Tod illustrate the various aspects of liberalism and the many issues within society and the groups looking for fair treatment, freedoms and rights.

The legacy of conservative control in Co. Monaghan ended with the general election of 1880, when two liberal Presbyterian candidates, solicitors John Givan (1837–95) and William Findlater (1842–1906), received the overwhelming support of the majority over Shirley and Leslie.[34] Their victory was achieved by a combination of Catholic votes that came as a result of the endorsement of Bishop Donnelly as well as strong support from liberal Presbyterians sparked on by the start of the Land War in 1879. Respectable middle-class Presbyterians comprised of tenant farmers and urban elites from Belfast and Derry supported tenant right, opposed the Ascendancy and elitism, and had a belief in non-sectarian education.[35] The Catholic middle class and tenants also shared these interests, and together they changed the face of Monaghan politics thereafter.

29 McGimpsey, '"To raise the banner in the remote north"', p. 309. 30 Kate Newmann, 'Isabella Tod (1836–1896): campaigner for women's rights', *DUB*; Georgina Clinton and Linde Lunney, 'Isabella Maria Susan Tod', *DIB*. 31 Wilson, *Ulster politics, the formative years*, p. 44. 32 Jessie Waddell to Charles Waddell, 10 June 1874 (Hope Collection). 33 *Pall Mall Gazette*, 7 July 1874. 34 Walker, *Parliamentary election results*, p. 126; Daire Hogan, 'Sir William Findlater', *DIB*; *Evening Herald*, 26 Jan. 1895. 35 Andrew R. Holmes, 'Covenanter politics: evangelicalism, political liberalism and Ulster Presbyterians 1798–1914', *English Historical Review*, 125:513 (2010), pp 364–5.

SECTARIAN MURDERS IN MONAGHAN: 1869-70

By combining newspaper reports and official judicial system reports such as the *Return of outrages* (1869) with Waddell's casebook, a clearer view of deaths that were suspected sectarian murders emerges.[36] Of the ten murders captured in Waddell's casebooks from 1869 to 1877, three appear to have been politically motivated, the last of which took place in 1870, just one month after sheriff Coote was dismissed from office.[37] On 28 August 1869, an inquest taken by Waddell made national news after he was attacked while trying to conduct it. The death of James Quigley, 23, received a great deal of press and attention. Quigley was a young man who had reportedly left home the morning of 21 August 1869 and was found lying on the roadside later that day.[38] His lip was cut, his eye and face were swollen, his right arm was 'powerless' and there was a wound over his shoulder blade on the right side.[39] Although he was attended by Dr O'Reilly from Clones, he died a week later from his injuries. An investigation was required, including an inquest. As the coroner and his entourage, a local constable and other members of the Royal Irish Constabulary, approached the townland of Crossreagh, where the body lay, they were attacked with stones by Quigley family members. Waddell's horse was kicked and they were driven away, unable to conduct the inquest.[40] 'The stoning of the coroner' was widely covered by newspapers across the United Kingdom. The *South London Press* reported that Quigley, a Catholic, died under very suspicious circumstances and it was believed that he received a savage and brutal beating.[41] The reporting of Quigley as a Catholic and the presence of members of the Royal Irish Constabulary suggests that there may have been a sectarian motive for the killing. The *Sheffield Independent* ran the story emphasizing the attack on Waddell and police, reporting 'the coroner, who is an aged man, was ill-treated'.[42] The violent response of the Quigley family, a unique incident in Waddell's career, could indicate that their actions arose from a distrust of the coroner and constabulary in the execution of justice. It was reported in later years by the *Northern Standard* that the Quigley family soon realized their error and begged the forgiveness of the coroner.[43] The murder was not recorded

---

36 *Return of outrages reported to the Constabulary Office in Ireland, during the year 1869, with summaries for preceding years; and return of outrages reported by the Constabulary in Ireland in the months of January and February, 1870*, 353 [C.60], C1 1870, lvii, 34. 37 This figure includes only adults and does not include infanticide or suicide. In cases of domestic murder, where evidence was overwhelming but a neutral verdict was returned, they are included in the total. Inquests include: CB2, no. 5.935, James Quigley, 28–30 Aug. 1869; CB2, no. 9.973, William McMahon, 9 Aug. 1870; CB2, no. 5.945, Phillip Treanor, 1 Dec. 1869; CB2, no. 3.1025, John McBride, 3 Apr. 1872; CB2, no. 10.1032, Michael Mooney, 17 June 1872; CB2, no. 10.1072, Mary McCarron, 10 Apr. 1873; CB2, no. 22.1158, William Magwood, 15 Dec. 1875; CB3, no. 2.1168, Catherine Byrne, 24 Feb. 1876; CB3, no. 2.1187, Sarah Maguire, 17 Aug. 1876; CB3, no. 7.1192, John Boylan, 19 Sept. 1876; CB3, no. 3.1207, Patrick Brides, 5 Mar. 1877. 38 CB2, no. 5.935, James Quigley, 28–30 Aug. 1869. 39 Ibid. 40 *BN*, 21 Aug. 1869. 41 *South London Press*, 4 Sept. 1869. Quigley's name was misreported as Griggy. 42 *Sheffield Independent*, 4 Sept. 1869. 43 *NS*, 10 May 1878.

in the official government report on 'outrages'.[44] This indicates that some of these murders were hidden from official government reporting.

Later that year, on 1 December 1869, another Waddell inquest made national news, one held on the body of Philip Treanor.[45] The murder was recorded in the *Return of outrages* (1869) and the inquest that followed had many of the characteristics of a political one, not only in terms of the press coverage, but also in the listing of jurors' names to indicate the need for public transparency.[46] Treanor, a 25-year-old Catholic farmer, considered a powerful young man, had been missing for several days when his body was found by the river. He appeared to have been assaulted.[47] On 27 November 1869, he had been at the market with a friend selling 112st of oats at 10d. per pound; he made £4 16s. 3d. and went for a few drinks that evening. It was reported that he was attacked by five men, four of whom were Protestant.[48] The post-mortem examination conducted by Dr Young revealed that Treanor had a broken nose, a fractured skull, and his hands and arms had wounds that indicated that he had been defending himself.[49] The doctor stated that the injuries took place prior to his entry into the water. The verdict of death stated that the deceased suffered wounds inflicted on his head and submersion in water by the hands of some person or persons yet unknown.[50]

Five prisoners were held during the course of the inquest, four of whom were suspected Orangemen. On 11 December 1869, the *Downpatrick Recorder* stated that there was great interest in the case and that a 'bitter feeling has been engendered by it'.[51] Four of the prisoners were defended by Belfast solicitor John Rea (1822–81), who was known for his disruptive and controversial tactics in the courtroom as well as his desire to support both Orangemen and Fenians as members of the working classes.[52] In what was described in the *Northern Standard* as 'an extraordinary scene', Mr Rea attempted to take charge of the inquest, stating that 'there is no necessity for going further and we consider that you should direct the jury to find an open verdict'.[53] Waddell stood his ground and maintained order, stating 'Now, I'll have no speeches.'[54] Rea encouraged the prisoners to leave just prior to the conclusion of the inquest, but the police rearrested them upon instruction of the resident magistrate, Mr Lucas Alexander Treston. After some debate they were released.[55] Rea shouted to the prisoners, 'Go home immediately and if any man attempts to interfere with you, knock him down!', which was followed by great cheering in the court.[56] The press coverage and editorials published in the conservative *Dublin Evening Mail* played to the defence of the four Protestants:

---

44 'Outrages' was a term used by British and Irish politicians to communicate 'Irish violence' that was politically subversive.   45 CB2, no. 5.945, Philip Treanor, 1 Dec. 1869; McGoff-McCann, *Melancholy madness*, pp 64–7; *BN*, 8 Dec. 1869; *DEM*, 17 Dec. 1869; *Armagh Guardian*, 10 Dec. 1869; *Northern Whig*, 15 Dec. 1869; *DD*, 18 Dec. 1869; *FJ*, 18 Dec. 1869; *Ulster Gazette*, 17 Dec. 1869.   46 *BN*, 8 Dec. 1869.   47 Ibid.   48 *NS*, 11, 18 Dec. 1869; *Newry Reporter*, 18 Dec. 1869.   49 CB2, no. 5.945, Philip Treanor, 1 Dec. 1869.   50 Ibid.   51 *Downpatrick Recorder*, 11 Dec. 1869.   52 Bridget Hourican, 'John Rea', *DIB*.   53 *NS*, 18 Dec. 1869.   54 Ibid.   55 Ibid.   56 Ibid.

> These resident magistrates [RMs] are virtually agents of the Castle, and officers of the police, are not proper justices ... they are merely the agents of bureaucratic government ... [which] in Ulster ... is brought to bear most heavily for the discouragement of Protestants.[57]

The editorial further stated: 'Stipendiarism is a failure, as well as a growing danger to public liberty'.[58] Salaried employees, like resident magistrates (as opposed to the fee-based pay of coroners, which was regularly criticized), were attacked for the way they were compensated and they too were believed to undermine justice and peace in the country if they opposed the conservative Irish elite.

Another murder that made national news was the shooting of the deputy master of Orange Lodge No. 1952, William McMahon, on 12 July 1870. According to the report in the *Northern Standard*, a peaceable meal was taken by twenty Orangemen at Fort Singleton, the home of justice of the peace and Monaghan grand juror, Whitney Upton Moutray, when they were interrupted by a gathering of three hundred Catholics with guns and pitchforks. After retiring to their lodge, the Protestant schoolhouse nearby, they were fired upon and McMahon was shot. Four persons were arrested, three men and one woman.[59]

One month later, on 9 August 1870, the inquest took place. Three Orangemen were interviewed, and they described how their gathering of twenty men was surrounded by a crowd of approximately fifty Catholics, one of whom they identified as Peter Murray, who shouted, 'Here they are! Shoot them!'[60] Evidence also included that the Orangemen were playing party tunes, with drums and fifes, breaking the law established by the Party Processions Act. The crowd opened fire on the procession and McMahon was shot. Dr Stewart of Glaslough attempted to stop the bleeding, but McMahon subsequently died from his injuries. The verdict was that his death on 8 August 1870 resulted from a gunshot wound inflicted on the 12 July last by some person or persons unknown.[61]

Two unique events followed the McMahon inquest, unlike the Baird and Clarke sectarian murder investigations that took place in 1868–9, with new measures enacted to try to impose justice. First, Waddell's inquest taken on McMahon was followed up by an additional magisterial inquiry, which resulted in charges being laid against two Catholics, Peter Murray, a 14-year-old boy, and his cousin, a young woman, Margaret Murray.[62] The panel of magistrates included three resident magistrates – Mr McCartney, sub-investigator Mr Carleton and Lucas Alexander Treston – as well as local justices of the peace J.W. Johnstone, John Cunningham and Whitney Upton Moutray.[63] Moutray's participation in the 12 July 1870 incident as an Orangeman, combined with his position and influence as a justice of the peace serving the inquiry, emphasizes the bias and injustice that persisted. Second, as a result of a change in legislation to the Party Processions Act,

---

57 *DEM*, 18 Dec. 1869. 58 Ibid. 59 *NS*, 16 July 1870. 60 CB2, no. 9.973, William McMahon, 9 Aug. 1870. 61 Ibid. 62 *NS*, 20 Aug. 1870; *FJ*, 27 Feb. 1871. 63 Ibid.

which allowed victims' families to appeal for recompense for loss or harm in cases of sectarian murder, widow Mary McMahon made a claim for compensation.[64] She was requesting £1,000 for the loss of her husband and the resulting destitution she found herself in, along with her three children.[65] At the crown court following the Monaghan assizes on 23 February 1871, Justice Fitzgerald found, after reviewing the evidence, that there was no case against the boy and his cousin. He also highlighted Moutray's participation in the Twelfth of July activities as not being the behaviour of a gentleman, asked the 'Orangemen to abstain from this stupid mummery, this utterly childish marching with dirty yellow handkerchiefs', and stated that the only way to dissuade either party from participating in such behaviour was to make them pay for it with a fine.[66] The judge instructed that the £500 awarded to the McMahon family be paid not from the county as a whole, but rather specifically by the barony of Trough. The restitution imposed a value on a life and served as a reminder to local authorities that they could be held accountable for not policing sectarian violence.

MURDER IN CO. MONAGHAN (1870–7)

After a flurry of sectarian murders, this category of death ceased to appear in Waddell's casebook. Rather, the last seven years of Waddell's career as coroner reveal the social and moral values of the community and the rural and domestic power structure, where women and children, the elderly and the poor, the sick, and the physically and mentally weak remained at risk. They also reveal continuing abuses of local power and authority and reflect the difficulty of defining and finding justice in Monaghan's polarized society. While many of the inquests taken exhibit sudden and suspicious death as a result of diseases, accidents or natural causes, as confirmed by post-mortem examinations conducted by medical men, others contain evidence of murder.

Domestic murder recorded in Waddell's casebooks is again examined with a focus on inquests that took place in the 1870s, specifically when murder happened in the home. Domestic murder trends are consistent over the thirty-one years of Waddell's casebooks, showing that women who murdered their children were often excused by coroners' juries; while juries simply refused to name the men suspected of having killed women and children or hold them responsible, while it did name women guilty of adult murder. In many of these cases, prosecutors opted not to initiate criminal trials. Under common law, a married woman's civil identity became that of her husband, along with her children and property.[67] Men's domestic rights were protected and were safeguarded by other men within jurisprudence. An evaluation of the inquest verdicts in cases of domestic abuse where women and children were murdered by men supports the finding that their lives did not have as much

---

64 *NS*, 26 Nov. 1870, 4 Feb. 1871; 13 & 14 Vict., c. 2 (16 Aug. 1850), Party Processions Act. 65 *NS*, 4 Feb. 1871. 66 *FJ*, 27 Feb. 1871. 67 *Irish Times*, 17 Oct. 2012.

social or political value, particularly within a society divided by partisan politics. In addition to the values of the public jury, as reflected by such inquest verdicts, the administration also emphasized the value of naming suspects and gaining convictions in sectarian murders, and with that as a priority, many murders of women and children went without suspects being prosecuted or held accountable.

On 4 June 1873, Waddell held an inquest into the sudden death of 36-year-old Bridget McCabe of Liscumasky. It was reported that there had been 'quarrels and rows between the deceased and her husband, and her mother and sisters told Waddell 'there was very much bad feeling 'twas clear from all the evidence'.[68] Waddell made a personal note in his casebook, 'I could get [evidence] that their disputes never went further than scolding and exchanging of foul names'.[69] Dr Reed told the coroner that McCabe's death resulted from 'neglect' and 'previous disease', having given birth to a child the day before her death.[70] No further action was taken and the doctor's assessment concluded the matter. A salient feature of such investigations was the medicalization of the condition rather than the identification of a crime. On 17 August 1876, an inquest was held on the reported murder of Sarah Maguire. Since it was five days before the post-mortem was conducted, it was impossible to identify any bruising, but the examination did reveal that there was an excessive amount of putrefaction of the head, face and neck along with cuts on her fingers.[71] It also showed that she had pneumonia in both her lungs. Testimony revealed that Sarah had been the victim of her brother, John Maguire, who had cut her with a scythe when the two went to work in a meadow.[72] According to witness testimony, the pneumonia could be explained by the fact that John said Sarah had laid down in the wet grass of the meadow for an hour or more. It was 'commonly said that she and her brother John quarrelled', and 'the voice of the county said he had caused his sister's death'.[73] Due to the absence of both of the prosecution solicitors, Mr Haire Foster and Mr Dungeon, on several occasions, which resulted in several adjournments, the inquest was delayed until 20 September 1876, when the jury reached a verdict of death by natural causes.[74] A lack of commitment on behalf of the local prosecution to protect the rights of Sarah Maguire illustrates the lack of support for women and children in cases of domestic abuse. The case also supports the body of evidence that Monaghan officials were averse to following the instructions of the administration when it came to local crimes.

On 4 September 1875, the inquest held in Clones on one-day-old infant Mary Maguire made clear that the child had been beaten. Dr Henry's post-mortem examination found two plasters on the back and front of the child, a black mark behind the left ear, a black eye and skull fractures in three places.[75] He and Dr

68 CB2, Inquiry Bridget McCabe, 4 June 1873. 69 Ibid. 70 Ibid. 71 CB2, no. 2.1187, Sarah Maguire, 17 Aug. 1876. Waddell included a note on his 1876 government return identifying the inquests taken. It stated, 'This case was ordered by government and the proceedings of it directed by the authorities representing it.' 72 Ibid. 73 Ibid. 74 Ibid. 75 CB2, no. 7.1143, Mary Maguire, 4 Sept. 1875.

O'Reilly concluded that the infant died as a result of violence. Regardless of the clear evidence that the infant's father, Peter Maguire, was responsible for the murder, the coroner's jury returned a verdict that 'Mary Maguire came to her death on the 31 August 1875 by extensive injuries received to her head, but how or by what means the jury have no evidence to show.'[76] Overall, these verdicts indicate that the domestic domain was owned by men and crimes committed within it were glossed over in verdicts from male coroners' juries.

The pattern of verdicts of infanticide inquests demonstrates that Waddell's juries continued to return neutral verdicts (i.e., death by natural causes) that exculpated mothers who murdered their infants. A total of 97 inquests held on infants were taken by Waddell throughout his 32-year career and in only eight was the mother identified by name.[77] Throughout the 1870s, patterns from previous decades remain the same in cases where the mother was known and regardless of evidence of concealment of pregnancy or overwhelming evidence of strangulation or beating, the mother was not blamed and a neutral verdict was reached. An example of such an inquest took place on 8 February 1871. Testimony at the inquest held on the body of infant McCullogh, child of servant Jane McCullogh, revealed that other servants were unaware Jane was pregnant until told by the master that she was confined.[78] Dr Lancaster Joyce deposed that having taken a post-mortem examination, the deceased was not merely born dead but was 'dead fully 24 hours prior to birth'.[79] The verdict was death from natural causes.[80] Another such example was that of the infant child of single mother Susan Maginis, who lodged with Rose and Felix Fitzpatrick.[81] At the inquest on 27 May 1871, the couple testified that they did not know Maginis was pregnant until the night the child was born, and although the mother tried to feed it, it was too little, it would not suck and it died. The verdict of death was from natural causes.[82] In both cases, the evidence provided by doctors and witnesses focused on the pre-conditions of the infants that indicated they were not well enough to survive.

Evidence from two inquests that name the mother suggests that the social status of the single mother of a dead infant influenced the outcome of the inquest. On 17 January 1877, Waddell held an inquest on the body of a male infant whose mother, Mary O'Hare, was a servant of Andrew Trimble at Cornacassa, land steward to justice of the peace James Hamilton esq. of Cornacassa House.[83] Trimble and his wife both testified as witnesses stating that they were unaware of her pregnancy and that the body of the child was found in O'Hare's bedroom. Dr Woods examined the body of the infant, and while he said he saw no marks of violence,

---

76 Ibid.   77 The inquests that name the mother as the primary contributor to the child's death include: CB1, no. 8.91, Catherine Magin, 2 Aug. 1847; CB2, no. 24.615, infant child, 7 Jan. 1861; CB2, no. 21.445, infant child, 7 Jan. 1857; CB2, no. 10.541, infant child, 7 Apr. 1859; CB2, no. 24.615, infant child, 7 Jan. 1861; CB2, no. 10.940, female infant, 4–6 Oct. 1869; CB3, no. 14.1199, infant male child, 17 Jan. 1877; CB3, no. 15.1200, infant child, 17 Jan. 1877.   78 CB1, no. 26.990, infant McCullogh, 8 Feb. 1871.   79 Ibid.   80 Ibid.   81 CB2, no. 11.1001, infant child, 27 Feb. 1871.   82 Ibid.   83 CB3, no. 14.1199, infant male child, 17 Jan 1877; *NS*, 3 Nov. 1877.

he found that the child died from suffocation on mucus as 'the poor Mother was altogether ignorant of the necessary attendance required in her situation'.[84] The verdict from the jury stated, 'We find that Mary O'Hare gave birth to a child in the house of Mr Andrew Trimble at Cornacassa on 16th inst. and from the evidence given at the inquest, we find death resulted from natural causes.'[85] A different inquest and outcome took place on that same day, 17 January 1877, on an infant child in Monaghan town. According to Head Constable Haverty, a woman named Mary Conlon, who lived on Jail Hill, who had been in a family way, was reduced in size and the belief was that she had given birth and placed the child in a box and buried it.[86] The box was secured and brought to the police barracks. Surgeon Young carried out a post-mortem examination and determined that the child had 'feebly respired after birth but its death was not caused by violence but most probably by the difficult labour and want of proper care on the part of the mother and her attendants'.[87] The verdict returned that death resulted from neglect and want of care on the part of the mother Mary Conlon and its 'dead body was placed by its mother where 'twas found'.[88] While the circumstances of both inquests are very similar and evidence suggests both women killed their infants, the case of the servant at Cornacassa with the backing of the trusted and empowered land steward and his wife resulted in a verdict of natural causes; while the unmarried mother from Jail Hill was named and considered guilty of neglect.

In cases of familial domestic murders that resulted in the naming of suspects in inquest verdicts, it was done with the intention of supporting a conviction at a subsequent trial. The connection between the inquest naming a suspect and a criminal trial was an expectation placed on coroners by the public and the administration in order to measure the value of their work. On 17 June 1872, Waddell held an inquest on Michael Mooney, an elderly Catholic man murdered by family members as they fought over the use of a field for grazing their cattle. Both attackers, his son-in-law's father and brother, John and Francis Mulligan, were identified as having caused his death in the verdict.[89] They were later convicted of the crime, Francis received five years penal servitude while John received a mitigated sentence of two months.[90] On 10 April 1873, an inquest was taken on the body of Mary McCarron, a woman who was killed by her mentally ill daughter, Catherine.[91] Described as 'out of her mind of the past six years' and regularly tied up in the house with a rope, Catherine had escaped her bondage, taken hold of a large stick, and beaten her mother. The verdict stated that Mary McCarron had come to her death from 'certain wounds inflicted on her by her daughter, Catherine McCarron'.[92] Another inquest was held for a 60-year-old Presbyterian man who stood less than four feet in height, William Magwood, who was found beaten to death on the roadside with his skull crushed.[93] Evidence revealed that Magwood's mother was dying and he

84 Ibid. 85 Ibid. 86 CB3, no. 15.1200, infant child, 17 Jan. 1877. 87 Ibid. 88 Ibid. 89 CB2, no. 10.1032, Michael Mooney, 17 June 1872. 90 *NS*, 20 July 1872; McGoff-McCann, *Melancholy madness*, pp 266–7. 91 CB2, no. 10.1072, Mary McCarron, 10 Apr. 1873. 92 Ibid. 93 CB2, no. 22.1158, William Magwood, 15 Dec. 1875; *NS*, 27 Dec. 1875.

planned to sell the farm to the displeasure of his nephews and other members of the family. The verdict stated that Magwood's death on the night of 13 December 1875 resulted from 'severe injuries inflicted on or sustained by him but under what circumstances the jury has not had evidence to show'.[94] Although unnamed in the inquest verdict, Magwood's nephew, George Magwood, was later identified and charged with the murder by police, who had enough evidence to take the case to trial.[95] George was later discharged and the crown dropped the case against him.[96] Evidence that contributed towards identifying a suspect in murder cases was not always immediately available at the time of the inquest. Given that inquests most often took place immediately after death, further investigation by police was often necessary to identify a suspect to hold and try to convict.

The public and the administration evaluated the coroner for his ability to identify suspects in murder cases as well as his contribution towards their conviction in the criminal justice system. As opposed to their English counterparts, Irish coroners were measured by their ability to find and name those who might be guilty of committing murder rather than their ability to secure evidence for a future investigation or find an accurate cause of sudden, accidental and suspicious death. While McMahon stated that coroners had significant influence over juries and evidence suggests that they guided and drove verdicts, this view does not take into consideration that the very nature of the role of coroner put these men in conflict with the local elite.[97] Additionally, this study provides evidence that Waddell and juries trusted in the doctors' findings. The verdicts in Waddell's casebooks indicate that if coroners had such power over juries, it would have resulted in a much higher number of named murderers in coroners' inquests. Instead, the lack of named murderers indicates that verdicts reflected more accurately the voice of the people and their social values rather than the coroner's guidance in determining the outcome.

THE POLITICS OF THE RAILWAY: DEATHS ALONG THE LINE

Alongside the fight for political power, innovation and investment opportunities continued to present themselves as the country continued to implement legislation and build infrastructure that modernized Irish society. Following the introduction of the railways in 1834, construction continued each decade and brought with it opportunity for private investment and local employment. As the railways expanded across the country, there were few safety procedures implemented during construction and fatalities became a common occurrence. Before 1846, compensation to the families of those killed on the railway was through the coroner's court, whereby they could award monies using a deodand. In England, railway companies were often penalized with a levy by coroners' juries returning verdicts that

---

94 CB2, no. 22.1158, William Magwood, 15 Dec. 1875.   95 *NS*, 24 Dec. 1875.   96 *Dublin Weekly Nation*, 22 July 1876.   97 McMahon, *Homicides and pre-Famine and Famine Ireland*, p. 169.

found the companies liable for the deaths of its workers. On 3 January 1842, the *Freeman's Journal* reported that following the death of a victim of a catastrophe on the Great Western Railway near Sonning in Berkshire, the coroner's jury had levied a deodand on the engine and trains of £100 and further recommended that 'the passenger truck be in the future placed further from the engine'.[98] In the same edition, another article highlighted a fifth inquest from another large accident and although the jury unanimously agreed that the railway was guilty of grossly improper management, there were no assets left to offer a deodand.[99] Deodands were also determined by coroners' juries in Ireland. One such inquest reported by the *Warder and Dublin Weekly Mail* on 25 February 1835 was held by Dublin county coroner John McCarthy on the body of a man who was killed on the Dublin and Kingstown Railway. Passenger William Thompson died having either fallen or leapt off the carriage and the jury ruled on a deodand of £40.[100]

As a result of the volume and inconsistency of deodands levied on railway companies by coroners' juries, the power of awarding financial compensation was taken away from the inquest with the Coroners' Act of 1846. From then onwards, compensation for the death of passengers and railway workers, if a suit was brought, was determined in civil court. The abolition of the deodand from the inquest had helped redefine the role of the coroner, removing not only any doubt about his own personal gain in compensation (coroners had received a percentage from a coroner's sale of assets) but also removing that power from the coroners' juries. This helped refocus the objective of the inquest, which was to find an accurate cause of death.

While the railway contributed to the modernization of Irish society by transforming the landscape, it was also an industry that became politicized. The Trillick derailment, which took place in Tyrone on 15 September 1854, resulted in the deaths of two firemen after an unknown group placed large boulders on the tracks to disrupt the travel of Lord Enniskillen and the Apprentice Boys, a loyalist group from Londonderry.[101] The incident was considered by elites to be politically motivated, a deliberate act of sectarianism, and six Catholic railway workers were held in prison for over a year, accused of the crime.[102] It might be considered one of the first acts of modern transportation terrorism in Ireland. The effects of the incident were extensive and many of those who used the train no longer felt safe.[103] Such fear likely added to the political divide.

The railway also offered potential economic prosperity for those able to invest. Lee highlights that of £12.5m invested in Irish railways between 1831 and 1852, nearly 80 per cent came from private investors, while the other 20 per cent was split between the government and private lenders.[104] The local elite in Co. Monaghan

98 *FJ*, 3 Jan. 1842.   99 Ibid.   100 *Warder and Dublin Weekly Mail*, 25 Feb. 1835.   101 *The Evening Freeman*, 20 Sept. 1845; Desmond Fitzgerald, 'The Trillick derailment 1854', *Clogher Record*, 15:1 (1994), pp 31–47.   102 Fitzgerald, 'The Trillick derailment', p. 31, 36; *FJ*, 20 Sept. 1854.   103 Fitzgerald, 'The Trillick derailment', p. 33; *BN*, 25 Sept. 1854.   104 Joseph Lee, 'The provision of capital for early Irish railways, 1830–53', *Irish Historical Studies*, 16:61 (1968), p. 40.

were keen to avail of the opportunity as well as improve the infrastructure in the county. One public meeting took place on 19 October 1844 in Monaghan and was well attended by landed proprietors, merchants, politicians and Orangemen, including Charles Powell Leslie, Edward Lucas, Henry Mitchell, Thomas Anketell, Robert Murray (coroner), Waddell, and many more.[105] This large group of men were interested in ensuring that the Ulster Railway Company build a railway line through Monaghan town from Armagh and stated they 'had no hesitation in saying that many of their proprietors would be large shareholders in the proposed undertaking' to ensure its construction and completion.[106] This investment opportunity was available to the few who had the means to do so, and as such further added to the politicization of the railway.

When combined with political polarization in Co. Monaghan, investigation into fatal accidents on the railway brought doubt, mistrust and, potentially, miscarriages of justice. The local elite, who were MPs, magistrates, justices of the peace or civil servants such as coroners, and who were also investors, were presented with a conflict of interest if involved in an investigation of the death of a railway labourer. Folklore suggests seven to eleven men were killed when a wall of earth buried them alive and that the deaths were covered up. The incident is believed to have taken place in July 1856 in the parish of Killeevan on the Dundalk–Clones–Enniskillen line, while they were constructing a railway bridge at Ballynure.[107] It was said that a relief tunnel was dug to try to free the men, and that a mausoleum exists, unmarked, where it is believed those who died were buried.[108] That same month, in a different parish, Waddell conducted inquests on two men who were killed when a wall of earth described as 'a mass of stuff' struck and hit the men, knocking them down while constructing the Armagh–Monaghan railway line in the nearby parish of Donagh. Bernard Clarken died on 24 July 1856 after being buried by the wall of earth falling on top of him, while just six days later, on 30 July 1856, Francis McMurrer was killed in the exact same manner.[109] While there is no evidence in Waddell's casebook to suggest a cover-up, and Waddell regularly investigated railway deaths, the folklore does indicate that there was a scepticism and distrust of the railway companies, likely due to the politics of their investors as compared to those involved in the construction of the railways. Waddell recorded twenty-seven fatalities involving the railways from 1847 to 1872; twenty-two of the inquests returned neutral verdicts, while just five blamed the railway company for negligence.

In 1871 and 1872, Waddell carried out five railway inquests. In them, the jurors focused on public safety. There was the inquest on 22 August 1872 on the body of John Gormley, a 25-year-old shoemaker who was run over by a goods train.[110] He had been sleeping on the railway tracks. Regardless of his negligence, the coroner's

---

105 *NS*, 19 Oct. 1844.   106 Ibid.   107 *NS*, 17 Oct. 2002; *NS*, 14 Aug. 2003.   108 Ibid.
109 CB2, no. 2.426, Bernard Clarken, 25 July 1856; CB2, no. 3.427, Francis McMurrer, 31 July 1856.   110 CB2, no. 8.1042, John Gormley, 22 Aug. 1872.

jury returned a verdict that stated they 'also think that the railway officials are to blame for not prosecuting trespassers on the line, as this is not the first case of similar serious accidents'.[111] While the inquest no longer determined a monetary value to offer to the families of victims, it was used as the voice of the people, reflecting societal values of the time. Additionally, such a verdict supported surviving family members who might attempt to retrieve compensation in civil court.

THE DISTRICT LUNATIC ASYLUM AND THE MENTALLY ILL

An evaluation of inquest verdicts in cases of suicide, using the prism of blame, reveals the social values of the coroners' juries. There were ten suicides in Waddell's casebooks from 1870–7, and each followed the same pattern in identifying the cause of death, highlighting post-mortem evidence that wounds were self-inflicted, and declaring that the deceased had suffered from either temporary insanity or having been 'affected in his mind'. On 14 June 1872, an inquest was held on the body of Jane Devine, a servant of Mr James Fiddes of Hollywood. Dr Woods of Scotstown, who knew the deceased, testified that

> she had laboured under melancholy madness resulting from a predisposition to that state of mind. It ran in her family and was increased by her state of bodily health, a well-developed attack of English Cholera. The verdict of death was from suffocation of drowning and which was her own act whilst labouring under a fit of melancholy madness.[112]

Some who suffered from mental illness or 'lunacy' were sent to the local district lunatic asylum. The annual *Lunatic asylums Ireland* report (1877) stated that of the 765 deaths that took place inside asylums that year, four of them were suicides and a coroner's inquest was held on each. One verdict defending the environmental and structural integrity of the asylum stated,

> Verdicts exonerating character returned, in one instance, however, with an expression of opinion by some members of the jury, that the window from which the deceased threw himself was constructed with due strength against such an occurrence.[113]

Investigation into death at the asylum bore a cost, which was imposed on the local elite, and therefore, similar to the gaol, a value was placed on the lives of the mentally ill, who were often neglected and hidden from society. This value would take on more meaning as that population grew and costs continued to rise, and reflected

---

111 *Belfast Weekly News*, 31 Aug. 1872. 112 CB2, no. 11.1033, Jane Devine, 14 June 1872. 113 *Lunatic asylums Ireland: the twenty-sixth report on the district, criminal, and private lunatic asylums in Ireland; with appendices*, 449 [C.1750], HC 1877, xli, 7.

Lee's findings that modernization of Irish society expanded not only with technology, but with the ability to take care of all its members.[114]

The process of institutional reform, innovation and expansion manifested itself through the creation of gaols and workhouses as well as public district lunatic asylums. Politicians initiated the legislation required to provide care for the mentally ill in Ireland based on a belief that it would be better to hold them in public asylums purpose-built specifically for their care, rather than in gaols or private facilities.[115] In 1817, 1821 and 1826, Lunacy (Ireland) Acts were passed that gave power to county grand juries to establish new institutions for mentally ill people who were poor, or who had been charged with offences.[116] The district lunatic asylums were designed and constructed in three phases. The first was prior to 1825 and incorporated Bentham's panopticon principle, similar to Irish gaols, with central 'moral' observation, but with variations of a radial plan to accommodate the separation and isolation of inmates based on systems of classification, prioritized by gender. The next two phases in the construction of asylums took place in 1845–55 and 1862–9, with architectural competitions launched across Ireland prioritizing features of design based on local requirements and a focus on building larger asylums due to demand for accommodation and overcrowding.[117]

In 1864, architect John McCurdy (1824–85) won the design competition for Monaghan district lunatic asylum (see Map 4), which was to be the largest of its kind in Ireland at that time.[118] The main building combined cell blocks and thousands of yards of corridors, along with rooms and beds able to accommodate 340 patients.[119] Other buildings erected included two detached infirmaries and the house of the first Monaghan chief medical superintendent, Dr John C. Robertson.[120] Management and staff were hired and a board of governors was appointed. Positions were filled, including an engineer; a land steward; first-, second- and third-class male attendants and female nurses; a hall porter; a cook; a laundress; kitchen, laundry and hall maids; and a gatekeeper.[121]

The asylum began admitting patients in May 1869.[122] Twenty were transferred from local gaols in Monaghan, another 20 were admitted by governors and medical officers, and another 52 inmates were admitted as a result of justices' warrants.[123] The asylum also received a transfer of 113 patients from the Armagh asylum in the first three months, and by 31 December 1869, the population of the Monaghan asylum was comprised of 171 patients (91 male, 80 female).[124] Similar to gaols, the

---

114 Lee, *The modernisation of Irish society*, p. 1. 115 Joseph Robins, *Fools and mad: a history of the insane in Ireland* (Dublin, 1986), p. 60. 116 57 Geo. III, c. 106 (25 June 1817), Lunacy Act (Ireland); 1 & 2 Geo. IV, c. 33 (28 May 1821), Lunacy (Ireland) Act; 7 Geo. IV, c. 14 (31 May 1826), Lunacy (Ireland) Act. 117 Ibid. 118 'McCurdy, John', *Dictionary of Irish architects*, dia.ie. 119 Mulligan, *The buildings of south Ulster*, pp 479–80. 120 Ibid. 121 *Lunatic asylums Ireland: the nineteenth annual report on the district, criminal and private lunatic asylums in Ireland, with appendices*, 287 [C.202], HC 1870, xxxiv, 102. 122 NS, 22 May 1869. 123 *The nineteenth annual report of lunatic asylums in Ireland*, 287 [C.202], HC 1870, xxxiv, 102. 124 Ibid., 80; *Lunatic asylums Ireland: the twentieth annual report of the district, criminal and private lunatic asylums in Ireland, with appendices*, 427 [C.440], HC 1871, xxvi, 25–6.

Table 13: Supposed causes of 'mental disease' (1872)	
Moral causes	Physical causes
Poverty and reverse of fortune	Intemperance and irregularity of living
Grief, fear and anxiety	Cerebral diseases or afflictions
Love, jealousy and seduction	Congenital idiocy, & c.
Domestic quarrels and afflictions	Effects of climate and sunstroke
Relgious excitement	Febrile affections
Study and mental excitement	Bodily injuries and disorders
Ill-treatment	Abuse of medicine
Pride	Sedintary habits
Anger	Hereditary

Source: HC, *Twenty-second report on the district, criminal and private lunatic asylums in Ireland, with appendices* (1873).

inmates that made up the population were individually categorized using multiple labels in order to better identify their conditions (see Table 13). General subjective labels included 'lunatics', 'imbeciles' and 'epileptics'. The diagnosis or category of each patient would indicate their status as curable or incurable. Inmates were also classified as 'convalescent', 'quiet and orderly but insane', 'moderately tranquil', 'noisy and refractory', 'imbecile and epileptic' and 'suicidal'. The many different categories and labels for patients that required different and special needs contributed to the demand for increased space within the institution, and the growing population required regulation and investigation to ensure proper treatment.

In the first eight months after it opened, from May through December 1869, eight deaths were reported at the Monaghan asylum, but only one inquest was held – on 66-year-old inmate Terence McDonald, on 13 September 1869.[125] This indicates that only certain deaths, those under sudden or suspicious circumstances, were investigated by the coroner. McDonald had been admitted to Monaghan asylum on 14 June 1869 and was diagnosed as 'melancholic with decided propensities to self-destruction'.[126] He was found on the morning of 4 September 1869 with a superficial wound about two inches long, self-inflicted, on the right side of his neck. Three days later, he again tried to commit suicide, with a piece of tin torn from the edge of a chamber utensil.[127] After the second attempt, he was moved from the dormitory to a single room and a special attendant was put in charge of him. Though he ate well, McDonald did not sleep. On the afternoon of 11 September 1869, he died. The verdict of death was exhaustion of the nervous system.[128] Only

125 *Lunatic asylums Ireland: the twenty-first report on the district, criminal and private lunatic asylums in Ireland, with appendices*, 323 [C.647], HC 1871, xxvii, 20; CB2, no. 9.939, Terence McDonald, 13 Sept. 1869. 126 Ibid. 127 The chamber pot and/or lid appears to have been made of metal. By tearing a loose piece of the metal from it, McDonald was able to make a weapon. 128 Ibid.

one witness provided evidence, consulting surgeon A.K. Young, who told the jury that he saw the deceased shortly after his attempt to commit suicide and on several occasions up to the time of his death.[129] Notably, the testimony from the special attendant is absent. While the annual *Lunatic asylums Ireland* report (1870) credited Dr Robertson with 'very satisfactory results' after being open just eight months, it would take another calendar year to glean more insight into the treatment of patients and the running of the institution.[130]

From January 1870 through December 1870, Waddell conducted two more inquests at the asylum. The first death was reported to the coroner by Dr Robertson, on 26 January 1870 and the inquest was conducted two days later on the body of inmate James Lamb, who became faint while eating his dinner of meat, soup and potatoes in the dining hall.[131] House steward John Patterson told the inquest jury that he suddenly saw two of the attendants catch hold of Lamb and carry him out into the open air, but he appeared weak and died two minutes later.[132] The verdict was death from serious appoplexy (cerebral haemorrhage or stroke). The second inquest conducted by Waddell that year took place on 17 December 1870 on the body of 65-year-old inmate Owen Coyle, who had been found dead in his bed.[133] Dr Robertson deposed that Coyle had been admitted on 17 March 1870, labouring under general paralysis, and on the day of the 15 December, Robertson had seen him and observed that his paralysis would worsen. Second-class attendant Robert Gibson deposed that he had put Coyle to bed that night a little earlier than usual at his request, and in the morning he found him dead. The verdict was that he died from paralysis.[134]

The following year, when the next annual *Lunatic asylums Ireland* report (1871) was published, it revealed the disturbing news that mortality at the Monaghan district lunatic asylum had been unusually high at 16 per cent.[135] The total number of patients under treatment from January to December 1870 had been 271, admissions during the year reached 100, and 30 patients died.[136] The report also revealed that several of the attendants at the Monaghan asylum had been brought up on charges of misconduct.[137] Attendant John Kane had his leave withdrawn for three months as punishment for drunkenness. He was then found guilty of gross insubordination to Dr Robertson and immediately dismissed.[138] Attendant John Renning was dismissed for cruelty, having struck a patient with a strap.[139] Three more attendants – Boyd, Keenan and Gordon – were found guilty of gross misconduct for leaving the asylum at night.[140] Boyd and Keenan were dismissed, but Gordon was given a fine and a reprimand and allowed to stay.[141] Lastly, the board of governors were complaining of great expenses for repairs on the building

129 CB2, no. 9.939, Terence McDonald, 13 Sept. 1869. 130 *The nineteenth annual report of lunatic asylums in Ireland*, 287 [C.202], HC 1870, xxxiv, 23. 131 CB2, no. 21.951, James Lamb, 28 Jan. 1870. 132 Ibid. 133 CB2, no. 20.984, Owen Coyle, 17 Dec. 1870. 134 Ibid. 135 Based on the daily average number of residents being 191. 136 *The twentieth report of lunatic asylums in Ireland*, 437 [C.440], HC 1871, xxvi, 25. 137 Ibid., p. 26. 138 Ibid., p. 25. 139 Ibid. 140 Ibid. 141 Ibid.

which was just over a year old. There were leaks, damp walls, defective plastering and problems with sewage. The report stated that great interest was taken by the governors in the affairs at the asylum and that they were highly efficient.[142]

While the inspectors and the board reflected upon the report for the previous year, including the several grave instances of misconduct by attendants, the *Lunatic asylums Ireland* report (1872) praised the admirable working order of the Monaghan asylum throughout 1871.[143] This time Dr Robertson was satisfied with the general good conduct of the asylum staff, which was also confirmed by his board of governors.[144] The report stated that there was nothing particular to observe on admissions, discharges or deaths, with the exceptional case of a suicide.[145] It stated that

> The patient, L.M., is reported to have been sick and in a dying state, he was not known or suspected to have any suicidal tendency and was found suspended by a piece of his bed-sheet, which had been tied to the fastenings of the window shutter of the single-bedded room in which he slept. An inquest was held, and a verdict in accordance with the above facts returned.[146]

Waddell's casebook shows that he held an inquest on inmate Laurance Meighan on 6 April 1871. Dr Robertson testified before the coroner's jury that Meighan had been admitted on 3 December 1870 as 'a melancholy lunatic and imbecile in mind and in very bad health (consumption)', but 'before and since his admission' he had never threatened to commit suicide.[147] First-class attendant Alexander Gordon (presumably the same Gordon previously threatened with dismissal) deposed that there had been no change in the deceased's health over the preceding several weeks. He stated that on 5 April 1870, Meighan ate a hearty supper and there was no change in his manner at bedtime,

> but on opening his room the next morning I saw him suspended by a strip taken from the sheet of his bed clothes and well twisted. I promptly took him down but by then he was quite dead. Though there was no reason to apprehend suicide of the deceased, yet [*sic*] there was always a strict supervision kept over him in common with all the other inmates of this establishment.[148]

The verdict was that he had died the morning of 6 April 1871 from strangulation voluntarily inflicted by himself.[149] The coroner, in an unusual gesture, wrote an extra sentence after the verdict, 'Deceased was of very weak mind.'[150] With no other evidence, the inquest verdict placed the blame in the hands of the deceased.

---

142 Ibid., p. 26. 143 *Lunatic asylums Ireland: the twenty-first report on the district, criminal and private lunatic asylums in Ireland, with appendices*, 647 [C.647], HC 1872, xxvii, 20. 144 Ibid., 20–1. 145 Ibid. 146 Ibid. 147 CB2, no. 6.996, Laurance Meighan, 6 Apr. 1871. 148 Ibid. 149 Ibid. 150 Ibid.

The report also identified that another patient died from suffocation in an epileptic fit.[151] This again matched up with Waddell's casebook. The coroner held an inquest on 40-year-old asylum inmate Thomas McCormick on 18 January 1871. Dr Robertson testified before the coroner's jury that McCormick was admitted to the asylum on 16 June 1869 suffering from epilepsy.[152] He stated that he saw the inmate daily until last week, when his condition changed and he was steadily becoming worse. At 2 a.m., on the morning of 17 January 1871, attendants Edward Cosgrove and Joseph Brown heard him having a seizure and settled him. When they went back to check on him at 7 a.m., he was found lying on his face dead.[153] Cosgrove told the jury, 'I attended [him] as carefully as if he had been my father.'[154] The verdict was death from suffocation from having turned on his face during an epileptic fit.[155] After McCormick's inquest, Waddell only conducted four further inquests at the asylum over the next six years; instead, he consistently held inquiries on inmates there, a total of 99.[156] These inquiries captured the diagnoses of the inmates' conditions (i.e. epilepsy, melancholia) combined with the disease or natural cause of death. Very different than inquests, inquiries did not require a jury but rather an update from the medical superintendent and the verification of the coroner.

Demand for Waddell's attendance at the deaths of inmates of the asylum was due to the increase in the asylum population and resulted in a permanent assignment. He was called to attend asylum deaths at the discretion of Dr Robertson and paid £1 for each inquiry, as was recorded in the margin of his casebook. On 8 November 1876, a letter from Waddell's cousin Kate Murch confirmed her receipt of his last letter, and stated, 'I was very pleased to ... hear the account of your health and it is very nice that you have been appointed Coroner for the Asylum'.[157] It is possible that given Waddell's age (he was 78 years old at the time of his appointment to the asylum) this assignment was created for him so he could continue serving a useful purpose without travelling too much. At the time of Waddell's last inquiry taken at the Monaghan asylum in September 1877, the institution was holding 414 inmates: 216 men and 198 women.[158]

POVERTY AND STARVATION IN CO. MONAGHAN: 1873-7

Although the administration continued to erect public buildings and enforce legislation on grand juries to ensure the safe protection of inmates at institutions, the Irish Poor Law continued to put beggars and mendicants at risk.[159] Emigration,

---

151 *The twenty-first report lunatic asylums in Ireland*, 647 [C647], HC 1872, xxvii, 20. 152 CB2, no. 22.936, Thomas McCormick, 18 Jan. 1871. 153 Ibid. 154 Ibid. 155 Ibid. 156 This is the total number of inquiries held at the asylum taken from CB2 and CB3. 157 Murch to Waddell, 8 Nov. 1876 (Hope Collection). 158 *Lunatic asylums Ireland: the twenty-seventh report on the district, criminal and private lunatic asylums in Ireland, with appendices*, 395 [C2037], HC 1878, xxxix, 42. 159 The terms used to capture the mobile poor changed over time. After 1850, mendicancy became associated with vagrancy and crime, and was seen as a lifestyle choice. Crossman, *Poverty and the poor in Ireland*, p. 199.

employment opportunities and more stringent laws against mendicancy resulted in an increase in elderly and child patients, the sick and the insane in institutions.[160] Meanwhile, the administrators of the workhouse system were condemned for the poor conditions and treatment of inmates.[161] The conservative position of the Monaghan Poor Law guardians on the issue of offering outdoor relief did not change and, as such, several inquests capture the ongoing suffering of the poor who entered – and those who refused to seek entry to – Co. Monaghan workhouses in the 1870s. While the Clones Poor Law Union did offer some outdoor relief, it was minimal. Waddell's inquests reveal the continuing pattern whereby people died because they were too ashamed to enter the workhouse and there was a lack of, or inadequate, outdoor relief.

Two inquests captured the phenomenon of the elderly who waited until near death to enter the workhouse, a trend that had continued from previous years. First, on 31 January 1873, Waddell conducted an inquest at Clones workhouse on the body of 60-year-old Mary Maguire, who had died the first night of her admission.[162] Thomas Wilson, relieving officer for the Clones Poor Law Union, stated he 'did not know her but gave her the ticket on the strength of the statement of one in whom he places every confidence'.[163] Wilson appears to be communicating that Maguire knew of her condition and was not upfront about the serious nature of her illness, and as a result the Poor Law union would have to pay for the attendance of Dr Henry to care for her, and thus the county must accept the expense. Such costs were a topic of focus at the Monaghan quarter sessions in July 1876. The *Leinster Express* reported on a Poor Law guardians meeting in Co. Monaghan that took place on 22 July 1876.[164] It highlighted how a Monaghan Poor Law guardian who issued a visiting ticket to a person who was not a fit subject for poor relief is fixed with the liability to pay the doctor's fees if the ticket is cancelled.[165] The Monaghan quarter sessions held thereafter agreed that the 'guardian that issues the ticket will be held responsible if it can be shown that the ticket was issued to an improper person'.[166] Another inquest was taken a month later, on 3 February 1873, on 90-year-old Bridget Smith, who was admitted to the Clones workhouse at 1.30 p.m. but died less than six hours later.[167] Described by workhouse matron Ann Colstan as 'very weak, filthy and also very cold and very old', after being put into a warm bath and bed, Smith was almost speechless.[168] Dr Henry attended. Although he left some stimulants for the patient, she died shortly thereafter. The verdict was death from old age, infirmity and exposure to the cold.[169]

In 1876, a commission report revealed disputes over outdoor relief, which remained a prominent issue. It was stated in the *Lunacy Inquiry Commission report* (1876) that there was evidence from Monaghan that outdoor relief was used for

160 Laurence M. Geary, 'The medical profession, health care and the Poor Law in nineteenth-century Ireland' in Virginia Crossman and Peter Gray (eds), *Poverty and welfare in Ireland, 1838–1948* (Dublin, 2011), p. 200. 161 Ibid. 162 CB2, no. 2.1064, Mary Maguire, 31 Jan. 1873. 163 Ibid. 164 *Leinster Express*, 22 July 1876. 165 Ibid. 166 Ibid. 167 CB2, no. 3.1065, Bridget Smith, 3 Feb. 1873. 168 Ibid. 169 Ibid.

payment of rent and that it was so meagre that the recipients were forced to subsist on charity.[170] Inquests taken by Waddell support these findings. On 19 December 1874, Waddell held an inquest into the death of Mary Prunty. The 43-year-old spinster, according to her brother Francis, supported herself by her own industry (likely begging) and was generally of good health.[171] She lived alone in a 'wretched cabin that could not turn out neither cold, nor rain nor snow'.[172] The verdict was death from exposure to the extreme severity of the weather for some days past and most probably super-inducing an attack of paralysis.[173] Prunty lived in the Monaghan Poor Law Union and therefore had no option of outdoor relief, which could have saved her life.

However, another inquest supports the findings of the government commission's investigation and provides evidence that recipients of outdoor relief were dying. On 6 April 1876, Waddell held an inquest on the body of 70-year-old Peter Began, who 'when unable to work was able to get on the relief fund'.[174] Susan Welsh testified that Began, when he was able to work, supported himself by his own industry and slept on a bed in Bernard Welsh's barn.[175] When he was unable to go to work, he received 1s. 6d. per week from the Carrickmacross Poor Law Union relief fund, but he also required help from the neighbours to stay afloat.[176] However, Welsh stated that 'as of late he complained much of shortness of breath'.[177] Dr Martin of Ballybay called in to see him on 3 April 1876, but upon his arrival Began died. The verdict was death from old age and other natural causes.[178]

In 1877, twenty-five years after the end of Great Famine, another failure of the potato crop arrived in Ireland. The agricultural depression and its effect on Co. Monaghan is illustrated by Ollerenshaw's study on the performance of Belfast banks in 1877–81.[179] It reveals that deposits at the Northern Bank branch in Clones declined 56 per cent during this period, the largest drop of all branches in the county, and the branch at Ballybay saw a 49 per cent drop.[180] Ollerenshaw states that Monaghan was one of the areas most effected by the agricultural depression.[181] Two inquests taken by Waddell in 1877 provide evidence of a lack of resources and raise questions about community empathy towards beggars and strangers. While some testimony indicates that care was given by some, other evidence reflects attitudes that mirror those captured in Waddell's inquests during the Great Famine. On 2 February 1877, an inquest taken on the elderly Mary McCabe demonstrates the support and compassion she was shown. Francis Kelly stated that he knew the deceased as 'she often stopped with me though no relative. She was over 70 years of age, supported by the charity of neighbours. She had seen better times'.[182] Witness Eliza Smith stated that McCabe was a stranger to her. Having seen her earlier in

---

170 *Poor Law Union and Lunacy Inquiry Commission (Ireland), report, minutes of evidence with appendices*, p. 127, HC 1878–9 (2239) xxxi, 35.   171 CB2, no. 17.1123, Mary Prunty, 19 Dec. 1874.   172 Ibid.   173 Ibid.   174 CB3, no. 7.1173, Peter Began, 6 Apr. 1876.   175 Ibid.   176 Ibid.   177 Ibid.   178 Ibid.   179 Philip Ollerenshaw, *Banking in nineteenth-century Ireland: the Belfast banks, 1825–1914* (Manchester, 1987), pp 116–18.   180 Ibid.   181 Ibid.   182 CB3, no. 18.1203, Mary McCabe, 2 Feb. 1877.

the day, Smith went to the shop, and after she arrived home, McCabe was in her house. Smith offered the old woman some warm tea to try to revive her a little and, immediately after, McCabe shouted 'my heart, my heart' and, falling over, she died.[183] The verdict of death was from old age, infirmity and the great severity of the weather.[184]

On 10 August 1877, Waddell held an inquest on 'a man, a stranger, a mendicant', this being the first and only time he used the latter term in his casebook in 31 years.[185] Charles Simpson told the coroner's jury that on the evening of 9 August 1877, while cutting the grass in one of his fields, he saw the deceased lying at the foot of the field, dead. The man had previously told Simpson and witness William Slowey that he was a 'going beggar', that his father had been a shoemaker in Glasgow, but he had epilepsy, which prevented him from taking up the trade.[186] He told Slowey that he did not look for shelter, but slept out in the fields.[187] The verdict of death considered that he had died three weeks earlier but could not give a cause. A note added by Waddell stated that 'the jury have no reason [to] think that he came to his death from other than natural causes and from the complaint to which he was subject'.[188] The fact that Waddell described the man as a mendicant indicates that he was seen locally as a threat. He was exposed to the outdoors with no shelter and no obvious source of food, was not taken in by the witnesses or provided with support, and died alone in the fields. The lack of charity offered to the man may reflect attitudes throughout Co. Monaghan towards beggars and strangers and the shift in moral obligation for their care.

THE PROFESSIONAL CORONER

In addition to the suffrage movement and tenant farmers fighting for their rights, middle-class professionals were also looking for opportunities within previously unavailable public sectors. Eighteenth-century and early nineteenth-century employment depended upon the patronage and support of the elite and success relied upon it. However, by the second half of the nineteenth century, the professional advancement of the middle-class had become dependent upon education, apprenticeship, personal qualities and merit-based competition. The characteristics of these groups of professionals, similar to those in England, included the determination to make a living, a commitment toward improving the moral code of their society and a desire to improve their status by social climbing.[189] Irish administrative history highlights that the many changes to civil roles within local government were born from the need to innovate and improve society, particularly in regards to recruitment methods and qualification practices in the civil service, which opened up job opportunities for the middle class. The year 1870 was one

---

183 Ibid. 184 Ibid. 185 CB3, no. 3.1218, a man, a stranger, a mendicant, 10 Aug. 1877. 186 Ibid. 187 Ibid. 188 Ibid. 189 W.J. Reader, *Professional men: the rise of the professional classes in nineteenth-century England* (London, 1966), p. 1.

of 'momentous' change for the civil service as placements for successful candidates were now determined by open competitive examination instead of nepotism or patronage.[190] Additionally, salary levels for many Irish government workers significantly increased, and those for whom it did not formed committees to fight for equal pay as compared to their English counterparts and requested 'the removal of the brand of inferiority'.[191]

Inspired by the wave of public administrative changes, the Irish coroners formed a society and appointed a committee to draft and submit the Irish coroners' bill of 1870.[192] The bill was first introduced to Parliament on 4 March 1870 by Armagh conservative MP John Vance (1808–75), an Orangeman, and Louth coroner T.M. Callen.[193] It proposed improvements to the office with multiple clauses whereby coroners would enjoy the same authority and remuneration as their English equivalents, including the hiring of coroners' deputies, a fixed salary, an increase in payments for poor witnesses and for the removal of bodies, and mandatory retirement at the age of 60 with a pension of two-thirds their salary.[194] Additionally, it sought to introduce a one-day poll – instead of a two-day poll – for elections of coroners and that the whole constituency vote rather than just the ratepayers.[195] The bill also proposed that coroners be allowed to discharge a jury and swear in a new jury if a verdict was not delivered within a reasonable amount of time.[196] Coroners faced difficult situations when they held juries longer than was reasonable. Such a situation arose on 25 November 1871 as an empanelled jury deliberated with 73-year-old Waddell on the circumstances surrounding the death of Edward Molloy, a man killed by a special train passing through Clones that same month.[197] The case had already taken three full days to conduct and upon having concluded it, Waddell had also opened up an inquest on Mrs Letitia Andrews.[198] At 5 p.m. on the evening of the Molloy case, he called for a further adjournment, upon which the jury became 'very noisy insisting that I [Waddell] should sit and finish the case'.[199] According to a rare personal note in the casebook, Waddell wrote,

> On this I told them this I could not do for two reasons: First that it would take a long day yet to close it and second, I had another in hand to proceed with at 5 p.m. but they would hear no reason and I must finish then and if I would not, they would attend no more adjournments. On my essaying to pass from my seat to the door, the jury would not move from their standing attitude to allow me to pass out of the room. I then stepped on the chair on

190 McDowell, 'Administration and the public services' p. 571. 191 McDowell, *The Irish administration, 1801–1914*, p. 43. 192 *County coroners (Ireland)* ..., p. 1, HC 1870, lxiv, 339. 193 *Hansard 3*, cxcix, 4 Mar. 1870, c. 1241. 194 *County coroners (Ireland): a bill to amend the law relating to the appointment, duties and payment of county coroners, and expenses of inquests in Ireland*, p. 1, HC 1870, lxiv, 339. 195 Ibid. 196 Ibid. 197 CB2, no. 11.1014, Edward Molloy, 16 Nov. 1871. 198 CB2, no. 13.1014, Letitia Andrews, 22 Nov. 1871. 199 CB2, Week of 25 Nov. 1871, William Charles Waddell documentation of issues with jury.

which I had been sitting and thence on the table, walked across it towards the room door and so left the room, informing the Sergeant in reply to their threat of farther attendance that I would call them on a fine of £5. On my leaving the room amid a great hubbub, they put their Foreman in the chair by the way of acting independent of me, but the four legal gentlemen engaged on the inquest arose and left the room. The Head Constable would call no further witness as the last witness had concluded his evidence and the Foreman would have brought himself into trouble had he presumed to administer the oath to my witness. Shortly after this disgraceful scene was brought to a close the Jury left the inquest room for their own houses. When I met them two days after, according to adjournment, I took no notice of their conduct.[200]

The Irish coroners bill was defeated on 11 May 1870.[201] Although the bill had been supported by the majority of Irish members, an overwhelming majority of English and Scottish MPs voted against it, refusing to extend to Ireland 'some of those advantages enjoyed by the coroners of England and Scotland'.[202] Evidence suggests that the English and Scottish MPs rejected the bill due to the fact that, uniquely in Ireland, there was a property qualification for coroners. Middle-class professionals from medical and legal backgrounds without property did not qualify, and therefore it was still an office best secured by the landowning social elite. Providing these men with benefits equal to their English and Scottish counterparts was an unpopular decision, so the bill was rejected.

On 14 June 1870, the *Freeman's Journal* published an article that claimed the reason for the defeat of the bill was the need for the government to re-evaluate and reconstruct the whole system of county administration, starting with the grand jury, 'for grand jurors are virtually self-elected', and this conflicted with the Gladstonian liberal ideology that 'representation is the foundation of popular government'.[203] This view exposes that the administration, including English and Scottish MPs, did not want to empower Irish coroners due to their compromised position as members of, or servants to, the local elite. The *Mayo Examiner* also provided an explanation as to why the coroners' bill was declined. It stated, coroners were appointed by the same method as county MPs,

> The same course of canvassing, proposing and seconding is gone through; and when two or more gentlemen are candidates for the office, and demand

---

200 Ibid.   201 *FJ*, 14 June 1870; *Divisions of the house: return of the number of divisions of the house in the session of 1870; stating the subject of the division, and the number of members in the majority and minority, tellers included; also, the aggregate number in the house on each division; distinguishing the divisions on public business from private, &c. (in continuation of parliamentary paper, no. 0.100, of session 1868–9)*, p. 5, HC 1870 (131) lvi, 5.   202 Peel, *The case of the Irish coroners stated*, p. 3; *Return of the number of divisions of the house in the session of 1870*, p. 5, HC 1870 (131) lvi, 5.   203 *FJ*, 14 June 1870.

a poll, the polling is carried on for two days instead of one. This mode of proceeding has been found not only tedious and expensive, but frequently unsatisfactory. It leads to the appointment, not of the man best qualified for the office, but of one who has the most money to spend, and the largest amount of local influence at command.[204]

Evidence suggests that the bill may have passed had it called for changes to the qualifications for the role of coroner. In Ireland, the primary challenge for the administration and high-ranking Irish medical and legal professionals was to find a member of the local elite who would take the office and could be relied upon in cases of political (sectarian) murder.[205] This was contrary to the then prevalent liberal ideology of opening local government roles to educated middle-class professionals. By incorporating professionals and doing away with the property criteria, a wider and more diverse pool of talent would be made available. In 1870, of the 91 coroners, 18 were solicitors and 18 had medical qualifications, while the rest were likely men who met the property qualifications, were supported by members of the local elite, or were themselves local elites, such as Waddell.[206]

In February 1871, the secretary of the Coroners' Society, Armagh coroner and Orangeman Thomas George Peel (alias 'Orange Peel'), submitted a memorial to Lord Lieutenant Earl Spencer on behalf of the coroners of Ireland.[207] It was signed by 83 of the 91 coroners, including Waddell and Hugh Swanzy (see Appendix 2). It claimed that the public supported the coroners' bill, reinforced by national newspapers, both liberal and conservative.[208]

The Coroners' Society continued the pursuit of their rights for the next ten years. Peel published two political pamphlets on behalf of the society. The first was published in 1872, *The case of the Irish coroners stated* and the second, in 1874, *The crown, the coroners and the people*.[209] Both articulated arguments for passing the bill and the challenges that coroners faced that necessitated such change. Peel reflected on having lost the vote and re-established the mission and purpose of the coroners in Ireland, emphasizing their 'wide influence on the community which they have used for the promotion of law, order and morality'.[210] He presented the arguments surrounding the barriers and difficulties facing the coroner and identified the areas in which they had unequal status as compared with English coroners. Peel highlighted processes that interfered with the execution of the role, including the decision-making power of the grand jury, who could still deny payment of fees for inquests if they thought there was an 'obvious cause of death'.[211] This was considered a major deterrent to securing the right men for these positions

---

204 *Mayo Examiner*, 11 Apr. 1870. **205** Clark, 'General practice and coroners' practice', p. 49. **206** Adam Bisset Thom, *Thom's Directory of Ireland* (1870), p. 49. **207** *Coroners (Ireland): copy of a memorial addressed to the lord lieutenant by the coroners of Ireland, requesting that a measure on their behalf may be brought before Parliament early in the present session*, p. 439, HC 1871 (86) lviii, 480; *Nation*, 18 Nov. 1876. **208** Peel, *The case of the Irish coroner stated*, p. 3. **209** Ibid.; Peel, *The crown, the coroners, and the people*. **210** Peel, *The case of the Irish coroner stated*, p. 4. **211** Ibid.

and treating them with the respect such a qualified candidate would deserve. Also outlined were the efforts of Dublin medical practitioners to use their positions to create disharmony about the lack of coroners' roles secured by doctors.[212] The argument that a medical practitioner was best suited for the role of coroner coincided with advances in medical science and early forensic medical examination, and initiated debate regarding choosing men from professional backgrounds to fill the role. Also, in 1873, the jurisdiction of police magistrates was widened and the legislation changed regarding the procedure and process of investigation of deaths.[213] The accused was no longer allowed to attend the inquest but rather was kept from it. This change to the law undermined the authority of the coroner and the dynamic and purpose of the inquest. As to any resistance to this treatment of prisoners, Peel wrote, 'It is seldom that Irishmen can agree upon one question, no matter how broad it may be. Upon this, however, they are united.'[214]

The biggest challenge facing Irish coroners was the fight for their very existence, as the bill had triggered debate about getting rid of the office altogether,[215] and using resident magistrates to hold inquests instead. On 14 July 1873, Peel's letter to the editor of the *Freeman's Journal* included one cogent fact underlying the proposal, 'The average Irish coroner costs £80 per annum. A resident magistrate costs £700. Abolish the office of coroner and you will have these gentlemen as plenty as blackberries in harvest.'[216] Such a solution was expensive and would prove unpopular. He also quoted coroner and barrister-at-law Mr Payne, who, when fighting for the rights of the coroner, stated, 'If the institution of the coroner's court be defective, improve it as much as possible, but let the people beware how they suffer popular institutions to be taken from them.'[217]

William Charles Waddell died on 4 May 1878 and was succeeded as coroner by Dr Robert Hamilton Reed (1847–81) of Slieveroe, Ballybay, Co. Monaghan. Reed, a Presbyterian, was a licensed physician, surgeon and fellow from the King and Queen's College, Ireland, the medical officer for Kilmore dispensary district, and ran an extensive private practice.[218] He was also the worshipful master of the Masonic Lodge 351 in Monaghan.[219] Reed served as coroner for just three years, until he died suddenly on 16 September 1881 at just 34 years old.[220] He left behind a wife and three young children. It was reported that Lord Rossmore and Colonel Lloyd attended the funeral, which took place at Cahans meeting house, Lisnaveane, along with more than seventy members of the Masonic Lodge.[221] Such personal and professional associations indicate that Reed was more liberal than Waddell, reflecting a shift in attitudes of the local elite and voters. In 1882, a government return identified the religious persuasions of those men who held positions within the commission of the peace (including magistrates, justices of the

212 Ibid. 213 *FJ*, 17 Oct. 1873. 214 Peel, *The crown, the coroners and the people*, p. 11. 215 Ibid. 216 *FJ*, 17 Nov. 1873. 217 Peel, *The crown, the coroners and the people*, p. 5. 218 Sharon Odie Brown, 'Robert Hamilton Reed and Margardet Jackson', *The silver bowl*, thesilverbowl.com; *The Irish medical directory for the year 1873* (Dublin, 1873), p. 128. 219 Ibid. 220 *NS*, 24 Sept. 1881. 221 Ibid.

peace, resident magistrates and coroners).[222] In Co. Monaghan this included just 7 Catholics, along with 59 Anglicans and 1 Presbyterian.[223] The report also revealed that of 95 coroners in Ireland at that time, 22 were also medical professionals and a further 16 came from legal backgrounds.[224] While representation of Catholics and Presbyterians remained low, the rise of the professional, which supported the modernization of Ireland, is evident in the increase in medical and legal professionals serving in the role of coroner.

The Coroners' Act of 1881 required that professionals who desired to run for election as coroner must have qualifications as barristers, solicitors, doctors or justices of the peace.[225] This breakthrough in making the coroner's office one for professionals rather than just men of privilege was a significant contribution to the modernization of society. As stated by Lee, the growth of equality of opportunity, whereby merit superseded birthright, and the development of mass political consciousness was the true definition of modernization, and contributed toward the growth of the nation.[226] While the nature of Ireland's politically polarized society remained, the changes to the qualifications for the role of coroner were intended to help depoliticize the inquest and improve the respect for justice and the value of life.

CONCLUSION

The work of the coroner revealed the changing social, economic and political landscape in the 1870s, and the abuses and protection of society's weakest. Although political murders often concluded with no suspect arrested and convicted, new methods of compensation for victims held local authorities accountable for a lack of policing. The inquests also reveal the victims of domestic murder and how social values reinforced the protection of a man's rights in his home, as well as a lack of protection for unwanted infants. Co. Monaghan conservatives imposed restrictive criteria for outdoor relief, which resulted in deaths captured by Waddell. The significant number of inquiries at the asylum emphasize the importance of the investigation of the deaths of mentally ill people and the desire for knowledge of their treatment behind the walls of the institution. The rise of the middle-class professional included the Irish coroner, and the fight for equal respect as measured through compensation and resources equivalent to their English counterparts, resulted in the abolition of a property qualification for the role.

[222] While the return captured religious persuasions, it did not identify them against individual men or their positions. [223] Commission of the Peace (Ireland), *Return to an order of the Honourable the House of Commons dated 14 November 1882;- for, return 'for each county, city and borough in Ireland, of the names of the persons holding the Commission of the Peace, the aggregate number of such persons that are Protestants, specifying their denominations, the number that are Roman Catholics, and the number that are members of any other religious persuasions'*, p. 331, HC 1884 (13) lxiii, 72–3. [224] Ibid., pp 1–118. [225] 44 & 45 Vict., c. 35 (1 Aug. 1881), Coroners (Ireland) Act. [226] Lee, *The modernisation of Irish society*, pp i–ii.

Conclusion

On 1 September 1894, the *Freeman's Journal* reported that a meeting had taken place at the Gresham Hotel in Dublin attended by coroners representing each county and city throughout Ireland.[1] It was there they formed the Irish Coroners' Association.[2] The coroners appointed officers and organized law, executive and parliamentary committees, created rules and engaged in discussion on various subjects set out in their agenda. These included a letter received from the honorary secretary of the English Coroners' Society, Mr Athelstan Braxton Hicks (1854–1902), the Surrey coroner, which wished for the success and prosperity of their newly formed order and made the suggestion that they form a committee to confer with the English society on 'all matters affecting coroners'.[3] The Irish Coroners' Association then passed a resolution to do just that.[4] This group of professional coroners, many identified by their medical and legal backgrounds, now had the support of their English colleagues, signifying the advancement of the standing of their office and an endorsement of their efforts to further enhance the position of coroner in Ireland. Professionalism and the rise of the middle class contributed to the inevitable extinction of the landed elite's monopoly over public administration and employment patronage. The final piece of legislation impacting the coroner before Irish independence was the Local Government (Ireland) Act (1898), which dissolved the grand juries, instituted county councils and deemed the coroner to be a civil servant, with a salary, who would be appointed based on his professional qualifications.[5]

ADMINISTRATIVE ORGANIZATION OF JUDICIAL OFFICES

The office of coroner survived amid local government reform and dissolution of many other judicial offices. The judiciary used its power as 'an instrument for intervention in political and economic life', and participation in judicial office served as social conditioning for members of the local elite.[6] The confessional complexities of Ireland and limited roles for Catholics resulted in a contradictory

---

1 *FJ*, 1 Sept. 1894. Mr Athelstan Braxton Hicks was a barrister-at-law, an expert in medical jurisprudence and wrote extensively on infanticide. He was a member of the British Medical Association and the Coroners' Society. He was the son of Dr John Braxton Hicks, well-known obstetrician from London. 2 Due to a lack of evidence, it is unclear if the Irish Coroners' Association was merely a 'rebrand' of the Coroners' Society formed three decades earlier. 3 *FJ*, 1 Sept. 1894. 4 Ibid. 5 61 & 62 Vict., c. 37 (3 Aug. 1898), Local Government (Ireland) Act. 6 McDowell, *The Irish administration, 1801–1914*, pp vii–viii; Gray, 'Conceiving and constructing the Irish workhouse, 1836–45', p. 22.

system of justice and legal organization predominately under the control of the Protestant local elite. Under the Union, sheriffs, justices of the peace and grand juries exercised administrative and judicial functions. However, they were subject to significant legislative reform in the course of the nineteenth century, which resulted in significant changes to their authority and power.

The role of the coroner sat within the organizational structure of the judiciary and local government. It was a separate function with unique authority from that of justices of the peace and magistrates, primarily because the coroner ran the only publicly independent court. The coroner was an independent judicial office holder who selected his own jury and held a public inquest. He could allow for public questions and participation if he chose. The grand jury had to accept and allow his independent authority as per the law under the administration. He worked within a framework of law but outside the petty and assizes courts judiciary, while being at the same time, a member of the judicial system. Legislative change also reinforced the coroners' authority within local government and his authority and autonomy apart from the grand jury. While the law supported the position and actions of coroners, the conservative Monaghan grand jury was representative of other grand juries that were resentful of the costs. The Monaghan grand jury also opposed Whig-influenced policies including investigating the deaths of the poor. As a result, they often refused to pay Waddell for his work. This required him to hire a lawyer and take them to court to retrieve the monies owed. Paradoxically, Waddell, a Presbyterian, was a member of the local elite, and shared similar conservative politics to his peers, who were also officers of local government. While most coroners were members of the Protestant landed elite, the office of coroner had denominational flexibility when compared to others in local government. The examination of Waddell serving in the role of coroner exposed the complicit behaviour of the local elites.

THE CORONER DURING THE GREAT FAMINE

Coroners served a crucial and important function during the Great Famine. They held a conspicuous position in local government and one that was more widely exposed to public opinion when investigating deaths during a humanitarian crisis. The inquests taken during the years of the Famine that were published in local and national newspapers revealed how the legislation imposed by Peel's and Russell's administrations, combined with delays in implementing relief measures and local mismanagement, directly contributed to the deaths of many of society's poorest members. Although the Irish coroners shared a common sphere of activity, the results of their investigations varied depending upon their geographic location, the political composition of the local elite and inquest participants. Newspapers were selective about which verdicts of 'death due to starvation' they chose to cover during the Famine. While some verdicts named Lord John Russell and the administration, others exposed pervasive ideologies towards the poor that blamed

Conclusion

the victims for their poverty and the circumstances surrounding their death. The coroners also differed in their performance when executing their duties based on the inclinations and abilities of each man serving in the role. Some coroners announced their own temporary suspensions when conducting inquests in cases of 'obvious' starvation so as not to impose unnecessary costs onto the grand jury and ratepayers. Opinions as to the importance of inquests held by the coroner during the Famine varied; while some clergymen sought the attendance of the coroner and saw value in capturing evidence of the humanitarian crisis, some laymen stopped asking the coroner to investigate deaths, seeing it as a futile exercise.

Waddell's performance as a coroner during the Famine in Co. Monaghan revealed the conflict that existed between the execution of his duties in that role and his personal and professional politics. Waddell's background as a landed Presbyterian gentleman who also worked as a land agent, merchant and farmer, and his historical pedigree and conservative politics demonstrate that he secured the coronership through patronage and political allegiance. However, the 'truth' revealed in his inquests often put him at odds with the interests of the local elite of which he was a member. Waddell captured inquests that revealed deaths resulting from restrictive local criteria used by local inspectors and relief officers, the reluctance of the Monaghan elite to take out loans for relief and to offer employment to save lives, and the lack of financial support from the Monaghan board of guardians, who refused to offer outdoor relief – despite his own participation as an elected official on the board. The deaths he recorded during the Famine marked a significant moment at the start of Waddell's transformation into a professional coroner, separating him from his personal allegiances and patronage. His role thrust upon him the authority and autonomy of conducting an independent public court, and his responsibility to report on the findings.

Waddell's professionalism was evident early on in his career through his detailed documentation of his investigations, with named witnesses and descriptive testimony providing evidence of the circumstances surrounding each death. He used experienced, educated local doctors whose medical expertise was followed and respected, and this was reflected in inquest verdicts that supported their findings. Waddell often documented the reasons for ordering post-mortems, which demonstrated his understanding of the process he was to follow. His documentation was used as a vital tool for reporting to the authorities, particularly in cases forwarded to the assizes and, at the end of each year, in his annual report to the Chief Secretary's Office.

The entirety of Waddell's body of work during the years of the Famine, over three hundred inquests, reveals a sad and dramatic time of change, during which he must have experienced conflicting emotions when faced with the tragic situations in which death occurred. His investigations exposed the fractures in the moral compass of members of rural society, who, fearing for their own survival, stopped offering charity to strangers and wandering beggars who sought food and shelter. Testimony revealed the emotional and difficult choices made by the destitute when refusing to ask for – or being refused – entry to the workhouse meant no possibility of survival.

Waddell's inquests exposed the severity of the Famine crisis and how Co. Monaghan's institutions struggled to support the surging number of people living in poverty. When workhouse populations surged, some inmates chose to leave these institutions to return to their townlands, and died of disease or starvation shortly thereafter. These findings suggest that the living conditions behind the walls of the workhouses were intolerable. The population of the Monaghan gaol also rose significantly as tenants found themselves unable to pay rent. The gaol was considered by some as a haven for survival, but overcrowding and disease caused the deaths of elderly and infirm inmates and sometimes put healthier inmates at risk of death.

Local elite ideology towards the poor contributed towards the mass scale of deaths, as they attempted to improve behaviour through inadequate legislation and divisive relief strategies. Inquests captured deaths from starvation as a result of the delayed response to implementing measures, the dissolution of the Relief Commission and the closure of food depots and soup kitchens. Waddell's inquests revealed the failings of the Labour Rate Act (1846), which offered employment to sick and starving men, leaving them with no other choice but to avail of employment on the public works – which could result in their deaths. There was direct evidence that death by starvation was caused by the Gregory clause (1847), which restricted relief to those tenants in possession of less than a quarter-acre of land. Land was also cleared through evictions, which resulted in deaths from starvation, and Waddell's inquests exposed the lack of humanity among the members of the local landed elite. Although Waddell's personal attitudes are not recorded, his professional performance as a coroner contributed towards the gradual transformative change of the office that occurred over time.

The political stratagems implemented by the conservative *Northern Standard* newspaper played a part in restricting and controlling coverage of Waddell's inquests revealing the local crisis. Circumstantial evidence suggests that the lack of local inquests published in the *Northern Standard* up until June 1847 was an attempt to play down the severity of the crisis in Co. Monaghan. The infrequency of inquest reports may have negatively impacted public opinion about the necessity of Waddell's work and the value of his findings. After Russell's administration placed the financial burden of supporting the destitute during the Famine upon the landed elite, Waddell's inquests were more frequently published in the newspaper and were used to stir sympathy for local authorities as the crisis continued across the county.

EROSION OF THE LOCAL ELITE

The function of the coroner contributed to the erosion of the power of the local elite that started during the Famine and continued gradually through the years in post-Famine Ireland. In the years after the Famine, Waddell's investigations of institutional death in workhouses, gaols and asylums exposed local corruption and mismanagement by institutional officers. Most senior level positions – gaol governor, head medical superintendent and workhouse master – as well as those of junior officers, were secured by patronage or nepotism. Evidence of malpractice and misadventure on behalf of institutional officials resulted in their dismissal and proved embarrassing to local elites. These deaths also stirred social and political consciousness as they highlighted the injustice towards the socially disadvantaged and the lack of adequate representation of both the majority Catholic population and the liberal middle class in the management of these institutions. We find evidence of unethical behaviour by institutional leaders that directly contributed to the deaths of infants at the workhouse, infanticide at the gaol, abuse of mentally ill asylum patients by their attendants and unfair practices towards gaol inmates. The evidence within these inquests contributed to the mistrust of local authority figures, and added to further political and social polarization, while at the same time igniting liberal political will to support legislative and social change for equal representation in local government.

THE INCIDENCE OF MURDER AND SECTARIANISM

Waddell's inquests established patterns in the types of murders that took place, both domestic and sectarian. When examining domestic murder, using O'Halpin and Breathnach's work, this study attempted to identify community emotion by locating the prism of blame in cases of infanticide. By expanding the application of the prism of blame to a wider variety of deaths, specific spheres of blame, culpability and community belief were discovered. Two new spheres of blame in cases of domestic murder have been defined. In the 'maternal sphere', inclusive of mothers and infants, the coroners' juries refused to convict mothers of murdering children. In the 'fraternal sphere', men who murdered women (usually their wives, but not always) were rarely convicted by coroners' juries, which were composed entirely of men. These results support the community beliefs that domestic life was private and male authority was not to be undermined within the home. Evidence suggests that economic pressures contributed to an increase in these domestic homicides and those of financially independent women who were at risk without male protection.

When examining sectarian murder, community emotion was identified in coroners' inquests and, unlike domestic murder, guilty verdicts were returned naming the accused. Sectarian murder appeared infrequently in Waddell's casebooks. In just five cases, a gun was used to shoot and kill a victim.[7] Testimony revealed that sectarian murders were most often pre-meditated and politically motivated. In each incidence, the role of coroner was in conflict with the political agenda of the

---

7 While other inquests captured drinking, accidental drowning, or victims who had been beaten and left for dead, evidence was inconclusive that these were politically motivated. Therefore, deaths at these inquests cannot be categorized as sectarian.

local elites as the latter were eager to secure a verdict. The cases of sectarian murder covered by Waddell also shared similar characteristics to others that occurred in Co. Monaghan. It was revealed to be a common trait of such cases that while the coroner's jury found the accused guilty at the inquest, he was never convicted at criminal trial. Evidence suggests that government in Co. Monaghan was corrupt, and the complicit behaviour captured included jury tampering, fraud and abuse of authority. Regardless of overwhelming evidence of guilt and a guilty inquest verdict, convictions at the assizes were not secured and guilty men were acquitted. The coroner's inquest, driven by Waddell, resulted in more accurate verdicts in cases of sectarian murder, with jurors returning a verdict of guilty against the accused.

THE INCIDENCE AND IMPACT OF POVERTY

The deaths captured in inquests by Waddell, specifically during the Famine, provide new insights into some of the causes of the vast scale of poverty in Co. Monaghan. Legislation, politics and ideology worked against society's poorest, as shown through analysis of inquests during the Famine years of 1846 to 1852. The increase in deaths of cottiers, beggars and landless tenant farmers was proven to be a direct result of poor legislation and slow implementation of relief. The behaviour of the Monaghan grand jury and Monaghan Poor Law guardians and their unwillingness to secure loans to fund employment for the poor in time to save lives contributed to the deaths of many. The work of Ó Gráda demonstrated that the Monaghan grand jury and Monaghan board of guardians prioritized cost savings over caring for the needy.

Studying Waddell's inquests in chronological order helped to show how the removal of relief (such as the soup kitchens) induced significant distributional shifts of starvation and death, and how price shocks, the shortage of food, increase in evictions, the lack of employment and restrictive distribution of relief all contributed to deaths. Workhouses and the Monaghan gaol were functioning at more than 200 per cent capacity at the height of the crisis. They could not provide a safe environment for inmates. In the post-Famine years, institutional provision for the destitute remained available but with more restrictive requirements for entry. Waddell's inquests during the agricultural depression of the late 1870s, including incidents of beggars found dead in fields, continued to reflect how these deaths were a result of local relief policy and a lack of relief offered to the poor.

Institutional provision for the destitute often proved inadequate in order to save lives. An examination of local relief management in Co. Monaghan provided further evidence of the social conditions that contributed to the deaths in Waddell's casebook. The Poor Law of 1838 was not able to support the vast numbers of starving people during the humanitarian crisis of the Great Famine. Workhouse records and statistics published in local newspapers reflect the overpopulation of these institutions, and the inadequate facilities that failed to support the destitute.

Incidents captured through Waddell's inquests showed inmates leaving the workhouse only to return to their neighbourhoods and townlands to die, most often from starvation and disease soon after their departure. Such deaths expose the poor conditions within these institutions, but also the reluctance of inmates to remain and die inside them.

The role of the coroner in institutional deaths, such as in the Monaghan gaol, helped expose the circumstances that caused death and the vast numbers of inmates incarcerated as paupers. Disease was the primary cause of death for those behind the walls of these institutions and a trend of restrictive spending on clothing was a direct cause for the increase in disease. The inquests taken in relation to the workhouse and gaols put Waddell at odds with local authorities, who resented the exposure. These deaths also reflected the impact of government legislation and restrictive local relief policies, such as the decision taken to provide no outdoor relief in the Monaghan Poor Law Union, which put more pressure on the adjoining Poor Law unions. In the late 1860s and throughout the 1870s, inquests captured at the Monaghan district lunatic asylum also reflected that inmates died from disease, most likely as a result of poor conditions such as overcrowding.

THE SIGNIFICANCE OF THE FINDINGS

The implications of the findings in this study are important and should lead others to attempt similar case studies for other regions. Ciarán Reilly created a framework for land agents in the nineteenth century using John Plunket Joly, land agent during the Great Famine in King's Co.[8] This book attempts to do for coroners what Reilly has done for land agents. For its framework it uses Waddell as a case study through which to examine coroners and their work. First, it investigates his social profile and function as the coroner within Co. Monaghan, and the landscape and people. It identifies the social status of the Waddell family and its place within the political hierarchy of the local elite. Waddell's landed ancestry and Presbyterian faith gained him membership and access to the local elite.

The challenges and problems affecting the coroner offered new insights into the function of the role and Waddell's work during and after the Great Famine. The inquests also show the social conditions of the region where they took place. The coroner in his role is key to providing these new historical insights, particularly with regard to the wider community. The study of the deaths within the social and political context creates a new history for the county and the Famine there. The work of the coroner in the post-Famine years allows for a new social history of rural communities, providing insight into patterns of domestic and sectarian murder. The inquests contained themes of poverty, destitution, institutional care for paupers and the importance of the survival of the coroner as a judicial officer.

---

8 Ciarán Reilly, *John Plunket Joly and the Great Famine in King's County* (Dublin, 2012); idem, *The Irish land agent, 1830–60: the case of King's County* (Dublin, 2014).

These themes, when placed within the political and social context, help develop a cause-and-effect relationship between them.

The studies of the Irish land agent and of the Irish coroner are comparable but different as the latter has been absent from existing academic research. By outlining the qualifications and functions of the coroner, this study brings to light the social significance of the role in administrative history. It also shows the struggle for the survival of the office, its evolution as a professional office, its contribution to knowledge via forensic study and criminal investigation, and its overall contribution to the modernization of Irish society. Examining Waddell's work in chronological order allows for the identification of themes that can be aligned with a wider social and political narrative. This structure can also be used for researchers examining coroners' inquests in other periods in Irish history.

WADDELL'S CHARACTER

William Charles Waddell is an important figure in the study of coroners and Co. Monaghan in nineteenth-century Ireland. His well-kept, unique set of records, which have survived over 150 years, reveals aspects of his character and this study also reveals his social identity. In many ways, Waddell was representative of other middle-class men of his time. He was ambitious and served in multiple private and public roles including those of land agent, landlord, shopkeeper, Poor Law guardian, member of the road sessions committee, and coroner. A deep dive into his ancestry shows that Waddell was a descendant of planted Scottish Presbyterians. He had ancestors with both conservative and radical politics, but was himself considered gentry by the Monaghan Protestant elite in 1846. Waddell's own public politics are best reflected by his time served in the yeomanry and his membership of the Brunswick Club, which had given him an opportunity to declare his political alignment by supporting similar interests to those of his Protestant counterparts. Most notable was Waddell's participation as a juror in the trials of the infamous Orangeman and Protestant hero Sam Gray. He helped at different times to both acquit his son and convict Gray, whose political career ended after he attempted to murder a Presbyterian man. Evidence suggests that Waddell's support of the conservative administration in the campaign against Gray was further enhanced by a need for justice for his Presbyterian brethren.

Waddell's Presbyterian values and identity are clear. In January 1842, his selection and participation on a committee to discuss the Presbyterian question, led by C.P. Leslie, indicates that he was seen as a leading member of the Presbyterian community. Another example was reflected in a letter he received from Revd Thomas Witherow in December 1857, which revealed explicitly for the first time Waddell's sympathy with liberal Presbyterian values. Additionally, Waddell's wealthy uncle Charles Hopes, with whom he shared a close relationship, was a representative elder in the synod of Ulster, as well as serving as a Monaghan grand jury member for over fourteen years and high sheriff in 1853. Furthermore, Waddell's status as a

Presbyterian coroner for several decades from 1846 through 1878 not only reflects upon his reputation and public standing but lends new insight into the unique status of Presbyterians in local government in south Ulster. Circumstantial evidence suggests that some Presbyterians in Co. Monaghan had a special relationship with, and social status within, the local Protestant elite. Waddell had two social identities, one as a supporter of Protestant Orangemen and the other as a man with Presbyterian alliances, both personal and professional. Such a variation in his political relationships makes it difficult to identify Waddell by one political agenda.

Examining his participation as a guardian in the Monaghan Poor Law Union highlights an area of contradiction in his character. In 1839, upon his election to that post, it was reported in the *Northern Standard* that he had threatened tenants of his uncle in his role as land agent. The Monaghan Poor Law Union was composed of primarily conservative-minded men who voted to prevent outdoor relief to paupers during (and after) the Famine, which caused the deaths of many. Serving in the role of coroner, Waddell exposed the poor local management of the crisis, as reflected in many deaths that followed. It was reported in his obituary in 1878 that he often paid for coffins for paupers out of his own pocket.[9] It is difficult to imagine that such a traumatic event and the role Waddell played in it would not affect or change his outlook.

Waddell's relationships with his family were not always harmonious. The Waddells and Hopes had a long-established record of keeping marriage and business partnerships within their families. In this regard, Waddell prioritized family tradition, as evidenced by his marriage to Maria, who was his first cousin. Although Waddell was the second eldest son, with younger siblings, it was he who was responsible for the land agency and management of leaseholds across inherited townlands. He also resided in the family property at Lisnaveane House, one of two Waddell family ancestral homes. Many leases named Waddell as the owner of lands on which various tenants paid rent, including extended family members. Complicated leases, emigration and debt increased some family tensions, as reflected in a letter written by a cousin desiring to keep their property out of Waddell's 'ravenous grasp'. He was perceived as having 'unlimited covetousness and power', which indicates that the Waddells of Lisnaveane did not always live together in harmony. His success as a land agent, landlord and public figure was gained with the support of his uncle, Charles Hopes. This appears to have contributed to tensions within the family, in particular, with those members who were not financially solvent and were indebted to Waddell.

Ultimately, Waddell's role as the coroner of the northern district of Co. Monaghan and the body of work he left behind help define his judgment, integrity and character. The nature of his work put him at risk of public scrutiny as well as social exclusion should an inquest verdict conflict with the politics of the local elite. He was involved in many controversial investigations exposing injustice: an

9 *NS*, 11 May 1878.

inquest held on a man killed in a sectarian murder exposes the risks he faced, and suggests a liberal shift in his politics. Reported in newspapers throughout Ireland and Great Britain, Waddell had first refused and then accepted a verdict of wilful murder against Protestant David Baird for Thomas Hughes' murder. Conservative newspaper commentary compared his actions to coroners' juries that had returned 'liberal' verdicts. The *Dublin Daily Express* compared them to juries' verdicts of manslaughter against Lord John Russell during the Famine. In addition, the *Northern Standard* editor, John Holmes, called Waddell's actions 'eccentric' and accused him of playing a 'little game'.[10] However, a magisterial inquiry into Waddell's action of adjourning and then reconvening the jury during the Hughes inquest supported his actions. The warrant for Baird's arrest was upheld.

The evidence suggests Waddell was a gentleman with the confidence and strength of mind to prioritize his professional integrity over political pressure and the interests of his class. Although not a professional coroner in the modern sense, with medical or legal training, the casebooks reveal a man who evolved into the role.

10 *NS*, 25 July 1868.

Appendix 1: The coroners of Ireland (1871)

In 1871, these coroners in Ireland signed a memorial to change legislation to improve the office for themselves and future professionals who would hold it.

Name	County
Edward D. Atkinson	Co. Armagh
J.M. Magee	Co. Armagh
Thomas G. Peel	Co. Armagh
David Campion	Co. Carlow
John McFuddin	Co. Cavan
William Pollock	Co. Cavan
James Berry	Co. Cavan
Francis O'Donnell	Co. Clare
John Cullinan	Co. Clare
John Frost	Co. Clare
Eugene Hogan	Co. Cork
James Somerville	Co. Cork
John Moore	Co. Cork
C.J. Daley	Co. Cork
William Lane	Co. Derry
M. Lloyd	Co. Derry
D. Kelly	Co. Derry
D. Gaily	Co. Derry
F.G. Lang	Co. Donegal
John M.B. Evans	Co. Donegal
George M. Mitchell	Co. Donegal
T. Crawford	Co. Donegal
J.A. Ward	Co. Down
R.J. Tyrrell	Co. Down
George A. Hume	Co. Down
Alexander Markham	Co. Down
Henry Harty	Co. Dublin

Name	County
F.J. Davys	Co. Dublin
William Raphael	Co. Dublin
B. Leslie, J.P.	Co. Fermanagh
Samuel Gamble	Co. Fermanagh
George Cottingham	Co. Galway
E.K. Lynch	Co. Galway
Martin Pelly	Co. Galway
James D. McDonagh	Co. Galway
John Roche	Co. Kerry
John C. O'Reardon	Co. Kerry
R.C. Hurtnell	Co. Kerry
Robert T. Hayes	Co. Kildare
Robert C. Carter	Co. Kildare
Thomas Izod	Co. Kilkenny
W.J. Maher	Co. Kilkenny
W.A. Gowing	King's Co.
John Corcoran	King's Co.
Terence Keown	Co. Leitrim
Robert Corscadden	Co. Leitrim
W.C. Murphy	Co. Limerick
Thomas Costello	Co. Limerick
Thomas Ambrose	Co. Limerick
John Quinn	Co. Longford
J.M. Callen	Co. Louth
Thomas L. Moore	Co. Louth
Edmond C. Kelly	Co. Mayo
Robert Moysten	Co. Mayo
James Rutledge	Co. Mayo
M. Marmion	Co. Meath
Hugh Martin	Co Meath
W.C. Waddell	Co. Monaghan
Hugh Swanzy	Co. Monaghan
Robert O'Kelly	Queen's Co.
William Clarke	Queen's Co.
Thomas P. Peyton	Co. Roscommon

Appendix 1: The coroners of Ireland (1871)

Name	County
Richard Garnett	Co. Roscommon
J.C. Davies	Co. Roscommon
Alexander Burrough	Co. Sligo
John McDonagh	Co. Sligo
Michael Maher	Co. Tipperary
Thomas O'Mera	Co. Tipperary
J.W. Morrissy	Co. Tipperary
John J. Shee, J.P.	Co. Tipperary
W.O. Orr	Co. Tyrone
Robert McCrea	Co. Tyrone
R. Buchanan	Co. Tyrone
Edward T. Tener	Co. Tyrone
H.T. Denneley	Co. Waterford
W.H. Gore	Co. Waterford
Patrick Connell	Co. Westmeath
T. Fetherson	Co. Westmeath
R.B. Ryan	Co. Wexford
J.B. Allen	Co. Wexford
M.H. Jones	Co. Wicklow
P. Newton	Co. Wicklow

Sources: Thomas G. Peel, T.C., *The case of the Irish coroners stated* (Belfast, 1872); *Coroners (Ireland): copy of a memorial addressed to the lord lieutenant by the coroners of Ireland, requesting that a measure on their behalf may be brought before Parliament early in the present session,* p. 439, HC 1871 (86) lviii, 480.

Appendix 2: Inquests and inquiries in William Charles Waddell's casebooks

1846

CB1, no. 1, Patrick Boyland, Drummond, Magheracloone parish, barony of Farney, 7 May 1846.
CB1, no. 10, Margaret Quinn, Cooldarragh, Drumsnat parish, barony of Monaghan, 29 July 1846.
CB1, no. 16, Mary Byrne, Carrickmacross, Magheross parish, barony of Farney, 3 Dec. 1846.
CB1, no. 1.17, John Carahar, Drumanan, Aghabog parish, barony of Dartree, 9 Dec. 1846.
CB1, no. 2.21, John Cambell, Feragh, Monaghan parish, barony of Monaghan, 19 Dec. 1846.

1847

CB1, no. 10.29, Paul Murphy, Drumcrew, Clontibret parish, barony of Cremorne, 8 Feb. 1847.
CB1, no. 12.31, Mary Sherry, Clare Oghill, Clontibret parish, barony of Cremorne, 13 Feb. 1847.
CB1, no. 13.32, Unknown child, Aghnasedagh, Monaghan parish, barony of Monaghan, 15 Feb. 1847.
CB1, no. 14.33, James McKierney, Mullaghfinnog, Errigal Trough parish, barony of Trough, 19 Feb. 1847.
CB1, no. 15.34, _____ Daroley, Tullylish, Tyholland parish, barony of Monaghan, 20 Feb. 1847.
CB1, no. 16.35, Body of a strange man, Mulnacrern [Mullanacross], Errigal Truagh parish, barony of Truagh, 27 Feb. 1847.
CB1, no. 17.36, Charles Coyle, Cornanure, Tullycorbet parish, barony of Monaghan, 2 Mar. 1847.
CB1, no. 21.40, Mary Ann McDermot, Cladowen, Clones parish, barony of Dartree, 13 Mar. 1847.
CB1, no. 19.38, Patrick McCabe, Greaghlatacapple, Magheross parish, barony of Farney, 10 Mar. 1847.
CB1, no. 23.42, Pat McPhillps, Gallagh, Clontibret parish, barony of Cremorne, 15 Mar. 1847.
CB1, no. 26.45, Laurance Daily, Cornamucklagh, Clontibret parish, barony of Cremorne, 25 Mar. 1847.
CB1, no. 27.26, James Williamson, Tanmacnally, Ematris parish, barony of Dartree, 31 Mar. 1847.
CB1, no. 28.47, James Henry, Sheetrim, Muckno parish, barony of Cremorne, 2 Apr. 1847.
CB1, no. 32.51, Catherine Collen, Mullaghcroghery, Magheross parish, barony of Farney, 9 Apr. 1847
CB1, no. 33.52, Ann Collen, Mullaghcroghery, Magheross parish, barony of Farney, 9 Apr. 1847.

Appendix 2: Inquests and inquiries in William Charles Waddell's casebooks 217

CB1, no. 56.37, Peter Reed, Aghaloughan, Donagh parish, barony of Trough, 26 Apr. 1847.
CB1, no. 59.40, Patt Banagan, Sreenty, Magheross parish, barony of Farney, 4 May 1847.
CB1, no. 41.60, Francis Mulligan, Castleblayney, Muckno parish, barony of Cremorne, 6 May 1847.
CB1, no. 42.61, Elizabeth Grimes, Drumgavny, Tullycorbet parish, barony of Cremorne, 7 May 1847.
CB1, no. 44.63, Isaiah Moore, Unshinagh, Ematris parish, barony of Dartree, 13 May 1847.
CB1, no. 47.66, Michael Hughes, Drumneill, Clontibret parish, barony of Cremorne, 18 May 1847.
CB1, no. 49.68, William Harker, Monaghan Infirmary, parish and barony of Monaghan, 21 May 1847.
CB1, no. 51.70, Rose Sweeny, Killycarnan, Tydavnet parish, barony of Monaghan, 26 May 1847.
CB1, no. 53.72, Thomas Hughes, Castleblayney, parish of Muckno, barony of Cremorne, 28 May 1847.
CB1, no. 57.76, James McEneny, Monaghan gaol, town, parish and barony of Monaghan, 1 June 1847.
CB1, no. 60.79, James Gillespie, Monaghan parish and barony of Monaghan, 7 June 1847.
CB1, no. 61.80, Ann Gray, Carrickmacross, Magheross parish, barony of Farney, 10 June 1847.
CB1, no. 63.82, Thomas Chessar, Killeevan, Killeevan parish, barony of Dartree, 11 June 1847.
CB1, no. 64.83, Margaret Chessar, Tullaghan, Tedavnet parish, barony of Monaghan, 12 June 1847.
CB1, no. 4.87, Bernard Kelly, Aghalisk, Kilmore parish, barony of Monaghan, 29 June 1847.
CB1, no. 8.91, Catherine Magin, Monaghan gaol, town, parish and barony of Monaghan, 2 Aug. 1847.
CB1, no. 25.108, Brian Martin, Monaghan gaol, town, parish and barony of Monaghan, 9 Dec. 1847.
CB1, no. 26.109, Owen McGarrell, Monaghan gaol, town, parish and barony of Monaghan 24 Dec. 1847.
CB1, no. 27.110, Patt Maginn, Monaghan gaol, town, parish and barony of Monaghan, 28 Dec. 1847.
CB1, no. 28.111, Francis Woods, Monaghan gaol, town, parish and barony of Monaghan, 30 Dec. 1847.

1848

CB1, no. 29.112, Phillip Mayne, Monaghan gaol, town, parish and barony of Monaghan, 1 Jan. 1848
CB1, inquiry, John Quinn, Monaghan gaol, town, parish of Monaghan, 3 Jan. 1848.
CB1, no. 33.116, John McPhillips, Monaghan gaol, town, parish and barony of Monaghan, 6 Jan. 1848.
CB1, no. 1.117, Bernard Carr, Monaghan gaol, town, parish and barony of Monaghan, 6 Jan. 1848.
CB1, no. 2.118, James McCarron, Monaghan gaol, town, parish and barony of Monaghan, 10 Jan. 1848.
CB1, no. 4.120, John Smith, Monaghan gaol, town, parish and barony of Monaghan, 12 Jan. 1848.

CB1, no. 5.121, Dan Finley, Monaghan gaol, town, parish and barony of Monaghan, 12 Jan. 1848.
CB1, no. 9.125, Mary Lambert, Monaghan town, parish and barony of Monaghan, 24 Jan. 1848.
CB1, no. 10.126, Pat Connolly, Monaghan workhouse, parish and barony of Monaghan, 24 Jan. 1848.
CB1, no. 12.1128, John Casey, Drumnagavlin, Clones parish, barony of Dartree, 2 Feb. 1848.
CB1, no. 13.129, Thomas Clements, Smithborough, Clones parish, barony of Dartree, 4 Feb. 1848.
CB1, no. 17.133, Bernard Rudden, Killark, Currin parish, barony of Dartree, 27 Feb. 1848.
CB1, no. 18.134, Terance Conolly, Drum, Currin parish, barony of Dartree, 28 Feb. 1848.
CB1, no. 22.138, William Quigley, Newbliss, Killeevan parish, barony of Dartree, 21 Mar. 1848.
CB1, no. 24.140, Owen Treanor, Tedavnet, Tedavnet parish, barony of Monaghan, 3 Apr. 1848.
CB1, no. 27.143, Joseph Abraham, Telayden, Donagh parish, barony of Trough, 20 Apr. 1848.
CB1, no. 29.145, James Clark, Monaghan gaol, town, parish and barony of Monaghan, 16 May 1848.
CB1, no. 32.148, James Duffy, Monaghan gaol, town, parish, and barony of Monaghan, 15 June 1848.
CB1, no. 33.149, Ann Cavenagh, Cortannel, Aughnamullen parish, barony of Cremorne, 27 June 1848.
CB1, no. 4.153, John Mitchell, Drumbenagh, Tedavnet parish, barony of Monaghan, 27 July 1848.
CB1, no. 11.160, Thomas Wright, Clones workhouse, parish and barony of Clones, 26 Oct. 1848.
CB1, no. 1.117, Bernard Carr, Monaghan gaol, town, parish and barony of Monaghan, 6 Dec. 1848.
CB1, no. 13.162, Alice Connolly, Aghnahola, parish of Currin, barony of Dartree, 14 Dec. 1848.
CB1, no. 14.163, Mick Smith, Kilnamaddy, parish of Monaghan, barony of Monaghan, 23 Dec. 1848.

1849

CB1, no. 20.169, Pat Keenan, Leitrim, Tyholland parish, barony of Monaghan, 21 Feb. 1849.
CB1, no. 2.170, Mary Hughes, Monaghan gaol, Monaghan parish, barony of Monaghan, 16 Mar. 1849.
CB1, no. 3.172, Mathew Cassidy, Monaghan gaol, town, parish and barony of Monaghan, 24 Mar. 1849.
CB1, no. 6.175, Mary Boyland, Killymarly, Monaghan parish, barony of Monaghan, 3 Apr. 1849.
CB1, no. 9.178, Bernard Rorc, Annaghybane, Ematris parish, barony of Dartree, 26 Apr. 1849.
CB1, no. 10.179, Mick Cuningham, Tonystackan, Tydavnet parish, barony of Monaghan, 26 Apr. 1849.
CB1, no.16.185, Mick Burk, Kilmore East, Ematris parish, barony of Dartree, 8 June 1849.
CB1, no. 17.186, Thomas McCarvle, Killycoonagh, Killeevan parish, barony of Dartree, 10 June 1849.
CB1, no. 18.187, Darby Ferguson, Clones poorhouse, Clones parish, barony of Dartree, 12 June 1849.

Appendix 2: Inquests and inquiries in William Charles Waddell's casebooks 219

CB1, no. 19.188, Thomas Madill, Bragan, Errigal Trough parish, barony of Trough, 17 June 1849.

CB1, no. 21.190, William Barker, Monaghan gaol, town, parish and barony of Monaghan, 25 June 1849.

CB1, no. 5.196, George Smith, Monaghan gaol, town, parish and barony of Monaghan, 1 Sept. 1849.

CB1, no. 6.197, Patrick Calaghan, Monaghan poorhouse, town, parish and barony of Monaghan, 2 Sept. 1849.

CB1, no.12.203, John Armstrong, Monaghan gaol, town, parish and barony of Monaghan, 11 Sept. 1849.

CB1, no. 7.198, Ann Martin, Monaghan gaol, town, parish and barony of Monaghan, 4 Oct. 1849.

CB1, no. 8.199, Ann Treanor, Monaghan, parish and barony of Monaghan, 2 Nov. 1849.

CB1, no.12.181, Catherine McCourt, Drumfernasky, parish Errigal Trough, barony of Trough, 3 May 1849.

CB1, no. 13.182, Catherine Trainor, Drumfernasky, parish Errigal Trough, barony of Trough, 3 May 1849.

CB1, no. 17.298, Andrew English, Monaghan gaol, town, parish and barony of Monaghan, 18 Dec. 1849.

CB1, no. 18.209, John Reidy, Monaghan gaol, town, parish and barony of Monaghan, 29 Dec. 1849.

1850

CB1, no. 19.210, Bernard Cosgrove, Clones, Clones parish, barony of Dartree, 13 Jan. 1850.

CB1, no. 20.211, John McGorman, Roosky, Monaghan parish, barony of Monaghan, 8 Feb. 1850.

CB1, no. 4.215, Ann Magaghy, Milltown, Ematris parish, barony of Dartree, 19 Mar. 1850.

CB1, no. 21.212, Catherine Connolly, Drum, Currin parish, barony of Dartree, 19 Feb. 1850.

CB1, no. 6.217, Silvester Gartland, Monaghan gaol, town, parish and barony of Monaghan, 27 Mar. 1850.

CB1, no. 9.220, Thomas Keery, Monaghan gaol, town, parish and barony of Monaghan, 29 May 1850.

CB1, no. 11.222, Peter Walsh, Monaghan gaol, town, parish and barony of Monaghan, 15 June 1850.

CB1, no. 2.225, George McMeighan, Monaghan gaol, town, parish and barony of Monaghan, 2 July 1850.

CB1, no. 14.237, Michael Gartland, Monaghan gaol, town, parish and barony of Monaghan, 14 Oct. 1850.

1852

CB1, no. 276.17, Ann Fee, Smithborough, Clones parish, barony of Monaghan, 2 Jan. 1852.

CB1, no. 287.5, Jane Hanna, Coleshill, Kilmore parish, barony of Monaghan, 23 Apr. 1852.

CB1, no. 294.12, Infant child, Monaghan town, parish and barony, 22 June 1852.

CB1, no. 305.11, Sarah McGarvey, Clones, Clones parish, barony of Dartree, 27 Nov. 1852.

1853

CB1, no. 309.15, Hamilton Clark, Lislynchahan, Ematris parish, barony of Dartree, 8 Jan. 1853.
CB1, no. 329.15, Thomas Riddle, Monaghan gaol, town, parish and barony of Monaghan, 28 May 1853.
CB1, no. 332.2, Infant child, Monaghan gaol, town, parish and barony of Monaghan, 12 Aug. 1853.
CB1, no. 342.12, Brian Rooney, Monaghan gaol, town, parish and barony of Monaghan, 5 Oct. 1853.

1855

CB1, no. 13.401, Robert Gillespie, Clones workhouse, barony of Dartree, 19 Oct. 1855.
CB1, no. 14.402, Jane Armstrong, Clones workhouse, Clones parish, barony of Dartree, 19 Oct. 1855.

1856

CB2, no. 2.426, Bernard Clarken, Mullaloughan, Donagh parish, 25 July 1856.
CB2, no. 3.427, Francis McMurrar, Derrylea, Donagh parish, 31 July, 1856.

1857

CB2, no. 21.445, Infant child, Clones, Clones parish, barony of Dartree, 7 Jan. 1857.
CB2, no. 6.470, Michael Muldoon, Clones, Clones parish, barony of Dartree, 27 Aug. 1857.

1859

CB2, no. 10.541, Infant child, Kilcorran, Clones parish, barony of Dartree, 7 Apr. 1859.

1861

CB2, no. 24.615, Infant child, Derrins, Currin parish, 7 Jan. 1861.

1866

CB2, no. 5.824, Mary Magee, Clones, parish of Clones, 10 Sept. 1866.

1867

CB2, enquiry, Jane Gordon, Dundrannan, parish of Ematris, 12–19 Jan. 1867.

1868

CB2, no. 1.892, Thomas Hughes, town, parish and barony of Monaghan, 14 July 1868.
CB2, no. 17.900, James Clarke, town, parish and barony of Monaghan, 26 Nov. 1868.

Appendix 2: Inquests and inquiries in William Charles Waddell's casebooks 221

1869

CB2, no. 5.935, James Quigley, Crossreagh, Killeevan parish, 28–30 Aug. 1869.

CB2, no. 9.939, Terence McDonald, Co. Monaghan asylum, town, parish and barony of Monaghan, 13 Sept. 1869.

CB2, no. 10.940, Female infant, Monaghan infirmary, town, parish and barony of Monaghan, 4–6 Oct. 1869.

CB2, no. 5.945, Phillip Treanor, town, parish and barony of Monaghan, 1 Dec. 1869.

1870

CB2, no. 21.951, James Lamb, Monaghan lunatic asylum, town, parish and barony of Monaghan, 28 Jan. 1870.

CB2, no. 9.973, William McMahon, Knockakirwan, Errigal parish, 9 Aug. 1870.

CB2, no. 20.984, Owen Coyle, Monaghan lunatic asylum, town, parish and barony of Monaghan, 17 Dec. 1870.

1871

CB2, no. 22.936, Thomas McCormick, Monaghan lunatic asylum, town, parish and barony of Monaghan, 18 Jan. 1871.

CB2, no. 26.990, McCullogh infant, Cargaghramer, Tullycorbet parish, 8 Feb. 1871.

CB2, no. 6.996, Laurance Meighan, Monaghan lunatic asylum, town, parish and barony of Monaghan, 6 Apr. 1871.

CB2, no. 11.1001, Infant child, Drumsloe, Drummully parish, 27 May 1871.

CB2, inquiry, C.P. Leslie, 27 June 1871.

CB2, no. 11.1014, Edward Molloy, Clones, Clones parish, 16 Nov. 1871.

CB2, no. 13.1014, Letitia Andrews, Clones, Clones parish, 22 Nov. 1871.

1872

CB2, no. 3.1025, John McBride, Maghernakill, Donamoyne parish, barony of Farney, 3 Apr. 1872

CB2, no. 11.1033, Jane Devine, Hollywood, Tydavent parish, 14 June 1872.

CB2, no. 10.1032, Michael Mooney, Carn, Aghabog parish, 17 June 1872.

CB2, no. 8.1042, John Gormley, town, parish and barony of Monaghan, 22 Aug. 1872.

1873

CB2, no. 2.1064, Mary Maguire, Clones workhouse, Clones parish, barony of Dartree, 31 Jan. 1873.

CB2, no. 3.1065, Bridget Smith, Clones workhouse, Clones parish, barony of Dartree, 3 Feb. 1873.

CB2, no. 10.1072, Mary McCarron, Rakelly, Errigal Trough parish, 10 Apr. 1873.

CB2, inquiry, Bridget McCabe, Liscumasky, Aghabog parish, 4 June 1873.

1874

CB2, no. 17.1123, Mary Prunty, Corcreeghy, Kilmore parish, 19 Dec. 1874.

1875

CB2, no. 7.1143, Mary Maguire, Clones, Clones parish, barony of Dartree, 4 Sept. 1875.
CB2, no. 22.1158, William Magwood, Scotstown, Tedavnet parish, 15 Dec. 1875.

1876

CB3, no. 2.1168, Catherine Byrne, town, parish and barony of Monaghan, 24 Feb. 1876.
CB3, no. 7.1173, Peter Began, Corraskea, Aughnamullen parish, barony of Cremorne, 6 Apr. 1876.
CB3, no. 2.1187, Sarah Maguire, Boughill, Killeevan village, Killeevan parish, barony of Dartree, 17 Aug. 1876.
CB3, no. 7.1192, John Boylan, Clones, Clones parish, barony of Dartree, 19 Sept. 1876.

1877

CB3, no. 14.1199, Infant male child, Cornacassa, Monaghan parish, barony of Monaghan, 17 Jan. 1877.
CB3, no. 15.1200, Infant child, town, parish and barony of Monaghan, 17 Jan. 1877.
CB3, no. 18.1203, Mary McCabe, Mullanlary, Donagh parish, barony of Trough, 2 Feb. 1877.
CB3, no. 3.1207, Patrick Brides, parish of Currin, barony of Dartree, 5 Mar. 1877.
CB3, no. 3.1218, A man, a stranger, a mendicant, Crosslea, Currin parish, barony of Dartree, 10 Aug. 1877.

Bibliography

PRIMARY SOURCES

MANUSCRIPT SOURCES

Bodleian Library, Oxford

Clarendon deposit, Letter from Lord Clarendon, the lord lieutenant to Prime Minister Lord John Russell, 10 Aug. 1847 (Letterbox I).

Clogher Historical Society Collection, Monaghan

Arthur Richards Neville, Maps of the Clermont estate, 1791.
Rent roll for one year's rent, duties and agents fees due to the daughters of Colonel Murray out of their lands and tenements in the estate of Monaghan ending at and including 25 March rent 1798.

Clones Library, Clones, Co. Monaghan

Casebook of William Charles Waddell, vol. 1, 1846–55.
Casebook of William Charles Waddell, vol. 3, 1876–7.
Monaghan town rent rolls, Sept. 1828.
Carrickmacross workhouse minute books, 1848–50.

Longleat House, Bath estate (Irish) papers, Bath

Tristam Kennedy, 'Observations accompanying the accounts of the agents of the Bath estate in Ireland', year ending 1 July 1848 (Irish Papers box III, bundle 2).
Report accounts and rental of the estate of the most noble, the marquis of Bath situate in the barony of Farney, country of Monaghan for the year ending March 1855 drawn up by the agent William Steuart Trench (1 Mar. 1855).

National Archives of Ireland, Dublin: Chief Secretary's Office registered papers

CSO/OPMA/1015 (2), Coroner's Districts, Jan. 1846–Mar. 1846.
CSO/RP/1820/659, Charles Clarke Hughes, MD, member of the Royal College of Surgeons, Dublin, and Drury Jones, alderman, one of the coroners for County City Dublin to Charles Grant, 21 Mar. 1820.
CSORP/PR/1821/72, The coroners of Cork to Charles Grant, chief secretary of Ireland, 14 Apr. 1821.

CSO/RP/SC/1821/138, Peter Browne, dean of Ferns, Glebe House, Ahascragh to William Gregory, 1 June 1819.

CSO/RP/SC/1821/138, Peter Brown, dean of Ferns, Glebe House, Ahascragh to Prince Frederick, 7 June 1819.

CSO/RP/SC/1821/138, Colonel Thomas Sorrell, Royal Hospital Dublin to Charles Grant, chief secretary for Ireland, 15 Sept. 1821.

CSO/RP/1821/220, James McCarthy, coroner for Co. Dublin to Charles Grant, 13 Dec. 1821.

CSO/RP/1821/424, Paul Parks, one of the coroners of Co. Louth, Dundalk to William Gregory, the lord lieutenant's secretary, 22 May 1821.

CSO/RP/1822/1139, The coroners of Tipperary to Charles Grant, 1 Sept. 1819.

CSORP/1821/SC/1426, James Landy, chief magistrate of police, Co. Kildare to William Gregory, 6 Nov. 1821.

CSO/RP/1822/1936, William McCune, church warden, Downpatrick to Henry Grattan, MP, 16 Oct. 1822.

CSO/RP/1822/2849, James Waddell to Richard Wellsley, lord lieutenant of Ireland, 1 Nov. 1822.

CSO/RP/1828/940, John Atkinson, Castlebar, Co. Mayo to lord lieutenant, Henry William Paget, 24 June 1828.

CSO/RP/1828/1910/2, Michael Creagh, high sheriff, Co. Cork to chief secretary, 19 Dec. 1828.

CSO/RP/1828/1910/3, Michael Creagh, high sheriff, Co. Cork to chief secretary, 17 Dec. 1828.

CSO/RP/1828/1910/4, Michael Creagh, high sheriff, Co. Cork to chief secretary, 17 Dec. 1828.

CSO/RP/1828/1910/5, Michael Creagh, high sheriff, Co. Cork to chief secretary, 16 Dec. 1828.

CSO/RP/1828/1910/7, Michael Creagh, high sheriff, Co. Cork to chief secretary, 10 Dec. 1828.

CSO/RP/1828/1910/8, Michael Creagh, high sheriff, Co. Cork to chief secretary, 1 Dec. 1828.

CSO/RP/1829/1910/9, Michael Creagh, high sheriff, Co. Cork to chief secretary, 6 Jan. 1829.

CSO/RP/1830/34, William Thompson, Ballyshannon, Co. Donegal to chief secretary, Sir Francis Leveson Gower, 5 Jan. 1830.

CSO/RP/1830/1321, George Evans, Swords, Dublin to chief secretary, Sir Francis Leveson Gower, 25 May 1830.

CSO/RP/1839/109, *A return of all coroners inquests taken in the respective years 1835, 1836, 1837, 1838, and 1839 to the time of making up such returns, in the several counties, cities and towns in Ireland, respectively, specifying the names of the persons on whose bodies such inquests were held, also the times and places where, the same were severally taken, and the findings or verdict of the jury in each case, and in all cases of homicide distinguishing those in which the verdict was against persons described by name, and those in which the verdict was against persons unknown* (Ordered by House of Commons on 12 March 1839).

National Archives of Ireland, Dublin: Coroners returns

CSORP 1876, 1877/32, Return for the coroner's district of northern Co. Monaghan, 31 Dec. 1876.

CSORP 1876, 1877/32, Return for the coroner's district of southern Co. Monaghan, 9 Jan. 1876.

National Archives of Ireland, Dublin: Criminal record files

CRF/1841/McConkey/17, Revd Roper and Revd Henry Moffett to lord lieutenant, Hugh Fortescue, 18 Apr. 1841.

National Archives of Ireland, Dublin: Distress papers

1402/D.332, Fr John Mullen to Rt Hon. Sir Thomas Freemantle, MP or Richard Pennefather, 1 Apr. 1846.
1403/D.431, Fr John Mullen to Rt Hon. Sir Thomas Freemantle, MP, 15 Apr. 1846.
1411/D.6438, Frs. John Mullin, Paul McCusker, and Michael McQuaide, to his Excellency Lord Bessborough, lord lieutenant of Ireland, Oct. 1846 [undated].
1411/D.6711, Frs James Duffy, P. Carolan, and J. Rooney of Tydavnet to undersecretary, 15 Oct. 1846.
1414/D.8819, Monaghan grand jury, clerics and MP to Lord Lieutenant Bessborough, 27 Nov. 1846.
1472/D.969, Revd Roper to Sir Randolph Routh, 25 Jan. 1847.

National Archives of Ireland, Dublin: Prison registers

Book 1/10/2, Irish prison registers 1832.
Book 1/10/7, Irish prison registers 1846.
Book 1/10/31, Dublin-Kilmainham prison general register, 1840–50.
Book 1/13/42, Dublin-Bridewell, Richmond prison general register, 1847–83.
Book 1/14/1, Dublin-Smithfield prison general register, 1844–9.

National Archives of Ireland, Dublin: Relief Commission papers

3/1/4261, Lambert to Labouchere, 12 July 1846.
3/1/5011, Fr Paul McCusker to Undersecretary Thomas Redington, 29 July 1846.
3/1/5363, James Warner to Relief Commission, 12 Aug. 1846.
3/2/26/42, Grant to McGregor, 4 Dec. 1846.
3/2/28/32, Henry Lucas St George, rector of the parish of Dromore, Co. Tyrone to the Relief Commission Office, 16 Mar. 1847.
5/23, James J. Sanderson, county inspector to Dublin Castle, 24 Aug. 1846.

National Archives of Ireland, Dublin: Other

Griffith's valuation, 1864, Co. Monaghan.
Landed Estates court rentals 1850–85 (vol. 34, doc. 80).
Ordnance Survey map, 1836, Lisnaveane, Co. Monaghan.
Ordnance Survey map, 1836, Monaghan town gaol, Co. Monaghan.
Ordnance Survey map, 1837, Co. Monaghan.
Ordnance survey map, 1908, Monaghan town, Co. Monaghan.
Outrage papers, Monaghan (1851/244).
Tithe applotment books, 1826, 1834, Co. Monaghan.
Valuation Office books, Co. Monaghan Field Book (1837).

National Folklore Collection, University College Dublin, Dublin

The Schools Collection, vols 799, 951, 1798.

Offaly Historical and Archaeological Society, Tullamore, Co. Offaly

Inquest reports of James Dillon, King's Co. coroner (1846–54).

Public Record Office of Northern Ireland

CR3/25, Presbytery meeting notes for Cahans.
D1252/14/3, Will of Alexander Waddell, 1798, Lisnaveane, Co. Monaghan.
D1739/3/9, Tenant roll of Lord Massareene, Alexander Woddall, 23 Apr. 1698–6 Feb. 1811.
D3531/M/1–2, Shirley estate papers 1840–7.
Dio (RC) 1/11A/9, Callan to Donnelly [undated].
Dio (RC) 1/11B/11, Bishop Donnelly's diary.

Register of Deeds, Dublin, Ireland

25/29/635, Waddell to Waddell, 1855.
27/238, Waddell to Waddell, 1853.
29/269/767, Massareene to Waddell, 1852.
29/269/768, Massareene to Waddell, 1852.
13103, Waddell to Jackson, 1762.
50239, Waddell to Waddell, 1732.
35479, Waddell to Graham, 1726.
162539, Waddell to Jackson, 1759.
544542, Waddell to Waddell, October 1825.
552767, Waddell to Waddell, February 1827.
568807, William Charles Waddell, Maria Orr Hope, John Hopes Jr. and Charles Hope, Sept. 1829.

State Library of New South Wales, Australia

PXA 685/41–41, Letter of John Jackson Waddell.

Schomberg House, Belfast

Co. Monaghan Grand Orange Lodge minute books, 1843–75.

NEWSPAPERS AND PERIODICALS

Aberdeen Press and Journal
Armagh Guardian
Belfast Mercury
Belfast Morning News
Belfast Newsletter
Belfast Weekly News

Bristol Mercury
Brooklyn Eagle
Clare Journal and Ennis Advertiser
Cork Constitution
Cork Examiner
Downpatrick Recorder
Dublin Daily Express
Dublin Evening Mail
Dublin Evening Mail Supplement
Dublin Evening Packet and Correspondent
Dublin Evening Post
Dublin Medical Press
Dublin Morning Register
Dublin Weekly Nation
Dundalk Democrat
Evening Chronicle
Evening Freeman
Evening Herald
Fermanagh Reporter
Finn's Leinster Journal
Freeman's Journal
Halifax Courier
Irish Examiner
Irish Times
Kerry Evening Post
King's County Chronicle
Leeds Mercury
Leinster Express
Limerick and Clare Examiner
Liverpool Daily Post
Londonderry Standard
London Evening Standard
Longford Journal
Louth County Advertiser
Manchester Courier and Lancashire General Advertiser
Mayo Constitution
Mayo Examiner
Merthyr Telegraph and General Advertiser for the Iron Districts of South Wales
Morning Post
The Nation
Nenagh Guardian
Newry and Louth Examiner
Newry Examiner and Louth Advertiser
Newry Telegraph
Northern Standard
Northern Whig
Pall Mall Gazette
Saunders's News-Letter and Daily Advertiser
Sheffield Independent
Sligo Journal
South London Chronicle
South London Press
Sydney Morning Herald
The Times
Tyrone Constitution
Ulster Gazette
Vindicator
Warder and Dublin Weekly Mail
Wexford Conservative
Yorkshire Post and Leeds Intelligencer

OFFICIAL PUBLICATIONS

A collection of the public general statutes passed in the ninth and tenth year of the reign of her majesty, Queen Victoria: being the sixth session of the fourteenth Parliament of the United Kingdom of Great Britain and Ireland (London, 1846).
Abstract of the Census of Ireland for the year 1841, p. 2, HC 1843 (459) li, 319.
Census of Ireland for the year 1851: Part I, showing the area, population and number of houses, by townlands & electoral divisions, County Monaghan, 259 [1575], HC 1852–3, xcii, 285.
Census of Ireland. 1871: Part III, general report with illustrative maps and diagrams, summary tables and appendix, 1 [C.1377], C1 1876, lxxxi, 35, 111.
*Commission of the Peace (Ireland): Return to an order of the Honourable the House of Commons dated 14 November 1882;- for, return 'for each county, city and borough in Ireland, of the names of the persons holding the Commission of the Peace, the aggregate number of such persons that are

Protestants, specifying their denominations, the number that are Roman Catholics, and the number that are members of any other religious persuasions', 331, HC 1884 (13) lxiii.

Coroners (Ireland): Copy of a memorial addressed to the lord lieutenant by the coroners of Ireland, requesting that a measure on their behalf may be brought before Parliament early in the present session, 439, HC 1871 (86) lviii.

County coroners (Ireland): A bill to amend the law relating to the appointment, duties and payment of county coroners, and expenses of inquests in Ireland, HC 1870, lxiv.

Criminal and Judicial Statistics. 1877: Ireland, Part I, Police, criminal proceedings, prisons; Part II, Common law, equity and civil law, 265 [C.2152] HC 1878, lxxix.

Divisions of the house: Return of the number of divisions of the house in the session of 1870; stating the subject of the division, and the number of members in the majority and minority, tellers included; also, the aggregate number in the house on each division; distinguishing the divisions on public business from private, &c. (in continuation of parliamentary paper, no. 0.100, of session 1868–9), HC 1870 (131) lvi.

Evicted Destitute Poor (Ireland) Act: Abstract of return to an order of the honourable House of Commons dated 19 February 1849, for return 'of all notices served upon relieving officers of Poor Law districts in Ireland by landowners and others, under the Act of last session, 11 & 12 Vict., c.47, intituled "An Act for the Protection and Relief of the Destitute Poor evicted from their Dwellings"', HC 1849 (571) xlix.

First report of the commissioners for administering the laws of relief for the poor in Ireland, with appendices, 563, HC, 1847–8, xxxiii, 166.

First report of commissioners of public instruction, Ireland, sessional papers, HC 1835 (829), xxxiii.

First report from the select committee of the House of Lords appointed to inquire into the operation of the Irish Poor Law and the expediency of making any amendment in its enactments, and to report thereon to the house: together with minutes of evidence, p. 8, HL 1849 (192) xvi, 4.

First, second and special reports from the select committee on juries (Ireland); together with the proceedings of the committee, minutes of evidence, and appendix, 339, HC 1873 (283) xv.

Further return showing the progress of disease in the potatoes, the complaints of the scarcity which have been made, the applications for relief, HC 1846 (213) xxxvii.

Hansard 1, xxxiv, 22 May 1816, cc 681–3.

Hansard 3, ix, 25 June 1823, cc 1212–41.

Hansard 3, xv, 15 Feb. 1833, cc 718–58, 732.

Hansard 3, xvi, 19 Mar. 1833, cc 827–72.

Hansard 3, xxxvi, 22 Feb. 1837, cc 863–958.

Hansard 3, ci, 10 Aug. 1848, cc 54–5

Hansard 3, cxvii, 28 May 1851, cc 100–13.

Hansard 3, cxclll, 20 July 1868, c. 1482.

Hansard 3, cxcix, 4 Mar. 1870, c. 1241.

Hansard 3, ccxiv, 11 Mar. 1873, c. 1739–1868.

Hansard 3, cclx, 5 Apr. 1881, cc 751–2.

Hearth money rolls, 1663 and 1665.

Inspectors general report on general state of prisons of Ireland for the year 1807, HC 1808 (239) ix.

Inspectors general report state of prisons of Ireland, 1818 with appendix, HC 1819 (534) xii.

Irish law reports of cases argued and determined in the courts of queen's bench, common pleas, and exchequer of pleas, during the years 1843 and 1844, VI (Dublin, 1844).

Lunatic asylums Ireland: The nineteenth annual report on the district, criminal and private lunatic asylums in Ireland, with appendices, 287 [C.202], HC 1870, xxxiv, 102.

Lunatic asylums Ireland: The twentieth annual report of the district, criminal and private lunatic asylums in Ireland, with appendices, 427 [C.440], HC 1871, xxvi.

Lunatic asylums Ireland: The twenty-first report on the district, criminal and private lunatic asylums in Ireland, with appendices, 323 [C.647], HC 1871, xxvii.

Lunatic asylums Ireland: The twenty-sixth report on the district, criminal and private lunatic asylums in Ireland; with appendices, 449 [C.1750], HC 1877, xli.

Lunatic asylums Ireland, The twenty-seventh report on the district, criminal and private lunatic asylums in Ireland, with appendices, 395 [C2037], HC 1878, xxxix.

Minutes of evidence taken before the select committee of the House of Lords appointed to enquire into the state of Ireland since the year 1835 in respect of crime and outrage, which have rendered life and property insecure in that part of the empire, HC 1839 (468) xi, xii, 1.

Poor Law Union and Lunacy Inquiry Commission (Ireland): Report, minutes of evidence with appendices, HC 1878–9 (2239) xxxi, 35.

Prisons of Ireland: Report of inspectors general; 1823 with abstract from appendix of general observations on each prison in the several districts &c., HC 1823 (342) x.

Prisons of Ireland: Eighth report of the inspectors general on the general state of the prisons of Ireland, 1830, HC 1830 (48) xxiv.

Prisons of Ireland: Ninth report of the inspectors general, 1831, HC 1831 (172) iv.

Prisons of Ireland: Tenth report of the inspectors general on the general state of the prisons of Ireland, 1832, HC 1832 (152) xxiii.

Prisons of Ireland: Eleventh report of the inspectors general on the general state of prisons in Ireland, 1833, HC 1833 (67) xvii.

Prisons of Ireland: Twelfth report of the inspectors general on the general state of the prisons of Ireland, 1834, HC 1834 (63) xl.

Prisons of Ireland: Thirteenth report of the inspectors general on the general state of the prisons of Ireland, 1835, HC 1835 (220) xxxvii.

Prisons of Ireland: Fourteenth report of the inspectors general on the general state of the prisons of Ireland 1836: with an appendix, HC 1836 (118) xxxv.

Prisons of Ireland: Fifteenth report of the inspectors general on the general state of the prisons of Ireland 1836: with appendixes, HC 1837 (123) xxxi.

Prisons of Ireland: Sixteenth report of the inspectors general on the general state of the prisons of Ireland 1837: with appendixes, HC 1838 (186) xxix.

Prisons of Ireland: Seventeenth report of the inspectors general on the general state of the prisons of Ireland 1838: with appendixes, HC 1839 (91) xx.

Prisons of Ireland: Eighteenth report of the inspectors general on the general state of the prisons of Ireland 1839: with appendixes, HC 1840 (240) xxvi.

Prisons of Ireland: Nineteenth report of the inspectors general on the general state of the prisons of Ireland 1840: with appendixes, HC 1841 (299) xi.

Prisons of Ireland: Twentieth report of the inspectors general on the general state of the prisons of Ireland 1841: with appendixes, HC 1842 (377) xxii.

Prisons of Ireland: Twenty-first report of the inspectors general on the general state of the prisons of Ireland 1842: with appendixes, HC 1843 (462) xxvii.

Prisons of Ireland: Twenty-second report of the inspectors general on the general state of the prisons of Ireland 1843: with appendixes, HC 1844 (535) xxviii.

Prisons of Ireland: Twenty-third report of the inspectors general on the general state of the prisons of Ireland 1844: with appendices, HC 1845 (620) xxv.

Prisons of Ireland: Twenty-fourth report of the inspectors general on the general state of the prisons of Ireland 1845: with appendices, HC 1846 (697) xx.

Prisons of Ireland: Twenty-fifth report of inspectors general on the general state of the prisons of Ireland, 1846, HC 1847 (805) xxix.

Prisons of Ireland: Twenty-sixth report of the inspectors general on the general state of the prisons in Ireland, 1847; with appendices, HC 1848 (952) xxxiv.

Prisons of Ireland: Twenty-seventh report on the general state of prisons in Ireland 1848, with appendices, HC 1849 (1069) xxvi.

Prisons of Ireland: Twenty-eighth report of the inspectors general on the general state of prisons of Ireland 1849, with appendices, HC 1850 (1229) xxix.

Prisons of Ireland: Thirty-third report of the inspectors general of the general state of the prisons of Ireland, 1854, HC 1854–5 (1956) xxvi.

Reports from Poor Law inspectors as to the existing relations between landlord and tenant in respect of improvements on farms, drainage, reclamation of land, fencing, planting, and also as to the existence (and to what extent) of the Ulster tenant-right in their respective districts, &c., 37 [C.31], HC 1870, xiv, 101.

Report from the select committee on county cess (Ireland), p. 138, HC 1836 (527) xii.

Report from the select committee on outrages (Ireland); together with the proceedings of the committee, minutes of evidence, appendix and index, p. 91, HC 1852 (438) xiv.

Report of the commissioners appointed to take the census of Ireland, for the year 1841, 1, [504], HC 1843, xxiv.

Report of the inspectors general on the general state of the prisons of Ireland, 1824, HC 1824 (294) xxii.

Return of number of agricultural holdings in Ireland, and tenure held by occupiers, 5, 6 [C.32], C1.1870, lvi, 737.

Return of outrages reported to the Constabulary Office in Ireland, during the year 1869, with summaries for preceding years; and return of outrages reported by the constabulary in Ireland in the months of January and February, 1870, 353 [C.60], C1 1870, lvii, 34.

Return of the number and dates of any coroners' inquests that have been held on the bodies of any paupers that have died in the workhouses of any of the Unions in Ireland, in the years 1848, 1849 and 1850, HC 1851 (448).

Return of the number of divisions of the house in the session of 1870, HC 1870 (131) lvi, 5.

Return of the number of freeholders who stood registered and qualified to vote in each county in Ireland, on 1st January 1829 and 1st January 1830; distinguishing in each county the number registered in each case at each rate, HC 1830 (556) xxix.

PUBLISHED SOURCES

Anon., *A list of persons to whom premiums for sowing flax-seed in the year 1796 have been adjudged by the trustees of the linen manufacture* (Belfast, c.1796).

Anon., *The Irish medical directory of 1852* (London, 1852).

Anon., *The Irish medical directory for the year 1873* (Dublin, 1873).

Anon., *Irish workhouse rulebook, 1844* (Dublin, 1844).

Anon., *Pigot and Co.'s city of Dublin and Hibernian provincial directory* (London, 1824).

Bibliography

Anon., *Pigot and Co.'s directory of Monaghan town, 1826* (London, 1826).
Anon., *Slaters national commercial directory of Ireland 1846* (Manchester, 1846).
Balch, William Stevens, *Ireland, as I saw it: the character, condition and prospects of the people* (New York, 1850).
Boucicault, Dion, *Used up: a petite comedy, in two acts* (London, 1844).
Butt, Isaac, 'The Famine in the land, what has been done, and what is to be done', *Dublin University Magazine*, 29:172 (Apr. 1847), pp 501–40.
Carleton, William, 'The resurrections of Barney Bradley', *Dublin Penny Journal*, 2:88 (8 Mar. 1834), pp 285–8.
___, 'Barney Bradley's resurrection' in *The fawn of Spring Vale, the clarionet, and other tales*, iii: *The misfortunes of Barney Branagan, the resurrections of Barney Bradley* (Dublin, 1841), pp 261–328.
___, *The black prophet: a tale of Irish Famine, traits and stories of the Irish peasantry, the works of William Carleton* (New York, 1881), vol. 3.
Croly, Henry, *The Irish medical directory of 1843, including notices of the literary and scientific institutions of Ireland, with notes, historical, biographical and bibliographical* (Dublin, 1843).
Duffy, Charles Gavan, *My life in two hemispheres* (London, 1898).
Dutton, Matt, *The office and authority of sheriffs, under-sheriffs, deputies, county-clerks, and coroners in Ireland* (Dublin, 1721).
Elven, John Peter, *The book of family crests: comprising nearly every family bearing ... with surnames of the bearers, their mottos, an essay on the origina of arms, crests ... a glossary of terms and an index of subjects* (London, 1840), vol. 1.
Griffin, Gerald, *Card drawing, the half sir, and Suil Dhuv the coiner* (Dublin, 1891).
Hayes, Edmund, *Crimes and punishments: or, an analytical digest of the criminal statute law of Ireland* (Dublin, 1837).
___, *Crimes and punishments: or, a digest of the criminal statue law of Ireland, alphabetically arranged, with ... notes*, 2nd ed. (Dublin, 1842).
Huband, William George, *A practical treatise on the law relating to the grand jury in criminal cases, the coroner's jury, and the petty jury, in Ireland* (Dublin, 1896).
Hughes, John, *A lecture on the antecedent causes of the Irish Famine in 1847, delivered under the auspices of the general committee for the relief of the suffering poor of Ireland, by the Right Rev. John Hughes, D.D., bishop of New York, at the Broadway Tabernacle, March 20, 1847* (2nd ed.; New York, 1847).
Jacob, Giles, *Every man his own lawyer ... corrected and improved, with many additions, from the reports of Sir James Burrow, Sir William Blackstone, etc.* (10th ed.; Rivington, 1788).
Jervis, John, *Sir John Jervis on the office and duties of coroners: with forms and precedents* (London, 1827).
___, *A practical treatise on the office and duties of coroners* (London, 1829).
___, *On the office and duties of coroners: with forms and precedents* (3rd ed.; London, 1866).
Livingstone, Peadar, *The Monaghan story: a documented history of the County Monaghan from the earliest times to 1976* (Enniskillen, 1980).
Peel, Thomas G., *The case of the Irish coroners stated* (Belfast, 1872).
___, *The crown, the coroners and the people* (Armagh, 1874).
Rushe, Denis Carolan, *Historical sketches of Monaghan* (Dublin, 1895).
___, *History of Monaghan for two hundred years, 1660–1860* (Dundalk, 1921).
Shirley, Evelyn Philip, *The history of the county of Monaghan* (London, 1879).

Somerville, E.Œ, and Martin Ross, *Some experiences of an Irish R.M. with illustrations by Edith Somerville* (London, 1899).
Sullivan, Alexander Martin, *New Ireland* (3rd ed.; London, 1877), vol. 1.
Thom, Adam Bisset, *Thom's Directory for 1857* (Dublin, 1857).
_____, *Thom's Directory for 1870* (Dublin, 1870).
Wyse, Thomas, *Historical sketch of the late Catholic Association of Ireland* (London, 1829), vol. 2.

PRIVATE COLLECTIONS

Casebook of William Charles Waddell, Volume 2, 1856–76 (Alistair McCrory, Co. Down, Northern Ireland).
Journal of Ina Rogers, 1900 (Henry Skeath, Co. Monaghan, Ireland).
Letters of William Charles Waddell (Rory Hope, Adelaide, Australia).

SECONDARY SOURCES

Published Sources

Books

Bate, Johnathan and Eric Rasmussen (eds), *William Shakespeare: Hamlet* (Hampshire, 2008).
Bingley, C.W., *The Waddells of Ireland: a genealogical resource* (Belfast, 2014).
Bonsall, Penny, *The Irish RMs: the resident magistrates in the British administration in Ireland* (Dublin, 1997).
Broeker, Galen, *Rural disorder and police reform in Ireland, 1812–36* (London, 1970).
Burney, Ian A., *Bodies of evidence: medicine and the politics of the English inquest, 1830–1926* (Baltimore, 2000).
Cockburn J.S. and Thomas A. Green (eds), *Twelve good men and true: the criminal trial jury in England, 1200–1800* (Princeton, 2014).
Conley, Carolyn, *Melancholy accidents: the meaning of violence in post-Famine Ireland* (Lanham, MD, 1999).
Connolly, S.J., *Religion and society in nineteenth-century Ireland* (Dundalk, 1985).
Crossman, Virginia, *Local government in nineteenth-century Ireland* (Belfast, 1994).
___, *Politics, law and order in nineteenth-century Ireland* (Dublin, 1996).
___, *Politics, pauperism and power in late nineteenth-century Ireland* (Manchester, 2006).
___, *The Poor Law in Ireland, 1838–1948* (Dublin, 2006).
___, *Poverty and the Poor Law in Ireland, 1850–1914* (Oxford, 2013).
Crossman, Virginia and Peter Gray (eds), *Poverty and welfare in Ireland, 1838–1948* (Dublin, 2011).
Curran, Daragh, *The Protestant community in Ulster, 1825–45, a society in transition* (Dublin, 2014).
Day, Angelique and Patrick Williams (eds), *Ordnance Survey, counties of south Ulster, 1834–1838, Cavan, Leitrim, Louth, Monaghan and Sligo* (Belfast, 1998), vol. 40.
Delaney, Enda and Breandán Mac Suibne (eds), *Ireland's Great Famine and popular politics* (New York, 2016).
Donnelly, James S. Jr., *The great Irish potato Famine* (Stroud, 2010).
Dooley, Terence, *The Big Houses and landed estates of Ireland: a research guide* (Dublin, 2007).

Bibliography

Dowdall, Denise M., *Irish nineteenth-century prison records: survey and evaluation* (Dublin, 2013).
Farrell, Brian, *Coroners: practice and procedure* (Dublin, 2000).
Farrell, Elaine, *'A most diabolical deed': infanticide and Irish society, 1850–1900* (Manchester, 2013).
Farrell, Sean, *Rituals and riots: sectarian violence and political culture in Ulster, 1784–1886* (Lexington, 2009).
Garnham, Neal, *The courts, crime and the criminal law in Ireland, 1692–1760* (Dublin, 1996).
Geary, Laurence M., *Medicine and charity in Ireland, 1718–1851* (Dublin, 2004).
Gray, Peter, *Famine, land and politics: British government and Irish society, 1843–1850* (Dublin, 1999).
Hand, G.J., *English law in Ireland, 1290–1324* (London, 1967).
Havard, J.D.J., *The detection of secret homicide: a study of the medico-legal system of investigation of sudden and unexplained deaths* (London, 1960).
Holmes, Andrew R., *The shaping of Ulster Presbyterian belief and practice, 1770–1840* (Oxford, 2006).
Hoppen, K. Theodore, *Elections, politics and society in Ireland, 1832–1885* (Oxford, 1984).
___, *Ireland since 1800: conflict and conformity* (2nd ed.; London, 2013).
Howlin, Niamh, *Juries in Ireland: laypersons and law in the long nineteenth century* (Dublin, 2017).
Hunnisett, Roy Frank, *The medieval coroner* (Cambridge, 1961).
Kane, Anne, *Constructing national identity: discourse and ritual during the Land War, 1879–1882* (New York, 2011).
Kerr, Donal, *'A nation of beggars'? Priests, people and politics in Famine Ireland, 1846–1852* (Oxford, 1994).
Knight, George, *A Clones miscellany* (Clones, 2004).
Leckey John L. and Desmond Greer, *Coroners' law and practice in Northern Ireland* (Belfast, 1998).
Lee, Joseph, *The modernization of Irish society, 1848–1918* (Dublin, 1973).
Lyons, F.S.L., *Ireland since the Famine* (London, 1963).
MacDonagh, Oliver, *The nineteenth-century novel and Irish social history: some aspects* (Dublin, 1970).
___, *Early Victorian government, 1830–1870* (London, 1977).
___, *Ireland: the union and its aftermath* (London, 1977).
McDowell, R.B., *The Irish administration, 1801–1914* (London, 1964).
McGoff-McCann, Michelle, *Melancholy madness: a coroner's casebook* (Cork, 2003).
McMahon, Michael, *The murder of Thomas Douglas Bateson, County Monaghan, 1851* (Dublin, 2016).
McMahon, Richard, *Homicide in pre-Famine and Famine Ireland* (Liverpool, 2013).
Mokyr, Joel, *Why Ireland starved: a quantitative and analytical history of the Irish economy, 1800–1850* (Oxford, 1983).
Mulligan, Kevin V., *The buildings of Ireland: south Ulster, Armagh, Cavan and Monaghan* (New Haven, 2005).
Murnane, James H. and Peadar Murnane, *At the ford of the birches: the history of Ballybay, its people and vicinity* (Monaghan, 1999).
Nagy, Victoria M., *Nineteenth-century female poisoners: three English women who used arsenic to kill* (New York, 2015).
Nally, David, *Human encumbrances: political violence and the great Irish Famine* (Notre Dame, IN, 2011).

Nesbitt, David, *Full circle: a story of Ballybay Presbyterians* (Monaghan, 1999).
O'Dowd, Anne, *Spalpeens and tattie hokers: history and folklore of the Irish migratory agricultural worker in Ireland and Britain* (Dublin, 1991).
Ó Gráda, Cormac, *Ireland: a new economic history, 1780–1939* (Oxford, 1995).
Ollerenshaw, Philip, *Banking in nineteenth-century Ireland: the Belfast banks, 1825–1914* (Manchester, 1987).
Palmer, Stanley H., *Police and protest in England and Ireland, 1780–1850* (Cambridge, 1988).
Perkin, Harold, *The rise of professional society: England since 1880* (London, 1989).
Purdue, Olwen, *The MacGeough Bonds of the Argory* (Dublin, 2005).
Reader, W.J., *Professional men: the rise of the professional classes in nineteenth-century England* (London, 1966).
Reilly, Ciarán, *John Plunket Joly and the Great Famine in King's County* (Dublin, 2012).
___, *The Irish land agent, 1830–60: the case of King's County* (Dublin, 2014).
Robins, Joseph, *Fools and mad, a history of the insane in Ireland* (Dublin, 1986).
Sherry, Brian and Raymond McHugh, *Along the black pig's dyke: folklore from Monaghan and south Armagh* (Castleblayney, 1993).
Stratmann, Linda, *The secret poisoner: a century of murder* (New Haven, 2016).
Tarlow, Sarah, *Ritual, belief and the dead in early modern Britain and Ireland* (Cambridge, 2013).
Trench, William Steuart, *The realities of Irish life* (London, 1869).
Walker, B.M. (ed.), *Parliamentary election results in Ireland, 1801–1922* (Dublin, 1978).
___, *Ulster politics: the formative years, 1868–86* (Belfast, 1989).
Wright, Frank, *Two lands on one soil: Ulster politics before home rule* (Dublin, 1996).
Vaughan, W.E., *Landlords and tenants in mid-Victorian Ireland* (Oxford, 1994).
___, *Murder trials in Ireland, 1836–1914* (Dublin, 2009).

Book chapters

Andrews, J.H., 'Land and people, c.1780' in T.W. Moody and W.E Vaughan (eds), *A new history of Ireland*, iv: *eighteenth-century Ireland, 1691–1800* (Oxford, 1984), pp 236–64.
Bartlett, Thomas, 'This famous island set in a Virginian sea': Ireland in the British empire' in Peter James Marshall (ed.), *The Oxford history of the British empire: the eighteenth century* (Oxford, 1998), pp 253–75.
Brown, Michael and Seán Patrick Donlan, 'The laws in Ireland, 1689–1850: a brief introduction' in Michael Brown and Seán Patrick Donlan (eds), *The laws and other legalities of Ireland, 1689–1850* (Farnham, 2011), pp 1–31.
Clark, Michael J., 'General practice and coroners' practice: medico-legal work and the Irish medical profession, c.1830–1890' in Catherine Cox and Maria Luddy (eds), *Cultures of care in Irish medical history, 1750–1970* (Basingstoke, 2010), pp 37–56.
Comerford, R.V., 'Gladstone's first Irish enterprise, 1864–70' in W.E. Vaughan (ed.), *A new history of Ireland*, v: *Ireland under the Union, 1801–70* (Oxford, 1989), pp 431–50.
___, 'Ireland 1850–70: post-Famine and mid-Victorian' in W.E. Vaughan (ed.), *A new history of Ireland*, v: *Ireland under the Union, 1801–70* (Oxford, 1989), pp 372–95.
Connolly, Claire, 'The national tale', in Peter Garside and Karen O'Brien (eds), *The Oxford history of the novel in English, Volume Two, English and British fiction, 1750–1820* (Oxford, 2015), pp 216–33.
Connolly, S.J., 'Mass politics and sectarian conflict, 1823–30' in W.E. Vaughan (ed.), *A new*

history of Ireland, v: *Ireland under the Union, 1801–70* (Oxford, 1989), pp 74–107.
___, 'The Catholic question 1801–12' in W.E. Vaughan (ed.), *A new history of Ireland*, v: *Ireland under the Union, 1801–70* (Oxford, 1989), pp 24–47.
___, 'Union government, 1812–23' in W.E. Vaughan (ed.), *A new history of Ireland*, v: *Ireland under the Union, 1801–70* (Oxford, 1989), pp 48–73.
Crossman, Virginia, 'Peculation and partiality: local government in nineteenth-century rural Ireland' in Roger Swift and Christine Kinealy (eds), *Politics and power in Victorian Ireland* (Dublin, 2006), pp 133–42.
Cullen, L.M., 'Economic development, 1750–1800' in T.W. Moody and W.E. Vaughan (eds), *The new history of Ireland*, iv: *Eighteenth-century Ireland, 1691–1800* (Oxford, 1986), pp 123–58.
Donnelly, James S. Jr., 'The administration of relief, 1847–51' in W.E. Vaughan (ed.), *A new history of Ireland*, v: *Ireland under the Union, 1801–70* (Oxford, 2013), pp 316–31.
Dooley, Terence A.M., 'Estate ownership and management in nineteenth- and early twentieth-century Ireland' in Terence Dooley (ed.), *Sources for the history of landed estates in Ireland* (Dublin, 2000), pp 3–16.
Duffy, Patrick J., 'Placing migration in history: geographies of Irish population movements' in Brian S. Turner, *Migration and myth: Ulster's revolving door* (Belfast, 2006), pp 27–37.
___, 'Mapping the Famine in Monaghan' in John Crowley, William J. Smyth and Mike Murphy (eds), *The atlas of the Great Irish Famine* (New York, 2012), pp 440–9.
Garnham, Neal, 'Crime, policing and the law, 1600–1900' in Liam Kennedy and Philip Ollerenshaw (eds), *Ulster since 1600: politics, economy and society* (Oxford, 2013), pp 90–105.
Geary, Laurence M., 'The medical profession, health care and the Poor Law in nineteenth-century Ireland' in Virginia Crossman and Peter Gray (eds), *Poverty and welfare in Ireland, 1838–1948* (Dublin, 2011), pp 189–206.
___, '"The whole country was in motion": mendicancy and vagrancy in pre-Famine Ireland' in Jacqueline Hill and Colm Lennon (eds), *Luxury and austerity* (Dublin, 1999), pp 121–36.
Gray, Peter, 'British relief measures' in John Crowley, William J. Smyth and Mike Murphy (eds), *The atlas of the Great Irish Famine* (New York, 2012), pp 75–86.
MacDonagh, Oliver, 'Ideas and institutions, 1830–45' in W.E. Vaughan (ed.), *A new history of Ireland*, v: *Ireland under the Union, 1801–70* (Oxford, 1989), pp 193–217.
McDonagh, T., E. Slater and T. Boylan, 'Irish political economy before and after the Famine' in Terrence McDonough (ed.), *Was Ireland a colony? Economics, politics and culture in nineteenth-century Ireland* (Dublin, 2005), pp 212–34.
McDowell, R.B., 'Administration and the public services, 1800–70' in W.E. Vaughan (ed.), *A new history of Ireland*, v: *Ireland under the Union, 1801–70* (Oxford, 2013), pp 538–61.
___, 'The age of United Irishmen: reform and reaction' in W.E. Vaughan (ed.), *A new history of Ireland*, v: *Ireland under the Union, 1801–70* (Oxford, 2013), pp 289–338.
McEntee, Joanne, '"Gentlemen practisers": solicitors as elites in mid-nineteenth-century Irish landed society' in Ciaran O'Neill (ed.), *Irish elites in the nineteenth century* (Dublin, 2013), pp 99–112.
McLoughlin, Dympna, 'Workhouses and Irish female paupers 1840–70' in Maria Luddy and Cliona Murphy (eds), *Woman surviving* (Dublin, 1989), pp 117–47.
Mokyr, Joel and Cormac Ó Gráda, 'Famine disease and famine mortality: lessons from the Irish experience, 1845–50' in Tim Dyson and Cormac Ó Gráda (eds), *Famine demography: perspectives from the past and present* (Oxford, 2002), pp 19–43.

Ó Gráda, Cormac, 'Yardsticks for Irish workhouses during the Great Famine' in Virginia Crossman and Peter Gray (eds), *Poverty and welfare in Ireland, 1838–1948* (Dublin, 2011), pp 69–98.

Parkes, Susan M., 'Higher education, 1793–1908' in W.E. Vaughan (ed.), *A new history of Ireland*, vi: *Ireland under the Union, II 1870–1921* (Oxford, 2012), pp 539–70.

Quinault, Roland, 'Victorian prime ministers and Ireland' in Roger Swift and Christine Kinealy (eds), *Politics and power in Victorian Ireland* (Dublin, 2006), pp 54–68.

Reilly, Ciarán, '"Nearly starved to death": the female petition during the Great Hunger' in Christine Kinealy, Jason King and Ciarán Reilly (eds), *Women and the Great Hunger* (Hamden, 2016), pp 47–56.

Sim, Joe and Tony Ward, 'The magistrate of the poor? Coroners and deaths in custody in nineteenth-century England' in Michael Clark and Catherine Crawford (eds), *Legal medicine in history* (Cambridge, 1994), pp 245–67.

Skehill, Caroline, 'The origins of child welfare under the Poor Law and the emergence of the institutional versus family care debate' in Virginia Crossman and Peter Gray (eds), *Poverty and welfare in Ireland, 1838–1948* (Dublin, 2011), pp 115–26.

Smyth, William J., 'The creation of the workhouse system' in John Crowley, William J. Smyth and Mike Murphy (eds), *The atlas of the Great Irish Famine* (New York, 2012), pp 120–7.

___, 'The story of the Great Irish Famine 1845–52: a geographical perspective' in John Crowley, William J. Smyth, and Mike Murphy (eds), *The atlas of the Great Irish Famine* (New York, 2012), pp 4–12.

Vaughan, W.E., 'Ireland c.1870' in W.E. Vaughan (ed.), *A new history of Ireland*, v: *Ireland under the Union, 1801–70* (Oxford, 2013), p. 726.

Journal articles

Bourke, Joanne, 'Fear and anxiety: writing about emotion in modern history', *History Workshop Journal*, 30 (2003), pp 111–33.

Boyle, Phelim P. and Cormac Ó Gráda, 'Fertility trends, excess mortality and the Great Irish Famine', *Demography*, 23:4 (1986), pp 543–62.

Brady, Thomas, 'Introductory lecture on medical jurisprudence, delivered in the theatre of the Royal Dublin Society, on Saturday 16th November 1837 by Thomas Brady esq. MD, fellow and professor in the King and Queen's College of Physicians, Ireland' (Dublin, 1839).

Breathnach, Ciara and Eunan O'Halpin, 'Scripting blame: Irish coroners' courts and unnamed infant dead', *Social History*, 39:2 (2014), pp 210–28.

Brown, Lindsay T., 'The Presbyterians of County Monaghan part I: the unfolding story', *Clogher Record*, 13:3 (1990), pp 7–54.

___, 'The Presbyterian dilemma: a survey of the Presbyterians and politics in Counties Cavan and Monaghan over three hundred years: part II of a series on the Monaghan Presbyterians' in *Clogher Record*, 15:2 (1995), pp 30–68.

Burney, Ian A., 'A poisoning of no substance: the trials of medico-legal proof in mid-Victorian England', *Journal of British Studies*, 38:1 (1999), pp 59–92.

Butler, Richard J., '"The radicals in these Reform times": politics, grand juries, and Ireland's unbuilt assize courthouses, 1800–50', *Architectural History: Journal of the Society of Architectural Historians of Great Britain*, 58 (2015), pp 109–39.

Calvert, Leanne, '"Do not forget your bit wife": love, marriage and the negotiation of patriarchy in Irish Presbyterian marriages, c.1780–1850', *Women's History Review*, 26:3 (2017), pp 433–54.

Duffy, Patrick J., 'Management problems on a large estate in mid-nineteenth-century Ireland: William Steuart Trench's report on the Shirley estate in 1843', *Clogher Record*, 26:1 (1997), pp 101–22.

Fisher, Pam, 'Getting away with murder? The suppression of coroners' inquests in early Victorian England and Wales', *Local Population Studies*, 78 (2007), pp 47–62.

Fitzgerald, Desmond, 'The Trillick derailment 1854', *Clogher Record*, 15:1 (1994), pp 31–47.

Gray, Peter, 'Conceiving and constructing the Irish workhouse, 1836–45', *Irish Historical Studies*, 38:149 (2012), pp 22–35.

Griffiths, A.R.G., 'The Irish Board of Works in the Famine years', *Historical Journal*, 13:4 (1970), pp 634–52.

Guinnane, Timothy W. and Cormac Ó Gráda, 'Mortality in the North Dublin Union during the Great Famine', *Economic History Review*, 55:3 (2002), pp 487–506.

Holmes, Andrew R., 'Covenanter politics: evangelicalism, political liberalism and Ulster Presbyterians 1798–1914', *English Historical Review*, 125:513 (2010), pp 340–69.

Hoppen, Theodore K., 'Roads to democracy: electioneering and corruption in nineteenth-century England and Ireland', *History*, 131:264 (1996), pp 553–71.

Howlin, Níamh, 'Controlling jury composition in nineteenth-century Ireland', *Journal of Legal History*, 30:3 (2009), pp 227–61.

___, '"The terror of their lives": Irish jurors' experiences', *Law and History Review*, 29:3 (2011), pp 703–61.

___, 'The politics of jury trials in nineteenth-century Ireland', *Comparative Legal History*, 3:2 (2015), pp 1–20.

Hurren, Elizabeth T., 'Remaking the medico-legal scene: a social history of the late-Victorian coroner in Oxford', *Journal of the History of Medicine and Allied Sciences*, 65:2 (2009), pp 207–52.

Johnson, David, 'The trials of Sam Gray: Monaghan politics and nineteenth-century Irish criminal procedure', *Irish Jurist*, 20:1 (1985), pp 109–34.

___, 'Trial by jury in Ireland 1860–1914', *Journal of Legal History*, 17:3 (1996), pp 270–93.

Kelly, James, '"A most inhuman and barborous piece of villany": an exploration of the crime of rape in eighteenth-century Ireland', *Eighteenth-Century Ireland*, 10 (1995), pp 78–107.

Kinzer, Bruce L., 'John Stuart Mill and the Irish university question', *Victorian Studies*, 31:1 (1987), pp 59–77.

Leaney, Enda, 'Vested interests: science and medicine in nineteenth-century Ireland', *Field Day Review*, 2 (2006), pp 285–93.

Lee, Joseph, 'The provision of capital for early Irish railways, 1830–53', *Irish Historical Studies*, 16:61 (1968), pp 33–63.

Lynch, Linda G., 'Death and burial in the Poor Law union workhouses in Ireland', *Journal of Irish Archaeology*, 13 (2014), pp 189–203.

Lysaght, Patricia, 'Perspectives on women during the Great Irish Famine from the oral tradition' in *Béaloideas*, 64/5 (1996/7), pp 63–130.

MacDonald, Brian, 'A time of desolation: Clones Poor Law Union, 1845–50', *Clogher Record*, 17:1 (2000), pp 3–146.

___, 'Monaghan in the age of revolution', *Clogher Record*, 17:3 (2002), pp 751–80.

Mac Giolla Choille, Breandán, 'Fenians, Rice and Ribbonmen in County Monaghan, 1864–67' in *Clogher Record*, 6:2 (1967), pp 221–52.

Maume, Patrick, 'Monaghan reimagined: "The Orangeman" (1915) as Ulster-American origin narrative', *New Hibernia Review/Iris Éireannach Nua*, 6:1 (2002), pp 113–29.

Magennis, Eoin, 'Belturbet, Cahans and two Presbyterian revolutions in south Ulster, 1660–1770', *Seanchas Ardmhacha: Journal of the Armagh Diocesan Historical Society*, 21:2 and 22:1 (2007/8), pp 129–48.

McClelland, Aiken, 'Orangeism in County Monaghan', *Clogher Record*, 9:3 (1978), p. 403.

McEldowney, John F., 'The case of the Queen v. McKenna (1869) and jury-packing in Ireland', *Irish Jurist*, n.s., 12 (1977), pp 339–53.

McGimpsey, Christopher D., 'Border ballads and sectarian affrays', *Clogher Record*, 11:1 (1982), pp 7–30.

Murnane, James H., 'The Lawless sortie into County Monaghan, September to October 1828', *Clogher Record*, 13:3 (1990), pp 146–62.

Oldham, James C., 'The origins of the special jury', *University of Chicago Law Review*, l:1 (1983), pp 137–221.

Ó Mórdha, Brian, 'The Great Famine in Monaghan: a coroner's account', *Clogher Record*, 4:1/2 (1961), pp 29–41.

___, 'The Great Famine in Monaghan (continued)', *Clogher Record*, 4:3 (1962), pp 175–86.

Ó Mórdha, Pilip, 'Summary of inquests held on Currin, Co. Monaghan victims 1846–1855', *Clogher Record*, 15:2 (1995), pp 90–100.

___, 'Addenda to the "Summary of inquests held on Currin, Co. Monaghan victims 1846–1855"', *Clogher Record*, 15:3 (1996), pp 158–9.

Pietz, William, 'Death of the deodand: accursed objects and the money value of human life', *RES: Anthropology and Aesthetics*, 31 (1997), pp 97–108.

Reuber, Markus, 'The architecture of psychological management: the Irish asylums (1801–1922)', *Psychological Medicine*, 26 (1996), pp 1179–89.

Rice, Charles T., 'Fenianism in Monaghan: memoir of James Blayney Rice: personalities of the Fenian movement and interesting details of activities in Monaghan, 1865–1885', *Clogher Record*, 1:4 (1956), pp 29–84.

Sharp, David, 'Thomas Wakely (1795–1862): a biographical sketch', *Lancet*, 379:9829 (May 2012), pp 1914–21.

Thuente, Mary Helen, 'Violence in pre-Famine Ireland: the testimony of Irish folklore and fiction' in *Irish University Review*, 15:2 (1985), pp 129–47.

Wilkinson, Susan, 'Early medical education in Ireland', *Irish Migration Studies in Latin America*, 6:3 (2008), pp 157–63.

Unpublished sources

Dunne, Terence Martin, 'Cultures of resistance in pre-Famine Ireland' (PhD, National University of Ireland, Maynooth, 2014).

Fisher, Pam, 'The politics of sudden death: the office and role of the coroner in England and Wales, 1726–1888' (PhD, University of Leicester, 2007).

McCann, Michelle, 'The investigation of death: the coroner's office in nineteenth-century Ireland' (MA, St Mary's University, Twickenham, 2014).

McGimpsey, Christopher D., '"To raise the banner in the remote north": politics in County

Monaghan, 1868–1883' (PhD, University of Edinburgh, 1982).
Norton, Desmond, Stewart and Kincaid, 'Irish land agents in the 1840s', Working Papers, No. 200208 (University College Dublin, 2002).
O'Reilly, Lorraine, 'The Shirley estate, 1848–1906: the development and demise of a landed estate in County Monaghan' (PhD, Trinity College Dublin, 2014).
Smalley, Alice, 'Representations of crime, justice and punishment in the popular press: a study of the *Illustrated Police News*, 1864–1938' (PhD, Open University, 2017).

Online sources

Brown, Sharon Oddie, 'Robert Hamilton Reed and Margaret Jackson', *The silver bowl*, thesilverbowl.com.
Clinton, Georgina and Linde Lunney, 'Isabella Maria Susan Tod', *DIB*.
Crimmins, James E., 'Jeremy Bentham', *Stanford Encyclopedia of Philosophy*, plato.stanford.eu.
Crossman, Virginia, 'Henry William 1st marquis of Anglesey Paget', *DIB*.
___, 'The Poor Law in Ireland, 1838–1948', *Institute of Historical Research, University of London*, history.ac.uk, 30 Mar. 2018.
Curtis, L. Perry, 'Corrigan, Sir Dominic John, first baronet (1802–1880)', *ODNB*.
Delaney, Enda and Breandán Mac Suibne (eds), *Ireland's Great Famine and popular politics* (Abingdon, 2016).
Farrell, Stephen, 'County Monaghan (1820–32)', *History of Parliament*, accessed 25 Aug. 2018.
Geoghegan, Patrick M., 'William O'Connor Morris', *DIB*.
___, 'Thomas O'Hagan', *DIB*.
Gilliand, J., 'James Greenacre', *ODNB*.
Hogan, Daire, 'Sir William Findlater', *DIB*.
Hourican, Bridget, 'Denis Caulfield Heron', *DIB*.
___, 'John Rea', DIB.
Irish Architectural Archive, 'Behan, John', *Dictionary of Irish architects, 1720–1940*, dia.ie.
Irish Architectural Archive, 'John McCurdy', *Dictionary of Irish architects 1720–1940*, dia.ie.
Lawrence, Sir Thomas, 'Chalres Grey, second Earl Grey', *ODNB*.
Lee, Sidney revised by K.D. Reynolds, 'Thomas Chisholm Anstey (1816–1873)', *ODNB*.
Lunney, Linda, 'Thomas Witherow', *DIB*.
McCabe, Desmond, 'Louis Perrin', *DIB*.
McCabe, Desmond, 'Robert Torrens', *DIB*.
McElroy, Martin, 'Edward George Geoffrey Smith Stanley, 14th earl of Derby', *DIB*.
Murphy, David, 'Samuel McCurdy Greer', *DIB*.
Newmann, Kate, 'James Donnelly (1822–1893): bishop, Roman Catholic', *Dictionary of Ulster biography*, newulsterbiography.co.uk, accessed 28 Aug. 2018.
___, 'Isabella Tod (1836–1896): campaigner for women's rights', *Dictionary of Ulster biography*, ulsterbiography.co.uk, accessed 24 Feb. 2018.
Steele, David, 'Temple, Henry John, third Viscount Palmerston (1784–1865)', *ODNB*.
Vehling, Sara, 'Taking your breath away: why strangulation in domestic violence is a huge red flag', *MobileODT*, mobileodt.com, accessed 30 Oct. 2020.
Walker, Brian, 'William Johnston', *DIB*.

Index

Page numbers in **bold** refer to images.

Aberdeen, George Hamilton-Gordon, 4th earl of, 146
abortion, 35, 37
Abraham, Joseph, 126
accidents, 44–5
Act of Union (1801), 23, 31, 52, 53
Acton, Graham (surgeon), 34
Aghabog, 118, 124, 139
Aghnasedagh, 50–1
agricultural depression, 196
American War of Independence, 51
Andrews, Letitia, 198
Anglesey, Henry William Paget, marquess of, 34
Anketell, Matthew, 149
Anketell, Thomas, 134, 188
Anstey, Thomas Chisholm, MP, 140
Apprentice Boys, 187
Armagh asylum, 190
Armstrong, Ellen, 158
Armstrong, Jane, 158–9
Armstrong, Mr, 109
Arnold, John, 52
Articles of Eyre (1194), 23
Atkinson, John (surgeon/apothecary), 34
Aughnacloy, 131

Baird, David, 165, 166–8, 170, 212
    coroner's warrant for arrest, 167, 168, 212
    defence, funding of, 168, 172
    trial and acquittal, 171
Baird, John, 167, 171
Baird, John, Jnr, 170
Balch, William Stevens, 102–3
Ballybay, 51, 56, 60, 87, 149, 169, 196
Ballybay First Presbyterian, 52
Ballybay Orange Lodge, 59
Ballynakill, 81
Banagan, Patt, 91

Barber, Jane (midwife), 156
Barry, T.R. (constabulary sub-inspector), 79n44, 88, 95
Bashford, Mr, 97
Bateson, Thomas Douglas (land agent), 147, 148, 152–4
Bath estate, 113, 136, 147, 149
Beatty, Benjamin (schoolmaster), 11
Began, Peter, 196
beggars/vagrants, 102–3, 194
    attitudes towards, 86–7, 90, 98, 197, 205–6
    imprisonment, 112
    inquests, 124–5, 197
    legislation outlawing, 112
    mendicancy, laws against, 195
    relief restrictions, 124
    Russell's policies, effects of, 103
    starvation deaths of, 86–8, 98, 122, 124
    see also pauper debtors; paupers; poor people
Belfast Morning News, 166–7
Bell, James, 95
Bell, Mary, 95, 96
Bentham, Jeremy, 107, **108**, 190
Bessborough, John William Ponsonby, earl of, 79, 80, 132
Blackburn, George, 166, 170n194
Blackburn, Joseph, 166, 170n194
Blayney, Andrew Blayney, 11th Baron, 55, 80, 99
Board of Works, 74, 79
Boucicault, Dion, 26, 27
Bourne, Thomas, 39
Boyd (asylum attendant), 192
Boyland, Elizabeth, 139
Boyland, Patrick, 72–3, 76
Bradford, Moses, 61, 62
Brady, John (land agent), 163
Brady, Thomas, MD, 35–6

240

Brandrum House, 165
Breakey, H., 170n194
Breen, Patrick, 147
Brickie, Mr, 111
Brown, Hannah, 131–2
Brown, Joseph (asylum attendant), 194
Browne, Peter, dean of Ferns, 21–3, 29
Brunswick Constitutional Clubs, 54–5, 60, 64, 66, 210
Burk, Mick and Sarah, 129
Burney, Ian A., 109
Burnside, Samuel, 166
Butler, Richard J., 75
Butt, Isaac, 69, 153, 175, 176
by-election (1871), 176
Byrne, Mary, 109
Byrne, Paddy, 85

Caddagh, 150
Cahans, 58–9, 161, 201
Cahans Exodus, 51
Callaghan, Patrick, 38
Callen, T.M. (coroner), 198
Calvert, William, 99
Cambell, John, 82
Cambell, Patt, 73
Cambell's Hotel, 170, 171
Caraher, John and Elisabeth, 82
Carey, Michael, 141
Carleton, Mr (sub-investigator), 181
Carleton, William, 26–7
Carlisle's Hotel, 177
Carolan, Revd P., 79
Carr, Bernard, 116
Carrickmacross, 102–3
Carrickmacross bridewell, 109, 113
Carrickmacross Poor Law guardians, 97
Carrickmacross Poor Law Union, 196
Carrickmacross union, evictions, 136
Carrickmacross workhouse, 88–9, 97, 118, **119**
  inmates, 134, **135**, 137, **155**
Carricknabrock, 129
Carrigan, James, 86
Casebook (CB1) (1846–55), 12, 36, 72–3, 84–92, 98–100
  accidental death, 138–9
  Clones workhouse, inquests, 138–9
  deaths from exposure/starvation, 86–8, 128–9
  domestic abuse, 127
  infant deaths at workhouses, 156–9

inquest no. 1, 72–3, **73**
inquests (1848–50), 138–40
inquests (March to June 1847), 104–5
inquests (May 1846 to July 1847), **72**
inquests in Monaghan gaol, 114–16, 154
inquests, paupers, 122–6, 128–9
May 1846 to December 1852, **105**
murder, 95–6, 129–32
special verdict, 88
women, relief sought by, 93
Casebook (CB2) (1856–76), 12
  infanticide, 183–4
  inquests, Clones workhouse, 195
  inquests, Monaghan asylum, 191–2, 193–4
  murder cases, 182–6
  railway deaths, 188–9, 198–9
  sectarian murder, 166–7, 179–80, 181–2
  sudden death, 176, 183
  suicides, 189
Casebook (CB3) (1876–7), 13
  death from exposure, 196
  death from old age/infirmity, 196–7
  infant deaths, 184–5
  inquiries, Monaghan asylum, 194
  sectarian murder, 179–80
Casey, John, 123, 124
Castleblayney, 71, 79, 87, 154, 164
Castleblayney Poor Law Union, 118, 122, 136
Castleblayney workhouse, 118, **119**, 134, **135**, **155**
Castleshane Yeomanry, 55
Catholic Association, 54, 60
Catholic Church, 147
Catholic clergy, 77, 79, 89, 98, 164, 169, 170
Catholic emancipation, 31, 32, 53, 66
  opposition to, 52, 54, 60
  support for, 54, 146
Catholic hierarchy, 34
Catholics
  coroner, office of, 32, 43, 45, 202
  discrimination against, 147, 171
  education and, 34, 35, 174–5
  evictions, 57
  home rule and, 175–6
  House of Commons and, 32
  juries and, 171
  limited roles for, 203–4
  local government, lack of power in, 150
  medical training, 34
  offices held by (1823), **33**
  population in Monaghan, 175

tenant rights and, 149, 178
tithes and, 174
underground military organization, 162
voting and, 164, 178
Cavan Gaol, 112
Cavenagh, Ann, 41, 127
Cavenagh, Philip, 127
census (1851), 150
Chessar, Henry, 105
Chessar, Thomas and Margaret, 105, 137
Chief Secretary's Office, 16
Christian, James Stanley, 11
Church of Ireland, 164, 168–9, 174
Cinnemond, James, 166
Clarendon, George Villiers, 4th earl of, 102
Clarke, James, 170–1, 170n194
Clarke, John, 167, 171
Clarke, Richard, 166
Clarke, Samuel, 170
Clarke, Thomas, 51
Clarken, Bernard, 188
Clements, Nathaniel, 2nd earl of Leitrim, 26
Clements, Thomas, 123, 124
Clones board of guardians, 122, 123–5
Clones Library, 12
    Inquisitions by Coroner Hugh Swanzy, 1876–1877, County Monaghan, 13
Clones Poor Law Union, 136, 195
Clones workhouse, 118, **119**, 138, 158
    deaths of juveniles, 139
    departure of inmates, 126, 128
    infant deaths, 158
    inmates, 134, **135**, **155**
    inquests, 195
    inspection report, 159, 160
    mismanagement, 158–9, 160
    resignations, 134
Clonfad, County Fermanagh, 98
Clontibret, 11
Clover Hill House, Lisnaveane, 47, 50, 59, 151
Cochrane, Mr, 126
Cochrane, Mr (solicitor), 166
Coleshill, 105, 105n9, 137
Collen, Ann and Catherine, 93–4, 95–6, 130
Colstan, Ann (matron), 195
Commons, Mary, 83
Conlon, Mary, 185
Connellan, Daniel, 32
Connolly, Alice, 128
Connolly, Catherine, 139, 140
Connolly, James, 170n194

Connolly, Pat, 122
Conolly, Terance, 124
Conservatives, 76, 162, 164, 165, 168, 169, 170, 176
Coogan, Peter, 90
Cooke, Catherine, 40
Coomey, Patrick, 153, 154
Coony, Pat, 122–3
Coote, Thomas (high sheriff), 148, 165, 171, 172, 176, 179
Cootehill Board of Guardians, 135n152
Cootehill Poor Law Union, 118, **119**, 124, 136, 139–40
Cootehill workhouse, **135**, 139, **155**
Cordevlis, 150, 151
Cork city, 97–8
Cork, County, 28, 32–3
Cork Examiner, 98, 166
Cormeen, 118, 139
Corn Laws, 74, 75, 76
Cornacassa, 184, 185
Cornanure, 90
coroners
    abolition of office, 140–2
    authority, undermining of, 132, 134
    autonomy, 17, 26, 101
    Catholic clergy and, 89, 98
    Catholics and, 32, 43, 45, 202
    challenges faced by, 16, 209
    complaints about, 16, 21–2, 23, 29–31
    constabulary and, 38
    cost per annum, 201
    deaths of prisoners, 109
    debt collection, 21–2, 29
    denominational flexibility, 204
    deodands, 29, 43–4, 45, 186, 187
    districts, 43, 100
    election of, 70
    fees, 28–9, 34, 43, 46, 99–100
    grand juries and, 28–9, 30, 34, 42, 43, 46, 99–100, 101
    Great Famine and, 204–5
    history of, 23–4
    homicide cases and, 97
    juries and, 167–8, 186, 198
    jury selection, 37
    legislative change, 203, 204
    literary portrayals of, 26
    local elites and, 16, 17, 154, 186
    medically trained (1843), 36
    office of, 16–17, 23, 32, 45, 100

perception of, 16, 22, 24
politics of, 126–7
press coverage of, 70
primary duties, 24
property qualifications, 32, 33, 42–3, 45, 141, 199, 200
Protestants and, 31
qualifications/background, 141, 200, 202, 210
religious composition of, 31–3
reports submitted to the lord lieutenant, 97
reputation, 26–8
responsibilities, 23–4
role of, 14, 16, 23–4, 204
schedule of payments, 44
starvation deaths and, 97–8
work, value of, 97–101
see also inquests
Coroners' Act (1822), 32
Coroners' Act (1846), 42–5, 100, 187
Coroners' Act (1881), 202
coroners' bill (1870), 198, 199
Coroners' Society, 200
Coroners' Society of England and Wales, 35, 203
Corrigan, Sir Dominic John (physician), 21, 36
Corry, Thomas Stewart, 55
Cosgrove, Edward (asylum attendant), 194
Cottingham, Edward, Inspector General, 109
County Monaghan Grand Orange Lodge, 75, 148, 149, 162, 172
Coyle, Charles, 90
Coyle, Owen, 192
Crawford, William Sharman, 149
Creagh, Michael (high sheriff), 32–3
Cremorne, barony of, 51, 84, 100
Cremorne, Richard Thomas Dawson, 2nd Baron, 53, 54, 59, 77, 80, 169, 176
criminal trials, 41, 132, 133, 171
  convictions, 17, 38, 41, 42, 208
  juries, 42
  Protestants and, 60, 147
  Waddell as juror on, 59
Crossreagh, 179
Cunningham, John, 181
Cunningham, Mr, 63–4
Curran, Daragh, 70
Currin, 126

Daily, Laurence, 90
Dartree, barony of, 84, 100

Dawley, Michael, 116–17
Dawson, Hon. Vesey, MP, 80, 164
Dawson's Grove, 118, 139
de Burgh, Henry, 149
debt collection, 21–2, 29
debtors, 112, 116
  master debtors, 113, **114**
  pauper debtors, 113, **114**, 137, 138
  types of, 113
Deeghan, Peter, 166
deodands, 29, 43–4, 45, 186, 187
Derby, Edward George Geoffrey Smith-Stanley, 14th earl of, 146, 162
Derrydorraghy, 125
Devine, Jane, 189
Dickson, Andrew, 126
Dillon, James (coroner), 13, 44
diseases
  cholera, 111, 115, 128, 189
  dysentery, 85, 86, 91, 115
  Famine-related, 71, 72, 112, 117, 122, 134, 142
  fever/yellow fever, 91, 97, 104, 111, 115, 116
district lunatic asylums, 189–94
  construction phases, 190
  legislation, 190
  panopticon principle, 190
  suicides, 189
  see also Monaghan district lunatic asylum
doctors
  education, 34
  inquests and, 34, 36, 46
  social standing, 25
  see also post-mortem examinations
Dolly's Brae, County Down, 146
domestic abuse, 40–1, 127, 182–4
Donnelly, James, bishop of Clogher, 166, 168, 169, 176, 178
Donnelly, James S., Jnr, 120
Downpatrick Recorder, 180
Dromore, 89–90
Drum auxiliary workhouse, 118, 124, 139–40
Drumcrew, 85
Drumgavny, 99, 150, 151
Drumhillagh, 122
Drumanan, 82
Drumsnat, 122
Dublin city, 83
Dublin Daily Express, 167, 212
Dublin Evening Mail, 140, 141, 180–1

Dublin Evening Packet, 33
Dublin Evening Packet and Correspondent, 80
Dublin Evening Post, 149
Dublin grand jury, 141–2
Duffy, Sir Charles Gavan, 53, 54, 149, 161
Duffy, Revd James, 79
Duffy, John, 54
Dundalk Democrat, 153, 163, 166
Dundalk Poor Law Union, 118, 136
Dungannon Convention, 52
Dungeon, Mr (solicitor), 183

Elliott, Mr (workhouse master), 160
emigration, 77, 78, 92, 194
    Cahans Exodus, 51
    post-Famine, 146
    to Australia, 116, 154
    Waddell family and, 47–8
employment, 92, 195
    civil service, 197–8
    eligibility for, 79
    patronage/elite support, 197, 207
    professionals, 197
    wages, 80, 84
    women and, 92, 93
    see also public works
Emyvale, 75–6, 79, 170
Encumbered Estates Act (1849), 151
Enniskillen gaol, 112–13
Enniskillen, William Willoughby Cole, 3rd earl of, 187
Errigle Trough, 87
Evans, George, 34
Evening Chronicle, 98
Evicted Poor Protection Act (1848), 136, 137
evictions, 88, 90, 136–7, 146, 206
    Shirley estate, 55n35, 97, 137
    Waddell and, 57

Famine Casebook (CB1), *see* Casebook (CB1)
Farney, barony of, 72, 80, 100, 154, 177
Farrell, Elaine, 39
Fatal Accidents Act (1846), 45
Feehan, Bridge and William, 44
Fenianism/Fenians, 162, 165, 180
Ferguson, Darby, 138–9
Fermanagh Reporter, 98
Fiddes, James, 189
Findlater, William (solicitor), 178
Finley, Dr, 127
Fitzgerald, Justice, 182

Fitzpatrick, Felix, 184
Fitzpatrick, Rose, 184
Fleming, Thomas (surgeon), 73
food depots, 74, 76, 106, 128, 206
food shortages, 84, 85, 91–2
    see also grain prices; potato crop
Forster, Sir George, MP, 142n195, 148, 149, 162, 164
Forster, Sir Thomas, 55
Forsythe, Jane, 11
Fort Singleton, 181
Foster, Haire (solicitor), 183
Foster, Mrs, 137
Frederick, Prince, duke of York and Albany, 21, 22, 23
Freeman's Journal, 35–6, 61, 149, 150
    coroner, cost per annum, 201
    Coroners' Association, 203
    coroners' bill, defeat of, 199
    public works' food allowance, 83
    railway accidents, 187
French, Charles, 149

Galway workhouse, 83
gaols, 106
    conditions in, 112–13, 115
    county gaols, history of, 107–12
    deaths, 114, **115**
    deaths, coroners and, 109
    management of, 103, 107, 109
    panopticon model, 107, **108**
    prison reform, 107–9
Gartlan, Peter McEvoy, 154
Gault, Hugh, 82
Geary, Lawrence M., 35
general election (1852), 149, 162
general election (1857), 162
general election (1859), 162
general election (1865), 164, 169
general election (1868), 164–5, 168–70
general election (1874), 177
general election (1880), 178
Geraghty, Bernard, 166
Gibson, Robert (asylum attendant), 192
Gillespie, Robert, 158, 159
Givan, John (solicitor), 178
Gladstone, William Ewart, 145, 164, 169, 174, 175–6
Glaslough, 154, 176, 181
Glass, Joseph, 150
Glenn, John, 164

Golding, Edward (magistrate), 63, 99, 142n195, 147–8
Good, Daniel, 132
Gordon, Alexander (asylum attendant), 192, 193
Gordon, Jane and William, 40
Gormally, Patrick, 166
Gormley, John, 188–9
Gormley, Patt, 170n194
Gower, Francis Leveson, Chief Secretary, 32–3
Graham, Robert, 170n194
Graham, William and Amelia, 160
grain prices, **80**, 81, **82**, **84**
grand juries, 16
    coroners and, 28–9, 30, 34, 42, 43, 46, 99–100, 101, 126–7
    coroner's office, abolition of, 140–2
    Famine relief works, 74
    perception of, 25
    prison administration and, 107
    Protestant control of, 175
    public works and, 79–80
    sectarian ideology, 75
    selection of, 25
    see also Monaghan grand jury
Grant, Bryan, 153, 154
Grant, Charles (chief secretary), 28–9
Grant, John (constabulary sub-inspector), 81
Gray, Edward Warren, 164
Gray, James, 61, 81, 101, 118
Gray, John, 149, 150, 162
Gray, Sam, 59, 164, 169
    trials, 60–2, 63–4, 66, 210
Gray, William, 169, 170
Greaghlatacapple, 88, 89
Great Famine (1846–52), 13, 69, 206
    coroners and, 204–5
    evictions, 88
    Famine-related deaths, 71–2, **72**
    inquests, rise in, 43, 71
    maize depots, 74
    Poor Law guardians and, 58
    relief works, 74
Greenacre, James, 131–2
Greenan, Bernard, 88
Greer, Samuel MacCurdy, 161
Gregory Clause (1847), 125, 142, 206
Gregory, William, 21, 29, 30
Greves, Captain, 58
Grey, Charles Grey, 2nd Earl, 37–8
Griffin, Gerald, 26, 27–8

Grimes, Elizabeth, 99

Hamilton, Anne, 105
Hamilton, James, 148, 184
Hanna, Jane, 105n9
Hanna, William, 137
Hanratty, Patrick, 38
Harrison, Mr (coroner), 30
Haverty, Head Constable, 185
Hennessey, William, 170n194
Henry, Dr, 159, 183–4, 195
Heron, Denis Caulfield (lawyer), 145
Hewlett, Richard, 125
Hicks, Athelstan Braxton, 203, 203n1
Higgins, Thomas, 125
high sheriff, role of, 25
Hill, Pat, 95
Hilton Park, 41, 162, 177
Hodgins, Thomas, 147
Hollywood, 189
Holmes, Arthur Wellington, 75, 123, 132, 148, 160
Holmes, John, 160, 167–8
home rule, 175–6, 177
Hope, Charles, 56
Hope, John, 134–5
Hope, John Jnr, 56
Hope, Maria Orr (*later* Waddell), 56
    see also Waddell, Maria Orr
Hope, Susanna (*later* Waddell), 53
Hopes, Charles (WCW's uncle), 55–6, 57, 59, 137, 151–2, 154, 210–11
Hoppen, K. Theodore, 70, 148
Hoskins, Dr, 158–9
Hosty, Andrew (coroner), 26
House of Commons, 32, 138, 140, 178
Hughes, Charles Clarke (coroner), 29n40
Hughes, Revd James, 157
Hughes, John, 69
Hughes, Michael, 91
Hughes, Terry, 90
Hughes, Thomas
    inquest, 165–8, 170
    killing of, 165, 170, 212
Hume, Joseph, MP, 32
Hunt, Charles (magistrate), 153, 154
Hurst, Revd J. and Mrs, 86–7

infanticide, 35, 39–40, 71, **72**, 183–4, 202
Inniskeen, 118
inquests, 45, 71

accidental death, 71, 72, 99, 145, 188–9
chronic disease/illness, 71, 72
death from exposure, 196
doctors' attendance at, 34
Famine, rise during, 43
Famine-related, 71–2, 72, 81–2, 84–8, 104, 105
infant deaths in workhouses, 156–9
infanticide, 35, 39–40, 71, 72, 130, 183–5, 202
jurors, 37–9
jury composition for prison deaths, 109
jury, moral/civic responsibility of, 159–60
literary portrayals of, 26–8
May 1846 to July 1847, 72
Monaghan asylum, deaths at, 191–2, 193–4
Monaghan, murder (1870–7), 182–6
murder, 71, 72, 94, 95–6, 127, 130–1, 163, 164, 165–6
old age/infirmity, 196–7
poisoning, 36, 40, 62
press coverage of, 100–1, 167, 180–1, 204
public view of, 26
railway deaths, 188–9
special verdicts, 88
sudden death, 71, 72, 183
suicides, 71, 72, 130, 140–1, 189, 193
suspects, naming of, 185
'the voice of the people', 82–3
verdicts, 46
insurance, compensation for human life, 44–5
Irish Coroners' Association, 203
Irish Republican Brotherhood, 176
Irish society
   modernization of, 15–16, 174, 190, 202
   polarization into factions, 162, 202
   post-Famine, 146–50
   pre-Famine, 24, 25, 38, 41, 86, 117
   violence, tolerance for, 41
Irwin, John, 170n194

Jackson family, 51, 52
Jebb, John, 166
Johnson, Clement, Inspector General, 112–13
Johnson, Mr, 86
Johnston, H.S., 149
Johnston, Mary Anne, 62
Johnston, William, 169–70
Johnstone, J.W., 181
Joly, John Plunket (land agent), 209
Jones, Drury (coroner), 29n40

Jones, George, 95
Jones, Jane, 132
Jones, Richard, 32
Joyce, Lancaster (doctor), 184
judiciary, 203, 204
juries
   coroners and, 198
   coroners' juries, perception of, 167–8
   special juries, 42, 64
Juries Act (Ireland) (1871), 172
jurors
   Catholics, number of, 171
   criminal trials, 42, 59, 61–2
   inquests and, 37–9, 42, 166
   intimidation of, 46
   naming of, 166
   Protestants, number of, 171
   qualified, 43, 59
jury system, reform of, 172
jury-packing, 147, 148, 153–4, 172, 176

Kairns, Catherine, 78
Kane, John (asylum attendant), 192
Kearan, Bernard, 166
Kearns, B., 170n194
Keenan (asylum attendant), 192
Keenan family, 97
Keenan, Pat, 128
Kelly, Bernard, 104, 137
Kelly, Francis, 153, 196
Kelly, Owen, 153
Kelly, Thomas, 166
Kelly, William, 73
Kennedy, Tristram (land agent), 113, 142n195
Killeevan, 87, 88, 188
Killylough, 125
Kilmainham gaol, 112, 117
Kilmore, 105, 201
Kilnahaltar, 137
King's County, 16, 40, 44, 83, 84, 209
King's County Chronicle, 141
Kirkpatrick, John and Catherine, 158, 160
Kirwin, Dr (coroner), 83
Kirwin, Henry (constabulary sub-inspector), 163

Labour Rate Act (1846), 79, 81, 206
Lamb, James, 192
Lambert, Alexander Clendining, 77
Lambert, Mary, 122–3
Lancet, 34

land
　post-Famine inheritance, 146
　post-Famine purchases, 151–2
　valuations, 91, 136
Land Act (1870), 174
land agents, 57–8, 134, 209
　Waddell's role as, 55, 56, 57, 58, 66, 211
land grabbers, 96
land reform, 169
landlords/landowners, 92, 134, 146
　bankruptcy, 151
　decline of, 169
　evictions, 91, 136
　influence of, 169
　Poor Law levies and, 104, 106
　poor rates and, 58
　public works and, 80–1
　tenants, voting and, 149–50
Landy, James (chief of police), 29, 30
Larkin, Simon, 73
Lawless, Hon. E., 141
Lawless, Honest Jack, 60
Lee, Joseph, 15–16, 174, 187, 190, 202
Leek, 126
legal profession, 25
Leinster Express, 141
Leitrim (townland), 165, 166
Leonard, Maria and Sally, 156, 157
Lepper, Surgeon, 156
Leslie, Charles Powell, MP, 54, 55, 58, 59, 162, 164
　death, 176
　Orange Order and, 148, 149
　tenants and, 150
Leslie, John, 176
Liberalism, 174–6, 177–8
Liberals, 55, 162, 164, 165, 169, 176
Limerick and Clare Examiner, 82–3
Lindsay, John, 165
linen trade, 51, 52, 53, 66, 92, 150
Liscumasky, 183
Lisnaveane, **49**, 50, 51, 150, 151, 178, 201
Lisnaveane House, 50, 56, 211
Lisnaveane Independent Rangers, 51, 52n13
Little, Robert (rate collector), 138–9
Little, Thomas, 170n194
Livingstone, Peadar, 149
Lloyd, Colonel, 201
Lloyd, Minchin (coroner), 160
local elite
　coroners and, 16, 17, 154, 186

　erosion of power, 206–7
　institutions, management of, 207
　patronage, 197, 207
　poor people and, 206
　Waddell's access to, 209
local government, 14, 16, 25–6
　changes to civil roles, 197
　criticism of, 16
　elections, 70
　perception of, 24
　Presbyterians, status of, 211
　property qualifications, 32
　Protestant monopoly of, 31
　reforms, 23–4
Local Government (Ireland) Act (1898), 203
Londonderry, 98, 160
Londonderry prison, 107
Londonderry Standard, Waddell's letter to, 16, 100, 160–1
Long, Frederic B., 156
Lough, William, 170n194
Loughran, John, 166
Louth Advertiser, 94
Louth Examiner, 95
Lowry, Charles, 166
Lucas, Edward, 149
Lucas, Fitzherbert Dacre, 142n195, 148
Lucas, Thomas (magistrate), 148
lunacy *see* mental illness
Lunacy Inquiry Commission report (1876), 195–6
Lunacy (Ireland) Acts, 190
Lunatic asylums Ireland report (1870), 192
Lunatic asylums Ireland report (1871), 192
Lunatic asylums Ireland report (1872), 193
Lunatic asylums Ireland report (1877), 189
Lundy, James (middleman), 95, 96, 97

McArdle, Mr (estate bailiff), 147
McAuley, Revd Matthew, 59, 161
McCabe, Bridget, 183
McCabe, Mary, 196–7
McCabe, Patrick, 88–9
McCarron, Mary and Catherine, 185
McCarthy, James (coroner), 29n40
McCarthy, John (coroner), 187
McCartney, Mr, 181
McClean, Dr, 127
McCleary, Francis, 166
McConkey, Mary Anne (*née* Slater), 62–3
McConkey, Richard, 62
McCormick, Thomas, 194

McCourt, Catherine, 130, 131, 132, 134
McCourt, Patrick, 133
McCready, Bernard, 170n194
McCready, John, 166
McCreesh, Denise, 38
McCrory, Alistair, 12
Mac Cuarta, Séamus Dall (poet), 77–8
McCullen, James, 95–6
McCullogh (infant), 184
McCullogh, Jane, 184
McCune, William (church warden), 29n40
McCurdy, John (architect), 190
McCusker, Revd Paul, 77, 78, 79
McDermot, Catherine, 87
McDermot, Mary Ann, 87–8
MacDonagh, Oliver, 107
McDonald, Brian, 80, **84**
McDonald, Terence, 191–2
McDowell, Dr, 115–16
McDowell, R.B., 107
McEnally, Revd Thomas, 88–9
McEntagart, Michael, 38
McGarrell, Owen, 115
McGimpsey, Christopher D., 164, 176
McGovern, Revd Edward, 88–9
McGowan, John, 163–4
McGregor, Colonel Duncan, 81
McGurk, Patrick, 166
McKelvey, Sergeant, 133
McKenna, Brian, 131
McKenna, Hugh, 126
McKenna, John, 170, 171, 172, 176
McKenna, John, Anthony, Sylvester, Edward and David, 38
McKenna, Patrick, 133
McKenna, Peter and Ellen, 132, 133–4
McKierney, James, 86
McMahon, Mary, 82
McMahon, Mary (widow), 182
McMahon, Mr (estate bailiff), 147
McMahon, Richard, 127, 129–30, 186
McMahon, William, 181
McMurrer, Francis, 188
MacNally, Charles, bishop of Clogher, 88
McPhillips, Cecelia and Pat, 11
McQuaid, Mr, 57
McQuaide, Revd Michael, 79
Madden, John, 41, 176
Madden, John, 162–3
Madden, Captain William Wolseley, 162–3, 165, 168, 177

Madill, Alice and Thomas, 129
Magee, Charles and Mary, 41
Maghera, 161
Magheross, 88
Maginis, Susan, 184
Maginn, Revd, 98
Maguire, John, 183
Maguire, Mary, 195
Maguire, Mary (infant), 183–4
Maguire, Peter, 184
Maguire, Sarah, 183
Magwood, George, 186
Magwood, William, 185–6
Manchester Courier, 26
Marron, Hu, 105n9
Martin, Brian, 115, 116
Martin, Dr, 196
Massareene, John Clotworthy, Viscount, 50, 151
Mayne, Richard, 148
Mayne, Thomas (gaol governor), 115, 117, 156–7
Mayo Examiner, 199–200
Mayo, Richard Bourke, 6th earl of, 168
medical jurisprudence, 35–6
Meegan, Larry, 38
Meighan, Laurance, 193
mental illness, 189–94
  causes of (1872), **191**
middle-class professionals, 197, 199, 200, 202
Midgley, Mr (coroner), 83
migration, seasonal, 77–8
Mitchell, Henry, 148
Mitchell, John, 40
Mitchell, Martha, 40
Mitchell, Mr (solicitor), 166
Mitchell, Thomas, 170n194
Mitchell, William (sub-sheriff), 171, 172, 176
Molloy, Edward, 198
Monaghan assizes, 133, 171, 182
Monaghan baronial sessions, 79–80
Monaghan board of guardians, 120, 122, 123–4, 208
Monaghan Brunswick Constitutional Club, 54
Monaghan, County, **15**
  local relief committees, 74
  maize depots, 74
  population, 53, 69–70, 150, 175
  valuation of farms, 136
Monaghan district lunatic asylum, 190–1
  admissions, 190–1
  attendants, misconduct by, 192, 193

Index 249

board of guardians, 192–3
  chief medical superintendent, 190, 192, 193, 194
  classification of inmates, 191
  deaths, 191, 209
  inmates (1869), 190–1
  inquests, 191–2, 193–4, 209
  inquiries, 194
  mental disease, causes of, **191**
  mortality rate (1871), 192
  repairs to building, 192–3
  staff, 190, 192, 193, 194
Monaghan fever hospital, 104
Monaghan gaol, 107
  Board of Superintendence, 111
  conditions in, 104, 111, 113–14, 117
  death of infant, 156–7
  deaths in, 114–15, **115**, 154, 209
  debtors in, 116
  fever in, 116
  governor, 111–12
  hangings, 153
  inmates, **114**, 137–8, **155**
  inquests, 114–15
  inspection report, 156
  new gaol, construction of, 109–12, **110**
  pauper debtors in, 137–8
  population, rise in, 206
  prisoners awaiting transportation, 116–17
Monaghan grand jury, 74, 109–10, 127, 141–2, 148, 204, 208
  Bateson murder, 152, 153
  Monaghan gaol, building of, 109–10
Monaghan Independent Club, 54, 152
Monaghan Literary and Scientific Society, 35
Monaghan Local Relief committee, 123
Monaghan Poor Law guardians, 195, 208
Monaghan Poor Law Union, 58, 104, 122
  deaths of paupers, 122–3
  evictions, 136, 137
  outdoor relief, refusal to offer, 128, 195, 196, 209, 211
  restrictive criteria, relief and, 125
  Waddell and, 211
Monaghan quarter sessions, 195
Monaghan Savings Bank, 54
Monaghan town, 53, **110**, **121**
Monaghan workhouse, 104, 118, **119**
  children in, 157–8
  conditions in, 104, 134
  death rates, 122

departure of inmate, 126
diseases in, 122
inmates, 134, **135**, **155**
Montgomery, William and Elizabeth, 134
Mooney, Michael, 185
Moore, Isaiah, 92
Moorhead, Dr, 123
Moorhead, Martha, 177
Morant, George (magistrate), 89, 97, 137, 150
Morell, James, 52
Morphy, E.P., 148
Morris, William O'Connor, Justice, 171
Moutray, Whitney Upton, 181, 181–2
Muldoon, Michael, 162–4
Mulgerin, John and Ellen, 83
Mullaghcroghery, 93–4
Mullen, Revd John, 75–6, 79
Mulligan, Francis, 91
Mulligan, George, 166
Mulligan, John and Francis, 185
Mullock, William (coroner), 16
Murch, Kate, 194
murder
  coroners' inquests and, 36, 38–9, 72
  domestic murder, 40–1, 182–6, 202, 207
  'fraternal sphere', 40, 207
  gender politics and, 63
  'maternal sphere', 40, 207
  medieval penalty (éraic), 23
  Monaghan (1870–7), 182–6
  trials, 61–3
  of women, 78, 93–7, 103–4, 129–34
  women, naming in verdict, 40
  see also sectarian murder
Murdoch, J., 74, 75
Murphy, Alley, 85
Murphy, Bernard, 170n194
Murphy, Edward, 170n194
Murphy, John, 149
Murphy, Owen, 61, 62, 63
Murphy, Pat, 85
Murphy, Ruth, 82
Murphy, Terence, 85
Murphy, Thomas, Patrick, Hugh and Mary, 38–9
Murray, André Allan, 148
Murray, Margaret, 181
Murray, Peter, 181
Murray, Robert (coroner), 71, 100
Murray, William, 148
Murry, Bernard, 129

Naas gaol, 30
Nally, David P., 101
National Commercial Directory, 70
National Hibernian Bank, 56
National Insurance Company, 55–6
National Society for Women's Suffrage, 178
Naughton, Thomas, 170n194
Nenagh Guardian, 94
Newbliss, 126
Newry Telegraph, 47
Northern Bank, 196
Northern Standard, 55, 64, 154
    Baird, acquittal of, 171
    editorial columns, 75, 123–4
    'Famine Panic, The', 74
    gaol governor, praise for, 156
    inquest, 85–6
    inquest jury members, names of, 170
    inquest verdict on Baird, 167–8
    Leslie's death, 176
    Monaghan board of guardians, 122
    Monaghan fever hospital, 104
    Monaghan gaol, 117
    Monaghan grand jury, 74, 141–2, 153
    murder of Catholic, 162–3
    murder of women, 93, 95, 131, 132
    political stratagems of, 206
    potato crop, failure of, 78
    starvation deaths, 87, 98
    Twelfth of July celebrations, 148
    Waddell, attack on, 179
    Waddell's election as coroner, 70
    Waddell's inquests, 83–5, 87, 98–9, 124, 180
    workhouse, rumours about, 159

O'Connell, Daniel, 54, 66
O'Connor, John, *Workhouses of Ireland, The*, 135
Offaly Historical Society, 13
Ó Gráda, Cormac, 120, 122, 208
O'Hagan, Thomas (Lord Chancellor), 172
O'Hare, Mary, 184–5
Ollerenshaw, Philip, 196
Omagh, County Tyrone, 89
O'Neill, Revd, 166
Orange Lodge (No. 1952), 181
Orange Order, 59–60, 147, 148, 168, 171, 177
    government control, lack of, 61, 62
    Monaghan elite and, 153
    processions, 60, 61, 147

Twelfth of July marches, 60, 148, 165, 182
    see also County Monaghan Grand Orange Lodge
Orangeism, 75, 154, 162
Orangemen, 146, 162, 163, 164, 169, 175–6, 180
O'Reilly, Dr, 179, 184

Palmerston, Henry John Temple, 3rd Viscount, 146, 147, 162
Parkinson, Mr (crown solicitor), 166
Parks, Paul (coroner), 29n40
Parr, Mr (coroner), 30
Party Processions Act (1850), 60, 146–7, 169–70, 181
Patterson, John (asylum steward), 192
pauper debtors, 113, **114**, 137, 138
paupers
    attitudes towards, 104, 123, 124, 133, 140
    deaths of, 17, 43, 72, 99, 122, 124, 142
    imprisonment, 112, 209
    inquests, 122, 140, 142, 158, 209–10
    relief policies, effects of, 103, 120, 122, 124, 140, 211
    workhouses open to, 118
    see also beggars/vagrants; poor people
Payne, Mr (barrister), 201
Peel, Sir Robert, 74, 75, 76
Peel, Thomas George (coroner), 200–1
Pennefather, Richard (undersecretary), 75, 76
Perrin, Louis, Judge, 152–3
Phillips' handy atlas, **15**
Pickens, Margaret, 124
Pigot, David Richard (Chief Baron), 100
Pittar, Elizabeth, 152
police magistrates, **33**, 201
police service, 23, 30, **33**, 186
Pollock, Head Constable, 176
Poor Law, 194
    appeal for reform, 140
    implementation of, 123
    indoor relief, 58, 104, 128
    levies, landlords and, 104
    outdoor relief, 58, 122, 123, 128, 137
    qualifications for relief, 106
    restrictive criteria, 125
    valuations of property, 58
Poor Law Act (1838), 43, 58, 117, 157, 208
Poor Law Commission, 106
Poor Law Extension Act (1847), 106, 120, 124
Poor Law guardians, 43, 97, 120

cost-saving decisions, 120, 122, 142
non-elected ex-officios, 58
Poor Law inspectors, 159, 159n97, 175
Poor Law rates, 43, 106, 118, 128, 134–6
poor people
    attitudes towards, 84, 90, 91
    local elite ideology towards, 206
    moral obligation towards, 86
    relief policies, inadequacy of, 101, 208–9
    relief rations, inadequacy of, 91–2
    survival, fight for, 90–1
    see also beggars/vagrants
Poor Relief Act (Ireland) (1838), 74
post-mortem examinations, 34, 35, 86, 180, 183, 185
    Waddell's reasons for ordering, 127, 160, 205
potato crop
    failure (1845–52), 74, 75, 76, 78–9, 103, 128–9
    failure (1877), 196
poverty, 208–9
Power, Sir William Tyrone, 177–8
pregnancy, concealment of, 39
Presbyterian clergymen, 169
Presbyterians, 50, 51, 52, 54, 55
    general election (1880), 178
    intimidation of, 164
    perception of, 53
    population in Monaghan, 60, 175
    Protestants and, 58, 211
    status in local government, 211
    synod of Ulster, 56, 210
    Tenant League and, 149
    Waddell and, 161, 173, 210–11
Pringle, Alexander, 126
Prison Acts (1810, 1826), 107, 111
prison reform, 107–9
Protestants, 163, 174
    Brunswick clubs and, 54–5
    coroner, office of, 31
    grand juries, control of, 175
    juries and, 171
    jury selection, control of, 60, 147
    landowning elite, 41, 52, 140, 148
    local government, monopoly of, 31
    medical jurisprudence, 36
    medical/scientific fields, 35
    population in Monaghan, 175
    Presbyterians and, 58, 211
    self-defence, right to, 167
    Waddell's summons and, 167–8
Prunty, Mary, 196
public works, 74, 79, 80, 81
    food allowance, 83
    funding, 74, 79–80, 84
    half-pay, 81
    labourer's wage, 81
    landowners and, 80–1
    number of persons employed, 92
    women and, 93
Public Works Act (1846), 79

Queen's Colleges, 34
Quigley, James, 179
Quigley, William, 126
Quin, Neal, 153, 154
Quinn, John, 78
Quinn, Margaret, 40, 78

Rafferty, John, 166
railways
    compensation for deaths, 186–7
    fatalities, 186–9, 198–9
    investors, 187–8
    public safety, 188–9
    Trillick derailment, 187
    Ulster Railway Company, 188
Rankin, Revd John, 150
Rate in Aid Act (1849), 134
Rea, John (solicitor), 168, 180
Redington, Thomas, 77
Reed, Ally, 93
Reed, Robert Hamilton (physician/surgeon), 201
Reed, Thomas (doctor), 82, 85, 183
Reilly, Ciarán, 92–3, 209
Reilly, Mr (solicitor), 166
Relief Commission, 74, 76, 77, 79
    dissolution of, 106, 206
relief committees, 74, 77, 79, 88, 97, 123
relief policy, failure of, 82, 88, 101
relief works see public works
Renning, John (asylum attendant), 192
Rennocks, Elizabeth, 158, 159
resident magistrates, 25, 28, 112, 132–3, 180–2, 201
Reynolds, John, MP, 138
Ribbonism/Ribbonmen, 117, 146, 147, 148, 152, 154, 162
Rice, James Blayney, 165
Richard I, King, 23

Richardson, Captain, 149
Richmond gaol, 117
Robb, James, 94
Robertson, John C., 190, 192, 193, 194
Robinson, Henry (inspector), 159
Rockcorry, 51, 92
Rogers, Hessy, 38
Rogers, Ina, 56n42
Rogers, Revd, 52n13
Rooney, Bernard, 154
Rooney, Revd J., 79, 125
Roper, Revd, 84
Rorc, Bernard, 128–9
Rose, Mr (landlord), 58
Ross, County Galway, 77
Rossmore, Warner William Westenra, 2nd Baron, 54, 58, 80, 149, 201
Routh, Sir Randolph, 74, 83, 84
Rowland, John (gaol governor), 111–12
Royal Canal Company, 55
Royal Irish Constabulary, 179
Rudden, Bernard, 124–5
Rush, John, 38
Rushe, Denis Carolyn, 64
Russell, Archdeacon, 11
Russell, Lord John, 76, 77, 79, 83, 88, 98, 162
  change in government, 146
  legislative changes, impact of, 103
  Party Processions Act and, 147
  policy changes, impact of, 106, 124, 128, 204, 206

St Coleman's Church of Ireland, 11
St George, Revd Henry Lucas, 89–90
Sanderson, James J. (county inspector), 78–9
Scanlin, Timothy (sub-constable), 122
Scottish Presbyterians, 50, 53, 210
Scottish Seceder Church, 51
secret societies, 41, 57, 152–3, 41
sectarian murder, 17, 41–2, 162–3, 207–8
  compensation claim, 182
  Monaghan (1868), 165–6, 170–2
  Monaghan (1869–70), 179–82
sectarian organizations, 162–4
sectarian tensions, 57, 75, 146–7, 162, 181
Select committee of the House of Lords on crime, 39
Select committee on Outrages in Ireland (1852), 147
sexual assaults, 94–5
Shakespeare, William, *Hamlet*, 140–1

Sheffield Independent, 179
Shegog, William, 138–9
Sherry, Mary, 86
Shevlin, Peter, 164
Shirley, Evelyn John, 54, 55, 80, 89, 177
  estate, 93, 95, 96–7, 136
  evictions, 55n35, 137
  reward offered by, 93
Simpson, Charles, 197
Singleton, Richard (county inspector), 166
Skelton, Benjamin, 166, 170n194
Sligo, 98, 141
Slowey, Charles, 170n194
Slowey, William, 197
Smith, Bridget, 195
Smith, Eliza, 196–7
Smith, George, 62, 63
Smith, Margaret, 94
Smith, Mick, 128
socil changes, post-Famine, 146
Somerville, E.Œ, and Ross, Martin, 26, 28
Sommerville, Francis, 57
Soup Kitchen Act (1847), 88, 92, 106
soup kitchens, 88, 91–2, 106, 124, 206, 208
South London Press, 179
Spencer, John Poyntz, 5th Earl, 200
Spike Island, 117
Steen, John, 164
Steenson, George, 166
Stewart, Robert Wilson (doctor), 176, 181
Strokestown, County Roscommon, 92–3
suicide, 71, 72, 130, 140–1, 189–90, 193
Swan, William, 170n194
Swanzy, Hugh (coroner), 13, 71, 142, 164, 200
Sweeny, Rose, 91–2

Tabeteau, Joseph, 39
Tailor, Mary Catherine, 170
Taylor, John (doctor), 124, 139–40
Tedavnet, 125
Temple, John (gaol governor), 157
Temple, William, 166
Templetown estate, 147, 148, 152, 153
Temporary Relief Act (1847), 88, 106
Tenant League, 148–9, 150, 161
tenants, 91, 146
  fixity of tenure, 169, 174
  Gregory clause and, 125, 142, 206
  relief, qualification for, 106
  rights, 169
  tenants at will, 173

Index

Ulster tenant right, 91, 112, 148, 174, 175, 178
voting, landlords and, 149–50, 175
Thompson, Letitia (matron), 139
Thompson, William, 187
Thompson, William (surgeon), 34
Tipperary, County, 28–9
Tithe War, 31
tithes, 174
Tod, Isabella, 178
Torrens, Robert, Judge, 62
Torres, Judge, 117
Trainor, Catherine (*née* Trainor), 130–1, 132, 134
Trainor, Ellen (*née* McKenna), 133
Trainor, James, 133
Traynor, Patrick, 90
Treanor, Ann, 137
Treanor, John, 170n194
Treanor, Owen, 125
Treanor, Philip, 180
Treanor, Rose, 137
Trench, William Steuart, 149
Treston, Lucas Alexander (magistrate), 166, 180, 181
Trevelyan, Charles, 76, 81, 128
trials
witness tampering, 148
see also jurors
Trillick, County Tyrone, 187
Trimble, Andrew, 184, 185
Trinity College Dublin, 34
Trough, barony of, 74, 75, 77, 100, 132, 134, 182
Tullaghan, 105
Tullycorbet, 100
Turpin, Dick, 116
Twistleton, Edward, Chief Poor Law Commissioner, 128
Tydavnet, County Monaghan, 79
Tyholland, 165, 166

Ulster, seasonal migration, 77–8
Ulster gaols, deaths (1845–52), 115
Ulster Protestant Defence Association, 169
Ulster Railway Company, 188
Ulster tenant right, 91, 112, 148, 174, 175, 178
unemployment, 104, 128
United Irishmen, 52, 65
University Education (Ireland) Bill (1873), 174–5

Vagrant Act (1847), 112
Van Diemen's Land (Tasmania), 112
Vance, John, MP, 168, 198
Vaughan, W.E., 16, 42
Vindicator, 62
voters
40-shilling freeholders, 55
property qualifications, 160–1
tenants pressured by landlords, 149–50
£50 freeholders, 55

Waddell, Alexander, 47, 49–50, 65
Waddell, Captain Alexander Stuart, 47–8, 54, 59
Waddell, Br.J., 168
Waddell, Captain Alexander, 52
Waddell family, 47, 49, 50–2, 151
religion, 50, 54, 152
Waddell, Hope Masterson, 161
Waddell, James, 47, 48
Waddell, James (WCW's father), 53, 54
Waddell, Jessie, 178
Waddell, John Jackson, 47–8, 51, 59, 151, 154
Waddell, Maria Isabella (*later* Tod), 178
Waddell, Maria Orr (*née* Hope) (WCW's wife), 56–7, 59, 211
Waddell, Robert, 47, 48
Waddell, Robert (WCW's grandfather), 51–2, 53
Waddell, Susanna (*née* Hope) (WCW's mother), 53
Waddell, William Charles, 11, 65, 150–2, 209
attack on, 179
background, 53, 55, 56n41, 66, 205, 210
Brunswick Club, membership of, 64, 66, 210
casebooks, 12–14
Catholic emancipation, opposition to, 54
Catholic tenant evicted by, 57
character, 210–12
children, 56
coroner, election as, 70–1
coroner, role of, 66, 211–12
correspondence from wife Maria, 150n33
cousin's perception of, 48, 211
death, 201
fees for inquests, 99–100
jury duty, 59, 61, 62, 64, 66, 210
land agent, employment as, 55, 56, 57, 58, 66, 211

landownership, 49–50, 51
Londonderry Standard, letter to, 16, 100, 160–1
marriage, 56–7, 211
mileage fees, reduction in, 142
Poor Law guardian, 58, 211
Presbyterian community and, 161, 173, 210–11
professional/personal politics, 160–2, 210
professionalism, 205
property owned by, 160–1, 161n107
religion, 205, 209, 210
residence, 56, 66, 211
right to vote, 55
see also Casebook (CB1); Casebook (CB2); Casebook (CB3)
Wakely, Thomas (coroner), 34–5, 42
Warder and Dublin Weekly Mail, 187
Warner, James, 77
Waters, Bryan, 81
Watkins, James, 166
Welsh, Bernard, 196
Welsh, James, 104
Welsh, Susan, 196
Westenra, Henry Robert, 54
Whelen, Terance, 78
Whig-Liberal administration, 76
Whiteboy Act, 153
Whitla, Robert, 170n194
Wilkinson, George (architect), 118, **120**
Williamson, James, 90–1
Wilson, Thomas, 195
Witherow, Revd Thomas, 161, 210
women
    begging for food, 87–8
    domestic abuse, 40–1, 127, 182–4
    employment and, 92, 93

family survival, role in, 92
married women, civil identity of, 182
murders of, 93–7, 103–4, 127, 129–34
relief applications, 92–3
sexual assaults, 94–5
suffrage, 178
unmarried mothers, 39, 157, 184–5
Woodall, Alexander, 50–1
Woods, Dr, 184–5, 189
Woods, Francis (nurse), 115, 116
Woods, John, 166
Woods, John, 170n194
Woods, Patt, 170n194
workhouses, 117–20, **120**
    admissions, 89, 106
    bureaucracy, 139
    children in, 157–8
    conditions in, 103, 105, 209
    construction, funding of, 117–18
    cost-reduction measures, 158
    deaths at, 118, 138–9
    departures, 125–6, 128, 209
    distress in (1849), 134–6
    funding, 118
    infant deaths, 156–9
    inquests, **119**, 138–9
    legislation, 118
    management of, 103
    matrons, duties of, 157
    medical attendants at, 157–8
    populations (1846–9), **135**
    populations (1853–5), **155**
Wright, William (attorney), 100
Wyse, Thomas, **33**, 60

Young, Andrew K. (surgeon), 130, 133–4, 176, 180, 185, 191